Islamic Central Asia

Islamic Central Asia

An Anthology of Historical Sources

Edited by

Scott C. Levi and Ron Sela

Indiana University Press   BLOOMINGTON & INDIANAPOLIS

This book is a publication of

Indiana University Press

601 North Morton Street
Bloomington, IN 47404-3797 USA

www.iupress.indiana.edu

Telephone orders   800-842-6796
Fax orders   812-855-7931
Orders by e-mail   iuporder@indiana.edu

Every reasonable effort has been made to trace ownership of copyright materials. The publisher would welcome any information that would enable us to correct any copyright references in future printings.

⊗ *The paper used in this publication meets the minimum requirements of the American National Standard for Information Sciences— Permanence of Paper for Printed Library Materials, ANSI Z39.48-1992.*

MANUFACTURED IN THE UNITED STATES OF AMERICA

Library of Congress Cataloging-in-Publication Data

Islamic Central Asia : an anthology of historical sources / edited by Scott C. Levi and Ron Sela.
    p. cm.
  Includes bibliographical references and index.
  ISBN 978-0-253-35385-6 (cloth : alk. paper) — ISBN 978-0-253-22140-7 (pbk. : alk. paper) 1. Asia, Central—History—Sources.
2. Asia, Central—Civilization—Islamic influences—Sources. 3.
Islam—Asia, Central—History—Sources. I. Levi, Scott Cameron. II.
Sela, Ron.
  DS327.3.I75 2009
  958—dc22
                                    2009024093

1 2 3 4 5 15 14 13 12 11 10

Contents

Part 1 | Central Asia in the Early Islamic Period, Seventh to Tenth Centuries

Part 2 | Encounter with the Turks

Part 3 | The Mongol Empire

Part 4 | Timur and the Timurids

Part 5 | Central Asia in the Sixteenth and Seventeenth Centuries

Part 6 | Central Asia in the Eighteenth and Nineteenth Centuries

Acknowledgments

This volume was produced with funds provided by the Ohio State University Department of History and College of Arts and Humanities, and the Indiana University Department of Central Eurasian Studies and Islamic Studies Program. We are especially grateful for the original contributions to this anthology made by Devin DeWeese, Paul Losensky, and David Knighting, as well as to the generous counsel by our colleagues Akram Khabibullaev, Mika Natif, and Christopher Atwood, and the anonymous reviewers of this volume. Scott Tyler at Indiana University Graphic Services prepared the detailed map accompanying this volume. We are grateful for Yuri Bregel's permission to base our map on maps that he had prepared and published in his *Historical Central Asia Maps* (Papers on Inner Asia Special Supplement no. 1, Bloomington, 2000). We thank our editors at Indiana University Press, Rebecca Tolen and Laura MacLeod, for their support and dedication to this project. Lee Keeling provided valuable technical assistance in preparing several parts of the manuscript. Scott Levi would also like to thank Ali Shahhosseini for his friendship and valuable guidance in preparing for publication the original translation of the excerpt from Muhammad Hakim Khan's *Muntakhab al-tavarikh*.

Chapter 1: F. C. Murgotten, tr., *The origins of the Islamic state, being a translation from the Arabic accompanied with annotations geographic and historic notes of the Kitâb Futûh al-Buldân of al-Imâm Abu-l 'Abbâs, Ahmad ibn-Jâbir al-Balâdhuri*, vol. 2 (New York: Columbia Studies in the Social Sciences, 1916).

Chapter 2: (1) Reprinted by permission from *The History of al-Tabari (Ta'rikh al-rusul wa'l-muluk)*, vol. XXIII, *The Zenith of the Marwanid House: The Last Years of 'Abd al-Malik and the Caliphate of al-Walid, A.D. 700–715/A.H. 81–96*, translated and annotated by Martin Hinds, the State University of New York Press © 1990, State University of New York. All rights reserved.

(2) Reprinted by permission from *The History of al-Tabari (Ta'rikh al-rusul wa'l-muluk)*, vol. XXV, *The End of Expansion: The Caliphate of Hisham, A.D. 724–738/A.H. 105–120*, translated and annotated by Khalid Yahya Blankinship, the State University of New York Press © 1989, State University of New York. All rights reserved.

Chapter 3: Richard N. Frye, *The History of Bukhara: Translated from a Persian Abridgement of the Arabic Original by Narshakhī* (Cambridge, Mass.: Mediaeval Academy of America, 1954).

Chapter 4: Indiana University Press, which has published this book, acknowledges the material derived from *Hudūd al-'Ālam, 'The Regions of the World': A Persian Geography*, as edited by C. E. Bosworth (London, 1970). This work is published by the Trustees of the E. J. W. Gibb Memorial Trust, who have granted their consent to reproduce it here.

Chapter 5: Reprinted by permission from *The Life of Ibn Sina: A Critical Edition and Annotated Translation*, by William E. Gohlman, the State University of New York Press © 1974, State University of New York. All rights reserved.

Chapter 6: Jamil Ali, tr., *The Determination of the Coordinates of Positions for the Correction of Distances between Cities: A Translation from the Arabic of al-Bīrūnī's Kitāb Tahdīd Nihāyāt al-Amākin Litashīh Masāfāt al-Masākin*, Beirut: The American University of Beirut, 1967. Reproduced by permission of the publisher.

Chapter 7: Talat Tekin, *A Grammar of Orkhon Turkic*, Indiana University Uralic and Altaic Series, vol. 69 (Bloomington/The Hague: Mouton, 1968). Reproduced by permission of the Denis Sinor Research Institute for Inner Asian Studies.

Chapter 8: *The life and works of Jahiz; translations of selected texts, by Charles Pellat,* translated from the French [Ms.] by D. M. Hawke (Routledge & Kegan Paul © 1969). Reproduced by permission of Taylor & Francis Books UK.

Chapter 9: A. P. Martinez, "Gardizi's Two Chapters on the Turks," *Archivum Eurasiae Medii Aevi* 2 (1982): 109–217. Reproduced by permission of the author.

Chapter 10: James E. McKeithen, "The Risalah of Ibn Fadlan: an Annotated Translation and Introduction" (Ph.D. diss., Indiana University, 1979). Reproduced by permission of the author.

Chapter 11: Mahmud al-Kashgari, *Compendium of the Turkic dialects (Diwan Lughat at-Turk)*, ed. and tr. by Robert Dankoff and James Kelly, in Sources of Oriental Languages and Literatures, series ed. Sinasi Tekin (Cambridge, Mass.: Harvard University Department of Near Eastern Languages and Civilizations, 1982).

Chapter 12: *Istoriia Kazakhstana v persidskikh istochnikakh. T. 1. Al-Mulkhakat bi-s-surakh* (Almaty: Daik-Press, 2005). Translated from the Arabic by R. Sela.

Chapter 13: Yusuf Khass Hajib, *Wisdom of Royal Glory (Kutadgu Bilig): A Turko-Islamic Mirror for Princes*, tr. by Robert Dankoff (Chicago: University of Chicago Press, 1983). © 1983 by The University of Chicago. All rights reserved. Reproduced by permission of the publisher.

Chapter 14: al-Utbi, *The Kitab-i-Yamini: Historical Memoirs of the Amir Sabaktagin and the Sultan Mahmud of Ghazna*, tr. by James Reynolds (London: Oriental Translation Fund, 1858).

Chapter 15: Ibn Khallikan, *Biographical Dictionary*, tr. by Bn MacGuckin de Slane, 4 vols. (Paris: Oriental Translation Fund of Great Britain and Ireland, 1843).

Chapter 16: Nizam al-Mulk, *The Book of Government or Rules for Kings: The Syar al-Muluk or Siyasat-nama of Nizam Al-Mulk*, tr. by Hubert Darke (Routledge & Kegan Paul © 1978). Reproduced by permission of Taylor & Francis Books UK.

Chapter 17: Kai Kāūs ibn Iskandar, *A Mirror for Princes: The Qābūs Nāma,* tr. by Reuben Levy (New York: E. P. Dutton & Co., 1951).

Chapter 18: Karl A. Wittfogel and Fêng Chia-Shêng, *History of Chinese Society, Liao (907–1125)* (Philadelphia: American Philosophical Society, 1949). Reproduced by the generous permission of the publisher.

Chapter 19: *The Secret History of the Mongols: A Mongolian Epic Chronicle of the Thirteenth Century,* tr. by Igor De Rachewiltz (Leiden: E. J. Brill, 2006). Reproduced by permission of the publisher.

Chapter 20: Hayton. *La flor des estoires de la terre d'Orient. Recueil des historiens des croisades, [1] Documents arméniens* (Paris, 1906). Tranlsated from the Old French by R. Sela.

Chapter 21: Al-Nasawi. *Histoire du sultan Djelal ed-Din Mankobirti, prince du Khorezm.* Texte arabe publié d'apres le manuscrit de la Bibliotheque Nationale par O. Houdas (Paris: E. Leroux, 1891). Translated from the Arabic by R. Sela.

Chapter 22: Li Chih-Ch'ang, *The travels of an Alchemist,* tr. by A. Waley (G. Routledge & Sons © 1931). Reproduced by permission of Taylor & Francis Books UK.

Chapter 23: H. G. Raverty, tr., Minhaj al-Din Juzjani, *Tabakat-i-Nasiri,* 2 vols. (London: Gilbert & Rivington, 1881).

Chapter 24: Rashīd al-Dīn Tabib, *Jāmi al-Tavārīkh,* tr. by J. A. Boyle, *The Successors of Genghis Khan* (Columbia University Press, © 1971). Reprinted with permission of the publisher.

Chapter 25: 'Ala-ad-Din 'Ata-Malik Juvaini, *Genghis Khan: The History of the World-Conqueror,* tr. and ed. by J. A. Boyle (Manchester: Manchester University Press, 1958).

Chapter 26: Mirza Haydar Dughlat, *A History of the Moghuls of Central Asia, being the Tarikh-i-Rashidi of Mirza Muhammad Haidar, Dughlat,* ed. by N. Elias and tr. by E. Denison Ross, 2nd ed. (London: Curzon, 1898).

Chapter 27: H. A. R. Gibb, tr., *The Travels of Ibn Battuta,* A.D. 1325–1354, vols. 2 and 3 (Cambridge, 1958–71). "The Hakluyt Society was established in 1846 for the purpose of printing rare or unpublished Voyages and Travels. For further information please see their website at: www.hakluyt.com."

Chapter 28: J. H. Sanders, tr., *Tamerlane: or Timur the Great Amir, from the Arabic Life by Ahmed ibn Arabshah* (London: Luzac & Co., 1936).

Chapter 29: Walter J. Fischel, tr., *Ibn Khaldun and Tamerlane: Their Historic Meeting in Damascus, 1401 AD (803 AH): A study based on Arabic Manuscripts of Ibn Khaldun's "Autobiography," with a Translation into English and Commentary* (Berkeley: University of California Press, 1952).

Chapter 30: Ruy González de Clavijo, *Clavijo: Embassy to Tamerlane 1403–1406,* tr. by Guy Le Strange (New York: Harper & Brothers, 1928).

Chapter 31: Khwandamir, *Habibu's-siyar,* ed. and tr. by W. M. Thackston, in Sources of Oriental Languages and Literatures, series ed. Sinasi Tekin (Cambridge, Mass.: Harvard University Department of Near Eastern Languages and Civilizations, 1994).

Chapter 32: Mir Ali Shir Nava'i, *Muhakamat al-Lughatain,* ed. and tr. by Robert Devereux, *The Muslim World* 54, no. 4 (1964): 270–87 and 55, no. 1 (1965): 28–45 (Blackwell Publishing Ltd., © 1964 and 1965). Reproduced by permission of the publisher.

Chapter 33: Jo-Ann Gross and A. Urunbaev, ed. and tr., *The letters of Khwâja Ubayd Allâh Ahrâr and his associates* (Leiden: E. J. Brill, 2002). Reproduced by permission of the publisher.

Chapter 34: (1) Jami, *Nafahat al-uns,* ed. Mahmud 'Abidi (Tehran, 1370/1991), pp. 408–409 (the same account is given, citing the *Nafahat,* in the *Rashahat,* cited below, I, pp. 207–208). Translated from the Persian by Devin DeWeese.

(2) 'Ali b. Husayn Kashifi, *Rashahat-i 'Ayn al-hayat,* ed. 'Ali Asghar Mu'iniyan (Tehran, 2536/1977), I, pp. 328–29. Translated from the Persian by Devin DeWeese.

(3) Mir 'Abd al-Avval Nishapuri, *Malfuzat-i Khoja Ahrar,* ed. 'Arif Nawshahi, (Tehran, 1380/2001), pp. 246, 416. Translated from the Persian by Devin DeWeese.

(4) Badr ad-Din Kashmiri, *Siraj al-salihin,* ed. Sayyid Siraj ad-Din (Islamabad: Markaz-i Taqiqat-i Fars-i Iran va Pakistan, 1376/1997), pp. 245–47. Translated from the Persian by Devin DeWeese.

Chapter 35: 'Abdallah b. M. Nasrallahi, *Zubdat al-athar* (Misr: Matba'a Hindiyah, 1934). Translated from the Chaghatay by R. Sela.

Chapter 36: Zahiru'd-din Muhammad Babur Padshah Ghazi, *Babur-nama: Memoirs of Babur,* tr. by Annette Beveridge (London: 1921).

Chapter 37: Anthony Jenkinson, *Early Voyages and Travels to Russia and Persia . . . ,* ed. by E. Delmar Morgan and C. H. Coote, 2 vols., 1st ser., nos. 72–73 (London: Hakluyt Society, 1886). The editors thank Dr. Daniel Waugh and Lance Jenott for their permission to include here, slightly modified, their edited version of Jenkinson's account as presented on the Silk Road Seattle website (http://depts. washington.edu/silkroad/).

Chapter 38: P. P. Ivanov, *Khoziaistvo dzhuibarskikh sheikhov,* ed. by I. P. Petrushevskii, tr. by E. E. Bertel's (Moscow, 1954). Translated from the Persian by R. Sela.

Chapter 39: Henry Beveridge, tr., *The Akbarnama of Abu-l-Fazl,* vol. 3 (Calcutta: Asiatic Society of Bengal, 1897–1918).

Chapter 40: (1) A. N. Kononov. *Rodoslovnia turkmen: sochinenie Abu-l-Gazi khana Khivinskogo* (Moscow/Leningrad: Izd-vo AN SSSR, 1958). Translated from the Chaghatay by R. Sela.

(2) Aboul-Ghâzi Bèhâdour Khân. *Histoire des Mongols et des Tatares par Aboul-Ghâzi Bèhâdour Khân.* Publieé, traduite et annotée par le Baron Desmaisons. 1871–72. Translated from the Chaghatay by R. Sela.

Chapter 41: Ivan Khokhlov in *Sbornik kniazia Khilkova* (St. Petersburg, 1879). Translated from the Russian by David Knighting.

Chapter 42: Sayyida Nasafi, *Kulliyat-i asar,* ed. Jabulqa Dad 'Alishayif (Dushanbe, 1990). Translated from the Persian by Paul Losensky.

Chapter 43: Shah Mahmud Churas, *Khronika,* ed. and tr. by O. F. Akimushkin (Moscow, 1976). Translated from the Persian by R. Sela.

Chapter 44: *Timur-nama. Kulliyat-i farsi,* ed. Mirza Muhammad Qasim ibn Mirza ʿAbd al-Khaliq Bukhari (Tashkent, 1912). Translated from the Persian by R. Sela.

Chapter 45: Jonas Hanway, *An historical account of the British trade over the Caspian Sea* (London: T. Osborne, 1753).

Chapter 46: ʾAbd al-Karim al-Kashmiri. *The memoirs of Khojek Abdulkurreem . . . who accompanied Nadir Shah, on his return from Hindostan to Persia,* tr. by Francis Gladwin (Calcutta: W. Mackay, 1788).

Chapter 47: Muhammad Vafa Karminagi, *Tuhfat al-khani,* ms of the St. Petersburg Branch of the Institute of Oriental Studies, Russian Academy of Sciences, C 525. Translated from the Persian by R. Sela.

Chapter 48: Mirza Badiʿ-divan, *Madzhmaʾ al-arkam ("Predpisaniia fiska") (Priemy dokumentatsii Bukhare XVIII v.),* faksimile rukopisi, vvedenie, perevod, primechaniia i prilozheniia A. B. Vilʾdanovoĭ (Moscow: Nauka, 1981). Translated from the Russian by R. Sela.

Chapter 49: Yuri Bregel, ed. and tr., *Documents from the Khanate of Khiva (17th–19th centuries),* Papers on Inner Asia 40 (2007). Reproduced by permission of the Denis Sinor Research Institute for Inner Asian Studies.

Chapter 50: Haji Muhammad Hakim Khan b. Said Muhammad Khakimkhon, *Muntakhab at-tavarikh,* ed. by A. Mukhtarov (Dushanbe: Donish, 1985). Translated from the Persian by Scott C. Levi.

Chapter 51: Alexander Burnes, *Travels into Bukhara . . . ,* vol. 3 (London: John Murray, 1834).

Chapter 52: Mohan Lal, *Travels in the Panjab, Afghanistan & Turkestan to Balk, Bukhara, and Herat, and a visit to Great Britain and Germany* (London: Wm Allen & Co., 1846).

Chapter 53: Aleksei Levshin, *Opisanie Kirgiz-kazachʾikh, ili Kirgiz-kaisatskikh, ord i stepei* (1833) (Almaty: Sanat, 1996). Translated from the Russian by R. Sela.

Chapter 54: N. P. Ignatiev, *Mission of N. P. Ignatʾev to Khiva and Bukhara in 1858,* tr. by John Evans (Newtonville, Mass.: Oriental Research Partners, 1984). Reproduced by permission of the publisher.

Chapter 55: Muhammad Yusuf Bek Bayani, *Shajara-i Khorezmshahi,* Tashkent, Institute of Oriental Studies of the Academy of Sciences of Uzbekistan, MS no. 9596. Translated from the Chaghatay by R. Sela.

Note on Translation and Transliteration

This anthology contains excerpts from many different sources in diverse languages, written over a period of more than a millennium. The translators of these excerpts have employed varied approaches toward the text and they, and their editors, also tended to adhere to different systems of transliteration. For example, a simple word like "khan" could be rendered "xan," "qan," "chan," "han," and so forth. In order to avoid potentially very confusing consequences, we have chosen—in consultation with Indiana University Press—to provide a coherent and somewhat simplified system of transliteration throughout the text, both for original translations and for materials that had already been published. We follow a modified scheme of the *Encyclopaedia of Islam* and the Library of Congress, avoiding most diacritical marks. Furthermore, we have endeavored to provide clear and approachable translations, although some of the materials presented in this volume engage very complicated subject matters and are presented in distinct styles. We have also tried to avoid footnotes as much as possible. The reader will find a glossary at the end of the volume for explanations of different terms that are not provided in parentheses.

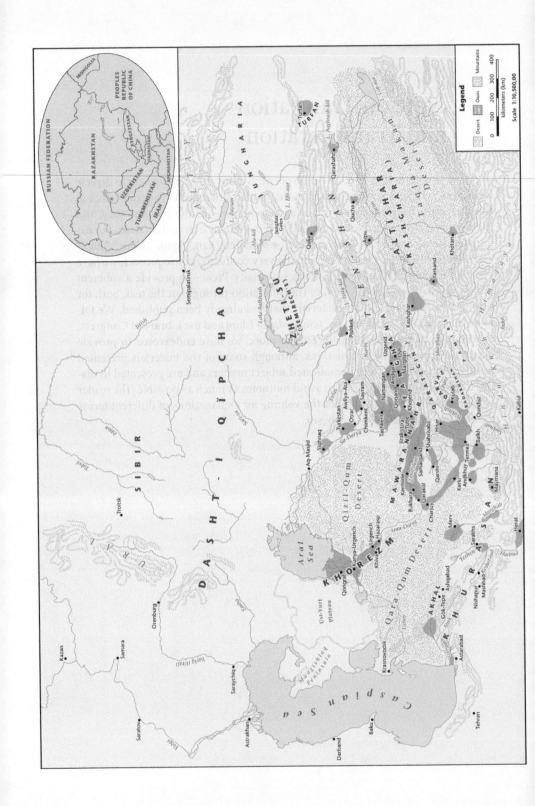

Islamic Central Asia

Introduction

This anthology is designed primarily to complement an introductory study of Central Asia's history. In recent years, the awareness of Central Asia's significance and unique history has grown rapidly among academics, policy makers, and the public. The unexpected increase in books and articles on Central Asia, many of them written by laypersons, has served also to add to the range of courses taught about this subject, mostly by specialists in other areas. Such an outpouring of attention has underlined the need for new pedagogical resources for the instruction of Central Asian history, and has prompted us to compile an anthology of historical sources to serve both the academic and non-academic communities. The final product includes extracts from a diverse array of sources that illustrate important features of the social, cultural, political, and economic history of Islamic Central Asia. Many of these are original translations, never before available in English, that we have produced ourselves, or solicited our colleagues to contribute.

Geographically, Central Asia stretches from the Caspian Sea in the west to East Turkestan (modern-day Xinjiang) in the east, from the Siberian plain in the north to northern Afghanistan and northeastern Iran in the south. Historically, this region has been labeled a crossroads of civilizations. Situated at the heart of the so-called Silk Road, the peoples of Central Asia witnessed numerous invasions, migrations, and exchanges of religions and cultures, goods and technologies. It is the birthplace of famous scientists, theologians, and jurists, and home to the fabled cities of Samarqand, Bukhara, and Khiva, as well as to epic nomadic traditions. Central Asia has been the center of world empires in antiquity and the medieval era, as well as the playing ground for the Anglo-Russian "Great Game" in the eighteenth and nineteenth centuries. Central Asia has been exoticized in the West—and in the East—and has captivated the imagination of many. While emphasizing some of the remarkable aspects of Central Asian history, this anthology also aims to examine the daily lives of people in the region, pointing to periods of great achievements and important transformations on the one hand, as well as crisis, strife, and relative isolation on the other.

As the present volume goes to press, it represents the first anthology of sources for the study of Central Asian history in the English language. It is not, however, the first such anthology ever produced. Those educated in Russian have long benefited from such publications. Already in the nineteenth century, V. G. Tizengauzen compiled a two-volume anthology of Arabic and Persian sources for the history of the Golden Horde, the westernmost part of the Mongol Empire, entitled *Sbornik materialov, otnosiashchikhsia k istorii Zolotoĭ ordy* (the first volume was published in St. Petersburg in 1884, the second posthumously published in 1941). More than a century later, Tizengauzen's work remains an especially useful research tool.

Other anthologies continued to be published in Soviet times, but with different objectives in mind and in different formats. In general, the authors of the Soviet anthologies aimed at introducing and consolidating the histories of each of their Central Asian "nationalities" by including extracts from diverse sources in Russian translation. Among such publications we note the *Materialy po istorii karakalpakov* (1935); *Materialy po istorii turkmen i Turkmenii* (1938–39); *Materialy po istorii kazakhskikh khanstv XV–XVIII vekov* (1969); and *Materialy po istorii kirgizov i Kirgizii* (1973). The more recent publication, *Materialy po istorii Sredneĭ i Tsentral'noĭ Azii X–XIX vv.* (1988), stands out for breaking away from the nationalist paradigm and engaging the region as a whole, and includes valuable materials in Russian translation, many of which are first-ever translations.

Other publications of this sort focused on a particular theme or topic and included, for instance, anthologies of travel literature, such as *Le Voyage en Asie centrale et au Tibet* (Paris: R. Laffont, 1992), an anthology of Western travelers' accounts of their travels in the region from medieval times to the first half of the twentieth century in French translation.

A carefully produced anthology can provide readers access to a wide variety of sources and can facilitate a more systematic and meaningful study of a particular subject. It must be recognized, however, that working with anthologies embodies certain risks: extracts can be taken out of context; materials are always difficult to sort out, edit, and restrict; and sources that are placed in the spotlight may assume more significance than they deserve, as readers may tend to propagate their reputation largely because of their availability in translation.

With this in mind, we have taken great care in selecting the extracts included in this volume, and we have allowed several factors to inform our selection process. Paramount among these is our desire to bring forth an assortment of primary sources that provides readers a sense of the richness and diversity of materials authored in and about the region, highlighting Central Asia's own rich textual tradition. This has presented a number of challenges as many of the Central Asian sources are available only in manuscript form, unedited and unpublished. This is especially true for the so-called early modern period (sixteenth to nineteenth centuries), the literature for which has been much less explored by the scholarly community than other periods in the region's history. In an effort to maintain a balanced presentation of the sources, we have therefore found it necessary to include significantly more original translations for the later period. Indeed, of the twenty-one excerpts that engage Central Asia's history from the sixteenth to the nineteenth centuries, twelve are original translations. We hope that these will prove to be useful resources for classroom instruction and for future research. We also hope that this effort will help to dispel the widely held belief—often propagated in classrooms and sometimes even found in scholarship—that Central Asians were illiterate until Russian colonization.

Secondly, we have made a deliberate effort to draw our extracts from multiple genres of sources, both narrative and documentary. These include: inscriptions, biographical dictionaries, geographical surveys, court chronicles, administrative manuals, memoirs, diplomatic correspondence, legal documents, hagiographies, travel literature, poetry, and more. This should illustrate for the reader that the study of history depends on analysis of a combination of sources and that each genre has its own strengths and weaknesses in constructing an improved understanding of the past.

Thirdly, we have tried not to rely too heavily upon the more well-thumbed sources that are readily available in English translation and have instead sought to direct attention to those sources that are also interesting and valuable, but perhaps less accessible. Of course, space limitations have also forced us to set aside many sources that we would have liked to include. To point to just one example, in the section on the Mongol Empire we elected not to include excerpts from the accounts of Marco Polo, William of Rubruck, and other European travelers, envoys, and Christian missionaries to the Mongol realm. Our reason for choosing to set this body of literature aside is that these accounts are relatively well known and available in affordable publications or on the Internet. We hope that readers will find our introductory essays useful also in terms of their review of available sources.

Our fourth aim has been to adequately represent the different geographical and cultural parts of this expansive and very diverse region. Although it is impossible to cover thoroughly all the areas of Central Asia in one modest volume, we have worked to include materials that would illuminate important historical features of the core sedentary heartlands of Central Asia as well as the vast pastoral-nomadic steppe, East Turkestan, the Turkmen territory east of the Caspian, the northern part of Afghanistan, and northeastern Iran. Additionally, we have tried to draw from sources that were produced outside of what we have defined as Central Asia in this volume, but that have had significant influence on the region in the course of its history and on the identity of its peoples. The Old Turkic inscriptions in Mongolia are one case in point.

Another of our goals in this volume has been to demonstrate the significance of studying Central Asia's history within the framework of the study of the Muslim world. Much of the recent scholarship on Central Asia exhibits an unfortunate tendency to approach the region and its history with very little knowledge of Islamic history. We hope that readers of this volume will gain an improved appreciation for the scale of Muslim existence in the region as reflected in almost every aspect of everyday life, from language to administration, and from sophisticated literary and historiographical traditions to the conducting of trade and the not-so-simple task of selling property. For more than a millennium, most of Central Asia has been part and parcel of the Muslim world.

The task of compiling an anthology is one of negotiation and compromise.

Editorial considerations and various constraints have prevented us from including many sources that we would like to have included, from different eras and regions. We also note that they account for some gaps or biases. For example, this book relies completely on written sources, and it cannot claim to address adequately societies where oral culture was predominant. We have made an effort to access available written records pertaining to nomadic peoples, but we note that, throughout most of the period in question, these were written by their sedentary neighbors, and often with a tone that was less than favorable. For this reason, and also because of the abundance of literary sources in the sedentary world, the book naturally assumes a more sedentary focus. The fact that this volume covers more than a millennium in the history of a vast and varied region further complicates our task. We have found it impossible to point to every unifying theme in the history of the entire region over such a long duration, as editors endeavor to do when they write the histories of national literatures, for example. One hopes that the study of Central Asia will flourish to demand more specific anthologies in the future.

We have organized this volume chronologically so that instructors might easily use it alongside a textbook on the history of Islamic Central Asia. We have also divided the readings according to the usual periodization, generally determined by easily identifiable, mostly political transitions. The volume begins with the Arab expansion into the region and the early period of Muslim adaptation and authority. Part 2 introduces the powerful incursion of Turkic peoples into the region and their incorporation into the Muslim world. Part 3 addresses the rise and establishment of the Mongol World Empire, as well as its breakup and lasting impact in Central Asian society. The house of Timur, ruling most of Central Asia from the late fourteenth century until the beginning of the sixteenth century, comprises part 4. Central Asia in the aftermath of the Uzbek migrations, during the sixteenth and seventeenth centuries, constitutes part 5. And part 6 deals with Central Asia from the early eighteenth century until the Russian conquest in the second half of the nineteenth century. We note that, after careful consideration, we elected to end our coverage with the rise of Russian authority in the region. Our hope is that a willing colleague will pick up the baton and produce another anthology of historical sources focusing entirely on the period stretching from the Russian conquest of Central Asia to the modern day.

We have introduced each of these six parts with a short essay that draws attention to the most significant developments of each period and provides a brief historiographical discussion to help readers appreciate the variety of sources available for the study of the period. In an effort to enhance the value of this anthology by making the sources excerpted here more meaningful to the reader, we have also taken care to preface each one with a few paragraphs detailing the specific historical context surrounding the circumstances of authorship. Ideally we would have included the texts in their original languages as well as in translation, but doing so would have made the volume prohibitively expensive for use as a pedagogical resource. Above all, we hope that this volume will encourage further inquiry into the fascinating history of Central Asia.

Part 1 | Central Asia in the Early Islamic Period, Seventh to Tenth Centuries

INTRODUCTION

Already by the middle of the seventh century AD, merely two decades after the installation of the first caliph, Abu Bakr, on the throne of the Muslim polity in Mecca, the armies of the Arab caliphate approached the banks of the Amu Darya River, a distance of more than 1,600 miles from their soon-to-be capital in Damascus. Having defeated the Sasanian Empire, the Arabs proceeded eastward and endeavored to cross the great river into the little known (to them) areas beyond it. This was not a trivial matter; indeed, the initial phase of the Arab conquest, although achieving some temporary success, did not yield any long-term results, and the Arabs were quickly pushed back to their base in the city of Merv.

The state of affairs beyond the Amu Darya was complicated. Different Iranian civilizations had deep roots in the region, and for centuries they had played a vital role in the trans-Eurasian exchange of goods and ideas. The population was heterogeneous: most spoke Iranian dialects, some spoke Turkic, and there were a variety of scripts in use. Their religious landscape was shaped by the Zoroastrian, Buddhist, Manichean, and Jewish traditions, and also by diverse Christian sects; their lands had witnessed the passage of great armies; and their politics, culture, and economy were profoundly influenced by the symbiosis between nomadic and sedentary populations. Politically fragmented, the ancient principalities of Soghdiana—the sedentary heartland of Central Asia including Samarqand, Bukhara and Ustrushana, Farghana, and Shash—raised tribute for the Turkic Qaghan in the beginning of the seventh century. To the southeast, in Tukharistan, and further to the east, along the Tarim river basin, the different city-states paid duty to Tang China until the middle of the seventh century, and then to the Tibetan Empire and the Turks.

The mostly Arab armies had to devise different strategies to cope with this mixture of civilizations, populations, political fragmentation, and ongoing imperial intrigue by Turks, Tibetans, and Chinese. Only with Qutayba b. Muslim, governor of the province of Khurasan for the Umayyads, did the Arab armies manage to make significant gains in the battlefield and emerge as the clear victors. Qutayba allied with several local rulers and sometimes with rivaling empires, recruited local troops into his own forces, and, depending upon the circumstances of his victory, treated the conquered population with different degrees of generosity and severity. The initial phase of the Muslim conquest of Central Asia included destruction of cities and old places of worship, construction of Islamic institutions, disputes over taxation, and a relatively tense interaction between the Arabs and the native inhabitants that also generated many rebellions.

At the same time, the new civilization brought with it new languages, a new religion, and new methods of administration, all of which would be incorporated—with many variations—into the fabric of the existing cultures. In the wake of the 'Abbasid Revolution of 750, the center of gravity in the Muslim world moved to Iraq. Nevertheless, the revolution also saw the advancement of several processes that drew more attention to Central Asia. Among these are the emphasis on the role of the region and people of Khurasan and that of Persians (and Arab intermarriages with Persians). Contrary to earlier Umayyad policies, the 'Abbasids encouraged an active policy of proselytization and increased conversion to Islam within the expanding boundaries of the caliphate. The defeat of the Chinese in the battle of Taraz (Talas) in 751 became a symbol for China's removal from Central Asian affairs for a millennium. Thus Central Asia's sedentary heartland became a province of the 'Abbasid Empire and gradually an integral part of the Muslim world.

At the same time, caliphal authority in Central Asia fluctuated. Political control over the region was usually not very strong and left to local governors, sometimes appointed by Baghdad, but more often rising from the region's population. Although attempts were made to keep the empire centralized, many local powers grew in strength and influence. These included the Tahirids, the 'Abbasids' governors of Khurasan who had ruled the province throughout much of the ninth century from their capital in Nishapur. The Samanids, rulers of Mawarannahr and parts of Khurasan in the ninth and tenth centuries, began as appointed subordinate governors to the Tahirids but quickly grew in power and influence to become almost autonomous rulers. The Samanid economy was based largely on agriculture and crafts (particularly textile production, paper making, and metalwork), although they also benefited from an extensive commercial network that included a thriving slave trade (see the following chapter), as well as their control over much of the silver production in that part of the world. They gained repute for standing as the barrier between the Muslim world, frequently conceptualized as the "civilized" world, and the nomadic entities of the north, often hailed as "barbarians" who supposedly aimed to destroy it from the outside. Thus, cultivating a reputation as protectors of the frontier zone against the Turks, the Samanids controlled or financed a series of frontier posts and engaged in the kind of frontier politics that was always a mixture of war and peace, trade and raids, as well as the dissemination of Islamic propagation among the "heathens." Internal feuds and their rivalry with their Turkic neighbors brought about their downfall.

The Samanids' economic power, their geopolitical standing, and the long tradition of erudition in the region also stimulated scholarship and learning in Samanid cities, particularly in the capital, Bukhara. During the Samanid era, Bukhara became famous for its concentration of libraries and for the numerous well-known and highly influential Muslim scholars who came from there. The sponsorship of literature in New Persian was also a noted development in that era.

This formative period of the Muslim Empire also witnessed the establishment of distinct patterns in Islamic historiography. Much was borrowed from
other existing traditions, and the outcome was a myriad of styles and sources
of inspiration that, under the new Islamic authority, together would also share
a very clear Muslim imprint. With the establishment of Baghdad as the political
and intellectual capital of the Muslim world of the eighth and ninth centuries,
attempts were made to systematically explore the empire and its boundaries, particularly the roads to the east and the interaction with nomads and other peoples
of the steppes. This marked the advent of what came to be called Arab geography. Extensive translations of scientific literature from territories that the Arabs
had conquered, or had other interactions with, also contributed to the flourishing climate of scientific learning. Additionally, the ninth century saw a wealth of
literary production as Muslim scholars were trying to understand their past and
their present. Muslim authors also wrote histories and biographical dictionaries, mostly in the style of *wafayat* (or obituaries), and even more prominent were
their theological discussions, legal opinions, geographies, travel literature, and
local histories, as well as political treaties and contributions to the genre of advice literature. Most of these were written in Arabic; some were later translated
into Persian. In addition to the textual sources, one should not underestimate
the immense value of archaeological, numismatic, and other evidence of material culture, a body of materials that keeps growing with new explorations and
excavations.

A | *Central Asia and the Arab Conquests*

1 Baladhuri: The Arab Conquests of Central Asia

INTRODUCTION

Ahmad ibn Yahya al-Baladhuri (d. 892), one of the leading Arab historians of the ninth century, probably spent most of his life in Baghdad, although he traveled and studied throughout the Middle East. He apparently enjoyed a high status at the caliph's court, particularly during the reign of the 'Abbasid caliphs al-Mutawakkil (d. 861) and al-Musta'in (d. 866). Al-Baladhuri composed a number of works, some based on genealogical tables, but his best-known work, the Futuh al-buldan *(Conquest of the lands) remains one of the most valuable sources that deal with the history of the Arab conquests. It was edited already in the 1860s by the Dutch Orientalist de Goeje, and was translated into English by Phillip Hitti and F. C. Murgotten under the title* The Origins of the Islamic State *beginning in 1916. According to tradition, al-Baladhuri died of over-indulging himself on the baladhur (hence, his nickname)—a kind of nut whose properties were believed to improve one's memory.*

In this excerpt, the author outlines the beginning of the Arab conquest of Central Asia in the early eighth century, a conquest that received new impetus with the appointment of Qutayba ibn Muslim to the position of governor of Khurasan in AD *712. The passage details Qutayba's and his successors' different strategies for conquest, for dealing with local rulers and notable land owners (di-hqan), for treating captives, and for engaging rebellions. The details are presented in Baladhuri's style of collecting and condensing "evidence," whether hearsay or written accounts (there were apparently many accounts of the conquest, sometimes limited to particular locales), always trying to trace the evidence back to the source, while avoiding literary flair, and offering little to no commentary on the facts reported.*

Qutayba governor of Khurasan. Al-Hajjaj [the governor of Iraq] then appointed as governor of Khurasan Qutayba ibn Muslim al-Bahili. He made an expedition against Akharun. When he was in Taleqan, the two *dihqan*s of Balkh met him and crossed the river with him. At the time he crossed the river, there also came to him the king of Saghaniyan with gifts and a golden key, paying him submission and inviting him to settle in his country. The king of Akharun and Shuman had been oppressing and raiding the king of Saghaniyan, and that is why he gave Qutayba these presents and this invitation. The king of Kafyan came to Qutayba with the same purpose as that for which the king of Saghaniyan had come to him, and both surrendered their lands to him.

Conquests by Salih. Qutayba withdrew to Merv, leaving his brother, Salih, as his lieutenant over Transoxiana. Salih conquered Kasan and Urasht, which is part of Farghana. With him in his army was Nasr ibn Sayyar. Salih conquered . . . and Khashka of Farghana, its ancient capital. The last of the conquerors of Kasan and Urasht was Nuh ibn Asad, the people thereof having risen in rebellion in the caliphate of the Commander of the Believers, al-Muntasir-billah.

Paykend reduced. The king of Juzjan sent envoys to Qutayba, who made peace with him on condition that he come to him. He did so, but later returned, and died in Taleqan. Then Qutayba, Nizak[1] being with him, raided Paykend in the year 87. He crossed the river from Zamm to Paykend, which is the nearest of the cities of Bukhara to the river. They rebelled and asked the Soghdians for aid, but Qutayba attacked them, invading their country and besieging them. They asked for terms, but he reduced the city by force.

Tumushkat and Karminiya. Qutayba raided Tumushkat and Karminiya in the year 88, leaving as his lieutenant over Merv his brother, Bashshar ibn Muslim. After capturing a few small forts, Qutayba made peace with them. He also raided Bukhara and reduced it by treaty.

Ibn al-Muthanna's account. Qutayba made an expedition against Bukhara. The inhabitants defended themselves against him, and he said, "Let me enter the city, and I will only pray two *rak'a*s therein." They gave him permission to do so, but he concealed some men in ambush, and upon entering the city, these overpowered the gate keepers, and the Muslims entered the city. Qutayba obtained much money thereby, dealing perfidiously with the inhabitants. He assaulted Soghd; killed Nizak in Tukharistan, and crucified him, and reduced Kesh and Nasaf [Nakhshab] by treaty.

The king of Khorezm. The king of Khorezm was weak, and Khurzad, his brother, had opposed him and overpowered him. The king sent to Qutayba, say-

---

1. Nizak was ruler of the northern Hephthalites, a part of nomadic confederation centered in Northern Afghanistan.

ing, "I will make thee such and such gifts, and deliver unto thee the keys, on condition that thou establish me securely as king over my country instead of my brother."

Khorezm consists of three cities encompassed by a moat. The strongest of them is Madinat al-Fil. 'Ali ibn Mujahid says that Madinat al-Fil is merely Samarqand. The king established himself in the strongest of the cities and sent to Qutayba the money specified in his agreement with him, and the keys. Qutayba dispatched his brother, 'Abd al-Rahman ibn Muslim, against Khurzad, whom he attacked and killed, getting possession of 4,000 captives. He put these to death, and established the former king of Khorezm on the throne in accordance with the agreement made with him. The people of his kingdom, however, said to the Muslim, "He (their king) is weak." And they assaulted and killed him. Qutayba appointed his brother, 'Ubaydallah ibn Muslim, governor of Khorezm.

Samarqand reduced. Qutayba raided Samarqand, where the kings of Soghd formerly used to live, although later they made their abode in Ishtikhan. Qutayba besieged the people of Samarqand, engaging in many battles. While the fighting was going on between them, the king of Soghd wrote to the king of Shash, who was staying in Tarbend. The latter came to him with a number of his soldiery. The Muslims met them and there was a very fierce engagement. Finally Qutayba, with a sudden charge, put the enemy to rout. Ghurak (ruler of Samarqand) capitulated, the terms being an annual payment of 1,200,000 *dirhams*, and that the Muslim might conduct prayers in the city. Qutayba entered the city, where Ghurak had prepared for him a feast. He ate and led in prayer; constructed a mosque, and departed, leaving in the city several Muslims, among them al-Dahhak ibn Muzahim, author of the commentary on the Qur'an.

Another version. Other authorities say that Qutayba granted peace for 700,000 *dirhams* and entertainment for the Muslims for three days. The terms of the surrender included also the houses of the idols and the fire temples. The idols were thrown out, plundered of their ornaments, and burned, although the Persians used to say that among them was one idol with which whoever trifled would perish. But when Qutayba set fire to it with his own hand, many of them accepted Islam. Al-Mukhtar ibn Ka'b al-Ju'fi says of Qutayba:

> He subdued Soghd with the tribes until
> He left the Soghdians sitting in nakedness.

'Umar orders an investigation. Abu 'Ubaida and others say: When 'Umar ibn 'Abd al-'Aziz became caliph, there came to him representatives of the people of Samarqand who complained to him that Qutayba had entered their city and settled the Muslims there fraudulently. 'Umar wrote to his *'amil* with orders to appoint them a *qazi* to investigate what they had related, and, if he decided in favor of expelling the Muslims, they should be expelled. The *'amil* appointed for them Jumai' ibn Hadir al-Baji, who decreed the expulsion of the Muslims, provided that the two parties should fight upon equal terms. But the people of the city of Samarqand were averse to warfare, and let the Muslims remain, and so they stayed among them. . . .

Sa'id al-Khudhayna. Afterwards Yazid ibn 'Abd al-Malik, when he became ruler, appointed Maslama ibn 'Abd al-Malik governor of Iraq and Khurasan. Maslama appointed Sa'id ibn 'Abd al-'Aziz ibn al-Harith ibn al-Hakam ibn Abu'l-'Asi ibn Umayya to govern Khurasan. This Sa'id was nicknamed Hudhayfa (the one with the clipped hair), because some one of the *dihqan*s of Transoxiana happened upon him in a yellow gown and with his hair done up, and said, "This is Hudhayfa," meaning "mistress." Sa'id was Maslama's nephew.

Sa'id's lieutenant defeated. Sa'id sent on as his lieutenant Sawra ibn al-Hurr al-Hanthali. Later he sent his son. The latter crossed over to Transoxiana and established himself at Ishtikhan. The Turks had attacked the city, but he entered into conflict with them, putting them to rout, and protecting the people from their exactions for a long time. Later on he met the Turks in battle again, and they defeated him and made a great slaughter among his followers; and Sa'id appointed Nasr ibn Sayyar to the command. . . .

Khudhayna replaced by al-Jurashi. Some of Khurasan's leading people sought audience with Maslama, complaining of Sa'id; so he dismissed him, and made Sa'id ibn 'Amr al-Jurashi governor of Khurasan. When the latter arrived there, he ordered his scribe to read aloud his commission. The scribe made some mistakes in pronunciation, and Sa'id said, "O people, the commander is guiltless of these mistakes which ye have heard."

Soghd subjugated. Al-Jurashi sent to Soghd, inviting its people to return to submission, and refrained from troubling them until his envoys could bring back their acquiescence in his succession to the rule. Then he marched against them. More than 10,000 of their main body deserted and left them, coming over to submit, and al-Jurashi conquered all of the strongholds of Soghd, subjugating the enemy completely.

Muslim succeeds al-Jurashi. Yazid ibn 'Abd al-Malik had designated Hisham ibn 'Abd al-Malik as heir apparent, and after him al-Walid ibn Yazid. When Yazid ibn 'Abd al-Malik died, Hisham succeeded to the throne, and appointed 'Umar ibn Hubayra al-Fazari governor of Iraq. The latter dismissed al-Jurashi, and appointed Muslim ibn Sa'id as his *'amil* over Khurasan. He raided Afshin and then made peace with him, the terms being 6,000 sheep and the surrender of his citadel to him. Then he withdrew to Merv.

Nasr ibn Sayyar. He made Nasr ibn Sayyar his lieutenant over Tukharistan. A number of the Arabs refused to acknowledge the latter's authority, and he resorted to force, but later ambassadors of both parties met and came to an agreement.

Muslim's rebellion. Then Hisham appointed as his *'amil* over Iraq Khalid ibn 'Abdallah al-Qasri, who made his brother, Asad ibn 'Abdallah, governor of Khurasan. News of this reached Muslim ibn Sa'id, who marched until he came to Farghana, and took possession of that city. He cut the trees and laid waste the cultivated land. The Turkish Khaqan came down upon him with his army, and he withdrew from Farghana and marched three stages on a single day, until his beasts could go no further. The Turks attacked the outskirts of his camp.

One of the poets says: "Thou, didst wage war on us rebelliously, fearing dismissal, But thou didst not escape from this vain world of trouble."

Al-Hasan fears the Turks. Asad proceeded to Samarqand and appointed as 'amil over it al-Hasan ibn Abu'l-'Amarrata. The Turks used to attack the outskirts of Samarqand and raid, and al-Hasan would retreat whenever they made a raid, and would not meet them. One day he was preaching, and cried out against the Turks in his sermon, saying, "O God, cut off the last remnant of them, and speedily destroy their power, and send down calamity (*sabr*) upon them." And the people of Samarqand reviled him, and said, "Nay, let God rather send down ice (*sabar*), and make their feet to slip."

Asad's conquests. Asad raided the Nimrud mountains, and Nimrud surrendered to him and accepted Islam. He raided Khuttal. When he arrived at Balkh, he ordered its city to be built and transferred the government offices thither. In his raids against Khuttal he could accomplish nothing, but brought suffering and hunger upon the people. Charges were preferred to him against Nasr ibn Sayyar, and he had him beaten and sent him to Khalid together with three men who were suspected of insurrection. Then Asad withdrew from Khurasan, leaving as his lieutenant over it al-Hakam ibn 'Awana al-Kalbi.

Ashras governor. Hisham appointed as 'amil over Khurasan Ashras ibn 'Abdallah al-Sulami. With him was a Nabatean scribe named 'Umayra, his *kunya* being Abu Umayya. This scribe incited him to evil. Ashras increased the assessments of Khurasan, ignored the *dihqan*s, invited the people of Transoxiana to accept Islam, and ordered the remission of the *jizya* for all converts to the faith. There was a rush to accept Islam, and the taxes decreased. When Ashras saw this, he seized the tribute money. The people disapproved of this, and became disaffected towards him. Thabit Qutna al-Azdi championed their cause. He was called Qutna ("cotton") because he had a sightless eye upon which he used to wear a piece of cotton. Ashras sent and scattered them, seized Thabit and imprisoned him. Later he let him go, on paying a sum of money, and sent him away somewhere, and the Turks made an attack upon him and killed him.

Al-Junayd governor. In the year 112 Hisham appointed al-Junayd ibn 'Abd al-Rahman al-Murri 'amil over Khurasan. He met the Turks and attacked them, sending out some skirmishers, who defeated the son of Khaqan while he was out hunting and drunk. They captured him and took him to al-Junayd ibn 'Abd al-Rahman, who sent him to Hisham, and continued the campaign against the Turks until he had overcome them. He wrote for reinforcements to Hisham, who sent to his assistance 'Amr ibn Muslim at the head of 10,000 men from Basra, 'Abd al-Rahman ibn Nu'aym at the head of 10,000 from Kufa. He also supplied him with 30,000 spears and 30,000 shields, and took charge of the payments, assigning stipends to 15,000 men.

Death of al-Junayd. Al-Junayd made many raids. During his administration the partisans of the Banu Hisham spread and their cause became strong. Al-Junayd died in Merv, and Hisham appointed as governor of Khurasan 'Asim ibn 'Abdallah ibn Yazid al-Hilali.

Abu 'Ubaidah says that the regions about Tukharistan became turbulent, and al-Junayd subdued them and brought them back to peace and the payment of tribute.

2   Tabari: Another Look
at the Arab Conquests

INTRODUCTION

Abu Ja'far Muhammad al-Tabari (839–923), a historian and commentator on the Qur'an, was born in Amul in Tabaristan (north-central Iran) to a fairly affluent family. He became an avid and prodigious student, and had traveled far and wide seeking education. Al-Tabari quickly became a scholar and a prominent religious authority in his own right, and spent most of his life following his travels in Baghdad, the intellectual capital of the Muslim world of the time.

Al-Tabari's Tarikh al-rusul wa'l muluk (History of the prophets and kings), or simply the History, is written in the genre of a universal history, stretching back to the Creation, and proceeding with the history of the Old Testament prophets, the kings of ancient Persia, the history of the Sasanian Empire, and the Prophet Muhammad. Then, al-Tabari's History is arranged annalistically, describing the events that occurred throughout the history of the Umayyads and 'Abbasids, down to the year 915. Tabari's work, written in Arabic, was later translated into Persian by the Samanid vizier Bal'ami, and both the original and the translation continued to inform many in Central Asia and elsewhere for generations to come. First published by de Goeje over a period of two decades (from 1879), the text continued to be republished and edited, with an ongoing English translation. Al-Tabari sometimes provides several parallel (often contradictory) accounts of the same event with the goal to show the evidence and not so much to construct a single, overarching narrative. The following segments cover some events that occurred during the first half of the eighth century, focusing on the conquests of Qutayba and their aftermath, and are especially interesting to compare and contrast with the earlier account by Baladhuri.

Events of the Year AH 93
(October 19, 711–October 6, 712)

When Qutayba took the peace tribute of the lord of Khorezm, al-Mujashshar b. al-Muzahim al-Sulami said, "I need [to say something to you]; let me be alone with you." Qutayba did so, and al-Mujashshar said, "If you want to conquer the Soghdians one of these days, do so now, for they feel secure from your moving against them this year. They are only ten days away." Qutayba said, "Has anyone advised you to suggest this?" He said, "No." Qutayba said, "Have you informed anyone of it?" He said, "No." Qutayba said, "If anyone speaks of it, I shall execute you." ...

Qutayba addressed [his army] and said, "God has conquered this place for you at a time when campaigning in it is possible. Now this region of Soghd has no one to defend it. They have broken the covenant that was between us. They have withheld that on the basis of which we made peace with Tarkhun, and have done to him that which has reached you. God has said, "Whosoever breaks his oath breaks it but to his own hurt, Go with God's blessing. I hope that Khorezm and Soghd will be like al-Nadir and Qurayza,[2] for God has said, *And other [spoils] you were not able to take; God has encompassed them already* (Qur'an 48:21).

He besieged them for a month; in the course of being besieged, [the Soghdians] fought [Qutayba's men] several times from a single direction. Fearful throughout the siege, the Soghdians wrote to the king of Shash and the Ikhshad of Farghana, "If the Arabs vanquish us, they will visit upon you the like of what they brought us."

[The king of Shash and the Ikhshad and their followers] agreed to go to [the Soghdians] and sent word to them, "Send [against the Arabs] those who may distract them, so that we may make a night attack on their camp."

['Ali] said: They chose horsemen from among the sons of the *marzban*s (Persian governors of frontier provinces), the Asawira (Persian cavalry), and heroic men of strength, and sent them off, having ordered them to stage a night attack on the [Arab] camp. The spies of the Muslims came bearing information (of this), and Qutayba chose three hundred—or six hundred—men of courage, put Salih b. Muslim in charge of them, and sent them along the road from which he feared that he might be approached. Salih sent out spies to bring him information [about the enemy), while he [himself] stopped two *parsang*s away from their camp. The spies returned and informed him that [the enemy] would be coming to him that night. Salih split his cavalry into three groups, kept two of them hidden, and [himself] stayed on the main road. The polytheists came by night, unaware of the position of Salih and confident that no one would engage them before [they reached Qutayba's] camp. They did not know about Salih until they ran into him.

['Ali] said: [Salih and his men] charged them and, when spear thrusts were being exchanged, the two hidden groups came out and fought.

According to ['Ali]—one of the Barajim (one of two clans by that name): I was present [on that occasion], and I have never seen people fighting more strongly or with more fortitude in adversity than the sons of those kings; only a few of them fled. We gathered together their weapons, cut off their heads, and took prisoners. We asked them about those whom we had killed, and they said, "You have killed none other than [here] a son of a king, or [here] one of the nobles, or [here] one of the heroes. You have killed men [among whom were those who were each] the

---

2. Two Jewish tribes of Medina.

equal of a hundred men; [in those cases,] we have written [their names] on their ears." Then we entered the camp in the morning, and there was not a single man among us who did not hang up a head known by name. We took as plunder excellent weapons, fine goods, and brisk riding animals, and Qutayba let us have all that as *nafal* [booty].

That broke the Soghdians. Qutayba set up mangonels against [the Soghdians], and shot at them, fighting them without desisting. He was well advised by those of the Bukharans and Khorezmians who were with him; they fought hard and gave of themselves unstintingly. Ghurak (ruler of Samarqand) sent [word] to [Qutayba], "You are fighting me with my brothers and family from [among] the non-Arabs. Send Arabs out to me." Qutayba became angry, summoned al-Jadali, and said, "Review the [army] and pick out the bravest people," and [al-Jadali] gathered the [army] together. Then Qutayba set, reviewing them himself. He summoned the platoon commanders and began to call for one man after another, saying, "What do you have?" The platoon commander would say, "(This is) a brave [man]." "And what is this?" "This is one of limited ability." "And what is this?" "This is a coward." Qutayba called the cowards "the Stinkers," took their good weapons, and gave them to the brave men and those of limited ability, and left them the most worn-out weapons. Then Qutayba took them forward and fought the enemy with them, using both horsemen and infantrymen. He bombarded the city with the mangonels and made a breach [in the wall] which [the enemy] blocked with sacks of millet. There emerged a man who stood on top of the breach and shouted abuse at Qutayba. Qutayba said to the archers who were with him, "Choose two of your number," and they did so. Qutayba said, "Which of the two of you will shoot at this man (on the understanding that,] if he hits him, he will receive ten thousand [*dirhams*] and, if he misses him, his hand will be cut off?" One of them held back, while the other came forward and shot him, right in the eye. [Qutayba] ordered that he be given ten thousand [*dirhams*].

As for [authorities] other than [Bahila], they say: Qutayba said, "The slaves have become frightened. Depart victorious," and they departed. He made peace with them the next day, on [the following terms]: [1] 2,200,000 [*dirhams*] per annum; [2] in that year, 30,000 slaves free of defect and including neither young boys nor old men; [3] that they would empty the city for Qutayba, and would not have in it any fighting men; [4] that there would be built for Qutayba in it a mosque, so that he might enter [it] and pray, and [that] a pulpit would be set up in it, so that he might preach a sermon, eat lunch, and go forth. . . .

['Ali] said: As for the Bahilis, they say: Qutayba made peace with them in return for one hundred thousand slaves, the fire temples, and the adornments of the idols. He took receipt of that on the basis of which he had made peace with them, and he was brought the idols, which were despoiled and then placed before him; gathered together, they were like an enormous edifice. He ordered that they be burned, and the non-Arabs said to him, "Among them are idols the burner of which will be destroyed." Qutayba said, "I shall burn them with my own hand." Ghurak came, knelt before him, and said, "Devotion to you is a duty incumbent upon me. Do not expose yourself to these idols." Qutayba called for fire, took a brand in his hand, went out, proclaimed "God is great," and set fire to them; [others then also] set fire [to them], and they burned fiercely. In the remains of the gold and silver nails that had been in them, they found fifty thousand *mithqals*.

['Ali] said: Muhammad b. Abi 'Uyayna said to Salm b. Qutayba in the presence of Sulayman b. 'Ali, "The non-Arabs revile Qutayba for perfidy; he acted perfidiously at Khorezm and Samarqand."

*   *   *

Events of the Year AH 110
(April 16, 728–April 4, 729)

ASHRAS AND THE AFFAIR OF THE PEOPLE OF SAMARQAND AND THOSE WHO FOLLOWED THEM IN IT

It is stated that Ashras said while governor of Khurasan, "Seek out for me a man possessing piety and excellence, that I may send him beyond the Oxus to call them to Islam." He was then advised to appoint Abu'l-Sayda' Salih b. Tarif, the *mawla* of the Banu Dabba. But this man said, "I am not skillful in Persian"; therefore they attached to his service al-Rabi' b. 'Imran al-Tamimi. Abu'l-Sayda' declared, "I am going forth on the condition that whoever becomes a Muslim will not have the *jizya* taken from him, and thus only the *kharaj* of Khurasan will be on the heads of the men." Ashras said, "Yes." Abu'l-Sayda' then said to his companions, "I am going forth. If the officials do not deal in good faith, will you help me against them?" They said, "Yes." Thus he traveled to Samarqand, where al-Hasan b. Abi al-'Amarrata al-Kindi was in charge of both the military forces and the financial office.

Abu'l-Sayda' called on the people of Samarqand and its environs to become Muslims, stipulating that the *jizya* would be removed from them. At this, the people hurried [to become Muslims]. Therefore, Ghurak wrote to Ashras saying, "The *kharaj* has fallen off drastically." Ashras then wrote to Ibn Abi al-'Amarrata saying, "In the *kharaj* there is power for the Muslims. I have heard that the inhabitants of Soghd and their likes have not become Muslims by [their own] desire, but rather they have only entered into Islam to escape the *jizya*. Therefore, see who has been circumcised, performs the ritual obligations, practices his Islam rightly, and can recite a chapter from the Qur'an. From him [alone] lift [the burden of] the *kharaj*."

Then Ashras dismissed Ibn Abi al-'Amarrata from the financial office, giving it [instead] to Hani' b. Hani', to whom he joined al-Ikhshid [title of the ruler of Samarqand]. Ibn Abi al-'Amarratah said to Abu'l-Sayda', "I have nothing to do with the *kharaj* anymore, but beware of Hani' and al-Ikhshid. Therefore, Abu'l-Sayda' began forbidding them from taking the *jizya* from whoever had become a Muslim. Hani' wrote [to Ashras], "The people have become Muslims and built mosques." Then the *dihqans* of Bukhara came to Ashras to say, "Who will you take the *kharaj* from, now that all the people have become Arabs?" Ashras wrote back to Hani' and to the [financial] officials, "Take the *kharaj* from whomever you used to take it from." Thus they brought back the *jizya* upon those who had become Muslims.

At this, seven thousand of the inhabitants of Soghd refused [to pay] and seceded, setting up camp seven *farsakh*s from Samarqand. These went out to them to support them: Abu'l-Sayda', Rabi' b. 'Imran al-Tamimi, al-Qasim al-Shibani, Abu Fatima al-Azdi, Bishr b. Jurmuz al-Dabbi, Khalid b. 'Ubaydallah al-Hajari, Bishr b. Zunbur al-Azdi, 'Amir b. Qushayr or Bashir al-Khojendi, Bayan al-'Anbari, and Isma'il b. 'Uqba.

Ashras removed Ibn Abi al-'Amarrata from the military command (as well), putting in his place al-Mujashshir b. Muzahim al-Sulami, joining to him Umayra b. Sa'd al-Shibani.

When al-Mujashshir arrived, he wrote to Abu'l-Sayda', asking that he come to him with his companions. When Abu'l-Sayda' and Thabit Qutna came, he imprisoned them both. Abu'l-Sayda' declared, "You have committed betrayal and gone back on what you said!" Hani' answered him, "It is not betrayal as long as bloodshed is prevented by it." He transported Abu'l-Sayda' to Ashras but kept Thabit Qutna in his own prison. When Abu'l-Sayda' was transported, his companions met and put Abu Fatima in command in order that they might fight Hani'. But Hani' said to them, "Wait until I write to Ashras, so that we may get his opinion and act according to his command." Thus they wrote to Ashras. Then Ashras wrote, "Impose the *kharaj* upon them."

After this, the followers of Abu'l-Sayda' went back [to their opposition], but their movement weakened, while their leaders were pursued, taken, and carried to Merv. Thabit remained imprisoned. Ashras appointed Sulayman b. Abi al-Sari, the *mawla* of the Banu Uwafa, as a colleague for Hani' b. Hani' in charge of the *kharaj*. Hani' and his agents pressed on with the collection of the *kharaj* insistently, treating the Iranian nobles with disregard. Al-Mujashshir gave Umayra b. Sa'd power over the *dihqans*, who were made to stand while their clothes were torn and their belts were tied around their necks. The agents also took the *jizya* from those of the humble who had become Muslims. As a result, [the people of] Soghd and Bukhara became apostates, calling upon the Turks to send an army [to support them]. . . .

According to 'Ali: Ashras went out to campaign and stopped at Amul, where he stayed for three months. He sent ahead Qatan b. Qutayba b. Muslim, who crossed the Oxus with ten thousand men. Thereupon the forces of Soghd and Bukhara, accompanied by the Khaqan and the Turks, approached, beleaguering Qatan in his camp, which was protected by a trench. The Khaqan began to choose a horseman every day who would cross the Oxus with a group of Turks. Some of the Turks suggested, "Attack their animals while they are unsaddled." Thus they crossed and made their raid while the Muslims were dispersed. Ashras then released Thabit Qutna on the surety of 'Abdallah b. Bistam b. Mas'ud b. 'Amr, sending him forth with the latter and the cavalry. They followed the Turks and fought them at Amul until they had rescued what the Turks held. Then (other)

Turks crossed the Oxus to their compatriots who were returning, (enabling them to escape). Then Ashras crossed with the Muslims to join Qatan b. Qutayba. . . .

THE BATTLE OF PAYKEND

The enemy approached, and, when they were close by, the Muslims met and fought them for a short time, then broke off the engagement. In that time, some men of the Muslims were slain. Then the Muslims renewed the battle, (this time) persevering. The polytheists were defeated. Ashras passed on with the troops until they camped at Paykend. At this, the enemy cut off their water; Ashras and the Muslims stayed in their camp that day and night. When they arose in the morning, their water being exhausted, they dug (for water) but did not find any and became thirsty. Thereupon they left for the city where the waters had been cut off from them, Qatan b. Qutayba being in charge of the Muslim vanguard. The enemy met and fought them to the point that the Muslims were exhausted from thirst. Seven hundred of them died and the troops were unable to fight. Only seven men were left in the battle line of al-Ribab. Dirar b. Husayn was almost captured owing to the exhaustion he suffered. Al-Harith b. Surayj urged the men on, saying, "O people, being killed by the sword is nobler in this world and greater in reward with God than death by thirst." At this al-Harith b. Surayj, Qatan b. Qutayba, and Ishaq, the son of Muhammad the brother of Waki', advanced with horsemen of the Banu Tamim and the Qays. They fought until they drove the Turks from the water, whereupon the men hurried to it, drinking and quenching their thirst.

Thabit Qutna passed by 'Abd al-Malik b. Dithar al-Bahili and said to him, "O 'Abd al-Malik, do you follow the traditions of the *jihad*?" The latter answered, "Wait for me while I wash and embalm myself!" Thabit stood waiting for him until he came out, then the two of them went on their way. Thabit said to his companions, "I am more knowledgeable about fighting those than you are," and urged them on. Thus they attacked the enemy. The fighting grew furious, and Thabit was slain along with a number of the Muslims.

B | *Central Asia under the Samanids*

3   Narshakhi: The Rise of the House of Saman

Introduction

Narshakhi's history of Bukhara is arguably the most impor-
tant source for the social and political history of Central Asia in the early Islamic
period. Unfortunately little is known about the author, Abu Bakr Muhammad
ibn Ja'far al-Narshakhi (c. 899–960), other than that he was from the village of
Narshakh, near Bukhara, and that he delivered his history to the Samanid Amir
Nuh ibn Nasr (r. 943–54) in the year 943. The chronicle, as it has come down to us,
was translated from Arabic into Persian in the twelfth century and modified several times to incorporate information from other works and to extend its coverage
beyond the lifetime of the original author. A detailed textual analysis can be found
in Frye's introduction to his translation of this valuable history of early Islamic
Central Asia.

The excerpt below details the events surrounding the rise of the Samanids
(819–1005), Central Asia's first Islamic ruling dynasty. The Samanids are believed
to be descendents of Saman Khudah, an influential dihqan from the vicinity of
the city of Balkh, in northern Afghanistan. Saman Khudah was both a powerful political figure and an early convert to Islam. As a reward for his services and
loyalty, the 'Abbasid Caliph al-Ma'mun (r. 813–33) reportedly granted to his four

grandsons the right to rule Samarqand, Farghana, Shash (Tashkent), and Herat. Arguably the greatest of the Samanid amirs was Isma'il (r. 892–907), who is cred-ited with moving the dynastic capital from Samarqand to Bukhara after the death of his older brother Nasr in 892. Narshakhi's account, reproduced below, recounts Isma'il's leadership qualities and strength of character, which he demonstrates by relinquishing regal authority back to Nasr even after defeating him in battle.

An Account of the House of Saman and Their Lineage

When Asad ibn 'Abdallah al-Qushayri (*sic*, al-Qasri) be-came the amir of Khurasan he came and remained there till he died in the year 166/782–83 (*sic*, 120/738). It is said that he was a man of good works and generous. He was so thoughtful that he took care of the great and old families (of Khurasan). He held in esteem the people of noble origin both of the Arabs and the natives. When Saman Khudah, who was the ancestor (of the Samanids), fled from Balkh and came to him in Merv, the amir showed him honor and respect. He (the amir) subdued his foes and gave Balkh back to him. Saman Khudah accepted Islam from him. He was called Saman Khudah because he had built a village which was called Saman. They called him by that name, just as the amir of Bukhara (was called) Bukhar Khudah. When a son was born to Saman Khudah, out of friend-ship for the (governor), he named him Asad. This Asad was the grandfather of the late amir Isma'il Samani. . . . From the time (of Asad) the power of the Samanids increased every day till it attained what it did.

An Account of the Beginning of the Rule of the Samanid Family, May God Show Mercy on Them

When the caliphate passed to Ma'mun, Ghassan ibn 'Abbad be-came the amir of Khurasan. Ma'mun ordered him to give the children of Asad ibn Saman Khudah districts (to rule) among the cities of Khurasan. He gave each an important city in recognition of what they had done. Ghassan ibn 'Abbad made Nuh ibn Asad the amir of Samarqand and Ahmad ibn Asad the amir of Merv. This was in the year 202/817–18. When Ghassan was recalled from Khurasan, Tahir ibn al-Husayn became the amir and confirmed these districts on them. He gave a robe of honor to Nuh ibn Asad the eldest, who was in Samarqand till he died. He (Nuh) made his brother Ahmad ibn Asad his successor. Ahmad ibn Asad was a learned and pious man. He lived in Samarqand until he died. He (Ahmad) named his son, Nasr ibn Ahmad ibn Asad, his successor. When he sat in his father's place there came a mandate from the caliph Wathiq bi'llah (*sic*) for (the rule of) the provinces of Transoxiana, in his name. The date was Saturday the first day of the month of Ramadan of the year 251/(Wednesday, September 26, 865 (*sic*—261/875)).

The Beginning of the Rule of the Past Amir Abu Ibrahim Isma'il ibn Ahmad al-Samani

He was the first ruler of the Samanids. He was really a worthy ruler, meritorious, intelligent, just, kind, and a man of vision and foresight. He always showed obedience to the caliphs, and he found it proper and necessary to submit to them. On Saturday, in the middle of Rabi' the second of the year 287 (April 900), he took 'Amr (ibn) Layth prisoner at Balkh, and conquered his kingdom. He ruled for a period of eight years. In the year 295/907 he died in Bukhara. . . .

He was born in Farghana in the month of Shawwal 234 (May 849). When he was sixteen years old his father died. The amir Nasr, who was his elder brother, held him in high esteem. He served the amir Nasr. When Husayn ibn Tahir al-Ta'i came to Bukhara from Khorezm in Rabi' the second of the year 260 (January 874), fighting occurred between him and the people of Bukhara. After five days he secured possession of the city. He made the people of Bukhara forsake city and village. He killed many people. He allowed the Khorezmians to plunder and confiscate. At night they broke into the houses by force. They committed serious crimes and seized property. The people of Bukhara came out to fight against them, and many people were killed. A third part of the city burned. When the inhabitants of the city began to prevail, he (Husayn) made a proclamation and made peace. When the people who had gathered and had engaged in battle heard the news of the peace, they dispersed. Some went to their villages. When Husayn ibn (al)-Tahir realized that the people had dispersed he wielded his sword and killed a great many people. . . .

Then Abu 'Abdallah, son of Khoja Abu Hafs, wrote a letter to Samarqand to Nasr ibn Ahmad ibn Asad al-Samani, who was the amir of Samarqand and Farghana, and requested an amir for Bukhara from him. He sent his brother Isma'il ibn Ahmad, to Bukhara. When the amir Isma'il came to Karmina he remained there several days and sent a messenger to Bukhara to Husayn ibn Muhammad al-Khawariji [Khorezmi], who was (then) the amir of Bukhara. His messenger went several times and returned before it was decided that the amir Isma'il should be amir of Bukhara and Husayn ibn Muhammad al-Khawariji his successor. His (Khawariji's) army gave allegiance on this condition. Amir Isma'il sent a diploma of successorship to Khawariji with a banner and robe of honor. Khawariji went throughout the city with the banner and robe, and the people of the city rejoiced. This was on a Tuesday, and on Friday the *khutba* was read in the name of Nasr ibn Ahmad. The name of Ya'qub (ibn) Layth was struck out before Amir Isma'il's entry into the city. That (occurred) on the first Friday of the blessed month of Ramadan of the year 260 (ca. 25 June 874). . . .

The Entry of the Amir Isma'il into Bukhara

It was on Monday, the twelfth day of the blessed month of Ramadan of the year 260 (ca. 1 July 874). Because of this the city was quiet and the people of Bukhara were delivered from trouble and enjoyed peace. In the same year the amir Nasr ibn Ahmad was sent a diploma for the rule of all of the districts of Transoxiana, from the Oxus river to the extremity of the lands of the East, from the caliph Muwaffaq bi'llah. The *khutba* of Bukhara was read in the names of the amir Nasr ibn Ahmad and the amir Isma'il, and the name of Ya'qub (ibn) Layth Saffar was dropped from the *khutba*. Amir Isma'il lived some time in Bukhara and after that went to Samarqand, without waiting for an order from the amir Nasr. He left his nephew Abu Zakariya Yahya ibn Ahmad ibn Asad as his deputy in Bukhara. When he arrived in Rishkhan [*sic*, Rabinjan] the amir Nasr received news and became angry at his coming without permission. He ordered him (Isma'il) to be received but himself did not come out. He did not honor him, but ordered him escorted to the fortress of Samarqand. The chief of police of Samarqand represented him (Nasr). Thus he (Nasr) showed his displeasure at him. Amir Isma'il went to greet him (Nasr) because he had not done so since his departure to Bukhara. Muhammad ibn 'Umar was made his (Nasr's) deputy. Amir Isma'il came with greeting and remained standing an hour; then he left. Amir Nasr did not speak a word with him. . . . [Narshakhi then describes the falling out between the brothers, which he attributes to Nasr's unfounded suspicions of Isma'il's intents.]

Amir Nasr went to Rabinjan, prepared his army, and returned. Amir Isma'il went before him to a village Wazbdin. They assembled there and joined battle on Tuesday, the fifteenth day of the month of the second Jumada of the year 275 (26 October 888). Amir Isma'il was victorious over the army of Farghana and [his brother] Abu'l-Ash'ath fled in defeat. The entire army was defeated. Amir Nasr remained with a few men, but he too was defeated. Amir Isma'il called to a group of Khorezmians to keep away from the amir Nasr, then he (Isma'il) descended from his horse and kissed his (Nasr's) stirrup. . . .

Nasr ibn Ahmad dismounted from his horse, put down a cushion and sat on it. Amir Isma'il arrived and jumped off his horse, came to Nasr and kissed the cushion and said, "Oh amir! This was the will of God which made me (victorious) over you. I see His great work today with my own eyes." Amir Nasr replied, "I was surprised at what you did, since you did not obey your amir and did not observe the mandate which God the Exalted placed on you." Amir Isma'il said, "Oh amir, I acknowledge that I committed an error, and it is all my fault. You are better (than I) in kindness, so that you will let pass this great sin, and forgive me."

They were speaking thus when another brother, Ishaq ibn Ahmad, arrived and did not dismount from his horse. Amir Isma'il said, "Oh fellow, why don't you dismount (before) your superior?" He scolded him and was angry at him. Ishaq quickly dismounted and fell at Nasr's feet. He kissed the ground and asked forgiveness, (saying), "My horse was unmanageable and I could not dismount quickly."

When these words were finished the amir Isma'il said, "Oh amir, it is best that you quickly return to your home before news of this arrives there and your subjects in Transoxiana revolt." Amir Nasr asked, "Oh Abu Ibrahim, are you going to send me back to my place?" Isma'il replied, "If I do not do this what should I do? (Between) a slave and his master no other arrangement is possible. Whatever you wish (is yours)." Amir Nasr spoke and tears rolled down his cheek. He repented that he had embarked (on the war) and the blood which had been spilt. Then he rose and mounted (his horse). Amir Isma'il and his brother Ishaq held the stirrups and sent him on his way. . . . On that same day that Nasr ibn Ahmad had been made a prisoner, he spoke to that group (the people of Samarqand) in the same (manner) as when he was the amir. He sat on the throne and they stood in service before him. Four years later the amir Nasr died, seven days before the end of the month of Jumada the first of the year 279 (21 August 892). He named amir Isma'il his successor over all of the provinces of Transoxiana. He placed another brother, and his own son, under him (Isma'il).

When the amir Nasr died the amir Isma'il went from Bukhara to Samarqand and brought the kingdom in order. He appointed his (Nasr's) son Ahmad ibn Nasr his deputy (in Samarqand). He undertook raiding expeditions from there. Amir Isma'il returned to Bukhara, and he had been there twenty years before his brother died and gave all of Transoxiana to him.

When the news of the death of the amir Nasr came to the Commander of the Faithful Mu'tadid bi'llah, (279–89/892–902) he gave the amir Isma'il a mandate for the dominion of Transoxiana in the month of Muharram of 280 (March or April 893). At the same time he (Isma'il) went to fight at Taraz, where he experienced great difficulty. Finally the amir of Taraz came out with many *dihqan*s and accepted Islam. Taraz was thus subjugated. A large church was transformed into a grand mosque, and the *khutba* was read in the name of the Commander of the Faithful Mu'tadid bi'llah. Amir Isma'il returned to Bukhara with much booty. . . .

[Several years later,] a letter from the Commander of the Faithful arrived in Samarqand requesting that 'Amr (ibn) Layth (be sent).[3] The heading of the letter was written as follows: "From 'Abdallah ibn al-Imam Abu'l-'Abbas al-Mu'tadid bi'llah, Commander of the Faithful, to Abu Ibrahim Isma'il ibn Ahmad, client of the Commander of the Faithful." When the letter reached the amir Isma'il he was grieved for the sake of 'Amr (ibn) Layth, but he was unable to ignore the order of the caliph. He ordered 'Amr (ibn) Layth placed in a litter and brought to Bukhara. Amir Isma'il could not even turn his face toward him, because of shame. He sent a man to ask if he ('Amr) had any wishes. 'Amr (ibn) Layth said, "Take care of my children and give something to those persons who carry me so they will think well of me." Amir Isma'il did that, and seated him in a litter and sent him to Baghdad. When he arrived in Baghdad the caliph entrusted him to Safi his servant, and put him in prison. He was imprisoned by Safi till the end of

3. Narshakhi explains that 'Amr ibn Layth was a recalcitrant noble of Khurasan who, despite having caused no end of trouble to Amir Isma'il, received extraordinarily kind treatment at his hands after Isma'il soundly defeated him.

the reign of Mu'tadid. He had been in prison two years when he was killed in the year 280/893–94 (*sic*, 289/902).

When the amir Isma'il sent 'Amr (ibn) Layth to the caliph, the latter sent back the investiture for Khurasan from the pass of Hulwan, including the provinces of Khurasan, Transoxiana, Turkestan, Sind, Hind, and Gurgan. All became his, and the amir appointed an amir over every city. He made appear the results of justice and good conditions. He chastised whoever showed tyranny to his subjects. There was no one of the house of Saman more capable of governing than he, for he was like an ascetic and allowed no favoritism in the affairs of state. He always showed obedience to the caliph. In his lifetime he was no refactory one hour to the caliph, and he held his commands in highest esteem.

Amir Isma'il became sick; it was prolonged and the moisture aggravated his trouble. The doctors said that the atmosphere of Juy-i Muliyan was wet, so he was carried to the village of Zarman, which was his private property. They said that this air would be better for him. The amir liked that village and always went there for hunting. A garden had been made for him. He was sick there for some time till he died. It was in a certain garden under a large tree. It was on the fifteenth day of the month of Safar of the year 295 (26 November 907). He had been the amir of Khurasan twenty years, and the length of his rule was thirty years. May God show mercy on him, for in his time Bukhara became the seat of government. After him all of the amirs of the house of Saman held court in Bukhara. None of the amirs of Khurasan before him had lived in Bukhara. He considered his residence in Bukhara as fortunate, and he did not find satisfaction in any district except Bukhara. Wherever he was, he said my city, i.e., Bukhara, (has) such and such. After his death his son took his place, and he (Isma'il) was surnamed al-Amir al-Mazi.

4   *Hudud al-'Alam:* The Frontiers of the Muslim World in the Tenth Century

INTRODUCTION

The Hudud al-'Alam *was compiled in 982–83 by an unknown author who dedicated the manuscript to a member of the Farighunid dynasty, vassals of the Samanids in northern Afghanistan. Although written in Persian, the work falls into the category of Arab geographies, a genre that emerged from the earlier Greek tradition and developed in sophistication from the early years of the* '*Abbasid caliphate (750–1258). For the study of Central Asian history, the* Hudud al-'Alam *holds a special place in that genre due to its author's dedicated attention to the peoples and places at the frontiers of the Islamic world.*

Minorsky's textual analysis suggests that the author drew material from an array of sources, both textual and oral, much of which is no longer in existence. The "borrowing" of information from other sources was common practice, and correlations in the texts suggest that some of these same sources also informed the works of such celebrated Arab geographers as Ibn Hawqal, al-Mas'udi, and others. Minorsky further deduces that the author drew heavily from the earlier texts of al-Istakhri and Ibn Khurdadhbih, and probably also from Jayhani's reportedly monumental, and unfortunately lost, seven-volume Kitab al-mamalik wa'l-masa-lik *(Book of kingdoms and routes). This is important as, beginning in 914, Jayhani is known to have served as the vizier for the Samanid ruler Nasr b. Ahmad (914–43) and, Minorsky notes in his preface, "he wrote letters to all the countries of the world and he requested that the customs of every court and divan should be written down and brought to him, such (as existed in) the Byzantine empire, Turkestan, Hindustan, China, Iraq, Syria, Egypt, Zanj, Zabul, Kabul, Sind, and Arabia." The likelihood that some of this information has been preserved in the* Hudud al-'Alam *further adds to this source's already substantial importance.*

The paragraphs below introduce readers to the "ethnic" geography of tenth-century Islamic Central Asia, as well as to the non-Muslim peoples in the neighboring sedentary and pastoral-nomadic regions. The author exhibits a particular interest in the Turkic peoples of the north and the commodities that these peoples produced. Among the numerous interesting observations included here is the author's repetition of the popular tradition that the Samanid dynasty was of the family of "Bahram Chubin," which is to say their lineage could be traced back to the Sasanian kings of pre-Islamic Persia (224–651).

Discourse on the Toquz-Oghuz Country and Its Towns

East of it is the country of China; south of it, some parts of Tibet and the Qarluq (Khallukh); west of it, some parts of the Qïrghïz; north of it, also the Qïrghïz (?) extend along all the Toquz-Oghuz country. This country is the largest of the Turkish countries and original . . . the Toquz-Oghuz were the most numerous tribe. The kings of the whole of Turkestan in the days of old were from the Toquz-Oghuz. They are warlike people possessing great numbers of arms. In summer and winter they wander from place to place along the grazing grounds in the climates which (happen to be) the best. From their country comes much musk, as well as black, red, and striped foxes, furs of the grey squirrel, sable-marten, ermine, weasel . . . and yaks. The country has few amenities, and their commodities are things which we have enumerated, as well as sheep, cows, and horses. The country possesses innumerable streams. The wealthiest (of the Toquz-Oghuz?) are the Turks. The Tatar too are a race of the Toquz-Oghuz.

1. Jinanjkath (Chinanjkath, "Chinese town"), capital of the Toquz-Oghuz. It

is a middle-sized town. It is the seat of the government and adjoins the limits of China. In summer great heat reigns in it but the winter there is very pleasant. . . .

Discourse on the Country of the Yaghma and Its Towns

East of the Toquz-Oghuz country; south of it, the river Khu-land-ghun which flows into the Kucha river; west of it are the Qarluq borders. In this country there is but little agriculture, (yet) it produces many furs and in it much game is found.

Their wealth is in horses and sheep. The people are hardy, strong, and warlike, and have plenty of arms. Their king is from the family of the Toquz-Oghuz kings. These Yaghma have numerous tribes; some say that among them 1,700 known tribes are counted. Both the low and the nobles among them venerate their kings . . . and in their region there are a few villages.

1. Kashghar belongs to Chinistan but is situated on the frontier between the Yaghma, Tibet, the Qïrghïz, and China. The chiefs of Kashghar in the days of old were from the Qarluq, or from the Yaghma . . .

Discourse on the Qïrghïz Country

East of it is the country of China and the Eastern Ocean; south of it, the Toquz-Oghuz borders and some parts of the Qarluq; west of it, (parts) of the Kimek country; [north of it, parts] of the Uninhabited Lands of the North. In the [outlying] part of their country there is no population, and that (region) is the Uninhabited Lands of the North where people cannot live on account of the intensity of cold. From this country are brought in great quantities musk, furs, *khadang*-wood, *khalanj*-wood, and knife-handles made of *khutu*. Their king is called Qïrghïz-Khaqan. These people have the nature of wild beasts and have rough faces and scanty hair. They are lawless and merciless, (but) good fighters and warlike. They are at war and on hostile terms with all the people living round them. Their wealth consists of Qïrghïz merchandise, sheep, cows, and horses. They wander along rivers, grass, (good) climates, and meadows. They venerate the Fire and burn the dead. They are owners of tents and felt-huts, and are hunters and game-killers.

1. Furi (*Quri?*), name of a tribe which also belongs to the Qïrghïz but lives east of them and does not mix with the other groups of the Qïrghïz. They are man-eaters and merciless. The other Qïrghïz do not know their language and they are like savages.

2. This side of the Furi there is a town K.M.JKATH where the Qïrghïz-Khaqan lives.

3. K.SAYM, name of a clan of the Qïrghïz who with their felt-huts have established themselves on the slopes of the mountains. They hunt for furs, musk . . . and the like. They are a different tribe from the Qïrghïz. Their language is nearer to that of the Qarluq and they dress like the Kimek.

Except at the residence of the khaqan, no class of the Qïrghïz has any villages or towns at all.

Discourse on the Qarluq Country and Its Towns

East of it are some parts of Tibet and the borders of the Yaghma and the Toquz-Oghuz; south of it, some parts of the Yaghma and the country of Transoxiana; west of it, the borders of the Ghuzz; north of it, the borders of the Tukhs, Chigil, and Toquz-Oghuz. This is a prosperous country, the most pleasant of the Turkish lands. It possesses running waters and a moderate climate. From it come different furs. The Qarluq are near to (civilized) people, pleasant tempered and sociable. In the days of old, the kings of the Qarluq were called *jabghuy,* and also *yabghu.* The country possesses towns and villages. Some of the Qarluq are hunters, some agriculturists, and some herdsmen. Their wealth is in sheep, horses, and various furs. They are a warlike people, prone to forays. . . .

Discourse on the Ghuzz Country

East of this country is the Ghuzz desert and the towns of Transoxiana; south of it, some parts of the same desert as well as the Khazar sea; west and north of it, the river Itil (the Volga). The Ghuzz have arrogant faces and are quarrelsome, malicious, and malevolent. Both in summer and winter they wander along the pasture-lands and grazing-grounds. Their wealth is in horses, cows, sheep, arms, and game in small quantities. Among them merchants are very numerous. And whatever the Ghuzz, or the merchants, possess of good or wonderful is the object of veneration by the Ghuzz. (The Ghuzz) greatly esteem the physicians and, whenever they see them, venerate them, and these doctors have command over their lives and property. The Ghuzz have no towns, but the people owning felt-huts are very numerous. They possess arms and implements and are courageous and daring in war. They continually make inroads into the lands of Islam, whatever place be on the way, and (then) strike, plunder, and retreat as quickly as possible. Each of their tribes has a (separate) chief on account of their discords with each other.

Discourse on the Turkish Pechenegs

East of this country are the limits of the Ghuzz; south of it, those of the Burtas and Baradhas; west of it, those of the Majghari and the Rus; north of it, (the river) Rutha. This country in all respects resembles (that of) the Kimek and is at war with all its neighbours. The (Pechenegs) have no towns; their chief is one of themselves.

Discourse on the Qïpchaq Country

The southern frontier of the Qïpchaq marches with the Pechenegs, and all the rest marches with the Northern Uninhabited Lands where there is no living being. The Qïpchaq are a clan which, having separated from the Kimek, has settled down in these parts, but the Qïpchaq are more wicked than the Kimek. Their king is (appointed) on behalf of the Kimek.

Discourse on the Country of Khurasan and Its Towns

It is a country east of which is Hindustan; south of it, some of its (own) marches and some parts of the desert of Kargaskuh; west of it, the districts of Gurgan and the limits of the Ghuzz; north of it, the river Jayhun. This is a vast country with much wealth and abundant amenities. It is situated near the centre of the Inhabited Lands of the world. In it gold-mines and silver-mines are found as well as precious things such as are (extracted) from mountains. This country produces horses and its people are warlike. It is the gate of Turkestan. It produces numerous textiles, gold, silver, turquoises, and drugs. It is a country with a salubrious climate and with men strongly built and healthy. The king of Khurasan in the days of old was distinct from the king of Transoxiana but now they are one. The *mir* of Khurasan resides at Bukhara; he is from the Saman family and from Bahram Chubin's descendants. These (princes) are called Maliks of the East and have lieutenants in all Khurasan, while on the frontiers of Khurasan there are kings called "margraves."

1. Nishapur is the largest and richest town in Khurasan. It occupies an area of 1 *farsang* across and has many inhabitants. It is a resort of merchants and the seat of the army commanders. It has a citadel, a suburb, and a city. Most of its water is from the springs and has been conducted under the earth. It produces various textiles, silk, and cotton. To it belongs a special province with thirteen districts and four territories.

20. Herat, a large town with a very strong *shahristan,* a citadel, and a suburb. It has running waters. Its cathedral mosque is the most frequented in all Khurasan. The town lies at the foot of a mountain and is a very pleasant place. Many Arabs live there. It has a large river which comes from the frontier region between Ghur and Guzganan and is utilized in the districts of Herat. It produces cotton stuffs, manna, and grape-syrup.

42. Merv, a large town. In the days of old the residence of the *mir* of Khurasan was there but now he lives in Bukhara. It is a pleasant and flourishing place with a citadel built by Tahmurath; in it there are numerous castles. It was the abode of the (Sasanian) kings. In all Khurasan there is no town [better] situated. Its market is good. Their land taxes are levied on the extent of irrigation. Merv produces good cotton, root of asafoetida, *filata*-sweets, vinegar, condiments, textiles of raw silk and of *mulham* silk.

67. Balkh, a large and flourishing town which was formerly the residence of the Sasanian kings. In it are found buildings of the Sasanian kings with paintings and wonderful works, (which) have fallen into ruins. . . . (Balkh) is a resort of merchants and is very pleasant and prosperous. It is the emporium of Hindustan. There is a large river in Balkh that comes from Bamiyan and in the neighbour-

hood of Balkh is divided into twelve branches; it traverses the town and is altogether used for the agriculture of its districts. Balkh produces citrons and sour
oranges, sugar-cane, and water-lilies. Balkh has a shahristan surrounded by a
mighty wall. In its suburb there are numerous marshes.

Discourse on the Region of Khurasanian Marches

East of this region lies Hindustan; south of it, the deserts of
Sind and Kerman; west of it, the borders of Herat; north of it, the borders of Gh-
archistan, Guzganan, and Tukharistan. Some parts of this region belong to the
hot zone and some to the cold. From its mountains the Ghur-slaves are brought
to Khurasan. It is a place with much cultivation. Indian articles are brought to
this region.

1. Ghur, a province amid mountains and rugged country. It has a king called
Ghur-shah. He draws his strength from the *mir* of Guzganan. In the days of old
this province of Ghur was pagan; actually most of the people are Muslim. To them
belong numerous boroughs and villages. From this province come slaves, armour,
coats of mail, and good arms. The people are bad-tempered, unruly, and ignorant.
They are white and swarthy.

19. Ghaznin, a town situated on the slope of a mountain, extremely pleasant.
It lies in Hindustan and formerly belonged to it, but now is among the Muslim
lands. It lies on the frontier between the Muslims and the infidels. It is a resort of
merchants, and possesses great wealth.

20. Kabul, a borough possessing a solid fortress known for its strength. Its
inhabitants are Muslims and Indians, and there are idol-temples in it. The royal
power of the *raja* of Qinnauj [possibly Kannauj, on the banks of the Ganges River,
capital of north India in the seventh century], is not complete until he has made a
pilgrimage to those idol-temples, and here too his royal standard is fastened.

22. In Ghaznin and in the limits of the boroughs which we have enumerated, live the Khalaj Turks, who possess many sheep. They wander along climates,
grazing grounds, and pasture-lands. These Khalaj Turks are also numerous in the
provinces of Balkh, Tukharistan, Bust, and Guzganan. Ghaznin and the districts
adjacent to it are all called Zabulistan.

Discourse on the Country Transoxiana
and Its Towns

East of this country are the borders of Tibet; south of it, Khurasan and its marches; west of it, the Ghuzz and the borders of the Qarluq; north of
it, also the borders of the Qarluq. This is a vast, prosperous, and very pleasant
country. It is the Gate of Turkestan and a resort of merchants.

The inhabitants are warlike; they are active fighters for the faith, and (good)
archers. Their creed is pure. This is the country where justice and equity reign.
In its mountains there are very numerous mines of gold and silver, as well as all
sorts of fusible substances, such as are found in the mountains, and all sorts of

drugs, such as are found in the mountains, e.g., vitriol, arsenic, sulphur, and ammoniac.

1. Bukhara, a large town, the most prosperous of the towns in Transoxiana. Here is the residence of the King of the East. The place is damp, produces plenty of fruit, and has running waters. Its people are archers and active fighters for the faith. It produces good woollen carpets as well as saltpetre, which are exported to (different) places. The territory of Bukhara is 12 *farsangs* by 12 *farsangs*, and a wall has been built round the whole of it, without any interruption, and all the ribats and villages are within this wall.

5. Soghd, a region. There is no place among the eastern regions more flourishing than this. It has running waters, many trees, and a good climate. The people are hospitable and sociable. It abounds in amenities, is prosperous, and mild, pious people are numerous there.

13. Samarqand, a large prosperous, and very pleasant town. It is the resort of merchants from all over the world. It has a city, a citadel, and a suburb. On the roof of their market a stream of water flows in a leaden (conduit). In Samarqand stands the monastery of the Manichaeans who are called *nighushak* ("*auditores*"). Samarqand produces paper which is exported all over the world, and hemp cords. The Bukhara river flows near the gate of Samarqand.

45. Farghana, a prosperous, large and very pleasant region. It has many mountains, plains, running waters, and towns. It is the Gate of Turkestan. Great numbers of Turkish slaves are brought here. In its mountains there are numerous mines of gold, silver, copper, lead, ammoniac, quicksilver, combustible schists, bezoar stone, lodestone, and numerous drugs. It produces . . . plants useful in the preparation of wonderful medicines. The kings of Farghana belonged formerly to (the class of) margraves and were called *dihqan*.

63. Ilaq, a large province stretching between the mountains and the steppe. It has a numerous population, and is cultivated and prosperous, (but) the people have little wealth. Its towns and districts are numerous. The people profess mostly the creed of those "in white raiment." The people are warlike and arrogant-looking. . . .

79. Chach (Tashkent), a large and prosperous district. The inhabitants are active fighters for the faith, warlike, and wealthy. (The locality) is very pleasant. It produces great quantities of *khalanj*-wood, and of bows and arrows made of *khadang*-wood. Its kings formerly belonged to the class of margraves.

C | *The Age of Learning*

5 Ibn Sina: Biographical Notes

INTRODUCTION

Perhaps more than any other individual, the renowned scientist and philosopher Abu 'Ali al-Husayn ibn Sina (980–1037) personifies the marvelous scholarly achievements of the medieval Islamic world. Ibn Sina was born in a small village near Bukhara, where his father, an adherent to the Isma'ili sect of Islam, served in the administration of one of the last Samanid rulers, Nuh ibn Mansur (r. 976–97). The family moved to Bukhara in 985, and it was there that Ibn Sina received his scholarly training.

As a youth, Ibn Sina was a voracious reader and gifted student. He memorized the Qur'an even before he was ten years old, and by the time he turned fourteen his knowledge had surpassed that of all of the private tutors that his father had hired for him. He devoured the classics, mastering such fields as Aristotelian metaphysics, Euclidean geometry, and, without even the benefit of a teacher, the medical sciences. After healing his amir of a terrible illness that had eluded all other doctors in Bukhara, Ibn Sina was permitted access to the Samanid library.

Ibn Sina was also an extremely prolific author, credited with 131 treatises, commentaries, and other works on philosophy, logic, astronomy, mathematics, theology, and more. Indeed, he is most famous for his work in medicine. His primary work in this field, Qanun fi'l-tibb (Canon of medicine), is an encyclopedic and orderly summary of much of the medical knowledge in the world at the time. In addition to introducing many revolutionary scientific techniques, it includes

*such pragmatic features as a pharmacological analysis of 760 different drugs, the
plants from which they are derived, and their various applications. The Canon
was translated into Latin in the twelfth century, and by some reports it remained
the most important source for the medical sciences in Europe even into the seventeenth century. In Europe Ibn Sina was known by the Latinized version of his
name, Avicenna, but his students referred to him as the Shaykh al-Ra'is, or Leader
of the Wise Men.*

*The following is taken from Gohlman's authoritative translation of Ibn Sina's
autobiography, which includes the useful biographical continuation authored by
al-Juzjani, one of Ibn Sina's most devoted students. This excerpt details the great
scholar's early training and leaves off as the author was just entering his early
twenties, at the very beginning of the eleventh century. These years marked the
Turkic-Muslim Qarakhanid overthrow of Samanid authority in Bukhara and
Mahmud of Ghazna's rise to power in Afghanistan and Iran. In the tense environment that followed these events, Ibn Sina lost his patronage and his security, and
was reduced to the life of an itinerant scholar. As the excerpt woefully concludes,
"When I became great, no country could hold me; When my price went up, I
lacked a buyer."*

My father was a man of Balkh; he moved from there to Bukhara in the days of
Amir Nuh ibn Mansur, during whose reign he worked in the administration, being entrusted with the governing of a village in one of the royal estates of Bukhara.
[The village,] called Kharmaythan, was one of the most important villages in this
territory. Near it is a village called Afshana, where my father married my mother
and where he took up residence and lived. I was born there, as was my brother,
and then we moved to Bukhara. A teacher of the Qur'an and a teacher of literature were provided for me, and when I reached the age of ten I had finished the
Qur'an and many works of literature so that people were greatly amazed at me.

My father was one of those who responded to the propagandist of the Egyp-
tians and was reckoned among the Isma'iliyya. From them, he, as well as my
brother, heard the account of the soul and the intellect in the special manner
in which they speak about it and know it. Sometimes they used to discuss this
among themselves while I was listening to them and understanding what they
were saying, but my soul would not accept it, and so they began appealing to me
to do it [to accept the Isma'ili doctrines.] And there was also talk of philosophy,
geometry, and Indian calculation. Then he [my father] sent me to a vegetable seller
who used Indian calculation and so I studied with him.

At that time Abu 'Abdallah al-Natili, who claimed to know philosophy, arrived in Bukhara; so my father had him stay in our house and he devoted himself
to educating me. Before his arrival I had devoted myself to jurisprudence, with
frequent visits to Isma'il the Ascetic about it. I was a skillful questioner, having become acquainted with the methods of prosecution and the procedures of rebuttal
in the manner which the practitioners of it [jurisprudence] follow. Then I began to

read the *Isagoge* under al-Natili,[4] and when he mentioned to me the definition of genus, as being that which is predicated of a number of things of different species in answer to the question "What is it?" I evoked his admiration by verifying this definition in a manner unlike any he had heard of. He was extremely amazed at me; whatever problem he posed I conceptualized better than he, so he advised my father against my taking up any occupation other than learning.

I continued until I had read the simple parts of logic under him; but as for its deeper intricacies, he had no knowledge of them. So I began to read the texts and study the commentaries by myself until I had mastered logic. As for Euclid, I read the first five or six figures under him; then I undertook the solution of the rest of the book in its entirety by myself. Then I moved on to the *Almagest*,[5] and when I had finished its introductory sections and got to the geometrical figures, al-Natili said to me, "Take over reading and solving them by yourself, then show them to me, so that I can explain to you what is right with it and what is wrong." But the man did not attempt to deal with the text, so I deciphered it myself. And many a figure he did not grasp until I put it before him and made him understand it. Then al-Natili left me, going on to Gurganj.

I devoted myself to studying the texts—the original and commentaries—in the natural sciences and metaphysics, and the gates of knowledge began opening for me. Next I sought to know medicine, and so I read the books written on it. Medicine is not one of the difficult sciences, and therefore I excelled in it in a very short time, to the point that distinguished physicians began to read the science of medicine under me. I cared for the sick and there opened to me some of the doors of medical treatment that are indescribable and can be learned only from practice. In addition I devoted myself to jurisprudence and used to engage in legal disputations, at that time being sixteen years old.

Then, for the next year and a half, I dedicated myself to learning and reading; I returned to reading logic and all the parts of philosophy. During this time I did not sleep completely through a single night nor devote myself to anything else by day. I compiled a set of files for myself, and for each proof that I examined, I entered into the files its syllogistic premises, their classification, and what might follow from them. I pondered over the conditions of its premises, until this problem was verified for me. And because of those problems which used to baffle me, not being able to solve the middle term of the syllogism, I used to visit the mosque frequently and worship, praying humbly to the All-Creating until He opened the

---

4. In the third century, the Syrian philosopher Porphyry (233–309) wrote the *Isagoge* as an introduction to Aristotle's collective works on the logic of classification. Originally written in Greek, the *Isagoge* was translated into Latin and Arabic, and it became as important as Aristotle's own work on the subject.

5. The Latinized form of *al-Kitab al-Mijisti* (The great book), an extraordinarily influential Greek work in mathematics and astronomy that dates to the middle of the second century of the Common Era. Its author, Ptolemy, advanced a geocentric cosmology that placed the Earth at the center of the universe.

mystery of it to me and made the difficult seem easy. At night I would return home, set out a lamp before me, and devote myself to reading and writing. Whenever sleep overcame me or I became conscious of weakening, I would turn aside to drink a cup of wine, so that my strength would return to me. Then I would return to reading. And whenever sleep seized me I would see those very problems in my dream; and many questions became clear to me in my sleep. I continued in this until all of the sciences were deeply rooted within me and I understood them as far as is humanly possible. Everything which I knew at that time is just as I know it now; I have not added anything to it to this day.

Thus I mastered the logical, natural, and mathematical sciences, and I had now reached the science of meta physics. I read the *Metaphysics* [of Aristotle], but I could not comprehend its contents, and its author's object remained obscure to me, even when I had gone back and read it forty times and had got to the point where I had memorized it. In spite of this I could not understand it nor its object, and I despaired of myself and said, "This is a book which there is no way of understanding." But one day in the afternoon when I was at the booksellers' quarter a salesman approached with a book in his hand which he was calling out for sale. He offered it to me, but I refused it with disgust, believing that there was no merit in this science. But he said to me, "Buy it, because its owner needs the money and so it is cheap. I will sell it to you for three *dirhams*." So I bought it and, lo and behold, it was Abu Nasr al-Farabi's book on the objects of the *Metaphysics*. I returned home and was quick to read it, and in no time the objects of that book became clear to me because I had got to the point of having memorized it by heart. I rejoiced at this and the next day gave much in alms to the poor in gratitude to God, who is exalted.

It happened that the Sultan of that time in Bukhara, Nuh ibn Mansur, had an illness which baffled the doctors. Since my name had become well known among them as a result of my zeal for learning and reading, they brought me to his attention and asked him to summon me. Thus I presented myself and joined with them in treating him, and so became enrolled in his service. One day I asked him to permit me to go into their library, to get to know it and to read its books. He gave me permission and I was admitted to a building which had many rooms; in each room there were chests of books piled one on top of the other. In one of the rooms were books on the Arabic language and poetry, in another, on jurisprudence, and likewise in each room [were books on] a single science. So I looked through the catalogue of books by the ancients and asked for whichever one I needed. I saw books whose names had not reached very many people and which I had not seen before that time, nor have I seen since. I read these books and mastered what was useful in them and discovered the status of each man in his science.

So when I had reached the age of eighteen I was finished with all of these sciences; at that time I had a better memory for learning, but today my knowledge is more mature; otherwise it is the same; nothing new has come to me since.

In my neighborhood there was a man named Abu'l-Hasan the Prosodist, who asked me to compose for him a comprehensive work on this learning [which I had attained.] So I wrote *The Compilation* for him, and gave his name to it, including in it all of the sciences except mathematical science. At that time I was twenty-one years old. Also in my neighborhood there was a man named Abu Bakr al-Baraqi, a Khorezmian by birth, and a lawyer by inclination; he was distinguished in jurisprudence, Qur'an commentary, and asceticism, having a liking for these sciences. He asked me to comment on the books [in these sciences], and so I wrote *The Sum and Substance* for him in about twenty volumes. I also wrote for him a book on ethics which I called *Good Works and Evil.* These two works exist only in his possession, and he has not loaned out either on one of them to be copied.

Then my father died and I was free to govern my own affairs, and so I took over one of the administrative posts of the Sultan. Necessity then led me to forsake Bukhara and move to Gurganj, where Abu'l-Husayn al-Suhayli, an amateur of the sciences, was a minister. I was presented to the Amir there, 'Ali ibn Ma'mun, at that time I was in lawyer's dress, with a fold of the mantle under my chin. They gave me a monthly salary which provided enough for someone like me. Then necessity led me to move to Nasa, and from there to Baward (Abiward), and then to Tus, then to Samanqan, then to Jajarm at the extreme limit of Khurasan, and then to Jurjan. My destination was the Amir Qabus, but at that time there occurred the seizure of Qabus, his imprisonment in one of his castles, and his death there.

Then I departed for Dihistan, where I became very ill, and from where I returned to Jurjan. Abu 'Ubayd al-Juzjani joined me there and recited to me an ode on my state of affairs which contains the poet's verse:

> When I became great, no country could hold me;
> When my price went up, I lacked a buyer.

6   al-Biruni: On the Importance of the Sciences

INTRODUCTION

Abu'l-Rayhan al-Biruni (973–c. 1050) was born in a neighborhood near the outskirts of Kath, the capital of Khorezm at the time. He was a contemporary of the famed physician Ibn Sina, just seven years his senior, and an equally remarkable example of the vibrant scholarly environment in Islamic Central Asia at the time. Both were extraordinarily prolific masters of philosophy, theology, mathematics, and multiple fields of science, including, especially in al-Biruni's case, astronomy. Among his great achievements was having argued, some six centuries before Galileo, that the Earth rotates on its axis and that it revolves around the sun. One might note that, unlike the Italian's sad fate in seventeenth-century Europe, al-Biruni was not forced to recant.

Ibn Sina and al-Biruni are known to have corresponded during their long careers, but whereas Ibn Sina fled the Ghaznavids in favor of Persian patronage, al-

Biruni remained in his homeland until 1017, when Mahmud of Ghazna's armies invaded and took him (and several other respected scholars) back to Ghazna as intellectual war-booty. For the rest of his life, al-Biruni served the Turkic slave-kings, and several times accompanied them on raiding missions into India. While there he dedicated himself to studying local languages, cultures, and religious practices, and in the year 1030 he completed what would become his most famous work, the monumental Ta'rikh al-Hind.[6]

The excerpt here is taken from an altogether different source: one of al-Biruni's scientific treatises that addresses some of the finer points of mathematical geography. The author begins his study by delivering a scathing critique of his lazy and ignorant contemporaries who exhibited ambivalence, and even hostility, to his scholarly pursuits. He points out that the Qur'an explicitly commands Muslims to acquire knowledge, and he elaborates upon multiple reasons why it is absolutely necessary for them to do so. These include satisfying even such simple requirements of the religion as knowing how to determine the qibla so that Muslims may conduct their prayers in the manner stipulated by Islamic law. For al-Biruni, willful ignorance of the laws of science is therefore not only foolhardy, it is intrinsically un-Islamic. This sentiment resonated several centuries later with the great conqueror Tamerlane's grandson and ruler of Samarqand, Mirza Ulughbeg (1394–1449). Renowned as the "astronomer-king," Ulughbeg adorned the magnificent madrasa that stands in the Registan Square in his capital city of Samarqand with celestial decorations and ornate calligraphy stating: "It is the duty of all Muslims to pursue knowledge."

In the Name of God, Most Gracious, Most Merciful

I feel I can almost trust the findings of the astrologers concerning the cycles and rules that govern the motions of hundreds and thousands of the stars, and that events all over the world are governed by those same rules; when I behold how the people of our time, in different parts of the world, reflect such forms of ignorance, and how proud of it they are; how antagonistic to people of excellent virtues they are; how they plot against a learned scholar and inflict on him all sorts of harm and persecution. . . .

The extremist among them would stamp the sciences as atheistic, and would proclaim that they lead people astray in order to make ignoramuses, like him, hate the sciences. For this will help him to conceal his ignorance, and to open the door for the complete destruction both of sciences and scientists.

The rude and stubborn critic among them, who calls himself impartial, would listen to scientific discourses, but his persistent stubbornness ultimately reveals

---

6. See Edward C. Sachau, trans., *Alberuni's India* (London: W. H. Allen, 1879, and reprint editions).

the meanness of his forebears. He would come forth with what he considers to be great wisdom, and say: "What is the benefit of these sciences?" He does not know the virtue which distinguishes mankind from all sorts of the animal kind: it is knowledge, in general, which is pursued solely by man, and which is pursued for the sake of knowledge itself, because its acquisition is truly delightful, and is unlike the pleasures desirable from other pursuits. For the good cannot be brought forth, and evil cannot be avoided, except by knowledge. What benefit then is more vivid? What use is more abundant? In spiritual as well as in worldly affairs, we cannot be sure, without knowledge, that what we seek and bring forth is the good, and that that which we avoid is evil.

If worldly possession is the benefit mentioned heretofore, then one can attain such a benefit in three ways: (a) Safe occupations which do not prosper without some knowledge and are morally sound vocations: such as the governorship of a district, business and commerce in general, and real estate brokerage. (b) Dangerous occupations: such as alchemy, falsification of documents, theft of jewelry, cheating in selling, theft of money, and robbing by choking. (c) The third way is pursued by him whose excessive greed has extinguished the lights in his heart and mind: such as selling wine, the prostitution of males and females, and the procurement of kith and kin for illicit sexual intercourse with strangers. Such a villain would not avoid such despicable pursuits; he would probably find all sorts of excuses for their approbation, and for him these are delightful activities, because they would provide him with the immense material benefits which he sought.

I do not think a benefit seeker is concerned about the good for his soul in the hereafter. Suppose he is concerned, then it is well known that primitive worship does not do his soul any good, because it is not based on intelligent knowledge which discriminates good from evil. Such primitive worship abounds in different parts of the world, and is practiced by different nations. Hence it is a cause for dissent, because truth can not be reached by worships based on different dogmas. If a worshipper is a truth seeker, then he is eventually led to an investigation of the old and new conditions of the world, and if he ignores that investigation, he can not pursue truth without reading intelligently about the rules of order in the universe and its parts, and without investigating the validity of those rules. This investigation will acquaint him with the Maker and His deserving qualities; and the knowledge of these qualities is the *sine qua non* for the recognition of a revealed prophecy, because their identification is essential to discriminate between a proper and a pseudo prophet. The pretenders to revelations are many, and since they do not agree among themselves, it is certain that some of them are false pretenders who would lead people astray.

This point of view is that which God Almighty would accept from His servants. He says, and what He says is luminous truth, *And contemplate the (wonders of the) creation in the heavens and the earth, Our Lord! Not for naught has Thou created (all) this!* (Qur'an 3:191). This noble verse contains the totality of what I have explained in detail, and until a man is truly disciplined by its instructions he can not truly realize the essence of wisdom in all forms of science and knowledge. There are two alternatives: either he would take it as a story and a tradition, or he would scientifically investigate and realize the truth it contains. But surely there is a great difference between an investigator of truth and a follower of tradition. God says, *Are those equal, those who know and those who do no know? It is those who are endowed with understanding that receive admonition* (Qur'an 39:9). A traditional follower of these principles is as ignorant as a traditionalist who follows what is derivable from them. God Almighty guides to the truth!

As to the sciences, man was naturally inclined to accept them, because during his lifetime he could only fulfill certain specific functions. The diversity of his needs, his insatiable desires, and his lack of instruments for defending himself against his many enemies, have all forced on him the inevitability of a civilized life with his human kind, that is, to cooperate in the division of labor, so that each may work for himself, as well as for others. Everyone needed something that can be divided into parts, and another which can be accumulated by duplication. Hence labor was divided according to need. But as labor and needs were disproportionate, and the times of labor involved were unequal, people devised systems of prices and exchanges which were based on the intrinsic worth of metals, jewels, and things resembling them, which are pleasant to look at, durable, and of rare occurrence. The exchanges and prices were made on the just basis of labor involved, which thieves and oppressors do not disregard, and which even waterfowls like the *burak* (swans?) and the pelicans uphold. When these birds fish in shallow water, they divide into two groups: one group flaps its wings on the water and drives the fish towards the other group which traps it, but does not devour it without sharing the catch with the chasing group. They actually gather the fish in sacks at the backs of their mouths, then discharge them and distribute them equally. Glory be to God Almighty!

Further, I say that a civilized person is keen to possess worldly valuables, *Heaped up hoards of gold and silver, horses, branded, and cattle and well-tilled land* (Qur'an 3:14). Hence the need arose for sciences which enable people to check the amount and area of possessions, when transferred from one owner to another, either by exchanges, or by inheritance. The principles of these sciences are called mathematics and formulae; they are embodied in the science of geometry, and its benefit has just been mentioned.

Also, as man breathes the air which may carry various kinds of infections, and as he lives on water and plants of various qualities, and as he is subject to heavenly and tellurian cataclysms which invade him from without, and storm upon him from within, and as the repulse of some of these mishaps is possible, and as there is an antidote to every evil (?), so man's experiments and investigations have led him to build up the sciences for medical and veterinary services. This organic science developed as time went on, and mankind and most animals have benefited by its development, but its achievements have remained insignificant when they are compared with those of absolute science. . . .

I say, further, that man's instinct for knowledge has constantly urged him to probe the secrets of the unknown, and to explore in advance what his future conditions may be, so that he can take the necessary precautions to ward off with fortitude the dangers and mishaps that may beset him. Also, as the influence of the sun in the atmosphere changes in cycles which revolve with the seasons, and as the influences of the moon on the seas and the rains are cyclic, which revolve with her quarters and the nychthemerons; so man has extended his experiments and observations to the stars in the universe, other than the sun and the moon, and built up the science of astronomy, with its special methods of observation, without much trouble, or external complications.

As man has the gift of speech, and as he is an argumentative dialectician on worldly affairs, and those of the hereafter; so his speech has to conform to certain rules, because the statements he makes may be either false or true. Therefore he devised the science of logic, which is based on the compound syllogism in dialectic to discover the truth or error in a given premise or proposition, and to correct an erroneous inference. . . .

The science of logic is attributed to Aristotle, and some of his theories and beliefs run contrary to the beliefs of Islam, because he was a theoretician and not a theologian. The Greeks and the Romans of his days were idolaters and star worshippers, so the extreme fanatics of our days call everyone whose name ends with (the letter) *sin* a rejecter of Islam and an atheist. The *sin* does not occur in the original Greek name; it appears in the transliteration into the Arabic, and is tacked on to the end to facilitate the pronunciation of the name, when it is used in the nominative case. But ignoring an achievement and distorting it out of hatred for its author, and ignoring the truth in one case because its author had erred in another are both contrary to what God, be He exalted, says, *Those who listen to the Word and follow the best (meaning) in it; those are the ones whom God has guided* (Qur'an 39:18). Yes, logic was written in words similar to the original Greek words, and in terms unfamiliar to the moderns, and because the subject itself is intricate, people have found it difficult to understand, and hence have avoided it. . . .

Let us put aside all that, and ignore the recalcitrant, and let us point out the great need for ascertaining the direction of the *qibla* in order to hold the prayer which is the pillar of Islam and also its pole. God, be He exalted, says, *So from whencesoever thou startest forth, turn thy face in the direction of the sacred Mosque, and wheresoever ye are, turn your face thither* (Qur'an 2:150). It is also intuitively known that this direction varies with the place at which the direction of the Ka'ba is to be determined. This is witnessed in the Sacred Mosque itself, and should be more evident, when considered from other places. If the distance from the Ka'ba is small, its direction may be determined by a diligent seeker, but when the distance is great, only the astronomers can determine that direction.

Every challenge calls for the right men. They (some researchers) have determined the longitudes of cities, which are the measure of their eastern or western displacements, and their latitudes, which are the measure of their northern or southern displacements. They have done this in accordance with the fundamental propositions of astronomy, based on the motion of the plumb line towards the center. These people were highly satisfied with themselves, because they were able to delve into such minute details of a science, and thought that they were masters of the whole science, and not only of its sources and principles. However, when they were asked to determine the direction of the *qibla* they were perplexed, because the solution of this problem was beyond their scientific powers. You see that they have been discussing completely irrelevant phenomena: like the directions in which the winds blow, and the ascensions of the lunar stations.

Even the professional astronomers find it a difficult problem to solve, and so you can well imagine how difficult it is for a non-astronomer! Most surprising of all these people is the man working on the determination of the local meridian, who thinks that it is the same plane all over the earth, and adds to this another proposition, that the sun culminates at the zenith of Mecca. He even composes a syllogism for it, and says: "The time for meridian crossing is the same all over the earth, and the sun culminates at the zenith of Mecca during its meridian passage. Hence a man facing the sun at meridian passage is turning his face towards Mecca."

I have no patience with this logician, because he built up his syllogism on two premises: the first of which is false, and the second is a particular premise, but he has considered it universal. It is useless to argue with such a man, because he is completely ignorant of the science of astronomy, but we shall follow his chain of reasoning and ask him about the application of his syllogism at Mecca itself. Why is it that the *qibla* at Mecca is not on the local meridian? Why is it that at places which are distant one mile east, or one mile west of Mecca, people do not pray by turning their faces to the meridian which is the same meridian for such places? To him it is the one meridian in reality, but to the astronomers it is the one meridian empirically. . . .

If the investigation of distances between towns, and the mapping of the habitable world, so that the relative positions of towns become known, serve none of our needs except the need for correcting the direction of the *qibla*, we should find it our duty to pay all our attention and energy for that investigation. The faith of Islam has spread over most parts of the earth, and its kingdom has extended to the farthest west; and every Muslim has to perform his prayers and to propagate the call of Islam for prayer in the direction of the *qibla*.

Part 2 | Encounter with the Turks

INTRODUCTION

One of the most consequential developments in the history of the Muslim world and particularly in the history of Central Asia was the influx of Turkic peoples into the region, and beyond. The Turkic encounter with, and subsequent integration into, the Muslim world occurred largely through the migrations—both voluntary and forced—of large numbers of Central and Inner Asian Turkic peoples to the Near and Middle East. Many of the Turks who made their way out of the steppe did so as conquerors, many others arrived as slaves, but the majority eventually embraced Sunni Islam. It did not take long—just a couple of centuries from their initial encounter—before a sizable portion of the Muslim world would be ruled by Turkic dynasties, many of which had as their founders slaves who served in different capacities, frequently in the military. In the Central Asian context, particular mention should be made of the Qarakhanids (999–1211), the first Turkic-Muslim dynasty in Central Asia; the Ghaznavids (977–1187), the dynasty centered in Ghazna (modern day Afghanistan) founded by Sebuktegin, a military commander for the Samanids; and the Saljuqids (Saljuqs), a Turkic dynasty that flourished in the eleventh and twelfth centuries, and ruled over much of Western Asia. The impact of the rising Turkic presence was at first felt perhaps most profoundly in the political arena and in the military, but it quickly influenced many other aspects of life as well, including language, customs and rituals.

The origin of the Turks is still debated. It is established that they emerged as a significant political power, rather than an ethnic category, in Mongolia in the middle of the sixth century. This was the Türk Qaghanate, and the historical sources indicated that the Ashina clan was their proverbial leader. Expanding to the east and to the west, the qaghanate clashed with other nomadic entities in the region and used a series of alliances and counter-alliances with nomadic and sedentary polities to establish its authority over vast portions of Central and Inner Asia. During this period, many Turks migrated to the northern and western parts of Central Asia, gradually mixing with and often subsuming earlier Iranian nomadic populations and polities.

The qaghanate was essentially divided in two, the eastern and western parts, each with its own administrative structure and distinct pattern of government. By the early seventh century, the eastern part succumbed to Tang China and practically disappeared, whereas the western part continued to prosper, although internal disputes eventually caused it to fragment as well. In the late seventh century, the so-called Second Qaghanate was born, still ruled by the Ashina clan, and, gaining strength, even fought alongside the Soghdians against the Arabs in 712–13 (they were defeated). It was during the Second Qaghanate that the Orkhon inscriptions were crafted, interpreted by some to indicate the celestial origins of the Turks. This qaghanate also fell after its leader, Bilge Qaghan, died in 734, and much of its remnants were incorporated into a new polity ruled by Uyghurs (744–840) and based in Ordu Baliq. After the destruction of the Uyghur state, a Turkic Qarluq ruler, related to the Ashina clan, established a new dynasty that became known in modern scholarship as the Qarakhanids. Conflicts quickly emerged between the Qarakhanids and their western neighbors, the Samanids. At first the Samanids were victorious and expanded into Qarakhanid territory, but this pattern was reversed throughout most of the tenth century.

Under the Samanids, Turkic slave troops (*ghulam*) were taken from the Central Asian steppes to serve as military soldiers in the sedentary state. Before long, this practice spread to other states as well. Turks were popularly considered to be better soldiers, and they were reputed to be loyal servants of their new masters. Replacing the old military systems, the new soldiers-turned-commanders rose to prominence and, by the end of the tenth century, they were the de facto lords of the land. Many of them also converted to Islam during that period. The most famous of these conversion narratives in Central Asia was—and still is—associated with the Qarakhanid ruler Satuq Bughra Khan.

Politically, the remains of the Samanid state were divided by the Ghaznavids to the south of the Amu Darya and the Qarakhanids to the north. By the middle of the eleventh century, the Saljuqs ended Ghaznavid expansion to the west. They conquered Khorezm and continued on to emerge victorious over Iran and Iraq and westward even into the Byzantine Empire. From the late 1080s, the Qarakhanids too became vassals of the Saljuqs, and, soon thereafter, a Turkic *ghulam* of the Saljuqs founded a new dynasty of kings in Khorezm, known as the khorezmshahs. Further to the north and east, in the 1130s, the Qara Khitai (Khitans) began to make their forceful presence known in Central Asia. Migrating from northern China, the Khitans expanded westward at the expense of the Qarakhanids, establishing their capital in Balasaghun, and, continuing their military conquest, forced much of the area to send them tribute. Of course, this did not prevent the seemingly subordinate dynasties from fighting amongst themselves.

Although the Turks arrived into the Muslim world as infidels (from the Muslim perspective), they soon became very much part of that world, and Muslim historians and geographers felt the need to explain their origins and find ways to include the Turks in the Muslim narrative. The Turks were therefore incorporated into the Muslim account of creation, and were accorded their place in history as descendants of Yafith (Japheth, one Noah's three sons). Muslim authors also sought to explain the Turks' influential presence within the boundaries of Muslim civilization, and at times they even devised for the Turks a Muslim heritage, regardless of whether or not there was any veracity to it.

In terms of historiography, or sources for the period, we have general histories and local histories written under Ghaznavid patronage, as well as important materials composed in the Qarakhanid realm. These include the *Diwan Lughat al-turk* (the famous Turkic dictionary), and multiple examples of the so-called "mirror for princes" genre of literature. Most of the sources for this era were also written in Arabic and include the fast-growing and popular genre of advice literature, lexicographical efforts to understand not only the Arabic language but Turkic as well, geographies and geographical manuals, and translations of the Arabic chronicles into the emerging New Persian.

A | *Turkic Peoples of the Steppe*

7   The Orkhon Inscriptions: The Early Turks

INTRODUCTION

Inscriptions from the eighth century AD (probably from the 730s), were discovered near Lake Tsaidam, to the west of the river Orkhon in modern-day Mongolia, in 1889 by the Russian explorer N. M. Yadrinstev. The two monoliths, dedicated to the Turkic rulers Kul Tegin and his brother Bilge Qaghan, contain long inscriptions in Old Turkic, carved in runic script, as well as inscriptions in Chinese. Studied first by the Russian-German Turkologist V. V. Radlov, the inscriptions were translated into Danish and French already in the late nineteenth century by the Danish philologist Vilhelm Thomsen (who disagreed with Radlov on some interpretations), and most English speakers since have been familiar with the rendering of the Danish translation into English.

The inscriptions, carved apparently by artisans especially brought from China, open with a statement from the patron, and then continue to describe his deeds and relate the history of his forefathers, Bumïn and Istemi, two centuries earlier. Events are recounted in a heroic fashion and relate the glorious deeds of past rulers as well as the circumstances that led to their downfall. The inscriptions not only detail campaigns of conquest and dealings with distant realms, but also serve as a warning of the dangers of not upholding proper governance and the proper veneration of the ancestors.

The Kul Tegin Inscription

I, the Heaven-like and Heaven-born Turkish Bilge Qaghan, succeeded to the throne at this time. Hear my words from the beginning to the end, first of all you, my younger brothers and my sons, and my folks and relatives, you, shadpit lords to the south, tarkans and buyruq lords to the north, you, Otuz (Tatar?), and you, Toquz-Oghuz lords and people! Hear these words of mine well, and listen hard! Eastwards to the sunrise, southwards to the midday, westwards as far as the sunset, and northwards to the midnight—all the peoples within these boundaries (are subject to me).

This many peoples I have organized thoroughly. These peoples are not rebellious now. If the Turkish qaghan rules from the Otukan mountains there will be no trouble in the realm. I went on campaigns eastwards up to the Shantung plain; I almost reached the ocean. I went on campaigns southwards up to Toquz-Arsin; I almost reached Tibet. Westwards I went on campaigns up to the Iron Gate beyond the Pearl River, and northwards I went on campaigns up to the soil of Yir Bayirqu. I have led (the armies) up to all these places. A land better than the Otukan mountains does not exist at all! The place from which the tribes can be (best) controlled is the Otukan mountains. Having stayed in this place, I came to an amicable agreement with the Chinese people. They (i.e., the Chinese people) give (us) gold, silver, and silk in abundance. The words of the Chinese people have always been sweet and the materials of the Chinese people have always been soft. Deceiving by means of (their) sweet words and soft materials, the Chinese are said to cause the remote peoples to come close in this manner. After such a people have settled close to them, (the Chinese) are said to plan their ill will there. (The Chinese) do not let the real wise men and real brave men make progress. If a man commits an error, (the Chinese) do not give shelter to anybody (from his immediate family) to the families of his clan and tribe. Having been taken in by their sweet words and soft materials, you Turkish people were killed in great numbers.

O Turkish people, you will die! If you intend to settle at the Choghay mountains and on the Togultun plain in the south, O Turkish people, you will die! . . .

If you stay in the land of Otukan, and send caravans from there, you will have no trouble. If you stay at the Otukan mountains, you will live forever dominating the tribes! O Turkish people, you always regard yourselves as satiated! You do not think of being hungry or satiated; if you once become satiated, you do not think of being hungry (again). On account of your being so, you went in (almost) all directions without a asking the advice of your qaghan who had nourished (you). You were completely ruined and destroyed in those places. (Of you), those who survived there, utterly exhausted, were marching in (almost) all directions. Since Heaven was gracious, and since I was granted with fortune, I succeeded to the throne. Having succeeded to the throne, I gathered all the poor and destitute people together. I made the poor people wealthy and the few people numerous; or, is there any falsehood in these words of mine? O Turkish lords and people, hear this! How you should live and dominate (other) tribes, I have recorded here; and how you would (otherwise) perish by being unfaithful (to your qaghan), this, too, I have recorded here. All words which I had to tell (you) I have recorded on this eternal stone. See these writings and get a lesson (from them)! You, faithful Turkish peoples and lords, you lords, you who have always been obedient to the throne, are you going to betray? I (had) the memorial (stone inscribed). I sent for painters from (the Chinese) emperor, and ordered them to decorate (the mausoleum). (The Chinese emperor) did not reject my request and (they) sent the court painters of the Chinese emperor. I got them to build an extraordinary mausoleum. I had the inside and outside (of the mausoleum) decorated with wonderful paintings and sculptures. I had the stone inscribed. I had (all) the words in my mind (recorded). See these writings and get a lesson (from them), all of you up to (the descendants) and subjects of (the On-Oq). I had the memorial stone inscribed. Since this is a (central?) place, and since it is in a much frequented place, I had the memorial stone inscribed and written in such a frequented place. See this memorial and learn its contents, as it is. I (inscribed?) that stone. The one who inscribed these inscriptions is his (that is, Prince Kul's) nephew (Prince) Yollugh.

When the blue sky above and the reddish-brown earth below were created, between the two human beings were created. Over the human beings, my ancestors Bumïn Qaghan and Ishtemi Qaghan became rulers. After they had become rulers, they organized and ruled the state and institutions of the Turkish people. (All the peoples living in) the four quarters of the world were hostile (to them). Having marched with the armies, they conquered all the peoples in the four quarters of the world and subjugated them. They made the proud enemies bow and the powerful ones kneel. They settled the Turkish people eastwards up to the Khingan mountains and westwards as far as the Iron Gate. They ruled (organizing) the Kok ("Blue") Turks between the two (boundaries). Wise qaghans were they, brave qaghans were they. Their *buyruqs* (that is, high officials), too, were wise and brave, indeed. Both the lords and peoples were peaceable. For this reason, they were able to keep the state under control. Having kept the state under control, they arranged the state rules and regulations.

They thus passed away. As mourners and lamenters there came from the east, from where the sun rises, the representatives of the people of the Bukli plain, the Chinese, the Tibetan, the Avar, the Byzantium, the Qïrghïz, the Uch-Quriqan, the Otuz-Tatar, the Qitan and the Tatabi.... This many peoples came and mourned and lamented. So famous qaghans were they. Then the younger brothers succeeded to the throne and the sons succeeded to the throne. But, apparently the younger brothers did not resemble their elder brothers, and the sons did not resemble their fathers. (Consequently) unwise qaghans succeeded to the throne, bad qaghans succeeded to the throne. Their *buyruqs*, too, were unwise and bad. Since the lords and peoples were not in accord, and the Chinese people were wily and deceitful, since they were tricky and created a rift between younger and elder brothers, and caused the lords and peoples to slander one another, the Turkish people caused their state which they had established to go to ruin, and their qaghan whom they had crowned to collapse. Their sons worthy of becoming lords became slaves, and their daughters worthy of becoming ladies became servants to the Chinese people. The Turkish lords abandoned their Turkish titles. Those lords who were in China held the Chinese titles and obeyed the Chinese emperor and gave their services to him for fifty years. For the benefit of the Chinese, they went on campaigns up to (the land of) the Bukli qaghan in the east, where the sun rises, and as far as the Iron Gate in the west. For the benefit of the Chinese emperor they conquered countries.

Then, the Turkish common people apparently said as follows, "We used to be a people who had an (independent) state. Where is our own state now? For whose benefit are we conquering these lands?" they said. "We used to be a people who had its own qaghan. Where is our own qaghan now? To which qaghan are we giving our services?" they said. By talking in this way (among themselves), they again became hostile to the Chinese emperor. But, after they had become hostile to him, they could not form and organize themselves well, and therefore they again submitted (to the Chinese).

(The Chinese), without taking into consideration the fact that (the Turkish people) have given their services so much (to the Chinese), said, "We shall kill and exterminate the Turkish people." (The Turkish people) were about to be annihilated. But, the Turkish god above and the Turkish holy earth and water (spirits below) acted in the following way: In order that the Turkish people would not go to ruin and in order that it would be an (independent) nation again, they (i.e., the Turkish god and the holy spirits) held my father, Ilterish Qaghan, and my mother, Il Bilge Katun, at the top of heaven and raised them upwards. My father, the qaghan, went off with seventeen men. Having heard the news that (Ilterish) was marching off, those who were in towns went up mountains and those who were on mountains came down (from there); thus they gathered and numbered to seventy men. Due to the fact that Heaven granted strength, the soldiers of my father, the qaghan, were like wolves, and his enemies were like sheep. Having gone on campaigns forward and backward, he gathered together and collected men; they all numbered seven hundred men. After they had numbered seven hundred men, (my father, the qaghan) organized and ordered the people who had lost their state and their qaghan, the people who had turned slaves and servants, the people who had lost the Turkish institutions, in accordance with the rules of my ancestors. He (also organized there) the Tolis and Tardush (peoples), and gave them a *yabghu* and a *shad*. To the south the Chinese people was (our) enemy, to the north Baz Qaghan and the Toquz-Oghuz people were (our) enemies; the Qïrghïz, Quriqan, Otuz-Tatar, Qitan and Tatabi . . . they all were hostile (to us).

My father, the qaghan, (fought against?) all these (peoples?). He went on campaigns forty-seven times and engaged in twenty battles. By the grace of Heaven, he took the realm of those who had had a realm, and captured the qaghan of those who had had a qaghan; he subjugated the enemies. He made the powerful enemies kneel and the proud ones bow. (My father, the qaghan) after he had founded (such a great) empire and gained power, passed away. My uncle, the qaghan, first erected Baz Qaghan as a *balbal* for my father, the qaghan. In accordance with the state rules, my uncle succeeded to the throne. After my uncle, the qaghan, succeeded to the throne, he organized and nourished the Turkish people anew. He made the poor rich and the few numerous. When my uncle, the qaghan, succeeded to the throne, I was *shad* over the Tardush people. Together with my uncle, the qaghan, we went on campaigns eastwards up to the Green River (i.e., the Yellow River) and the Shantung plain, and we went on campaigns westwards as far as the Iron Gate. (We went on campaigns up to the land of the Qïrghïz) beyond the Kogman (mountains). In all we went on campaigns twenty-five times and we fought thirteen times. We took the realm of those who had had a realm, and we captured the qaghan of those who had had a qaghan. . . .

You, Turkish and Oghuz lords and peoples, hear this! If the sky above did not collapse, and if the earth below did not give way, O Turkish people, who would be able to destroy your state and institutions? O Turkish people, regret and repent! Because of your unruliness, you yourselves betrayed your wise qaghan who had (always) nourished you, and you yourselves betrayed your good realm which was free and independent, and you (yourselves) caused discord.

8   al-Jahiz: The Peculiarities of the Turks

INTRODUCTION

A prolific Arab author, theologian, and polemicist from Basra (in Iraq), Abu 'Uthman 'Amr al-Basri (776–868/9), whose nickname, al-Jahiz, suggests a malformation of the eyes, was particularly famous for his observations on Man and Nature. It seems he held no official position, but still enjoyed considerable patronage and was able to produce, according to tradition, nearly two hundred literary compositions in numerous fields, from the animal kingdom to metaphysics, all written in elegant prose.

In his work on the merits of the Turks, al-Jahiz defends the decision to include Turks in the armies of the caliphate because their military skills, he writes, are far superior to those of anyone else. This excerpt begins with a comparison of different "warring" cultures with the aim of establishing the military superiority of the Turks over their Kharijite and Bedouin counterparts, and thus justify the caliphs' incorporation of the Turks into the imperial military system. This justification in itself was important but was not enough, so al-Jahiz also ends this section by a favorable comparison of Turks and Arab-Bedouin culture. Some elements in this essay may also resonate with the sentimental concept of the "noble savage" of eighteenth-century Europe.

The Merits of the Turks and of the
Imperial Army as a Whole

A Kharijite at close quarters relies entirely on his lance. But the Turks are as good as the Kharijites with the lance, and in addition, if a thousand of their horsemen are hard-pressed they will loose all their arrows in a single volley and bring down a thousand enemy horsemen. No body of men can stand up against such a test.

Neither the Kharijites nor the Bedouins are famous for their prowess as mounted bowmen. But the Turk will hit from his saddle an animal, a bird, a target, a man, a couching animal, a marker post, or a bird of prey stooping on its quarry. His horse may be exhausted from being galloped and reined in, wheeled to right and left, and mounted and dismounted: but he himself goes on shooting, loosing ten arrows before the Kharijite has let fly one. He gallops his horse up a hillside or down a gully faster than the Kharijite can make his go on the flat. The Turk has two pairs of eyes, one at the front and the other at the back of his head.

One of the criticisms of the Kharijite concerns his way of disengaging from combat, and of the Khurasani his method of engaging. The weakness of the Khurasanis is that as soon as they come up with the enemy they wheel round: if pursued they then take flight, and return again and again to the charge. These are reckless tactics, which may encourage the enemy to keep on their heels. When the Kharijites break off an engagement, it is broken off for good: once they withdraw they do not return to the charge, unless by chance. The Turk does not wheel round like the Khurasani; indeed if he turns his horse's head it is deadly poison and certain death, for he aims his arrow as accurately behind him as he does in front of him. Especially formidable is his trick of using his lasso to throw a horse and unseat its rider, all at full gallop. . . . He also commonly resorts to another trick with his lasso: he aims it nowhere near his adversary, and the fool takes this for clumsiness on the Turk's part or adroitness on his own!

They train their horsemen to carry two or even three bows, and spare bowstrings in proportion. Thus in the hour of battle the Turk has on him everything needful for himself, his weapon, and the care of his steed. As for their ability to stand trotting, sustained galloping, long night rides, and cross-country journeys, it is truly extraordinary. In the first place the Kharijite's horse has not the staying-power of the Turk's pony; and the Kharijite has no more than a horseman's knowledge of how to look after his mount. The Turk, however, is more experienced than a professional farrier, and better than a trainer at getting what he wants from his pony. For it was he who brought it into the world and reared it from a foal; it comes when he calls it, and follows behind him when he runs. It is so well trained that it recognizes the call meant for it, as a horse knows "*hoo!*," a she-camel "*hal!,*" a camel "*jahi!,*" a mule "*adas,*" and a donkey "*sasa,*" or as the village idiot knows his nickname or a child its name.

If the Turk's daily life were to be reckoned up in detail, he would be found to spend more time in the saddle than on the ground. The Turk sometimes rides a stallion, sometimes a brood mare. Whether he is going to war, on a journey, out hunting, or on any other errand, the brood mare follows behind with her foals. If he gets tired of hunting the enemy he hunts waterfowl. If he gets hungry, jogging up and down in the saddle, he has only to lay hands on one of his animals. If he gets thirsty, he milks one of his brood mares. If he needs to rest his mount, he vaults on to another without so much as putting his feet to the ground. Of all living creatures he is the only one whose body can adapt itself to eating nothing but meat. As for his steed, leaves and shoots are all it needs; he gives it no shelter from the sun and no covering against the cold. As regards ability to stand trotting, if the stamina of the border fighters, the posthorse outriders, the Kharijites, and the eunuchs were all combined in one man, they would not equal a Turk. The Turk demands so much of his mount that only the toughest of his horses is equal to the task; even one that he had ridden to exhaustion, so as to be useless for his expeditions, would outdo a Kharijite's horse in staying-power, and no Tukhari pony could compare with it.

The Turk is at one and the same time herdsman, groom, trainer, horse-dealer, farrier, and rider: in short, a one-man team. When the Turk travels with horsemen of other races, he covers twenty miles to their ten, leaving them and circling around to right and left, up on to the high ground and down to the bottom of the gullies, and shooting all the while at anything that runs, crawls, flies, or stands still. The Turk never travels like the rest of the band, and never rides straight ahead. On a long, hard ride, when it is noon and the halting-place is still afar off, all are silent, oppressed with fatigue and overwhelmed with weariness. Their misery leaves no room for conversation. Everything round them crackles in the intense heat, or perhaps is frozen hard. As the journey drags on, even the toughest and most resolute begin to wish that the ground would open under their feet. At the sight of a mirage or a marker post on a ridge they are transported with joy, supposing it to be the halting-place. When at last they reach it, the horsemen all drop from the saddle and stagger about bandy-legged like children who have been given an enema, groaning like sick men, yawning to refresh themselves and stretching luxuriously to overcome their stiffness. But your Turk, though he has covered twice the distance and dislocated his shoulders with shooting, has only to catch sight of a gazelle or an onager near the halting-place, or put up a fox or a hare, and he is off again at a gallop as though he had only just mounted. It might have been someone else who had done that long ride and endured all that weariness.

At a gully the band bunches together at the bridge or the best crossing-place; but the Turk, digging his heels into his pony, is already going up the other side like a shooting star. If there is a steep rise, he leaves the track and scrambles straight up the hillside, going where even the ibex cannot go. To see him scaling such slopes anyone would think he was recklessly risking his life: but if that were so he would not last long, for he is always doing it.

... The Kharijite's lance is long and heavy, the Turk's a hollow pike; and short hollow lances have greater penetrating power and are lighter to carry. This is why the Iranis keep long lances only for their foot-soldiers: these are the weapons used by the Persians of Iraq for fighting at the entries to trenches and from behind barricades. Not that they are to be compared with the Turks or the Khurasanis; in most cases they use them only at the entries to trenches or from behind barricades. The others are horsemen and riders, and horses and riders are the pivot of an army. They it is who withdraw and return to the charge, who fold the battalions around themselves as a letter is folded, and then scatter them like hair. No ambush advance-guard or rearguard duty but is always entrusted to the best of the mounted troops. Theirs are the glorious days, the famous battles, the vast conquests. Without them there could be no squadrons or battle formations. They it is who carry the standards and banners, the kettledrums, bells, and trappings. Theirs are the neighing, the dust flying, the spurring on, the cloaks and weapons flapping in the wind, and the thunder of hooves; they are the unerring in pursuit, the unattainable when pursued. . . .

National Characteristics

. . . Know that every nation, people, generation or tribe that shows itself outstanding in craftsmanship or pre-eminent in eloquence, the various branches of learning, the establishment of empires or the art of war, only attains the peak of perfection because God has steered it in that direction and given it the means and the special aptitudes appropriate to those activities. Peoples of varying habits of thought, different opinions, and dissimilar characters cannot attain perfection unless they fulfill the conditions needed to carry on an activity, and have a natural aptitude for it. Good examples are the Chinese in craftsmanship, the Greeks in philosophy and literature, the Arabs in fields that we mean to deal with in their proper place, the Sasanians in imperial administration, and the Turks in the art of war. Do you not see that the Greeks, who studied theory, were not merchants, artisans, sowers, farmers, builders, fruit-farmers, hoarders of treasure, or men bent on making money by hard work? Their rulers absolved them from the necessity to work by providing for their needs; and hence they were free to engage in research, and (thanks to their single-mindedness, ingenuity, and imaginativeness) to invent machines, tools, and musical instruments—music which brings peace to the soul, relaxation after travail, and blessed balm for the ulcer of anxiety. They built for men's profit and edification scales, balances, astrolabes, hourglasses, and other [instruments], and invented medicine, mathematics, geometry, music, and engines of war such as the mangonel, etc. They were thinkers, not doers: they designed the machine, made a template and drew a model of the tool, but could not use it; they confined themselves to giving directions about instruments, without handling them themselves. They loved science, but shrank from its application.

The Chinese for their part are specialists in smelting, casting, and metalworking, in fine colours, in sculpture, weaving, and drawing; they are very skilful with their hands, whatever the medium, the technique, or the cost of the materials. The Greeks are theoreticians rather than practitioners, while the Chinese are practitioners rather than theoreticians; the former are thinkers, the latter doers.

The Arabs, again, were not merchants, artisans, physicians, farmers—for that would have degraded them—, mathematicians, or fruit-farmers—for they wished to escape the humiliation of the tax; nor were they out to earn or amass money, hoard possessions or lay hands on other people's; they were not of those who make their living with a pair of scales, or [by giving short measure] in dried foods, and knew neither the *qirat* nor the *danaq*; they were not poor enough to be indifferent to learning, pursued neither wealth, that breeds foolishness, nor good fortune, that begets apathy, and never tolerated humiliation, which was dishonour and death to their souls. They dwelt in the plains, and grew up in contemplation of the desert. They knew neither damp nor rising mist, neither fog nor foul air, nor a horizon bounded by walls. When these keen minds and clear brains turned to poetry, fine language, eloquence, and oratory, to physiognomy and astrology, genealogy, navigation by the stars and by marks on the ground, and knowledge of anwa, to horse-breeding, weaponry, and engines of war, to memorizing all that they heard, pondering on everything that caught their attention and discriminating between the glories and the shames of their tribes, they achieved perfection beyond the wildest dreams. Certain of these activities broadened their minds and exalted their aspirations, so that of all nations they are now the most glorious and the most given to recalling their past splendours.

It is the same with the Turks who dwell in tents in the desert and keep herds: they are the Bedouins of the non-Arabs. . . . Uninterested in craftsmanship or commerce, medicine, geometry, fruit-farming, building, digging canals, or collecting taxes, they care only about raiding, hunting, horsemanship, skirmishing with rival chieftains, taking booty, and invading other countries. Their efforts are all directed towards these activities, and they devote all their energies to these occupations. In this way they have acquired a mastery of these skills, which for them take the place of craftsmanship and commerce and constitute their only pleasure, their glory, and the subject of all their conversation. Thus have they become in the realm of warfare what the Greeks are in philosophy, the Chinese in craftsmanship, and the Arabs in the fields we have enumerated.

9   Gardizi: The Turks in Early Muslim Traditions

INTRODUCTION

Abu Sa'id 'Abd al-Hayy Gardizi, a mid-eleventh-century Persian historian from Gardiz (a town in modern-day Afghanistan, east of Ghazna), may have been al-Biruni's student. His historical work, Zayn al-akhbar, was written in the reign of the Ghaznavid Sultan 'Abd al-Rashid (1049–1052), and contains a history of the pre-Islamic kings of Persia, of the Prophet and the caliphs to the year 1032, as well as a history of Khurasan until 1041. The part presented here, a chapter dealing with the Turks, was based primarily on the works of some

of the most important early Muslim geographers, including Ibn Khurdadhbih (a
Baghdad-based, ninth-century director of posts and intelligence in the 'Abbasid
Caliphate), al-Jayhani (a tenth-century prominent vizier of the Samanids), and
Ibn al-Muqaffa' (the eighth-century Iranian author and translator, and one of the
founding fathers of Arabic literary prose). The work was edited and translated into
Russian by the great Russian Orientalist Vasily Vladimirovich Bartol'd in 1897,
and has since received a number of translations and commentaries.

In this section, Gardizi follows Ibn al-Muqaffa' and others in incorporating
the Turks into the Muslim world by according them a place in the Muslim narra-
tive of creation. The account then describes the different units of the Turks, and a
comparison with the excerpt from the Hudud al-'Alam *is clearly warranted.*

The Origin and Characteristics of the Turks: The Legend of Japheth (Yafith)

In his book on *The Habitable Quarter of the World* 'Abdallah
Ibn al-Muqaffa' states that when the prophet Nuh (Noah), upon whom be peace,
came out from the ark, the world had become devoid of people. He had three
sons, Sam (Shem), Ham, and Yafith (Japheth), and he divided the earth among his
sons. The Land of the Blacks, such as Zanj, Abyssinia, Nubia, Barbary, and Fazz,
and the maritime and southern region of Persia he gave to Ham; Iraq, Khurasan,
Hijaz, Yemen, Syria, and the Iranian Realm became the portion of Sam; while the
lands of the Turks, the Saqlabs, and Gog and Magog as far as China fell to Yafith.
In as much as these lands of Turkestan were the farthest away from the areas of
cultivation he named them Tark (i.e., abandonment; neglected land fallen from
cultivation). Nuh, upon whom be peace, prayed and entreated the Lord, Almighty
and Glorious, that He might teach Yafith a Name of His, which when he called
upon Him by it, rain would at once come, and the Lord, Almighty and Glorious,
at once hearkened unto that prayer and so taught Yafith.

How the Turks Began to Use Rain Stones

When Yafith learned that Name, he wrote it on a stone which
he suspended about his neck out of precaution, lest he should forget it. Thereafter,
whenever he craved for rain, it would rain. Moreover, if he were to touch that
stone to water and give that water to a sick person, that person would become
better. That stone his descendants continued to hold as their inheritance until his
progeny, such as the Ghuzz, the Qarluq, the Khazar, and the likes of them, became
too many, at which time contention arose among them because of that stone.

[At that time] the stone was in the hands of the Ghuzz, and they agreed that
on such and such a day all the tribes would come together, and cast lots to see
to whose lot that stone would fall, to whom then they would give it. However,
the Ghuzz took another stone that was exactly alike in shape and inscribed that

prayer on it, and that counterfeit stone their chief hung about his neck. Then when they cast their lots on the appointed day and it fell to the Qarluq, they gave the Qarluq that falsified stone, while the original stone stayed with the Ghuzz. This is why when the Turks want rain they fashion themselves a special stone.

Now, the Turks are characterized by a certain sparseness of hair [in the beard] and canine disposition. The reason for this is that Yafith fell ill as a child and no medicine had any effect [on him] until a wise old woman told Yafith's mother to give him ant eggs and wolf's milk so that these might relieve him of his ailment. Accordingly, his mother kept giving him dosages of both of these things continually for one month until he recovered from this disease. However, when he began to have a beard, he turned out to be scanty-bearded as did his descendants, and this scantiness of beard befell him on account of those ants' eggs, while his bad-temper befell him on account of the wolf's milk. And it is from him that the stock of the Turkic peoples has descended, whom I will now relate nation by nation as I have found in books.

The Qïrghïz: How the Tribe Came to Be Formed; Their Connection with the Saqlabs for Which Reason They Are Ruddy-Skinned; The Legend of Their Saqlab or Royal Uyghur (?) Leader

As for the reason for the coming together of the Qïrghïz and their leader, (it was) that he was from the mass of the Saqlabs. He was Yaghlaqar. [Now] from the Byzantines (Rum) an envoy had come [to the Saqlabs], and this man had killed this envoy. The reason for his killing [him] was this, that the Byzantines are of the race of Sam, the son of Nuh, and the Saqlabs of the race of Yafith, and [thus] they go back to [a] dog, for they have been nurtured on bitch's milk. The story of this is [as follows:] When they took the ant's eggs for the sake of Yafith, the ant prayed God—Almighty and Exalted—that he might give Yafith no joy from his son. Thus when a son came to Yafith, [whose] name was Ashkenaz, [he was] blind in both eyes. At that time dogs used to have four eyes and there was a bitch which belonged to Yafith and had just given birth. Yafith had killed the whelp of that bitch, and Yafith's son used to suck the bitch's milk until he [reached the age of] four years. He used to hold the bitch's ear and would go about in the fashion of the blind. Then when the bitch had another whelp, she abandoned this son of Yafith and gave thanks to God—Almighty and Exalted—that she escaped from Yafith's son. [But] when it was the morrow, two of the dog's eyes had come back on this child and two eyes remained on the dog—and the trace[s] of [those other two eyes] have stayed still on the face[s] of dog[s]. This is the reason [the Saqlab] are called *sag-labi* and it was in [a] quarrel [over] this [matter] that [that the Saqlab leader] killed that [Byzantine] envoy and perforce had to depart from the Saqlabs.

Going thence, he came to the Khazars and the Khaqan of the Khazars treated him well until he died. The next Khaqan, however, who sat [on the throne] made heavy his heart against him. From that place, [too,] he had perforce to go and, departing thence, he went to Bashkir.

Now this Bashkir was a man from among the great men of the Khazars, and his abode was between the Khazars and the Kimek, with two thousand mounted warriors. Next, the Khan of the Khazars sent a person to Bashkir telling him to put out the Saqlab. He told [this] to the Saqlab and the Saqlab went to the province of the Toquz-Oghuz, for between him and some of them there was a tie of kinship. [But] when he arrived at a point in the road which [is] between the Kimek and Toquz-Oghuz the Khan [of the Toquz-Oghuz] became estranged from his own tribe, and took umbrage at them. When, accordingly, they were killed [by him], [having] scattered, they began to come by one[s] and two[s] to that Saqlab. All [of those who came] he received and treated well until they became numerous. [Then] a person was sent to Bashkir and [the Saqlab] joined with him in [an alliance] of friendship until such time as he became powerful. Thereafter he raided the Ghuzz. He killed many of them and took many of them prisoner, [thereby] procuring great wealth [for himself] both by means of his plundering and raiding, as well as on account of the prisoners, all of whom he sold back (i.e., for ransom). And that tribe who had gathered about him he named Qïrghïz. [Eventually,] news of him reached the Saqlab, and many folk came to him from the Saqlabs together with their families] and chattels. [These] mixed [well] with those others and formed bonds [with them] till all became one. (This is the reason why) the features and traits of the Saqlabs are to be found among the Qïrghïz [such as] reddishness of hair and whiteness of skin.

The Savage Khori Mongols

Now it is in these streams that there are wild people who do not associate with anyone [else] or know [how] to speak the language of any others, nor does anyone know their language. They are savages of human race who make everything out of skins, or who carry everything on their backs. All their utensils are [made] of the skins of wild animals. If they emerge from those swamps [wherein they live], they become like fish who have come out of water, so afflicted and aggrieved do they become. Their bows are of wood. But their clothing is of the skins of wild animals and their food is the meat of the animals they hunt. Their religion is such that they never lay hands on the clothing or goods of any [other] person. When they are going to make war, [therefore,] they sally forth with their families and chattels and make war. And when they gain victory over a foe, they do not touch his goods, but set fire to [them, instead], taking nothing away except his arms and [other things made of] iron. When they have sexual intercourse, they make the woman prop herself up on all four limbs and then couple [with her]. The bride-price [they pay] for women is wild animals, or else valleys in which there are many wild animals and trees. If [ever] one of them falls [into the hands of] the Qïrghïz, he eats no food, and when that one sees some of his fellows he flees. And so happens that if one of them dies, they carry his corpse [up] to a mountain and suspend it from a tree until it [decomposes and] disappears. Musk, skins, and narwhal horn are brought from the area of the Qïrghïz.

How the Qïrghïz Cremate Their
Dead like the Hindus

The Qïrghïz people, however, burn [their] dead like the Hindus, saying that fire is the purest of things and that whatever falls into it is purified, [so that] it cleanses the corpse of pollution and sin. Among the Qïrghïz some worship oxen, some the wind, some the hedgehog, some the magpie, some the falcon, and [some] others [yet], stately and handsome trees.

The Seers of the Qïrghïz and Their Yearly Oracles

There is a man or a people among them who every year on a pre-ordained day come and bring [together] all their minstrels and prepare all manners of merriment and the instruments thereof. This man is called *foghitun*. When these minstrels begin to play they go into a trance and then [people] ask them all of the things that are going to happen in that year, whether distress or abundance, rain or dearth, anxiety or security, or conquest of the enemy. And they tell all, and most of that [which they say] usually happens exactly as they have said it.

The Route to Tibet: The Tarim Basin:
Khotan, Kashghar, Kucha

The Tibet road starts out from Khotan towards Alshan and crosses over the mountains of Khotan. These mountains abound [in vegetation] and in them there are many four-legged beasts, such as oxen, sheep, and yaks. From these mountains it goes to Alshan, [going out] from which place there is a bridge [which has been] placed from one mountain side to another (i.e., suspended over a ravine). This bridge, so they say, was built by the people of Khotan in former times. From this bridge as far as the court of the Khaqan of Tibet there is a mountain which when you approach it, your breath is taken away owing to the [bad] air [that emanates] from it, so that people cannot breathe [as] their tongues become thickened and block their throats, in which [state] many people die, and the people of Tibet call that mountain "Poison Mountain."

When one goes from the town of Kashghar, one goes to the right of the road towards the East (i.e., Southwards) amidst the mountain ranges. When these have been crossed, one arrives at a country called Aghar. This country [extends] for forty *parsangs*; half of it is mountainous and half of it flat and plain. Kashghar has many villages and numberless hamlets, and that country in former times used to belong to the Khan of Tibet. From the province of Kashghar [this second route] goes to Saran-ka(?) and from thence to Alishur (Alti-shahr?). [Thence] it goes through desert until it comes to the River of Kucha, which goes to Kucha (apparently the Yarkend). On the banks of this river, towards the side of the desert, there is the village of Chamkhab, in which [there live] Tibetans. Next there comes a river which is crossed over by boat, [after which the road] comes to the Tibetan frontier. At the place where the road reaches the dominions of the Khaqan of Tibet there is an idol-temple in which there are many idols. Among these idols there is one seated on a dais (or throne) behind whose back there has been placed something like a fuller's beetle. That idol leans on that fuller's beetle, and when you put your hand behind that idol something like sparks of fire come out from it. To the left (i.e., north) of this place there is a desert plain in which there are many jujube trees on the banks of a river.

Barskhan: Its Persian Origin in the Time of Alexander

As for the origin of Barskhan, it was from the Persians. The reason for this was that when Alexander defeated Darius and conquered the Persians, the Kingdom of Persia, he was afraid because the Persian people were an intelligent resourceful and courageous people, very knowledgeable, subtle, perspicacious and prudent. [Therefore] Alexander concluded that he would [one day] depart and [then] they would rebel and, slaying his successors, take [back their] empire. Accordingly, he took one or two persons from every great house by way of hostages and took them with him. [Then] he set out for Turkestan and from there he intended to conquer China. But when he reached that place which today is called Barskhan, his scouts told Alexander that ahead of them there would be [only] desolate routes, narrow defiles, and [places] without fodder. Therefore the baggage he had with him should stay [behind where there was] fodder. Accordingly, Alexander gave orders that whatever was superfluous should be buried and that the beasts should be loaded with fodder. [At the same time] he commanded these sons of the aristocracy of Persia that they should abide there until he returned from China, when he would take them back with him to their own country. [In compliance] with his order they stayed there, but when the news came that Alexander had taken China and from there had gone to India, these sons of the Iranian nobility despaired of [ever again] reaching their native towns. Accordingly, they sent someone to China and brought [back] men such as masons, carpenters, and painters and ordered them to build towns there just like the cities of Persia, and they called that [town] Parskhan, meaning "[the city of] the prince of the Persians."

The Route to Barskhan

As for the road to Barskhan [it is as follows:] it goes from Navekaf to Kumbar-kat along the route of the Chigil thence to Jil. This Jil is a mountain and the meaning of the term is narrow. From there to Yar it is twelve *parsangs*, this Yar being a village from which three thousand men can be mustered. Amidst these are the tents of the Tegin of the Chigil. Amidst them there is no settlement [but] to the left (north) of the road [between them] is a lake which is called Issïq-köl (Lake Issyk Kul). Its circumference is a seven-day journey, for seventy streams come together (therein). Its water is brackish. From there to Tung is five *parsangs* and from Tung to Barskhan a three-day journey. There is nothing along this route except the tents of the Chigil people. The *dihqan* of Barskhan is called Managh. Six thousand men can be put into the field from Barskhan, and in the environs of Issïq-köl dwell all the Chigil people. To the south of Barskhan there are two summits one is called Yabghu, and the other Azar. From it a stream flows on the eastern side called Tafskhan which goes to the marches of China. This [second] summit is very high, so that birds which fly to China cannot cross over it.

10   Ibn Fadlan:
Journey to the Northern Lands

Introduction

Ahmad Ibn Fadlan was an Arab author and member of an embassy sent in the year 921 by the caliph al-Muqtadir (d. 932) to the king of the Bulghars on the Volga. Ibn Fadlan was charged with the duty of reading out a letter from the caliph to the Bulghar king, presenting the latter with gifts, and also supervising jurists and teachers whom the caliph had sent at the king's request to teach the Bulghars the laws of Islam. The embassy arrived at the court of the Bulghar king nine months after it had left Baghdad, having traveled through Mawarannahr, Khorezm, and the lands of the Oghuz, Pecheneg, and Bashkir.

Ibn Fadlan's book is the only information we have about this embassy. First published by the German Orientalist and numismatist C. M. J. Frähn in 1823 on the basis of an account found in Yaqut's thirteenth-century geographical diction-ary, Ibn Fadlan's story was later re-evaluated based on a unique manuscript discovered by the Bashkir historian Zeki Velidi Togan in the 1920s. Many scholars were later drawn to the pseudo-ethnographic nature of some of the passages, as well as the descriptions of the interaction between the Muslim embassy and the non-Muslim populations who were in the process of conversion to Islam.

When we had crossed it, we came to a tribe of the Turks who are known as Ghuzz. They turned out to be nomads, who have tents made of hair. They remain in a place for a while, then move on. You see their tents in one place, and then you see others similar to them at another place, [which is] in keeping with the practice of the nomads and their wanderings. And, indeed, they lead a miserable existence. They are moreover, like stray asses, and are not bound to God by religion, nor do they have recourse to reason. They do not worship anything, rather they call their chief men lords. When one of them consults his chieftain on something, he says to him, "O, my lord, what am I to do concerning such and such?" who conduct their affairs by mutual consultation. However, when they have agreed on a thing and have resolved to carry it out, the meanest and most despicable among them comes forth and nullifies that which they had unanimously agreed upon.

I heard them say, "La ilaha illa Allah, Muhammad Rasul Allah," in order to curry favor by this statement with whomsoever of the Muslims happens to pass by them, and not because they believe it. When one of them is wronged, or experiences something he happens to be averse to, he raises his head towards heaven and says, "Bir tengri," which means in Turkish, "God the One." For *bir* in Turkish means one, and *tengri* means God in the language of the Turks. They do not cleanse themselves after defecation or urination, nor do they wash after major ritual impurity. They have nothing whatsoever to do with water, especially in winter. Their women do not veil themselves before their [own] men nor before others, and in the same way, a woman does not conceal any part of her body from any man whatsoever.

When we happened to be staying with a man of them as guests, we came and sat down. The man's wife was with us, and while she was talking to us, she uncovered her pudendum and scratched it, while we were looking at her. We covered our faces saying, "I seek forgiveness of Allah." Her husband laughed and said to the interpreter:

"Tell them: 'She uncovers it in your presence and you see it, but she safeguards it, and it is not attainable. This is better than if she were to cover it, while making it accessible.'"

They do not know fornication. And of whomsoever they come to have knowledge of his having committed something of the sort, they split him in two. The manner in which they do it is to bring together the branches of two trees, tie him to the branches, and then release the two trees, so that the one fastened to them is split in two. One of them, as he heard me reading a portion of the Qur'an, expressed admiration for its recitation. He then said to the interpreter, "Tell him: 'Do not stop reading.'" This man said to me one day through the interpreter, "Tell this Arab: 'Does our Lord—Might and Majesty be His—have a wife?'" I was horrified at this, and I glorified God and implored His forgiveness. He then glorified God and sought His forgiveness just as I had done. Such is the custom of the Turk, who, whenever he hears a Muslim glorifying God, or making the Muslim confession of faith, he does the same. Formalities relating to marrying off their women are such as when one of them asks for the hand of a female relative of another, be it his daughter, sister, or someone whose guardian he happens to be, for such and such quantity of Khorezmian gowns. If the guardian approves of the offer, the suitor carries it to him. Sometimes the bride price is camels, or riding animals [such as horses, mules, and donkeys], or some other object. No one is allowed to go near his woman until he has paid the bride price agreed upon with her guardian. Upon the payment of the bride price to the guardian, the suitor proceeds unabashed until he enters the house where she happens to be, and takes her away in the presence of her father, mother, and brothers, and they do not prevent him from doing so.

When a man dies having a wife and children, his eldest son marries his wife if she is not his mother. None of the merchants, nor anyone else, is able to perform the ritual ablution after a major ritual impurity in their presence, except at night when they do not see him. For they become angry and say, "This person wants to cast a spell on us, because he has gazed into the water," and they fine him a certain amount of money.

No one from among the Muslims is able to pass through their country until he befriends one of them, and stays with him as his house guest. From the land of Islam, he brings a gown to his friend, a veil to his friend's wife, and some pepper, millet, raisins, and nuts. When the Muslim arrives at his friend's, the latter pitches a tent for him, and brings to him [a number of] sheep befitting his rank, in order that the Muslim assume the responsibility for slaughtering them. This is because the Turks do not kill animals by slitting the throat. They merely knock the sheep on the head until it is dead.

If one of them wishes to depart and some of his camels balk and will not move, or if he has need of money, he leaves the balking animals with his Turkish friend, takes what he needs of his friend's camels, mounts, and money, and departs. When he returns from the destination to which he is headed, he pays him his money, and restores to him his camels and mounts. Likewise, if a man happens to pass by a Turk whom he does not know, and says to him, "I am your guest, and I want some of your camels, riding animals, and money," the Turk hands over to him what he wants. If the merchant dies on the road, in the course of that trip, and the caravan returns, the Turk meets them and says, "Where is my guest?" If they say, "He died," he makes the caravan unload. He then goes to the noblest looking merchant that he sees among them, unpacks his baggage while he looks on, and takes from his money an amount equal to that which he had with the [deceased] merchant, without taking a single additional grain. Similarly, he takes some of his riding animals and camels, saying, "That man is your cousin, and you are the most fitting person to assume the obligation of paying his debt. If the merchant runs away, the Turk does the same thing and says, "He is a Muslim like you. You take [what you have given] from him." If the Turk does not meet his Muslim guest on the highway, he inquires about his country and his whereabouts. If he is guided to him, he journeys for several days in search of him until he arrives at where he is. The Muslim then delivers to the Turk what the latter had entrusted to him, as well as what he bestows upon him as gifts.

This is also the way the Turk is wont to behave when he goes into Jurjaniya, where he inquires about his guest, and stays with him until he departs. And were the Turk to die at the home of his Muslim friend, and the caravan, in which the Muslim friend of the Turk happened to be, were passing through the country of the Turks, they kill him, saying, "You killed him as a result of having imprisoned him. Had you not detained him, he would not have died." Likewise, if he were to give the Turk *nabidh* (a fermented drink) to drink, and he fell off a wall, they kill him in retaliation. If the Muslim friend of the dead Turk is not in the caravan, they seek out the most important man in the caravan, and kill him.

Sodomy is regarded as a great enormity among them. A man of the people of Khorezm came to stay with the tribe of the Kudharkin, who is a vice-regent of the King of the Turks. He lodged for a time with a host of his, while engaged in purchasing sheep. The Turk had a beardless son, and the man from Khorezm did not cease to coax the lad, and to seduce him until the latter yielded to him that which he desired. The Turk came, and found the two of them consummating the deed. The Turk submitted the matter to the Kudharkin, and he said, "Gather the Turks," and he called them together. When they had assembled, he said to the Turk, "Do you want me to render a just verdict or a false one?" The Turk said, "A just one." The Kudharkin said, "Bring your son," and he brought him. Said the Kudharkin, "The boy and the merchant must both be killed." The Turk was annoyed at this and said, "I will not give up my son." The Kudharkin said, "Then the merchant may ransom himself," and this he did. He paid a certain number of sheep to the Turk for what he had done to his son. He paid four hundred sheep to the Kudharkin for exempting him from punishment. He then left the land of the Turks. . . .

We halted in the country of a tribe of Turks called Bashkirs, and we were extremely wary of them. For they are the most wicked of the Turks, the dirtiest and the most audacious in the commission of murder. Thus when one man meets another, he cuts off his head, takes it with him and leaves the body. They shave off their beards and eat lice. One of them will examine the seam of his tunic and grind the lice with his teeth. One of them who had accepted Islam was with us and used to serve us. I saw him find a louse in his clothing. He crushed it between his fingernails and licked it, and he said when he saw me, "Good!"

Each of them sculpts a piece of wood the size of a phallus and hangs it on himself. If he is about to undertake a trip or to meet an enemy, he kisses it and prostrates himself before it saying, "O my Lord, do unto me such and such." I said to the interpreter, "Ask one of them as to their justification for this, and as to why he believes it to be his lord." He said, "I came out of something similar to it, and I do not know any creator of myself other than it."

Among them are those who maintain that they have twelve lords: a lord for the Winter; a lord for the Summer; a lord for the rain; a lord for the wind; a lord for trees; a lord for men; a lord for horses; a lord for water; a lord for the night; a lord for the day; a lord for death; and a lord for the earth. The Lord who is in Heaven is the greatest of them all, although he is in complete agreement with the others. Each one of them approves of what his partner does. May God be greatly exalted above what the iniquitous say.

We saw a group of them who worship snakes, a group who worship fish, and a group who worship cranes. They informed me that they were once engaged in a battle with a group of their enemies who had put them to flight, when the cranes let out a cry behind them and they became frightened and fled, after having first routed them. For this reason they came to worship the cranes. They said, "This is our Lord, and these are his actions. He put our enemies to flight." And they worship them for this reason.

B | *Qarakhanids: The First Turkic Muslim State in Central Asia*

11 al-Kashghari: On the Linguistic Distribution of the Turks

INTRODUCTION

Mahmud al-Kashghari, an eleventh-century lexicographer, hailed from Barskhan on the southern shores of Lake Issïq-köl (modern-day Kyrgyzstan). His family seems to have been well connected with the Qarakhanid dynasty, and Kashghari traveled extensively in the Turkic lands before making his way to Baghdad, where he began work on his Diwan Lughat al-turk *(Compendium of Turkic dialects) in 1072. Apparently, his second work on Turkic grammar has been lost. Kashghari had hoped that his Compendium would serve as a language manual for Baghdad-based scholars engaged with the Turkic world, so he used methods of Arabic grammar and lexicography to make the work more obliging for its intended users. Many of the observations made in the work are from the author's own personal experience.*

The Diwan Lughat al-turk *is very significant for the early history of the Turkic peoples, and contains many details on language, history, and geography. It survives in a unique manuscript from 1266. Most of the references in the work— addressing, among other things, designations of different Turkic groupings, ranks and titles, proper names, as well as proverbs and verses—are for the kind of Turkic spoken in Kashghar in the eleventh century, referred to by the author as Khaqani Turkic. Nevertheless, there is a comparative element to the Diwan that makes this work particularly appealing for the study of Turkic history of the era. The work has been edited and studied in Turkey since the early twentieth century, and its vocabulary appeared in several Turkic dictionaries.*

The slave, Mahmud ibn al-Husayn ibn Muhammad [al-Kashghari] states: When I saw that God Most High had caused the Sun of Fortune to rise in the Zodiac of the Turks, and set their Kingdom among the spheres of Heaven; that He called them "Turk," and gave them Rule; making them kings of the Age, and placing in their hands the reins of temporal authority; appointing them over all mankind, and directing them to the Right; that He strengthened those who are affiliated to them, and those who endeavor on their behalf; so that they attain from them the utmost of their desire, and are delivered from the ignominy of the slavish rabble; [then I saw that] every man of reason must attach himself to them, or else expose himself to their falling arrows. And there is no better way to approach them than by speaking their own tongue, thereby bending their ear, and inclining their heart. And when one of their foes comes over to their side, they keep him secure from fear of them; then others may take refuge with him, and all fear of harm be gone.

I heard from one of the trustworthy informants among the Imams of Bukhara, and from another Imam of the people of Nishapur: both of them reported the following tradition, and both had a chain of transmission going back to the Apostle of God, may God bless him and grant him peace. When he was speaking about the signs of the Hour and the trials of the end of Time, and he mentioned the emergence of the Oghuz Turks, he said, "Learn the tongue of the Turks, for their reign will be long." Now if this *hadith* is sound—and the burden of proof is on those two!—then learning it is a religious duty: and if it is not sound, still Wisdom demands it.

I have traveled throughout their cities and steppes, and have learned their dialects and their rhymes; those of the Turks, the Turkmen-Oghuz, the Chigil, the Yaghma, and the Qïrghïz. Also, I am one of the most elegant among them in language, and the most eloquent in speech; one of the best educated, the most deep-rooted in lineage, and the most penetrating in throwing the lance. Thus have I acquired perfectly the dialect of each one of their groups; and I have set it down in an encompassing book, in a well-ordered system.

I wrote this, my book, asking the assistance of God Most High; and I have named it *Diwan Lughat al-turk* (Compendium of the Turkic Dialects); in order that it be an everlasting memorial, and an eternal treasure; and have Dedicated it to His Excellency; of the Hallowed and Prophetic, Imamate, Hashemite, 'Abbasid line: our Master and Patron; Abu'-Qasim 'Abd Allah ibn Muhammad al-Muqtadi bi-Amr Allah; Emir of the Faithful and Deputy of the Lord of Worlds, May God prolong his abiding in everlasting glory and felicitous life. . . .

And I have set it out according to the order of the alphabet; and adorned it with words of wisdom and elegant speech, proverbs, verses of poetry, and sentences of prose. Thus did I soften its rough places, and make smooth its pits and hollows. I have spent long years of labor over it, causing each word to lie down in its proper place, and lifting each one out of obscurity; so that the one who seeks it may find it in its correct compartment, and the one who desires it may observe it in its allotted order. . . .

On What Is Mentioned in the Book and What Is Not

Of the names of mountains and deserts, and of rivers, lakes, and other bodies of water, I have mentioned those which are within the territories of Islam; since their names are on people's tongues, I have mentioned them because they are well known; but the majority of them I have left unmentioned, because of their obscurity. As for those that are in the lands of Polytheism, I have mentioned a few and have avoided the rest, since there is no profit in mentioning them.

Foreign words in this language are not mentioned.

The same for proper names of men and women, except that I have mentioned those that are well known and widespread, and which therefore require to be known exactly.

On the Classes of the Turks and an Outline of Their Tribes

The Turks are, in origin, twenty tribes. They all trace back to Turk, son of Yafith, son of Nuh, God's blessings be upon them—they correspond to the children of Rum, son of Esau, son of Isaac, son of Abraham, God's blessings be upon them. Each tribe has branches whose number only God knows. I shall mention only the great tribes and leave the little ones, except for the branches of the Oghuz-Turkmen—their branches I shall mention, along with the brands of their cattle, since people need to know them.

[In the following list] I outline the geographical position of each of their tribes in the eastern world. They are listed in order [from West] to East, both pagan and Muslim, beginning with those closest to Rum. First is: Bachanak (Pecheneg), then: Qifchaq (Qïpchaq), then: Oghuz, then: Yemak (Kimek), then: Bashghirt (Bashkir), then: Basmil, then: Qay, then; Yabaqu, then; Tatar, then: Qïrghïz. The last one is closest to Sin. All of these tribes are opposite Rum, extending toward the East.

Then: Chigil, then: Tukhsi, then; Yaghma, then: Oghraq, then: Charuq, then: Chomul, then: Uyghur, then: Tanut, then: Khitai which is Sin, then: Tawghach which is Masin. These tribes are middling between South and North.

On the Turkic Dialects

The most elegant of the dialects belongs to those who know only one language, who do not mix with Persians, and who do not customarily settle in other lands. Those who have two languages and who mix with the populace of the cities have a certain slurring in their utterances—for example, Soghdaq, Kanchak, and Arghu. The second category are such as Khotan, Tubut, and some of Tangut—this class are settlers in the lands of the Turks. I shall now outline the language of each of their groups.

The language of the people of Jabarqa is unknown because of their distance and the interposition of the Great Sea between them and Masin. The people of Masin and of Sin have a language of their own, although the sedentary population know Turkic well and their correspondence with us is in the Turkic script. Also the language of Yajuj and Majuj (Gog and Magog) is unknown because of the Barrier and the interposition of the mountains and the sea that is near Masin. Tubut have a language of their own. Khotan also have both a script and a language of their own. Both of these do not know Turkic well.

The Uyghur have a pure Turkic language, and also another language which they speak among themselves. [And they have two] writing systems, one in the Turkic script composed of twenty-five letters which I have enumerated above and in which their correspondence is written, and another which they have in common with Sin and in which they write their scriptures and registers—no one can read it except their priests. Those that I have named to this point are sedentary peoples.

Among the nomadic peoples are the Chomul—they have a gibberish of their own, but also know Turkic: also Qay, Yabaqu, Tatar, and Basmil—each of these groups has its own language, but they also know Turkic well. Then Qïrghïz, Qïpchaq, Oghuz, Tukhsi, Yaghma, Chigil, Oghraq, and Charuq—they speak pure Turkic, a single language. Approaching these is the language of Yemak and Bashghirt. As for the language of Bulghar, Suvar, and Bachanak, approaching Rum, it is Turkic of a single type with clipped ends (?).

The lightest of the dialects is that of Oghuz. The most correct is that of Yaghma and Tukhsi, and those who dwell on the rivers Ila (Ili), Artis (Irtïsh), Yamar, and Atil (Itil), as far as the country of Uyghur. The most elegant is that of the Khaqani kings and those who associate with them.

The people of Balasaghun speak both Soghdian and Turkic. The same is true of the people of Tiraz (Talas) and the people of Madinat al-Bayda' (Isfijab). There is a slurring in the speech of the people of the entire country of Arghu, which is considered to extend from Isfijab to Balasaghun. Kashghar has villages in which Kanchaki is spoken, but in the main city [they speak] Khaqani Turkic.

The main part of the lands of the Turks, from the area next to Rum up to Masin, is five thousand *farsakhs* long by three thousand wide, making a total of eight thousand *farsakhs*. I have indicated all this in the circle (map) in the shape of the earth so that it may be known . . .

The Turks take the names of twelve different animals and brand twelve [successive] calendar years by these names. Dates of births and battle are then reckoned according to the succession of these years. The origin of this custom is that one of their kings once required information about a battle that had occurred some years before his reign, and they [his ministers?] were mistaken about the year in which that battle fell. So he consulted with his people about it. He said, "Just as we were mistaken about this date, so will those who are after us be mistaken. Let us now therefore appoint a twelve-year cycle, corresponding to the number of the months and the number of the signs of the Zodiac, so that the reckoning [of years] from now on shall be according to their succession, and shall be an everlasting memorial." They said, "just as thou judgest."

Then he went out hunting, and ordered that the wild beasts be driven toward the valley of the Ila, a great river. They hunted the beasts and drove them into the water. Twelve different ones crossed the river, and he put the name of each of them on a year. The first is: *Sichghan* "Mouse." This was the first to cross, so he put it at the beginning of the cycle. The usage follows these names, *sichghan yili* "Year of the mouse"; then: *ud yili* "Year of the Ox"; then: *bars yili* "Year of the Leopard"; then: *tawisghan yili* "Year of the Hare"; then: *nag(lu) yili* "Year of the Crocodile"; then: *yilan yili* "Year of the Snake"; then: *yond yili* "Year of the Horse"; then" *qoy yili* "Year of the Sheep"; then: *bechin yili* "Year of the Monkey"; then: *taqaghu yili* "Year of the Hen"; then: *it yili* "Year of the Dog"; then: *tonuz yili* "Year of the Pig." ...

The Turks claim a piece of wisdom for each of the years, and draw an omen from it. They say: "If it is: *ud yili*—i.e., the Year of the Ox—there will be many battles, because of the goring of oxen. If it is the Year of the Hen there will be much food, but there will be strife among men, since the food of hens is grain, and they are constantly tossing about refuse [to find pieces of grain]. If it is the Year of the Snake, or the Year of the Crocodile, there will be rains and abundance of herbage, because the home of these animals is water. If it is the Year of the Pig there will be much cold and snow and discord." Thus do they claim something for each year.

The Turks do not have names for the seven days, since the week became known [only] with Islam. Also, the names of the months, in the cities, are given in Arabic. The nomads and the heathen infidels give them names according to four seasons; every three-month period has a name by which the passing of the year is known. For example, the beginning of spring, after Nayruz is called *oghlaq ay* meaning "Month of the kid"; then: *ulugh oghlaq ay* meaning "Month of the large kid"—since the second month is longer; then: *ulugh ay* meaning "Great month"— since it falls in mid-summer when milk is abundant and all the blessings of live-stock and of earth appear. And so for the rest; but I will not mention them, since they are seldom used—so understand!

12   Jamal Qarshi: The Conversion to Islam of Satuq Bughra Khan

INTRODUCTION

Jamal Qarshi was the nickname of Abu'l-Fazl Jamal al-Din Muhammad (b. 1230/31), a scholar and official in East Turkestan in the thirteenth century. Originally from Almaligh, he spent most of his life in the city of Kashghar, where he composed in 1282 a commentary, known as the Surah, *on al-Jawhari's famous Arabic dictionary al-Sihah (late tenth century). His* Mulhaqat al-surah *is a supplement to his commentary that contains many biographical entries, particularly on Qarakhanid personalities and also on several Mongol rulers of Turkestan. The supplement was completed in 1303.*

Qarshi's Mulhaqat *contains the first full narrative about the conversion of the Qarakhanid ruler Satuq Bughra Khan to Islam, probably in the middle of the eleventh century. Although fragments of the story appeared in several earlier works, Qarshi was the first to have managed to render the story in full, and attributes the story to the now lost work,* Tarikh-i Kashghar. *The conversion of Satuq Bughra Khan still serves as the main narrative and point of identification for different populations in East Turkestan (modern day Xinjiang), but in the past the story served to illustrate the conversion of the Qarakhanids to Islam.*

Mention of the Famous among the Turkic Khaqans in Mawarannahr and Its Environs during the Islamic Period

Satuq Bughra Khan al-Mujahid ʿAbd al-Karim ibn Bazir Arslan Khan ibn Bilge Bahur Qadr Khan of the people of Afrasiyab ibn Pushang ibn ʿAli ibn Risiman of the noble origin of Turä ibn Afridun ibn Anuyan ibn Zarasaf ibn Jam ibn Fars ibn Buri ibn Karkin ibn Yafith ibn the Prophet Nuh, peace be upon him. He was the first among the Turkic khaqans who took Islam in the area of Kashghar and Farghana during the reign of Caliph al-Muti'llah [r. 946–74], the commander of the faithful, in the state of the rightly guided Amir ʿAbd al-Malik ibn Nuh al-Samani [r. 951–54]. The capable, perfect, and able Imam Abu'l-Futuh ʿAbd al-ʿArif, son of the great and important Imam Shaykh Abi ʿAbdallah al-Husayn al-Fazli . . . stated in his work *Tarikh-i Kashghar:*

First among the lands of the Turks to embrace Islam was Shash [Tashkent] whose population adopted Islam in the time of Bilge Bahur Qadr Khan. Amir Nuh ibn Mansur al-Razi al-Samani conquered it and upon being paid a large tribute he withdrew and proceeded to the city of Isfijab. Correspondence between the two [between Nuh and Bilge] did not cease until Nuh ibn Mansur died. When the reign of Ismaʿil ibn Mansur began, he continued the correspondence, according to the tradition set by his brother.

And when Oghulchaq Qadr Khan, brother of Bazir Arslan Khan, became ruler of the Turks, he stopped heeding to messengers of Islam until Nasr ibn Mansur had escaped from his brother and arrived to Kashghar. Oghulchaq hosted him properly, and [Nasr ibn Mansur] told him, "I have taken refuge with you and your family, and I would serve you faithfully." . . .

Oghulchaq appointed him [Nasr] governor of the province of Artuj (Artush). Caravans began to arrive there from Bukhara and Samaqand, with heaps of merchandise, and he [Nasr] gave marvelous gifts to Qadr Khan endeavoring to win his favor.

He [that is, Abu'l-Futuh, narrator of the story], may Allah be pleased with
him, said: Some people had told me about their Islam that at that time, that infidel [Qadr Khan] found attractive brocade clothing and sugary sweets that he
had never seen before. He befriended him [Nasr ibn Mansur] and thus he grew
to depend on him. Then Nasr asked him to give him a plot of land the size of
a cow's hide for the construction of a mosque, so he could worship God. Qadr
Khan said, "Only for you, you can take that land over there to do as you please."
Nasr slaughtered a cow, stripped off its hide, and cut it into straps with which he
marked the plot of land for the mosque, now famous as the Central Mosque of
Artuj. That infidel [Qadr Khan] was astonished at his resourcefulness and solution to the question.

Oghulchaq was Satuq's uncle. When he [Satuq] was twelve years old, he possessed surpassing beauty, unblemished looks, bright character, mental clarity, excellent perception, and strong mind as were never observed before his time in any
of the sons of kings.

When caravans arrived from Bukhara, Satuq would go to Artuj to look at
them, what they were bringing, and also to trade. Nasr al-Samani treated him
generously. One day, when it was time for the midday prayer, the Muslims set
about to pray as was ordained by the *shar'ia*. Satuq was still unaware of that fortunate duty, so he observed from afar. When they concluded the prayer, he asked
al-Samani, "What were you doing?" He answered, "We are obligated to pray five
times a day in different times, every day and night." He asked, "Who commands
it to you?" Al-Samani began to describe the Creator, may he be glorified, with his
divine names and attributes, and the *shar'ia* of Islam as was told by Muhammad,
peace be upon him. . . .

At that point Satuq said, "This *is* God most high. How proper it is that he
should be worshiped, how truthful is his prophet, how right it is that he should
be followed, and how beautiful is this religion that really merits that one accepts
it." And he acknowledged Allah, may he be glorified, and Muhammad, peace be
upon him, and took on the faith, and swore to uphold Islam, and ordered his
slaves and courtiers to become Muslims at that hour.

Al-Samani kept this story from his [Satuq's] uncle Oghulchaq. He [Satuq] secretly studied the Qur'an, and the rules of the religion, and began his way on that
path. Secretly, he summoned to the faith a number of his relatives, of whom 50
young men had answered positively to his call, obeyed him, and followed him.

Oghulchaq soon began to suspect that Satuq had adopted Islam, and his confidants reported that they saw him one day perform ablutions and pray. They notified his uncle of this, and he revealed the secret to his wife. She was fond of Satuq,
so she secretly sent for him, warning him that, "On Saturday, your uncle wants
you to participate in the construction of a temple of idols for himself in order to
test you. It is necessary that you show great zeal in your work."

When it was time, while each of the workers was carrying one brick for the
construction, Satuq was carrying two, and while he was working he kept praying
secretly to God most high, saying, "O Lord, if you make me victorious over your
enemies and the enemies of your faith, and spread Islam through me, and deliver
the true words [of the Qur'an] into my hands, surely I will turn this place into a

mosque in which your servants will gather to obey you, and build a *mihrab* here to worship you, and a *minbar* to praise you, and I myself will become the Imam in order to seek your face and ask your contentment." Nowadays, that mosque is located in Artuj!

And so he demonstrated zeal and displayed diligence in his work, and the wife protested to her husband about the boy's burden in the building for his uncle, and his uncle was content with him and said, "Had he left our religion, he would not have done what he did, and he would have hurt my children behind my back."

And while he was experiencing these circumstances, he studied the Qur'an by heart, so by the time he was 25 years old, he already mastered it. [One day], pretending to go hunting, he set out on horseback in the company of the 50 young men to capture the fortress located in Yighach-Baliq. He besieged it and remained there for three months. He notified his uncle of what had happened; he thought that he would still be able to ward off his death. And when Satuq finally decided to meet him, he set out against him; he had with him 300 horsemen from Kashghar, and more than 1,000 warriors for the faith from Farghana. At first, they conquered At-Bashi, and their number rose to 3,000 horsemen. They attacked Kashghar and conquered it, and converted its population to Islam. And its infidels were delivered to the hand of fate, and the word of God became victorious. And he was able to execute the word of Allah and fulfill his promise. Praise be to God who made him victorious and [enabled him to] fulfil his promise. Satuq Bughra Khan the warrior for the faith passed away in 344/955–56, and his grave is located in Artuj, in one of the villages of Kashghar, and today it is built up and visited.

13   Yusuf Hass Hajib: Advice to the Qarakhanid Rulers

INTRODUCTION

Kutadgu Bilig (or Wisdom of Royal Glory) is a Turkic work written in 1069–70 in Kashghar and hailed as the oldest monument of Turko-Islamic literature. Authored by Yusuf Hass Hajib, a Balasaghun-based official in the service of the Qarakhanids, the work was dedicated to the Qarakhanid ruler Tabghach (Tamghach) Bughra Khan (r. 1074–1102). The composition belongs to the genre of advice literature, known also as mirror for princes, to borrow a Medieval European term. The range and styles of the genre have been fairly diverse, and in the Muslim world have borrowed significantly from similar traditions in other civilizations, particularly India and Iran. Kutadgu Bilig is the first attempt to fit the Islamic-Iranian concept into its Inner Asian Turkic context. As such, the work also preceded other contemporary masterpieces of advice literature such as the Qabus-nama and the Siyasat-nama (see below).

It is claimed that Hajib was influenced by the great Iranian epic, the Shah-nama, in his style and choice of verse pattern. Written in the form of a didactic poem and advancing the vision of the ideal ruler, the author introduces four central characters: Rising Sun, representing the king and the principle of justice; Full Moon, representing the vizier and the principle of fortune; Highly Praised, representing the sage and intellect; and Wide Awake, representing the ascetic and humanity's end.

The work survived in three manuscripts, all published in facsimile, and has been studied particularly by Turkish and Russian scholars. The following excerpt is taken from Robert Dankoff's English translation.

Highly Praised Explains the Qualifications of a Vizier

"For the prince, O king, the vizier is the hand by which he wields his authority. The prince cannot do without the vizier, and if the vizier is good, the prince can sleep in peace. It is the vizier who bears the prince's burdens, it is he who plants firmly the root of princely rule. Therefore he must be outstanding among men, mature of mind and stout in heart, great of intellect and profound in wisdom, that he may deal effectively with every matter, and redden the prince's cheeks.

"He ought to be of noble birth, also pious and upright, passing each day with rectitude. Being a vizier is a big job, for which one needs an exceptional man, one of sound and choice character, who is both intelligent and wise, both sensible and sensitive. A man of intellect sows good seed: wherever it falls, it grows, and does not wither. And he ought to be God-fearing and pious, for then the subjects will feel secure from him. A pious man is balm and medicine to all troubled souls; he acts with prudence, stays far from impropriety, and takes up affairs at their proper time. It is the vizier who by his words and deeds wields power in the realm as the prince's deputy. It is not meet, therefore, that he be base-born, for the base are impure. Rather he should be nobly born, for then he will be true. Hear these words, uttered by the legitimate head of state:

> The nobly born knows propriety;
> He serves the people with loyalty.
> The base-born only lies and cheats,
> Although he serves dainties and sweets."

How to Conduct Oneself with Commoners

"Commoners are quite different, both in their mentality and their character. They have no manners at all, no code of etiquette governing the relationships. Still, one cannot do without them. Therefore talk kindly to them, but do not become too intimate. The manners of commoners are black, so take care that you do not blacken yourself. By nature they are insubordinate and wild, and all their actions accord with these qualities. They only know how to fill their bellies, and have no other care but their throats. One who traveled much and had experience of vulgar manners once said: Commoners care solely for their bellies, and all their strivings are for the sake of their throats. How many people have perished for their throats, and now below black earth they eat fire in requital. Once a vulgar man fills his belly, his tongue loses its head, and if you do not keep control over him, he will lord it over you.

"Therefore, my brother, associate with them and give them food and drink continually, speak softly to them, and give them what they ask for. For he who gives is the true beneficiary. And be patient, do not talk too much, for words spoken rashly have little luster. A man who knew much wisdom and moderated his speech quoted this verse:

> Let not every word get out on your tongue;
> Speak only from necessity.
> I saw a wise man who, though he spoke little,
> Repented his loquacity."

Associating with Descendants of the Prophet

"Besides for the nobles and the prince's servants, you will have to meet with other people as well, my brother.

"One group is the descendants of the Prophet. Treat them with due reverence and you will be blessed with fortune. Love them with all your heart, and constantly favor them with alms. They are the 'People of the House,' kinsmen to the beloved Prophet, and you should love his kinfolk for his sake. So do not question their inner motives or examine their character and their origin, as long as they do not utter anything improper."

Associating with Scholars and 'Ulama'

"Another group is the 'ulama'. Their learning enlightens the way for the people. So love them sincerely, respect their pronouncements, and their sciences, or at least a part of them. They are the ones who distinguish right from wrong, who hold to the way that is straight and pure. As far as possible learn their doctrines, give them alms, and guard your tongue in their presence. For they are the pillar of true faith, and their learning is the foundation of the sacred law. If not for scholars and sages in this world, food would not sprout in the ground. Their learning is a lamp for the people, and as long as the lamp is bright one does not stray from the path at night.

"Give them a share of your wealth, accompanied by sweet words. Feed them hospitably and serve them cheerfully. Be reserved in their presence, do not indulge in slander and backbiting, for their flesh is poison. Rather, give them to eat of your bread and salt, treat them with reverence and esteem, heed their teachings, and do not speak ill of them or attribute to them wicked deeds. For you have need of their knowledge to serve as your guide to the path of righteousness. They are like the ram which leads the flock of sheep onto the straight path. Associate with them, therefore, and establish good relations. Then you will be fortunate in both the worlds."

Associating with Physicians

"There are several other groups besides, each having its own brand of wisdom and learning. One is the physicians. They provide treatment for all aches and ills. This group is indispensable to you also, for without them none of life's attending ills can be cured. While a man is alive he is subject to sickness and requires proper treatment and medicine. For a man, sickness is the companion of death, and death is the counterpart of life. So hold these physicians in good stead, and pay them their due, for they are necessary."

Associating with Dream Interpreters

"Another science is that of dreams. Whenever a man sleeps he dreams, and if the interpreter knows how to explain his dream favorably, it will turn out according to what he says. If the dream is auspicious, well and good; if inauspicious, the dreamer must give alms to the poor as a prophylactic measure. You should know that the merciful God, desiring His servant's welfare, gives signs in dreams, and has instituted the science of their interpretation. If the dream is good, then he may rejoice. But if he sees evil, then let him take refuge in the Lord and, giving alms to the poor, pray that God avert the evil from him. The outcome follows the explanation. Therefore, O interpreter, be subtle in your examination of the dream, and explain it favorably. Interpreters such as these are experts in their craft, wise, compassionate, and good. Treat them kindly, my brother. Consider them your own brothers or friends."

Associating with Astrologers

"After this come the astrologers. Theirs is a very subtle method. The calculation of years and months and days is with them, and this is a necessary calculation, O noble one. If you wish to learn it yourself, first study geometry; then the gate of reckoning will be opened. Learn multiplication and division, sums and fractions—they are the perfect test for a well-trained mind. Learn to double and to halve and to take the square root. Master addition and subtraction and apply them to land survey; then consider the seven heavens as a speck of dust. If you need still more, study algebra, then knock on Euclid's gate. Be they worldly matters or otherworldly, all are distinguished and grasped by a reckoning. If the reckoning is amiss, both worldly and otherworldly matters go afoul.

"Also, if you plan to undertake a certain business, you have first to determine the proper time. For there are lucky days and months and also unlucky ones. So inquire of the astrologer, and choose one that is lucky. That aged sage spoke well who said: Inquire of one who knows, and act accordingly. One who begins his enterprise with knowledge will gain his desire in the end, no matter what it may be. In every undertaking, knowledge first is helpful; if knowledge lags behind, the enterprise will not succeed. So inquire of the astrologers first. But do not be quick to rely on everything they say: God is the best Knower, and you should rely on Him alone. As for the astrologers, treat them kindly, do not abuse them with your tongue, nor wound their hearts."

How to Choose a Wife

"If you desire to marry, seek a good woman, and keep your eyes sharp. She should be of good stock in both family lines, also modest, devout, and chaste. Marry a virgin if you can, one who is untouched and who has seen no man's face but yours. Then she will love you, having known no one but yourself, and she will not bring with her any unbecoming habits. If you are going to marry, choose a wife below yourself in status. Do not marry a woman of nobler stock or you will end up her captive. A man of broad experience and ripe judgment coined the following in this connection: Choose one below yourself. Nor seek beauty in a wife: Find one who has virtue: She will brighten your life.

"O pious man of men! Do not marry: but if you do, choose a wife of equal standing to yourself. And do not look for beauty of face or form but good character. If her character is good, she will be perfect. But if you choose on the basis of looks alone, your ruddy countenance will turn sallow.

"When a man decides to marry, O chief of men, he must base his choice on one of four things. The first chooses a rich wife, following his greedy soul. The second desires a beautiful one, following his carnal eye. The third seeks one of noble stock, following his pride and desire for high status. The fourth desires a woman who is God-fearing and devout, and as soon as he finds such a one, he marries her. Give ear now, and I will tell you which of these is best. You who chose a wife for wealth: do not become her captive; for when her heart is set on something, she will lengthen her tongue and not let you rest until you get it for her. You who chose a wife for beauty: do not become a laughing stock; for every man loves beauty in his wife, but only God can be the guardian of a woman who possesses it. You who chose a wife for nobility and status: do not cheapen yourself by mixing with highborn stock; for their tongues are very long, and you will be a woman's slave. But you, prince of men, who chose a wife for her piety: if you found such a woman, then you have found all four of these together!

"So if you find a good and God-fearing woman, do not hesitate to marry her, my good man. Then if riches are your desire, she will save your money, make you wealthy, and redden your cheeks. As long as her character is upright, her beauty will show through; for the wise man knows that a woman's true beauty resides in her character. And if she is devout and chaste, then she is highborn. All three of those are gathered in this one point, O noble one. So if you are wise, you will choose a God-fearing wife, for then you will have all four of these qualities together. When you find a woman of this sort, O manly one, do not waste the opportunity, but go ahead and marry her."

C | Central Asia in the Eleventh and Twelfth Centuries

14   al-ʿUtbi: The Alliance of the Ghaznavids and Qarakhanids

INTRODUCTION

The Kitab al-Yamini *is a chronicle of the early Ghaznavid rise to power during the reigns of Amir Sebuktegin (r. 977–97), a Turkic military slave of high rank during the final years of Samanid rule, and his son, the first independent Ghaznavid ruler, Sultan Mahmud of Ghazna ("Yamin al-Dawla," r. 998–1030). The author of the chronicle, Abu Nasr Muhammad ibn ʿAbd al-Jabbar ʿUtbi ("al-ʿUtbi"), was born in the city of Rayy, in northern Iran, in 961. He later found employment in the Ghaznavid administrations of both Sebuktegin and Mahmud, and he completed his chronicle of their reigns around the year 1020.*

Although the author's ornate prose makes this a difficult text, even in a simplified English translation, the Kitab al-Yamini *provides a unique insight into Central Asia's political transformation in the years following the collapse of Samanid authority, as power in the region shifted for the first time from Persians to Turkic rulers. Two distinct groups vied for dominance in this environment: the Ghaznavids to the south and the Qarakhanids, known to their contemporaries as the Ilek (or Ilig) Khans, in Transoxiana. The Ghaznavids were a dynasty of Turkic slave-soldiers who had risen to elite status under the Samanids, only to assume regal authority for themselves as their patrons' authority waned. The Qarakhanids represented a more recent Turkic migration into the region from further to the east. Following the Qarakhanid ruler Satuq Bughra Khan's conversion in Kashghar in the middle of the tenth century, the Qarakhanids emerged as the first* significant Turkic-Muslim power in Central Asia. Several decades later they expanded westward into Farghana and Transoxiana, where they brought Samanid rule to an end and came into conflict with their new neighbors, the Ghaznavids, to the south.

The following excerpt describes the establishment of a peace treaty between Sultan Mahmud of Ghazna and the Qarakhanid ruler, or Ilek Khan, Nasr (r. 998–1015). While the two parties initially agreed that the Amu Darya River (at the time popularly known by its Arabic name, the Jayhun) would serve as the boundary between their two realms, it did not take long for conflict to arise. As the Ghaznavids focused their military conquest eastward, toward India, the Qarakhanids crossed the river and invaded. Our chronicler details how the Ghaznavids managed to reclaim their territory in Afghanistan and Iran.

Account of the Alliance of the Sultan with Ilek-Khan, and Their Subsequent Estrangement

When the Sultan had cleansed the Court of Khurasan from his adversaries, and had reduced the enemies of the family of Saman to non-existence, Ilek-Khan succeeded to Mawarannahr, and obtained the princes of the family of Saman, their children and comrades. And these regions were entirely stripped of all that race and pearl-stock. And he wrote to the Sultan, and congratulated him on his inheritance of the kingdom of Khurasan, and proposed a reparation of good-will and the thread of friendship. An alliance was made between them, and motives of good inclination and attachment were established. And his discriminating nature advanced from a sincere affection to a sincere unity; and, at the time when the Sultan went to repulse the attack at Nishapur, he had sent the Imam Abu'l-Ta'ib, who was Imam of *hadith* (or of the sacred traditions) upon an embassy to Ilek-Khan, and sent (also) Tuganjuk, Prince of Sarkas, to him and expressed a desire for a noble alliance with his nobles (or noble *race*) and presented before his greatness, his army and his fortress, curious valuables of pieces of pure gold, with jacinths and rubies, and chains of great and small pearls, and gifts of robes and eggs of amber, and vessels of gold and silver full of perfumes of camphor, and other productions of the provinces of India, made from frankincense-bearing trees, and Damascus scimitars, and war elephants adorned with many colored trappings and jeweled bits, in describing all which gems the mind would be confused, and in specifying all which incomparable things the eyes would become turbid. And celebrated horses, with ornaments and head-trappings of gold, and various other choice and desirable things. And when the Imam Abu'l-Ta'ib arrived at the Turkish territory they exhibited much agitation and eagerness at his approach, and expressed extreme readiness to pay homage and respect to his dignity, partly on account of their honour toward His Majesty the Sultan, and partly on account of the superabundant and excelling virtues of (the envoy) in all kinds of science, he being the singular scholar of his age. He was sound in controversial tact, and in casuistical divinity, and lunar calculations. He thus attained to the object desired (i.e., to demand a daughter of Ilek-Khan for the Sultan, in marriage), caused seeking to be joined with finding, and returned, having with diligent industry fully accomplished his pilgrimage; and he presented the unequalled pearl, which, as a diver, he had sought and found in Turkestan, before the Sultan's presence, with valuable specimens of the purchased articles of Turkestan, pure gold and silver, sweet musk, high-bred horses, moon-faced slaves, well-featured girls, white falcons, packets of peacock-feathers, ermines, and tawny skins, with exquisite china vessels, and many other beautiful fabrics, so that, between the two kingdoms, an interwoven alliance and affinity became fastened, as with nails, and between them, as between artificers and officers, a partnership was established in the adjustment of benefits and union. For a long period affairs continued to be fitly ordered and duly arranged between these Courts, until, through the hateful anger of fate, the straight road of affection became damaged by ill-will, and by the interlopings of Satan the stream of the fountains of love became diminished, and the bonds of that sincere regard became untied. Some of the beauteous words of Abu'l-Ta'ib have been cited, and at the end of this chronicle several of the subject-nobles of the Sultan (who in their paths were like bright stars, and in their fixed [orbits] like constellations, each one being a star of the stars of the age, and a moon of the moons of virtue, and a column of the pillars of science) will be commemorated. And these words are from many of the niceties of the judgment and novelties of the language of Abu'l-Ta'ib: "He who offers himself before his time offers himself to the air." And this apothegm is taken from "The Words" of Abu Mansur, the divine: "Even a dog has high thoughts, and he is of the lowest extremity of baseness in whom there is a seeking for power before the times of power," etc., etc.

Account of the Passage of the Jayhun (the Amu Darya) by Ilek-Khan

The state of a sincere alliance between the Sultan and Ilek-Khan remained firm, until the creeping scorpions of ill-will, and the disturbing manoeuvrers of hatred, cut off the progress of affection, so that the flames of dispute blazed up. And Ilek watched an opportunity of withdrawal and flight, and when the standards of the Sultan were far distant he made an expedition into the frontiers of Multan, and the extent of Khurasan was destitute of the protection of the State, and the guardianship of government, and he sent Sabashitagin, who was general of his army, with an abundant force to Khurasan, and entrusted the capital, Balkh, to Jaafartagin, with a band of warriors. And Arslan-Jazib, Prince of Tus, was established at Herat, having received orders before from the Sultan, that if any new attack should occur on his weak part, and if loss should be produced on both sides, he should take up his position at Ghazna, march from Herat, and come to Ghazna. And Sabashitagin came to Herat, and sent Hasan b. Nasr to Nishapur, to enquire into the property, and to value the sources of wealth. And the majority of the nobles of Khurasan encouraged them with friendship and aid, on account of the prolongation of the days of the Sultan's absence, and the interception of intelligence, and the concealment of his footsteps, and on account of the trembling of earthquakes (confused rumours), and contracted feelings, and daily reports, and vain words. And Abu'l-'Abas Fazl b. Ahmad, in order to guard the paths and govern the provinces of the kingdom, arrived from Ghazna, as far as the frontiers of Bamiyan, with the preparation for a complete intercepting cordon. And he committed the passes of ingress and egress of that country to men of action, and a cautious corps of observation. And quick messengers ran through the whole extent of the kingdom to the Sultan with tidings of the conduct of Ilek. And the Sultan laid aside all care for other regions, and like striking lightning and a furious wind traveled that expanse over the plains and through the warriors, over the deserts, and through the tribes of people, and in a short time arrived at Ghuzni, and afforded aid to his sons of the Empire, and the nobles of His Majesty, by his horses, mules and riders, and assembled from the great spearmen a body of glorious soldiers (Verse):

> Angels upon angels, or, if they were human, such as
> embroidered by the needle.

And came like a raging sea to Balkh, and Jaafartagin went out from this contingency flying like a devil from exposure to the storm of ashes. But the Sultan sent Arslan-Jazib with ten thousand cavalry on his road. And Sabashitagin when he arrived at the bank of the Jayhun, and beheld that foaming sea and roaring torrent, turned aside and came to Merv, in order to march through the desert. But the summer was hot, so that the wells were filled up, and the roads obliterated, and the path difficult to determine; therefore he began to move towards Sarkhas. But Muhsin b. Tabak, who was one of the Ghuzz chieftains, seized the road, and bestirred himself to resist him. Sabashitagin, therefore, finding no possibility of making a stand against the army of Arslan, and not even an opportunity of bathing (i.e., from the hot pursuit), was deprived of the power of proceeding, and went there from to Nasa. And as he was about to collect his baggage and march, upon occasion of one of his marches, Arslan-Jazib came down, and on account of his baggage, and the enormous weight of treasure and of goods which he had derived from the provinces of Herat, he was unable to retain those appendages, or to cope with those heroes. In order to preserve (this property) he wandered right and left until the conclusion of the affair was that he made it all the means of preserving his existence and a matter of life. Therefore he cast all this transported burden and heavy load from his back, and struck in towards Nishapur. The other army kept close after him until he halted at the frontiers of Jurjan. He threw himself amongst the cliffs and thickets of that land, and the surrounding people of Gilan struck him with the hand of slaughter and plunder, and brought to bear their killing strength upon his comrades and his troops. Several of his army fled to the safety of the protecting shadow of Shams al-Muali. He, by the route of Damistan, came as far as Nasa, and sent the remainder of his baggage to 'Ali b. Ma'mun Khorezmshah. And on the part of Ilek-Khan he entrusted him with the charge thereof, and enjoined him to preserve it, and earnestly recommended him to guard it from the impurities of treachery. And with respect to all the camp followers and the relics of the force, he dismissed them to the service of that Prince, and started for Merv, by way of the desert. The Sultan halted at Tus, for the inspection of the booty of Arslan-Jazib, and upon the arrival of intelligence that Sabashitagin came out by way of the desert, he turned on the road by which he might meet him, in order that he might perchance overtake him, and draw him into the snare of vengeance. But when the Sultan arrived he had passed to the desert. Upon this the Sultan dispatched after him 'Abdallah Tain, with an army of Arabs which was in his care; and his condition was such as Sa'id b. Hasan describes (Verse):

> I fled from a flowing rivulet and its scantiness
> Unto a superabundant water and its confused streams;
> And I was like one who eagerly rushes into a canal,
> When desiring to escape the thunder-rain

And, in the midst of a desert wherein there was no water, except Satan's saliva, and nothing brightly green except the flat of swords, they laid the sword upon his company and they took prisoners his brother, with seven hundred of his distinguished chiefs and captains. And the Sultan commanded that they should tie each one's sword below him, and place it upon his heel, and carry all to Ghazna, that all the world might take example from their misfortune and distress, and the fallaciousness of their confidence (Persian Verse):

> I have often contemplated and still no thought arrived, but this good one,
> Happy he who directs himself (to serve) this Lord.
> Let him who would be at ease implore God to make his burden light.
> The head of every one will be cheerful whose foot is on that threshold.

Sabashitagin, with a few individuals, saved his life, and passed the Jayhun, and appeared before Ilek-Khan, who had already sent Jaafartagin, with six thousand horse, towards Balkh, in order to divert the Sultan from the pursuit of Sabashitagin. But the Sultan regarded them not, until he had concluded his immediate engagement. Then he turned his reins towards them and suddenly assaulted them, and sent the Amir Abu'l-Muzaffar Nasr, with his hunting forces and reaping troops, who held on to them until they were all expelled from the territory of Khurasan.

As for Ilek Khan he could not rest from this calamity, and dispatched a "letter of succour" to Kadir-Khan, King of China, imploring aid. And a sea of Turkish forces came like a torrent, and occupied the utmost parts of his kingdom and cities. And the army of Mawarannahr came, in a body to join them, and five thousand bridles passed the Jayhun, madly proud of the resources and strength of Kadir-Khan, of his great numbers, extreme bravery, established ability, and extensive power (Verse):

> Around him is a sea, which dashes with its billows and wears
> out the margin of the cliff.
> The stone from a small hill comes to them,

It smoothes thereby the shore,
Until it joins the fragments of the misfortune and arranges them in order.

The news of their arrival reached the Sultan, at Tukharistan: he packed up and went to Balkh, that the food of their covetousness might be cut off from those regions, and the road of provisions and pay might be closed; and the Sultan was occupied in arranging the means of war, and he collected a numerous army, of various tribes of Turks, Khalajes, and Hindus and Afghans, and the Ghuzz troops, and they met at a wide place, four *farsangs* from Balkh (Verse):

The fifth of the east of the earth and the west responds,
And their murmur reaches the ear of Gemini.
Therein are assembled all people,
Nor can they understand the news without an interpreter.
Oh God, at the time of the way of sorrow thou seest it,
And (when) the warriors and lions survive not.

Ilek then marched down with his army to battle, and for that day the young men of the army only boasted and swaggered, until the carpet of night was spread, when they separated, with the promise to fight with each other on the morrow. And the Sultan was occupied in arranging the order of battle. He assigned the centre to the Amir Nasr, brother of the Prince of Jurjan, Abu Nasr Farighuni, and Abu 'Abdallah Taini, with a body of his picked Curds and brave genii. He sent the right to the great Sahib, the Amir Altuntash, and charged Arslan Jazib with the left, and strengthened the force of the centre with five hundred elephants. And as to Ilek Khan, he, having stationed himself in the centre, had Kadir-Khan, with the army of Chin, on the right, and Jaafartagin on the left. Thus they engaged, and the earth resounded with thunder-like shouts and was in a blaze, from the terrible lightning of swords, and they sewed patches of dust upon the blue lining of the heavenly vault, and rendered the field of battle brilliant with the torches of arms and the tapers of spears, and sprinkles of blood began to rain from those lightning scimitars. And Ilek-Khan, with five hundred Turkish *ghulams* (*quasi* grenadiers) fought so skillfully that in the front of the army they could split a hair with their arrows, and could take a mountain from its place by the strokes of their swords. Then the sea of war was raised to a storm and the ground of the field was shaken as by an earthquake. And the Sultan, when he witnessed the mighty strength and terrible power of that body, came down to a small hill and implored the Almighty to strengthen his right hand and forgive (*his errors?*) and he placed his hand upon the end of the skirt of Heaven and trusted in God's guardianship, and asked victory from Him; and he made vows of offerings and engaged himself to give pious alms, and humbly submitted himself to God (imploring) that He would speed on victory and conquest. Then he mounted his own special elephant, and, with clear mind and sincere assurance, made a charge upon Ilek-Khan's centre; and his elephant seized the standard-bearer of Ilek-Khan and tossed him into the air, and, with weighty fury and extreme might humbled the men under his foot, and with his trunk hurled them from the back of horses, and tore them to pieces with his teeth. Upon this the chiefs of the Sultan boiled with the eagerness of opportunity and the gladness of victory, and bestirred their scimitars to strike the mass. Then came the tongue of reproach and cursing, and they compelled the troops of the Turks to leave their position, and to take the path of flight, and the Sultan's army with fury and madness cast them back to Mawarannahr, and not a trace of them remained in Khurasan. And again, these verses of Salami contain a description of the event, and a delineation of the impress of the Sultan's deeds (Verse):

> "Oh sword of the religion of God thou art not pleasing to the enemy,
> even although they sword like thy rectitude cuts rightly," etc.

And when the Sultan had concluded this great victory, and had allayed the heat of his anxiety, and had put an end to the series of these accidents, he determined to carry out his design of attacking Nawastah Shah (or Zab-Sais). This Prince was one of those sons of some Kings of India, unto whom the Sultan, having displayed to them the profession of Islam, had intrusted several of the provinces which he had won from the infidels, and had given the reins of the government of regions unto the hand of his fidelity and had confidence in him, and had left him deputy and viceroy in those countries. But he divested himself of the collar of religion and the robe of Islam, and put on the cloak of infidelity, and became an apostate. The Sultan twisted him from his position by one direct attack, and expelled him broken and discomforted from those limits, and a second time adorned Bahjat Malik with that kingdom, under his own sovereignty. These two great victories, and important affairs, presented a clear demonstration and a cutting proof of the exalted dignity of the Sultan, of his perfect fortunes, of the support of God, and of the aid of heavenly kindness. And thus, beneath the canopy of empire and of victory he turned his face towards Ghazna. "For those grace of God makes to believe whom He will," for God has great grace.

15   Ibn Khallikan: Biography of the Vizier Nizam al-Mulk

INTRODUCTION

Abu'l-'Abbas Ahmad ibn Khallikan (1211–82) was born and educated in the city of Irbil, in northern Iraq. As an adult he moved between Aleppo, Damascus, and Mosul, and finally found himself in Cairo, where he secured a position as deputy to the chief jurist (the qazi al-quzzat). It was while Ibn Khallikan was in Cairo that he began work on the Wafayat al-Ayan, *his great biographical dictionary of the Islamic world. It took some eighteen years to complete the work, partially because of the enormity of the task but also because Ibn Khallikan's progress was interrupted in 1261, when the Mamluk Sultan Baybars (r. 1260–77) appointed him chief jurist of Damascus. He served in that post for ten years, until political disturbances led to his removal. Taking advantage of the situation, he returned to the libraries of Cairo so that he could resume work on the* Wafayat.

Ibn Khallikan was a highly respected scholar and jurist, and he harbored a great passion for history. According to his own account it was this interest that drove him to collect all available information that pertained to famous figures, both historical and his contemporaries. In 1274, he finally completed his masterpiece, a grand historical biography that documents the personal characteristics and lives of many of the most influential figures in Islamic history. The book is perhaps most useful in its treatment of Ibn Khallikan's contemporaries, although it is also a valuable resource for earlier periods as it includes a vast amount of information drawn from oral traditions and manuscripts that are difficult to access or, in some cases, no longer in existence.

The short section reproduced here is Ibn Khallikan's bibliographic entry for Nizam al-Mulk (1018–92), a highly influential figure who served as governor of Khurasan for the Ghaznavids and then vizier under two Saljuq Sultans, Alp Arslan (r. 1063–73) and Malik Shah (r. 1073–92). His importance is underlined in that, especially under the latter, he was widely reputed to have been more in control of the affairs of state than his Saljuq patron. Among his achievements, Nizam al-Mulk is credited with devising a number of new institutions and methods of governance that his Saljuq patrons embraced and implemented across their vast territory. He is most famous, however, as the author of the Siyasat-nama, *a work in the mirror for princes genre that is excerpted below.*

The vizier Abu 'Ali al-Hasan al-Tusi (native of Tus) was surnamed Nizam al-Mulk, Kawam al-Din (the regulator of the state, upholder of religion). Al-Samani says in his *Kitab al-ansab:* "Radkan: a small village near Tus; it is said that Nizam al-Mulk was from its neighbourhood." He was son to a *dihqan,* and, after studying the Traditions and jurisprudence, he entered as *katib* into the service of 'Ali Ibn Shadan, governor of the city of Balkh; but as heavy sums were extorted from him every year by his employer, he abandoned his post and fled to Dawud Ibn Mika'il al-Saljuqi, the father of Alp Arslan. This prince received from him such proofs of fidelity and attachment, that he gave him over to his son, Alp Arslan, saying: "Consider him as a parent, and disobey not his counsels." When Alp Arslan succeeded to the empire, Nizam al-Mulk took the direction of affairs, and administered with great talent; he remained in Alp Arslan's service ten years. On the death of that prince, his sons pressed forward to seize on the empire, but Nizam al-Mulk secured it to Malik Shah, son of Alp Arslan. From that period and during twenty years, all the power was concentrated in the hands of the vizier, whilst the sultan had nothing more to do than show himself on the throne and enjoy the pleasures of the chase. The caliph al-Muqtadi, having received a visit from Nizam al-Mulk, allowed him to be seated in his presence, and addressed him in these terms: "O Hasan! May God be pleased with thee in as much as the Commander of the faithful is pleased with thee." The court of the vizier Nizam al-Mulk was greatly frequented by doctors of the law and Sufis, towards the latter of whom he was very beneficent. Being asked the reason of the favour which he showed them, he answered:

> I was in the service of a certain emire, when a Sufi came to me and made me a pious exhortation, and said: "Serve Him whose service will be useful to you, and be not taken up with one whom dogs will eat tomorrow." I did not understand his meaning; but the emire used to drink from morning to evening, and had some dogs which were ferocious like beasts of prey, and devoured strangers at night; now, it happened that being once overcome with intoxication, he went out alone, and was torn to pieces by the dogs, which did not recognize him. I then knew that this Sufi had received a revelation on the subject, and I therefore treat these people with respect, in hopes that I may obtain a similar grace.

—On hearing the call to prayers, he immediately abandoned whatever occupation he might be engaged in; and when the Imam al-Haramain Abu'l-Ma'ali, and the author of the Epistle, Abu'l-Kasim al-Qushayri, came to visit him, he treated them with the utmost respect and made them sit down on the same sofa with himself. He built a number of colleges, convents, and mosques in different provinces. He was the first who set the example of founding a college, and he commenced, AH 457 (AD 1065) the construction of that of Damascus; in the year 459, it was agreed on by every class of persons that Abu Ishaq al-Shirazi should teach therein; but he did not present himself, and Abu Nasr Ibn al-Sabbagh, the author of the *Shamil*, taught for twenty days in his place, after which Abu Ishaq accepted. We shall give the full details of this circumstance in the life of Ibn al-Sabbagh, which see. At the hour of prayer, Abu Ishaq used to quit the college and perform his devotions in a mosque; "Because," said he, "I have been informed that the greater part of the materials employed in the construction of the college has been procured illegally."—Nizam al-Mulk learned and taught the Traditions, and he used to say: "I am conscious of not deserving that honour, but I wish to establish myself in the series of persons who have transmitted the sayings of the Prophet."—The following verses are declared to be his:

> After four-score, strength exists not; and the alacrity of youth is departed.
> With staff in hand I resemble Moses, but have not the gift of prophecy.

Some persons say, however, that these verses are by Muhammad Ibn Abi al-Saqr. Nizam al-Mulk was born on Friday, 21st of Zu'l-Qa'da, AH 408 (April, AD 1018), at Nawqan, one of the two cities of which Tus is composed. In AH 485, he set out with Malik Shah for Isfahan, and on Friday night, 10th of Ramadan (October, AD 1092), he broke his fast and mounted in his palanquin; on reaching a village called Sahna, near Nihavand, he remarked that a great number of the companions of the Prophet had been slain at that place in the time of the caliph 'Umar Ibn al-Khattab, "and happy," said he, "is the man who is with them!" He was then accosted by a boy of the province of Daylam, in the dress of a Sufi, who called to him to receive a memorial, and when the vizier reached out his hand to take it, he stabbed him to the heart with a dagger. Nizam al-Mulk was borne to his pavilion, where he expired, and the murderer took to flight, but having stumbled over a tent-rope, he fell and was immediately taken and put to death. The sultan rode forth without delay to tranquillize the army and console them. The body of the vizier was transported to Isfahan, and there interred. It is said that the assassin was suborned against him by Malik Shah, who was fatigued to see him live so long, and coveted the numerous fiefs which he held in his possession. The sultan survived him for thirty-five days only. This vizier was the ornament of the age in which he lived; his son-in-law, Shibl al-Dawla Muqatil al-Bakri, whose life will be found farther on, lamented his death in an elegiac poem containing the following passage:

> Nizam al-Mulk was a precious pearl, formed of pure nobleness by the merciful God: it was so fine that the age knew not its worth, and the Maker, jealous for its honour, restored it to its shell.

The assassination of Nizam al-Mulk has been attributed also to Taj al-Mulk Abu'l-Ghana'im; he was an enemy of the vizier and in high favour with his sovereign Malik Shah, who, on the death of Nizam al-Mulk, appointed him to fill the place of vizier. He was himself slain on Monday night, 12th Muharram, 486 (February, AD 1093); having been attacked and cut to pieces by the young *mamluks* belonging to the household of Nizam al-Mulk. He was aged forty-seven years: the tomb over the grave of the shaykh Abu Ishaq al-Shirazi was erected by him.

16   Nizam al-Mulk: A Mirror for Princes

INTRODUCTION

As mentioned in the introduction to the preceding reading, Abu 'Ali al-Hasan ibn 'Ali (1018–92), renowned as "Nizam al-Mulk" ("the regulator of the state"), rose to prominence as the Ghaznavid governor of Khurasan. Shortly after the Saljuq victory over the Ghaznavids at the battle of Dandanqan in 1040, Nizam al-Mulk sought, and found, employment in the Saljuq administration. In the mid-1050s he first became attached to the Saljuq Sultan Alp Arslan (r. 1063–73), who is reported to have become quite fond of his counsel and later appointed him to the post of vizier. Nizam al-Mulk reached the apex of his power as the vizier of Alp Arslan's son, Sultan Malik Shah (r. 1073–92), who was only eighteen years old when he succeeded his father. Nizam al-Mulk effectively governed in the name of his inexperienced sultan from the onset, and, despite his young protégé's periodic attempts to assert his own authority, he continued to do so with great success for the next two decades. Among his greater achievements was eliminating taxes not approved by Islamic law and implementing new land-revenue collection methods, designed to protect the rights of the peasantry from parasitic tax collectors.

Nizam al-Mulk ruled, without actually being the ruler, during what was arguably the most successful period of Saljuq dominance in the eastern Islamic world. In addition to overseeing Saljuq expansion into both Anatolia and Central Asia, he was a great patron of the arts and educational institutions. He invested in the future of Sunni Islam by financing the construction of many madrasas, the most famous of which was the Nizamiyya madrasa of Baghdad (1067). He also instructed his Turkmen benefactors, recent arrivals in the region, in the fine art of Perso-Islamic legal traditions in the hope that they might govern wisely, in accordance with Islamic law, and in harmony with their subjects, thereby bringing prosperity to their new lands. It was this goal, and his own advancing years, that prompted him to author in 1091–92 what would become his most famous legacy, the Siyasat-nama *(Treatise on government) as an instructional guide for later generations. This mirror for princes (one of several works in that genre included in this volume) references both Islamic traditions and historical anecdotes to instruct the Saljuqs in how they might govern a successful Perso-Islamic state and face the challenges of the time.*

On Recognizing the Extent of God's Grace towards Kings

1. It is for kings to observe His pleasure (His name be glorified) and the pleasure of The Truth is in the charity which is done to His creatures and justice which is spread among them. A kingdom which is blessed by its people will endure and increase from day to day, while its king will enjoy power and prosperity; in this world he will acquire good fame, in the next world salvation, and his reckoning will be the easier. Great men have said [in Arabic], "A kingdom may last while there is irreligion, but it will not endure when there is oppression." . . .

2. Tradition tells that when Joseph the prophet (the prayers of Allah and His peace be upon him) went out from this world, they were carrying him to Abraham's tomb (upon him be peace) to bury him near his forefathers, when Gabriel (upon him be peace) came and said, "Stop where you are; this is not his place; for at the resurrection he will have to answer for the sovereignty which he has exercised." Now if the case of Joseph the prophet was such, consider what the position of others will be.

3. It has come down in a tradition from The Prophet (may Allah bless him and save him) that on the day of the resurrection, when anyone is brought forward who [in his life] wielded power and command over God's creatures, his bands will be bound; if he has been just, his justice will loose his hands and send him to paradise; but if he has been unjust, his injustice will cast him into hell as he is, with his hands bound in chains.

6. Of a certainty The Master of the World (may Allah perpetuate his reign) should know that on that great day he will be asked to answer for all those of God's creatures who are under his command, and if he tries to transfer [his responsibility] to someone else he will not be listened to. Since this is so it behoves the king not to leave this important matter to anyone else, and not to disregard the state of God's creatures. To the best of his ability let him ever acquaint himself,

secretly and openly, with their conditions; let him protect them from extortionate hands, and preserve them from cruel tyrants, so that the blessings resulting from those actions may come about in the time of his rule and benedictions will be pronounced upon his age until the resurrections.

On Having Troops of Various Races

1. When troops are all of one race dangers arise; they lack zeal and they are apt to be disorderly. It is necessary that they should be of different races. Two thousand Daylamites and Khurasanis should be stationed at the court. Those that exist at present should be retained and the remainder be levied; and if some of these are from Gurjistan [Georgia] and Shabankara (in Fars), it will be suitable because men of these races are also good.

2. It was the custom of Sultan Mahmud [of Ghazna] to have troops of various races such as Turks, Khurasanis, Arabs, Hindus, men of Ghur and Daylam. When he was on an expedition, every night he used to detail several men of each group to go on guard and allotted each group their station; and for fear of one another no group dared to move from their places; they kept watch until daybreak in competition with one another and did not go to sleep. And when it was the day of battle, each race strove to preserve their name and honour, and fought all the more zealously lest anyone should say that such-and-such race showed slackness in battle. Thus all races endeavoured to surpass one another.

3. Since the fighting men were organized on this basis they were all valiant and intrepid. Consequently once they had taken up their arms they did not retreat one pace until they had defeated the enemy.

4. When once or twice an army has waxed valiant and gained victory over the enemy, thereafter a mere hundred of their horsemen will be a match for a thousand of the enemy and no force will ever again be able to oppose that triumphant army and all the armies of neighbouring countries will fear that king and submit to him.

On Keeping Turkmens in Service like Pages

1. Although the Turkmens have given rise to a certain amount of vexation, and they are very numerous, still they have a longstanding claim upon this dynasty, because at its inception they served well and suffered much, and also they are attached by ties of kinship. So it is fitting that about a thousand of their sons should be enrolled and maintained in the same way as pages of the palace. When they are in continuous employment they will learn the use of arms and become trained in service. Then they will settle down with other people and with growing devotion serve as pages, and cease to feel that aversion [to settled life] with which they are naturally imbued; and whenever the need arises 5,000 or 10,000 of them, organized and equipped like pages, will mount to perform the task for which they are detailed. In this way the empire will not leave them portionless, the king will acquire glory, and they will be contented.

17   *Qabus-nama:* A Different Mirror for Princes

INTRODUCTION

In 1082–83, an aging prince of the north Iranian Ziyarid dynasty, Kai Ka'us (r. 1049–87), produced the Qabus-nama, *another work in the mirror for princes genre intended to provide guidance for his son and successor, Gilan Shah. Like the* Siyasat-nama *written by Nizam al-Mulk, his more famous and powerful contemporary, the* Qabus-nama *provides readers with an array of practical advice drawn from the author's substantial experience navigating the pitfalls of statecraft. But while the* Siayasat-nama *promotes a Perso-Islamic view of the state, the* Qabus-nama *promotes a more Machiavellian outlook as to how rulers should conduct their affairs. One might surmise that the author developed such a jaded perspective on statecraft as the Ziyarid dynasty's authority in the region teetered under the weight of the newly arrived Saljuqs. But it also appears to be derived from the method of governance favored by the author's grandfather, Qabus b. Wushmgir (r. 997–1012), who was at the same time an educated patron of the arts and sciences—he even attracted Ibn Sina to his court—and a draconian despot whom Kai Ka'us honored by naming his book after him. In the end, at least for the Ziyarids, the wisdom of the* Qabus-nama *proved less than useful. Gilan Shah ruled for little more than three years before he was killed and his dynasty ended by a political power even more ruthless than his forebears: the Nizari Isma'ilis of Alamut (the Assassins).*

The following excerpt from the Qabus-nama, *one of forty-four chapters, instructs the reader in the fine art of purchasing slaves. Kai Ka'us divides his assessment into three categories of primary importance: physical appearance, general health, and the particular attributes associated with various ethnic groups (or races). Scrutinizing slaves very closely, he tells us, reveals much to the informed buyer about what one may expect in terms of the individual slave's applicability for specific types of tasks. More interesting for our present purpose is his assessment of the characteristics stereotypically associated with the various Turkic groups available in the slave markets of the eleventh-century Middle East.*

On the Purchase of Slaves

When you set out to buy slaves, be cautious. The buying of men is a difficult art because many a slave may appear to be good, who, regarded with knowledge, turns out to be the opposite. Most people imagine that buying slaves is like any other form of trading, not understanding that the buying of slaves, or the art of doing so, is a branch of philosophy. Anyone who buys goods of which he

has no competent understanding can be defrauded over them, and the most difficult form of knowledge is that which deals with human beings. There are so many
blemishes and good points in the human kind, and a single blemish may conceal
a myriad good points while a single good point may conceal a myriad faults.

Human beings cannot be known except by the science of physiognomy and
by experience, and the science of physiognomy in its entirety is a branch of prophecy that is not acquired to perfection except by the divinely directed apostle. The
reason is that by physiognomy the inward goodness or wickedness of men can be
ascertained.

Now let me describe to the best of my ability what is essential in the purchasing of slaves, both white and black, and what their good and bad points are, so
that they may be known to you. Understand then that there are three essentials
in the buying of slaves; first is the recognition of their good and bad qualities
whether external or internal, by means of physiognomy; second is the awareness
of diseases, whether latent or apparent, by their symptoms; third is the knowledge
of the various classes and the defects and merits of each.

With regard to the first requirement, that of physiognomy, it consists of close
observation when buying slaves. (The buyers of slaves are of all categories: there
are those who inspect the face, disregarding body and extremities; others look
to the corpulence or otherwise of the slave.) Whoever it may be that inspects the
slave must first look at the face, which is always open to view, whereas the body
can only be seen as occasion offers. Then look at eyes and eyebrows, followed by
nose, lips, and teeth, and lastly at the hair. The reason for this is that God placed
the beauty of human beings in eyes and eyebrows, delicacy in the nose, sweetness
in the lips and teeth, and freshness in the skin. To all these the hair of the head has
been made to lend adornment, since [God] created the hair for adornment.

You must, consequently, inspect everything. When you see beauty in the eyes
and eyebrows, delicacy in the nose, sweetness in the lips and teeth, and freshness
in the skin, then buy the slave possessing them without concerning yourself over
the extremities of the body. If all of these qualities are not present, then the slave
must possess delicacy; because, in my opinion, one that is delicate without having
beauty is preferable to one that is beautiful but not possessed of delicacy.

The learned say that one must know the indications and signs by which to
buy the slaves suited for particular duties. The slave that you buy for your private
service and conviviality should be of middle proportions, neither tall nor short,
fat nor lean, pale nor florid, thickset nor slender, curly-haired nor with hair over-
straight. When you see a slave soft-fleshed, fine-skinned, with regular bones and
wine-coloured hair, black eye-lashes, dark eyes, black eyebrows, open-eyed, long-
nosed, slender-waisted, round-chinned, red-lipped, with white regular teeth, and
all his members such as I have described, such a slave will be decorative and com-
panionable, loyal, of delicate character and dignified.

The mark of the slave who is clever and may be expected to improve is this:
he must be of erect stature, medium in hair and in flesh, broad of hand and with
the middle of the fingers lengthy, in complexion dark though ruddy, dark-eyed,

open-faced and unsmiling. A slave of this kind would be competent to acquire learning, to act as treasurer or for any other [such] employment.

The slave suited to play musical instruments is marked out by being soft-fleshed (though his flesh must not be over-abundant, especially on the back), with his fingers slender, neither lean nor fat. (A slave whose face is over-fleshy, incidentally, is one incapable of learning.) His hands must be soft, with the middles of the fingers lengthy. He must be bright-visaged, having the skin tight; his hair must not be too long, too short or too black. It is better, also, for the soles of the feet to be regular. A slave of this kind will swiftly acquire a delicate art of whatever kind, particularly that of the instrumentalist.

The mark of the slave suited for arms-bearing is that his hair is thick, his body tall and erect, his build powerful, his flesh hard, his bones thick, his skin coarse, and his limbs straight, the joints being firm. The tendons should be tight and the sinews and blood-vessels prominent and visible on the body. Shoulders must be broad, the chest deep, the neck thick, and the head round; also for preference he should be bald. The belly should be concave, the buttocks drawn in and the legs in walking well extended. And the eyes should be black. Any slave who possesses these qualities will be a champion in single combat, brave and successful.

The mark of the slave suited for employment in the women's apartments is that he should be dark-skinned and sour-visaged and have withered limbs, scanty hair, a shrill voice, little [slender] feet, thick lips, a flat nose, stubby fingers, a bowed figure, and a thin neck. A slave with these qualities will be suitable for service in the women's quarters. He must not have a white skin nor a fair complexion; and beware of a ruddy-complexioned man, particularly if his hair is limp. His eyes, further, should not be languorous or moist; a man having such qualities is either over-fond of women or prone to act as a go-between.

The mark of the slave who is callous [insensitive] and suited to be a herdsman or groom is that he should be open-browed and wide-eyed, and his eyelids should be flecked with red. He should, further, be long in lips and teeth and his mouth should be wide. A slave with these qualities is extremely callous, fearless, and uncivilised.

The mark of the slave suited for domestic service and cookery is that he should be clean in face and body, round-faced, with hands and feet slender, his eyes dark inclining to blue, sound in body, silent, the hair of his head wine-coloured and falling forward limply. A slave with these qualities is suitable for the occupations mentioned.

Each then, should have the essential characteristics which I have recounted. But I will also mention the defects and virtues which should be known in respect of each separate race. You must understand that Turks are not all of one race, and each has its own nature and essential character. Amongst them the most ill-tempered are the Ghuzz, and the Qïpchaqs; the best-tempered and most willing are the Khotanese, the Qarluqs, and the Tibetans; the boldest and most courageous are the Turghay (?), the most inured to toil and hardship and the most active are the Tatars and the Yaghma, whereas the laziest of all are the Chigil.

It is a fact well-known to all that beauty or ugliness in the Turks is the opposite of that in the Indians. If you observe the Turk feature by feature [he has] a large head, a broad face, narrow eyes, a flat nose, and unpleasing lips and teeth. Regarded individually the features are not handsome, yet the whole is handsome. The Indian's face is the opposite of this; each individual feature regarded by itself appears handsome, yet looked at as a whole the face does not create the same impression as that of the Turk. To begin with, the Turk has a personal freshness and clearness of complexion not possessed by the Indian; indeed the Turks win for freshness against all other races.

Without any doubt, what is fine in the Turks is present in a superlative degree, but so also is what is ugly in them. Their faults in general are that they are blunt-witted, ignorant, boastful, turbulent, discontented, and without a sense of justice. Without any excuse they will create trouble and utter foul language, and at night they are poor-hearted. Their merit is that they are brave, free from pretence, open in enmity, and zealous in any task allotted to them. For the [domestic] establishment there is no better race.

Slavs, Russians, and Alans are near in their temperament to the Turks but are more patient. The Alans are more courageous than the Turks at night and more friendly disposed towards their masters. Although in their craftsmanship they are nearer to the Byzantines, being artistic, yet there are faults in them of various kinds; for example they are prone to theft, disobedience, betrayal of secrets, impatience, stupidity, indolence, hostility to their masters, and escaping. Their virtues are that they are soft-natured, agreeable, and quick of understanding. Further they are deliberate in action, direct in speech, brave, good road-guides, and possessed of good memory.

The defect of the Byzantines is that they are foul-tongued, evil-hearted, cowardly, indolent, quick-tempered, covetous, and greedy for worldly things. Their merits are that they are cautious, affectionate, happy, economically-minded, successful in their undertakings, and careful to prevent loss.

The defect of the Armenians is that they are mischievous, foul-mouthed, thieving, impudent, prone to flight, disobedient, babblers, liars, friendly to misbelief, and hostile to their masters. From head to foot, indeed, they incline rather towards defects than to merits. Yet they are quick of understanding and learn their tasks well.

The defect of the Hindu is that he is evil-tongued and in the house no slave-girl is safe from him. But the various classes of the Hindus are unlike those that prevail amongst other peoples, because in other peoples the classes mingle with each other, whereas the Hindus, ever since the time of Adam (Upon whom be peace!), have practised the following custom: namely no trade will form an alliance with any outside it. Thus, grocers will give their daughters only to grocers, butchers to butchers, bakers to bakers, and soldiers to soldiers.

Each of these groups therefore has its own special character, which I cannot describe one by one because that would entail a book in itself.

However, the best of them, people benevolent, brave, or skilled in commerce, are [respectively] the Brahman, the Rawat, and the Kirar. The Brahman is clever, the Rawat brave, and the Kirar skilled in commerce, each class being superior to the one after. The Nubian and the Abyssinian are freer of faults, and the Abyssinian is better than the Nubian because many things were said by the Prophet in praise of the former.

These then are the facts concerning each race and the merits and defects of each.

Now the third essential is being completely alive to defects both external and internal through knowledge of symptoms, and this means that at the time of buying you may not be careless. Do not be content with a single look; many a good slave may appear vile at first sight and many an extremely vile one appear to be good. Further there is the fact that a human being's visage does not continually bear the same complexion. Sometimes it is more inclined to be handsome, at other times to be ugly. You must carefully inspect all the limbs and organs to ensure that nothing remains hidden from you. There are many latent diseases which are on the point of coming but have not yet appeared and will do so within a few days; such diseases have their symptoms.

Thus, if there is a yellowness in the complexion, the lips being changed [from the normal] in colour, and dry, that is the symptom of haemorrhoids. If the eyelids are continuously swollen, it is a symptom of dropsy. Redness in the eyes and a fullness of the veins in the forehead are the mark of epilepsy. Tearing out the hair, flickering of the eyelashes, and chewing of the lips are the signs of melancholia. Crookedness in the bone of the nose or irregularity in it are the symptoms of fistula; hair that is extremely black, but more so in one place than another, shows that the hair has been dyed. If here and there upon the body you perceive the marks of branding where no branding should be, examine closely to ensure that there is no leprosy under it. Yellowness in the eyes and a change [from the ordinary] in the colour of the face are the symptoms of jaundice.

When you buy a slave, you must take and lay him down, press him on both sides and watch closely that he has no pain or swelling. If he has, it will be in the liver or spleen. Having looked for such hidden defects, seek further for the open ones, such as smells from the mouth and nose, hardness of hearing, hesitation in utterance, irregularity of speech, walking off the [straight] road, coarseness of the joints, and hardness at the base of the teeth, to prevent any trickery being practised on you.

When you have seen all that I have mentioned and have made certain, then, if you should buy, do so from honest people and so secure a person who will be of advantage to your household. As long as you can find a non-Arab do not buy an Arabic-speaking slave. You can mould a non-Arab to your ways, but never the one whose tongue is Arabic. Further, do not have a slave-girl brought before you when your appetites are strong upon you; when desire is strong, it makes what is ugly appear good in your eyes. First abate your desires and then engage in the business of purchasing.

Never buy a slave who has been treated with affection in another place. If you do not hold him dear, he will show ingratitude to you, or will flee, or will demand to be sold, or will nourish hatred in his heart for you. Even if you regard him with affection, he will show you no gratitude, in view of what he has experienced elsewhere. Buy your slave from a house in which he has been badly treated, so that he will be grateful for the least kindness on your part and will hold you in affection. From time to time make your slaves a gift of something; do not allow them to be constantly in need of money in such a way that they are compelled to go out seeking it.

Buy slaves of a good price, for each one's value is in accordance with his price. Do not buy a slave who has had numerous masters; a woman who has had many husbands and a slave who has had many masters are held in no esteem. Let those you buy be well-favoured. And when a slave truly desires to be sold, do not dispute with him but sell; when a slave demands to be sold or a wife to be divorced, then sell or divorce because you will have no pleasure from either.

If a slave is deliberately (and not through inadvertence or mistake) lazy or neglectful in his work, do not teach him under compulsion to improve; have no expectation of that, for he will in no wise become industrious or capable of improvement. Sell him quickly; you may rouse a sleeping man with a shout, but a dead body cannot be roused by the sound of a hundred trumpets and drums. Further, do not assemble a useless family about you; a small family is a second form of wealth.

Provide for your slaves in such fashion that they will not escape, and treat them that you have well, as befits your dignity; if you have one person in good condition it is better than having two in ill condition. Do not permit your male slave to take to himself in your household someone whom he calls "brother," nor permit slave-girls to claim sisterhood with each other; it leads to great trouble. On bond and free impose the burdens which they are able to bear, that they may not be disobedient through sheer weakness. Keep yourself ever adorned with justice that you may be included amongst them that are honoured as such.

The slave must recognize your brother, sister, mother, or father as his master. Never buy a dealer's exhausted slave; he is as fearful of the dealer as the ass is of the farrier. Set no store by the slave who always, when called to any work, demands to be sold and never has any fears with regard to being bought and sold; you will gain nothing good from him. Change him quickly for another, seeking out one such as I have described. Thus you will achieve your purpose and suffer no troubles.

18   *Liao Shih:* Nomadic Khitan State and Society

INTRODUCTION

In the early tenth century, as Samanid Bukhara was earning praise as an Islamic cultural center in Central Asia, far to the north and east a pastoral-nomadic group from Manchuria known as the Khitan asserted control over the land that would three centuries later become the center of the great Mongol Empire. In the year 907, Abaoji of the Manchurian Yelü family was elevated to the position of qaghan, *or Great Khan, over the Khitan and within just a few years the Khitan had formed an empire that stretched across the region that today constitutes Manchuria, Mongolia, and northeastern China.[1] For some time the Khitan chose to take the name of Liao, and the dynasty is referred to by both names.*

Khitan (or Liao) dynastic rule in this region continued for more than two centuries, abruptly ending in the early twelfth century due to the invasion of another pastoral-nomadic power from Manchuria, the Jurchen. Many of the Khitan were absorbed into the Jurchen state, but, in 1125, Yelü Dashi led his loyal Khitan followers westward, where they asserted authority over East Turkestan, Semireche, and Transoxiana. Henceforth, these Khitan are referred to as either the Western Liao or, more commonly, the Qara Khitai (1141–1211). Back in the east, after displacing the Khitan the Jurchen rapidly withdrew from the steppe and ruled over northern China as the Qin (or Jin) Empire (1115–1234), until their state collapsed under the weight of the Mongol armies first led by Chinggis Khan himself (d. 1227) and then by his son and successor, Ögedei (r. 1229–41).

The readings below are English translations of entries extracted from the Chinese Liao Shih, *the Standard History of the Liao Dynasty. The volume by Wittfogel and Chia-Shêng includes several hundred English translations of original Chinese-language court records augmented with dozens of very useful essays that introduce readers to Khitan/Liao customs, traditions, and institutions having to do with pastoralism, agricultural production, trade, law, statecraft, military issues, religion, gender, and more. The authors note that scholarly objection to the idea of creating an official history for this "barbarian" dynasty delayed the compilation of the* Liao Shih *until 1343. They argue, however, that the veracity of the* Liao Shih *is strong, as its fourteenth-century compilers based their work primarily on the extensive daily government records of the Khitan/Liao and other, similarly reliable, contemporary sources for the early history of the Qara Khitai.*

Economic Base of the Northern People

[The people of] the Northern Desert made animal husbandry and hunting their occupations, just as the Chinese people encouraged agriculture from which they derived the means of subsistence. After Liao became an empire, it established the five capitals and set up the Southern and Northern Divisions and controlled the whole of China. But the customs of hunting still followed the old course.

---

1. The name "Khitan" is the etymological root of Cathay, an antiquated English word for China.

The Strength of the Ch'i-tan

In the ancient Ch'i-tan way of life their wealth consisted of horses and their strength of soldiers. The horses were released in the open country and the soldiers were demobilized among the people. Whenever a military campaign occurred, they were called to arms. The mounted archers and armored soldiers received their orders at the hour *mao* and assembled at the hour *ch'en*. The horses went after water and grass and the men depended on kumiss. They bent the powerful [bow] and shot living [animals] in order to provide for their daily needs. [They also had] dried food and fodder. Such was their way of living. On account of this, they held the upper hand and encountered no opposition wherever they went.

Animal Husbandry

[Entry from the year] 901—Previously, when T'ai-tsu was the *i-li-chin* of the I-lieh Administration, he took warning from the fact that the Yao-lien family had been weakened by isolation and therefore treated all tribes kindly, made the rewards and punishments equitable, and abstained from wanton military campaigns. He benefited his people by pursuing their interests. The herds flourished, and both the government and the people were sufficiently provided for. After he had ascended the throne, he attacked Ho-tung, subdued the commanderies and counties of Tai-pei, and seized more than a hundred thousand oxen, sheep, camels, and horses. Chancellor Yeh-lu Hsieh-chen in subduing the Nü-chih also captured more than two hundred thousand horses. The herds were distributed among pastures where water and grass were plentiful. Within a few years they increased beyond number. Taking over the horses from the rich at this time did not seem to increase the number, and granting more than ten thousand horses to the Greater and Smaller Hawk Armies did not seem to decrease it. Such were the results of [excellent] methods of animal husbandry. . . .

Afterwards, the kingdom of Tung-tan paid an annual tribute of one thousand horses; the Nü-chih ten thousand; the Chih-pu-ku and other countries ten thousand; the Tsu-pu, Wu-tu-wan, and T'i-yin twenty thousand each; Hsi Hsia and Shih-wei three hundred each; and the Yüeh-li-tu, P'ou-a-li, Ao-li-mi, P'u-nu-li, and T'ieh-li tribes three hundred each. Furthermore, the exportation of sheep and horses into Sung by way of Shuo Prefecture was prohibited, as well as the sale of horses from the T'u-hun and Tang-hsiang to [Hsi] Hsia.

As a result of this the herds flourished and grew to a total of more than a million. The stockbreeding officials were promoted according to their rank. During the almost two hundred years from T'ai-tsu down to Hsing-tsung the prosperity of the herds continued undiminished. During the early years of T'ien-tsu there were still several tens of thousands of herds of horses, each herd comprising not less than a thousand animals.

In the old system of the ancestors usually several tens of thousands of horses were selected for southern expeditions. They were grazed in Hsiung, Pa, Ch'ing, and Tsang in preparation for emergencies in Yen and Yün. Besides these, several tens of thousands of horses were selected for the quarterly hunting tours. The rest were assigned to different places for grazing. This system worked very well.

During the last years, because of frequent wars with Chin, six or seven out of ten barbarian and Chinese war horses were lost. Although the price increased many fold, horses could not be purchased anywhere. Then, in disregard of the law, government horses were purchased for the army and private sales of herds increased daily. Even the [emperor's] needs for hunting [horses] could not be satisfied. Consequently [Emperor T'ien-tsu] was defeated by Chin, deserted the people, and fled continuously until the fall [of the dynasty]. All the horses formerly kept north of Sung-mo became the possession of the scribe [Yeh-lü] Ta-shih.

Livestock Census

1069—In the beginning of Hsien-yung, [Hsiao T'ao-wei] was appointed grand guardian of the herds of horses. Having learned that herds nominally in existence were actually non-existent, he made a minute check of the old registers in order to eliminate the weak and the sick and to record the real number. The herdsmen were won over by their respect for him.

[Hsiao] T'ao-wei sent up a memorial saying, "The herds when small have been reported to be large, and when non-existent have been reported in existence. Superiors and inferiors deceive each other; evils accumulate and become habitual. It would be best to ascertain the real figures and to record the actual number. The government and private persons would both profit."

The proposal was approved. The livestock in consequence propagated abundantly year after year.

A Million Horses

1086—On the first day *ting-ssu* of the fifth month [in the second year of Ta-an], because the herds of horses had propagated so abundantly that they had reached a total of a million, the stockbreeding officials were rewarded and promoted according to their rank.

A Levy of Horses

1120—On the day *chi-yu* of the third month [in the tenth year of T'ien-ch'ing] one tenth of the horses possessed by the common people were taken to supply the armies of the Eastern Route.

The Land System of Liao

983–1012—During the T'ung-ho period Yeh-lü Chao stated that among the people of the northwest each year during the agricultural season, for each person engaged in patrol service, another cares for the public land and two render service to the *chiu* officers.

During that time garrison fields were set up along each of the borders. The soldiers on frontier duty cultivated the fields and stored up grain in order to provide food for the army. Therefore, in the seventh year of the T'ai-p'ing period it was decreed to the garrison fields that not a bushel of millet belonging to the government should be loaned out without authority, and that the military settlers engaged in tilling the public land need not pay taxes. This was the public land system.

Other people answered the call to till uncultivated land or to cultivate private fields. They had to pay out grain according to the [number of] *mou* as a tax to the government. In the fifteenth year [the government] called on the people to till the vacant land along the Luan River. Tax payments were to begin after the tenth year. This was the system concerning the uncultivated land under government administration.

It was further decreed that the families before and behind the mountains who had not yet paid taxes might occupy fields and establish property in the two counties of Mi-yün and Yen-lo and should pay taxes. This was the system of private land holding.

Masters and Slaves

1006—In the twenty-fourth year [of T'ung-ho] it was decreed that except in cases of plotting rebellion or treason or committing crimes punishable by hard labor or death, a slave could not act as first informant against his master. In case of slaves committing a crime deserving the death penalty, they were to be surrendered to the authorities. The master was not allowed to slay them on his own initiative.

Nobles and Commoners to be Punished Equally

1011—In the twenty-ninth year [of T'ung-ho], according to the old law, the descendants of the hereditary families of prime ministers and commanding prefects who committed a crime were sentenced to hard labor and beaten like the commoners but were exempted from the tattooing of the face. It was decreed that henceforth whenever they deserved tattooing for committing a crime they were to be punished equally according to the law.

High and Low Ch'i-tan May Not Intermarry

1019—On the day *kuei-ssu* [of the tenth month in the eighth year of K'ai-t'ai] it was decreed that the Horizontal Tents and the Three [Patriarchal] Households could not intermarry with the lesser tents and lineages. All marriages had to be reported to the throne before being concluded.

Sons of Concubines

1027—On the first day *ting-mao* of the tenth month [in the winter of the seventh year of T'ai-p'ing] it was decreed to all tents and households that the standing of a concubine's son should be decided according to the social standing of his mother.

On the day *ting-ch'ou* [of the twelfth month in the eighth year of T'ai-p'ing] it was decreed that a son of a concubine, even though he was already considered a free man, was not eligible for hereditary selection.

The Noble Lineages of Liao

1029—[On the day *ting-hai* of the twelfth month in the eighth year of T'ai-p'ing] it was decreed that the Two [sections of] Imperial Maternal Uncles and the Administrations of the Southern and Northern Kings were the noble lineages of the nation. Low and common persons were not allowed to hold offices in these groups.

Fire Informs Heaven of the Emperor's Accession

907—On the day *keng-yin* of the first month in the spring of the first year [of T'ai-tsu's accession] officials were ordered to erect an altar at Ju-yü-wang-chi-hui-kuo. Firewood was burned to announce to Heaven the accession to the imperial throne.

Invoking a Curse with Devil Arrows

913—On the day *chi-mao* [of the fourth month in the Summer of the seventh year of T'ai-tsu's accession, when the emperor] halted at a *mi-li*, he learned that his brothers had shot "devil arrows" in the direction of Mu-yeh Mountain to bring a curse upon him. So he seized the rebel Hsieh-li and, facing in their direction, invoked a curse upon them in the same way.

The Ch'i-tan Script

920—On the day *i-ch'ou* of the first month in the spring of the fifth year [of Shen-ts'e] the larger Ch'i-tan script was formulated for the first time. . . . On the day *jen-yin* [of the ninth month], the larger script was completed. An imperial decree ordered it to be circulated.

[Tieh-la] was endowed with a quick mind. T'ai-tsu said, "As to Tieh-la's cleverness—his quickness in accomplishing feats is beyond my powers. But for deliberateness in planning affairs I am his superior." Uyghur messengers came [to court], but there was no one who could understand their language. The empress said to T'ai-tsu, "Tieh-la is clever. He may be sent to welcome them."

By being in their company for twenty days he was able to learn their spoken language and script. Then he created [a script of] smaller Ch'i-tan characters which, though fewer in number, covered everything.

Schools for Uncivilized Settlers

1013—[On the day Chia-shen of the twelfth month in the first year of K'ai-t'ai] Kuei Prefecture reported that its inhabitants, who had originally been moved from Silla, were illiterate, and that schools should be set up to educate them. This request was approved by imperial decree.

System of Ritual

1046—In the fifteenth year [of Ch'ung-hsi] another imperial decree said, "The ancients who ruled the empire brought to light propriety and righteousness and standardized laws and regulations. Since the establishment of our dynasty there has been a ruler with enlightened virtue in every generation. Although the inside and outside incline toward our culture, yet a ritual has not been worked out and there is none to show to later generations. You should collaborate with [Yeh-lü] Shu-ch'eng to formulate a code of ritual by consulting the past and conforming to the present. If there are questions, you should discuss them with the northern and southern chancellors."

After [Hsiao] Han-chia-nu had received the order, he made an extensive study of old works. The customary practices and, traditional usages from the Son of Heaven down to the common people which might be put into effect without violating the past were written up in three chapters and presented to the emperor.

Clan Names and Marriage System

1074—The next year [in the tenth year of Hsien-yung, Yeh-lü Shu-chen] was transferred to the post of chief scribe. He submitted a memorial requesting the extension of the national [Ch'i-tan] clan names. It said, "Since our dynasty was founded, the laws and regulations have been made enlightened, but, as to our clan names, only two have been set up, namely the Yeh-lü and the Hsiao. Previously, when T'ai-tsu formulated the Larger Ch'i-tan Script, he wrote the tribal place-names into the end of the book as a supplementary chapter. I request that they be widely spread and that each tribe may set up clan names so as to make the marriages between men and women harmonize with the code of proper behavior."

The emperor, thinking that the old order should not be changed suddenly, refused consent.

Ethical Idealism versus Shamanism

Before 1077—Once, at a gathering with her brothers' wives, there was a dispute about the repression of evil spirits as a means of winning a husband's favor. [Hsiao] I-hsin remarked, "The repression of evil spirits is not as good as proper behavior."

When they all inquired the reasons for this, [Hsiao] I-hsin replied, "To cultivate yourself with purity, to honor elders with respect, to serve husbands with tenderness, to direct subordinates with generosity, and not to let gentlemen see one frivolous—this is proper behavior. It naturally gains the respect of one's husband. Are you not ashamed to gain favor by repressing evil spirits?"

The listeners were deeply mortified.

The Se-se Rain Ceremony

In case of drought an auspicious day was chosen for performing the Se-se Ceremony to pray for rain. Previous to this date an awning was setup with a hundred poles. When the day arrived, the emperor offered wine to the images of former emperors and then shot at willow trees. The emperor shot twice; the imperial princes and the ministers, in the order of their rank, each shot once. Those who hit the willow trees received as pledges the hats and robes of those who had marked the trees. Those who did not make a hit gave tip their hats and robes as pledges. The losers offered wine to the winners. Afterwards the hats and coats were returned to each person.

Further, on the next day willow trees were planted southeast of the awning. The shamans making the sacrifices of wine and glutinous and panicled millet and praying, planted the willow trees. After the emperor and the empress had worshipped the east, the younger men shot at the willow trees. Members of the imperial clan and of the Imperial Maternal Uncles and the various courtiers who participated in the ceremony were granted presents according to their rank. After three days, if rain fell, four horses and four suits of clothes were granted to the *ti-lieh-ma-tu;* if not, water was spilled upon him.

Legend of Tribal Origin

There was Mu-yeh Mountain on which temples for the earliest ancestors of the Ch'i-tan were built. Ch'i-shou Khaghan was [worshipped] in the southern temple and his *k'o-tun* in the northern temple. They modelled and painted likenesses of these two sage rulers and their eight sons.

Tradition has it that a divine man riding a white horse floated along the T'u River from the Ma-yü Mountains to the east. A heavenly maiden riding a cart drawn by a gray ox floated down the Huang River from P'ing-ti Sung-lin. On reaching Mu-yeh Mountain, where the two rivers joined courses, [the two persons] met and mated. They had eight sons. Later on their descendants gradually prospered. They split up into eight tribes. In each military undertaking and in the seasonal sacrifices of spring and autumn they had to use a white horse and a gray ox [as sacrificial animals] to show that their origin was not forgotten.

Part 3 | The Mongol Empire

INTRODUCTION

The Mongol conqueror Chinggis Khan (more well known as Genghis Khan) was named Temujin when, probably in 1167, he was born in the pastoral-nomadic steppe to the north of China. When Temujin was just nine years old, a band of Tatars poisoned his father, Yisugei, and the remaining years of Temujin's adolescence were extremely difficult. Shunned and alone, his mother, Ho'elun, managed to care for her children and keep them alive, although at times it seemed she was destined to fail. Being raised in such an environment taught Temujin the importance of strength, self-reliance, and persistence. In later years he also proved himself to be an insightful judge of character, a charismatic and visionary leader, a brilliant military strategist, and a ruthless conqueror.

In the early years of the thirteenth century, Temujin managed to attract a substantial following and establish himself as the dominant power in the steppe north of China. In 1206, the defeated nomadic tribal aristocracy was gathered together so that they might acclaim Temujin to be "Chinggis Khan": the Oceanic Ruler. They did so, and soon thereafter the Mongol armies erupted with the full might of the steppe. China was the first to experience the Mongol onslaught. Moving southwestward, in 1209 the Mongols forced the small Tibetan-Buddhist Hsi Hsia kingdom to acknowledge their suzerainty. Chinggis Khan then turned his attention to the considerably more substantial and potentially disruptive power to the east, the ethnically Manchurian Qin (1125–1234). The Qin themselves had just one century earlier departed the steppe to invade the Khitan territories in northeastern China, conquering some and forcing others to move westward where they became known as the Qara Khitai. In 1215, the invading Mongol army occupied the Qin capital of Zhongdu, modern Beijing, and forced the Qin to retreat and take up a defensive position further to the south. Soon thereafter, the Qin received a temporary reprieve as events in Central Asia drew the Mongol forces from their campaigns in China.

As Chinggis Khan's armies were becoming entrenched in northern China, he sent another force to the west. The Qara Khitai confederation fell under Mongol pressure in 1217, and soon thereafter Chinggis Khan dispatched envoys and a large and ostensibly peaceful trade mission to his new Central Asian neighbor, the Khorezmshah 'Ala al-Din Muhammad (r. 1200–1220). Ruling a territory that had recently grown to encompass Transoxiana, Khurasan, Afghanistan, and much of Iran, the khorezmshah arguably represented the most powerful force in the eastern Islamic world at the time. Nevertheless, provoked by Mongol raids in the north and suspicious that the Mongol envoys and caravan merchants were spies sent to determine the khorezmshah's strength and defensive positions, 'Ala al-Din's governor at the frontier outpost of Otrar had them massacred and confiscated their merchandise. Chinggis Khan realized that, in addition to the Qin, he faced another potentially serious threat to the west. Leaving behind a relatively small force to hold the Mongol advances in northern China, in 1219–20 Chinggis Khan personally led the Mongol invasion of Islamic Central Asia.

Chinggis Khan died in 1227, and he divided his inheritance among his sons as Mongol custom dictated. Jochi, his oldest son, predeceased his father, so Chinggis Khan granted western Siberia and the Qïpchaq Steppe to Jochi's son Batu (r. 1227–55). Although at the time of Chinggis Khan's death much of this territory remained to be conquered, the Mongols' western campaigns of 1236–41 were extraordinarily successful, and Batu's Golden Horde stretched even beyond Rus into Eastern Europe. To Chaghatay, the second oldest son, Chinggis Khan bequeathed the steppe lands to the north of sedentary Central Asia. During the reign of Ögedei (r. 1229–41), Chinggis Khan's third son and successor as *qaghan*, or great khan, the territory of the Chaghatay Khanate (1227–1363) was expanded to include the sedentary stretches of Transoxiana. As was the tradition, the fourth and youngest son, Tolui, was placed in charge of the "hearth" of the empire: the pastoral areas of Mongolia itself. While Tolui himself never rose to the position of *qaghan*, two of his sons, Möngke (r. 1251–59) and Qubilai (r. 1260–94), did. A third son, Hülegü, led the Mongol conquest of the Middle East where he established the Mongol Il-Khanate (1256–1353). While Hülegü's first task in the region was the elimination of the much-feared Assassins (the Nizari Isma'ilis), he is best known for conquering Baghdad, executing the caliph, and sending shock waves through the Islamic world by bringing an end to the 'Abbasid Caliphate in 1258.

At its peak, the Mongol Empire was the largest contiguous land empire in the history of the world. But after just three generations the authority of the *qaghan* deteriorated and the empire fragmented. The final *qaghan*, Qubilai, ruled both as the Mongol *qaghan* and as the founding emperor of the Chinese Yuan dynasty (1279–1368). But this dual role was abandoned after his death in 1294, and his successors continued on only as the Yuan emperors of China. By the end of the thirteenth century, the Chaghatay Khanate and the Il-Khanate were both independent Mongol polities in Central Asia and the Middle East. Further to the north, in Russia and Eastern Europe, the Golden Horde had been effectively independent already during the lifetime of Batu.

The institution of the *qaghan* as supreme ruler over the entire Mongol Empire was short-lived, but the independent Mongol Khanates had a greater duration, and the Mongol legacy lasted even longer still. In the territory of the Chaghatay Khanate and the Golden Horde, the ability of rulers to claim a Chinggisid ancestry remained a component critical to their claims to legitimacy even into the eighteenth century. Additionally, several Mongol khans deliberately promoted the spread of Islam among Turkic communities across the region. Proselytizing Sufis enjoyed Mongol patronage and flourished during the thirteenth and fourteenth centuries. In later years, Central Asian Sufis developed powerful dynastic families that wielded significant religious, political, and social influence, and these too have had a lasting impact on the practice of Central Asian Islam.

Because of its remarkable geographical expanse, lengthy duration, and general importance, there is a wealth of sources for the study of Mongol history. Naturally, this is less so for the earlier years, when most Eurasian peoples were completely unaware of the Mongols' existence. Historians must rely on careful analyses of the *Secret History of the Mongols* and oral traditions recorded years later in order to determine the circumstances surrounding the life of young Temujin and his rise to power in the steppe. But as the empire expanded in the early thirteenth century, historians are able to access a much greater variety of sources written in multiple languages—Mongolian, Russian, Chinese, Persian, and Arabic—that aid the study of Mongol history. Most of these can be categorized into one of several literary genres, including travel literature, diplomatic correspondence, court chronicles, and historical accounts produced by authors writing both inside and outside the boundaries of the empire. Some of these sources have all but escaped notice, while others have long elicited popular attention and scholarly interest. The multiple editions of Marco Polo's travels to the court of Qubilai Khan represent one obvious example of the latter. Recognizing the limitations of space, we have elected not to excerpt for inclusion here those sources that are widely known and readily available elsewhere.[1] We have instead given preference to those sources that are more obscure and sufficiently important, and will therefore offer greater benefit to the reader.

---

1. See also the accounts of European envoys to the Mongol court at Karakoram available in Christopher Dawson, ed., *Mission to Asia* (Toronto: University of Toronto Press, 1980).

A | *Temujin and the Rise of the Mongol Empire*

19 *Secret History of the Mongols:* Temujin's Origins

INTRODUCTION

Possibly the most well-known literary work in Mongolian, the Secret History of the Mongols *has been celebrated as the great written epic of the Mongols. Compiled probably around the middle of the thirteenth century by an anonymous author, the work seems to have been authored first in Uyghur-Mongolian script, but survived only in Chinese phonetic transcription accompanied by a translation. Archimandrite Palladius, head of the Russian ecclesiastical mission at Peking and an accomplished sinologist, translated the* Secret History *into Russian in the middle of the nineteenth century. Since then the work has appeared in many editions and translations, first in Chinese at the beginning of the twentieth century, and later in German, French, English, and other languages. The* Secret History *describes the origins of the Mongols down to the reign of Ögedei Khan (r. 1229–41), although most of the work is dedicated to narrating, in many anecdotes, the history of Chinggis Khan, from his birth to his death. The work emphasizes that young Temujin was destined to rule by heaven, but at the same time accords the protagonist a very human, earthly existence.*

The Origins of Chinggis Qahan

At the beginning there was once a blue-grey wolf, born with his destiny ordained by Heaven Above. His wife was a fallow doe. They came crossing the Tenggis. After they had settled at the source of the Onan river on Mount Burqan Qaldun, Batachiqan was born to them.

The son of Batachiqan was Tamacha; the son of Tamacha, Qorichar Mergen; the son of Qorichar Mergen, A'ujam Boro'ul; the son of A'ujam Boro'ul, Sali Qacha'u; the son of Sali Qacha'u, Yeke Nidun; the son of Yeke Nidun, Sem Sochi; the son of Sem Sochi, Qarchu.

The son of Qarchu, Borjigidai Mergen, had as wife Mongqoljin Qo'a. The son of Borjigidai Mergen, Toroqoljin Bayan, had a wife named Boroqchin Qo'a, a young lad named Boroldai Suyalbi, and two fine geldings, Dayir and Boro. Toroqoljin had two sons, Du'a Soqor and Dobun Mergen.

Du'a Soqor had a single eye in the middle of his forehead: with it he could see for a distance of three stages.

One day Du'a Soqor went up Burqan Qaldun with his younger brother Dobun Mergen. Du'a Soqor looked out from the top of Burqan Qaldun, and, as he did so, he saw in the distance a band of people on the move who, following the course of the Tunggelik Stream, were coming that way. He said, "Among those people on the move who are coming this way, there is a fine girl in the front seat of a black covered cart. If she has not been given to another man, we shall ask her for you, my younger brother Dobun Mergen!" So saying, he sent his younger brother Dobun Mergen to have a look.

When Dobun Mergen reached those people, he saw that indeed she was a beautiful and charming girl, and of excellent reputation. Her name was Alan Qo'a and she had not yet been given to any other man. . . .

After Alan Qo'a had come to Dobun Mergen, she bore him two sons who were named Bugunutei and Belgunutei. . . .

Before long, Dobun Mergen died. After his death, Alan Qo'a, although she had no husband, bore three sons who were named Buqu Qatagi, Buqatu Salji and Bodonchar Mungqaq.

Belgunutei and Bugunutei, the two sons born earlier to Dobun Mergen, said to each other, behind the back of their mother Alan Qo'a, "Although this mother of ours is without brothers-in-law and male relatives, and without a husband, she has borne these three sons. In the house there is only the man of the Ma'aliq Baya'ut. Surely these three sons are his." Their mother Alan Qo'a knew what they had been saying to each other behind her back.

One day in spring, while she was cooking some dried lamb, she had her five sons Belgunutei, Bugunutei, Buqu Qatagi, Buqatu Salji, and Bodonchar Mungqaq sit in a row. She gave an arrow-shaft to each of them and said, "Break it!" One by one they immediately broke the single arrow-shafts and threw them away. Then she tied five arrow-shafts into a bundle and gave it to them saying, "Break it!" The five sons each took the five bound arrow-shafts in turn, but they were unable to break them.

Then their mother Alan Qo'a said, "You, my sons Belgunutei and Bugunutei, are suspicious of me and said to each other, 'These three sons that she has borne, of whom, of what clan, are they the sons?' And it is right for you to be suspicious. Every night, a resplendent yellow man entered by the light of the smoke-hole or the door top of the tent, he rubbed my belly and his radiance penetrated my womb. When he departed, he crept out on a moonbeam or a ray of sun in the guise of a yellow dog.

> Why do you speak rashly?
> For him who understands, the sign is clear:
> They are the sons of Heaven.
> How can you speak, comparing them
> To ordinary black-headed men?
> When they become the rulers of all,
> The common people will understand!

Further, Alan Qo'a addressed these words of admonition to her five sons, "You, my five sons, were born of one womb. If, like the five arrow-shafts just now, each of you keeps to himself, then, like those single arrow-shafts, anybody will easily break you. If, like the bound arrow-shafts, you remain together and of one mind, how can anyone deal with you so easily?" Some time went by and their mother Alan Qo'a died.

After the death of their mother Alan Qo'a, the five brothers divided the live-stock among themselves.

[Several generations passed until we reach Temujin, born after a great battle in which his father, Yisugei Ba'atur, had defeated the Tatars.]

Then Yisugei Ba'atur captured the Tatars Temujin Uge, Qori Buqa, and other Tatars. At that time Lady Ho'elun was pregnant, and as she was staying at Deli'un Boldaq by the Onan, it was right there that Chinggis Qa'an was born. At the time of his birth he was born clutching in his right hand a clot of blood the size of a knucklebone. Because he was born when the Tatar Temujin Uge had been brought captive, for this very reason they gave him the name Temujin.

Yisugei Ba'atur had these four sons born of Lady Ho'elun: Temujin, Qasar, Qachi'un, and Temuge. One daughter was also born, named Temulun. When Temujin was nine years old, Jochi Qasar was seven, Qachi'un Elchi was five, Temuge Otchigin was three, and Temulun was still in the cradle.

When Temujin was nine years old, Yisugei Ba'atur set out to go to the Olqunu'ut people, relatives of Mother Ho'elun, taking Temujin with him and say-ing, "I shall ask his maternal uncles for girl in marriage for him." On the way, between Mount Chekcher and Mount Chiqurqu, he met Dei Sechen of the Ong-girat.

Dei Sechen said, "Quda Yisugei, in whose direction are you going, coming this way?" Yisugei Ba'atur said, "I have come here on my way to the Olqunu'ut people, the maternal uncles of this my son, to ask for a girl in marriage for him." Dei Sechen said, "This son of yours is a boy

> Who has fire in his eyes,
> Who has light in his face.

"Quda Yisugei, I had a dream last night, I did. A white gyrfalcon clasping both sun and moon in its claws flew to me and perched on my hand. I told the people about this dream of mine, saying, 'Before, when I looked, I could only see the sun and the moon from afar; now this gyrfalcon has brought them to me and has perched on my hand. He has alighted, all white. Just what sort of good thing does this show?' I had my dream, Quda Yisugei, just as you were coming here bringing your son. I had a dream of good omen. What kind of dream is it? The august spirit of you, Kiyat people, has come in my dream and has announced your visit. . . . Quda Yisugei, let us go to my tent. My daughter is still small, take a look at her, quda!" So said Dei Sechen, and having led him to his tent he made him dismount.

> When Yisugei saw his daughter, he saw a girl
> Who had light in her face,
> Who had fire in her eyes.

He was pleased with her. She was ten years old, one year older than Temujin, and her name was Borte. Yisugei spent the night there, and the following morning, when he requested his daughter for Temujin, Dei Sechen said, "If I gave her away after much asking on your part, you would respect me; if I gave her away without much asking, you would despise me. But the fate of a girl is not to grow old in the family in which she was born. I will give you my daughter, and you, for your part, leave your son here as my son-in-law." So they both agreed and Yisugei Ba'atur said, "I will leave my son as your son-in-law, but my son is very afraid of dogs. Quda, don't let him be frightened by dogs!" Then he gave him his spare horse as a pledge and went off, leaving Temujin as his son-in-law.

[On the way back, Yisugei was poisoned by his Tatar enemies and died. After a while, the Taychiut raided their camp, and after much turmoil captured Temujin, but he managed to escape heroically, with the aid of Sorqan Shira of the Suldus and his two sons.]

Once they (Temujin and his people) were reunited there, they left and set up camp at the Koko Na'ur of Mount Qara Jirugen mountain by the Senggur stream, in the Gurelgu Mountains south of Burqan Qaldun. Here they stayed, killing marmots and field-mice for food.

One day some robbers came and stole the eight horses, the light-bay geldings, that were standing by the tent and made off with them before their very eyes. Temujin and his brothers sighted the robbers, but being on foot fell behind.

Belgutei [Temujin's half-brother] was then away marmot-hunting on a short-tailed, short-haired chestnut horse. He arrived on foot in the evening after sunset, leading behind him the short-tailed, short-haired chestnut horse, which was so laden down with marmots that it staggered. When he was told that robbers had stolen the light-bay geldings, Belgutei said, "I will go after them!" Qasar said, "You cannot cope with them, I will go after them!" Temujin said, "Neither of you can cope with them, I will go after them!" Temujin got on the short-haired chestnut horse and went off in pursuit of the light-bay geldings, following the tracks left in the grass.

He spent three days and nights tracking, and in the early morning of the fourth day he met on the way a brisk lad milking mares in a large herd of horses. When Temujin inquired about the light-bay geldings, the lad said, "This morning, before sunrise, eight horses—light-bay geldings—were driven past here. I will show you their trail." He made Temujin leave the short-haired chestnut horse there, set him on a white horse with a black back, and he himself rode a fast dun mare. And without even going to his tent, he put down his leather bucket and pail, concealing them in the grass.

"Friend," he said, "you came to me being in great trouble, but men's troubles are the same for all. I will be your companion. My father is called Naqu Bayan. I am his only son and my name is Bo'orchu."

They spent three days and nights following the trail of the light-bay geldings. Then, in the evening of the fourth day, just as the sun was setting on the hills, they came upon people in a circular camp. They saw the eight horses, the light-bay geldings, standing at the edge of that large camp, grazing.

Temujin said, "Friend, you stay here. As for me—the light-bay geldings are those there—I will go out and drive them off." Bo'orchu said, "I came with you as your companion. How can I stay here?" They raced in together and drove the light-bay geldings off.

The men came after them in separate groups and began to pursue them. Away from the rest, one man on a white horse and holding a pole-lasso drew closer and caught up with them. Bo'orchu said, "Friend, give me the bow and arrows. I'll trade shots with him!" Temujin said, "I am afraid you'll come to harm because of me. I'll trade shots with him!" He swung around and they began to shoot arrows at each other. The man on the white horse stood up, aiming at him with his pole-lasso. His companions, who had fallen behind, caught up with him, but the sun sank, dusk came down, and those men behind, overtaken by darkness, halted and were left behind altogether.

They rode all that night and then rode for three more days and nights before they reached their destination. Temujin said, "Friend, would I ever have got these horses of mine back without you? Let's share them. How many do you say you'll take?" Bo'orchu said, "I became your companion because you, a good friend, were in trouble and approached me, and I wished to be of help to a good friend. Am I now to take the horses as booty? My father is called Naqu Bayan. I am the only son of Naqu Bayan. The property of my father is ample for me. I won't take the horses. What sort of help would my help be? I won't take them."

They arrived at the tent of Naqu Bayan. Naqu Bayan was all in tears for the loss of his son Bo'orchu. When they suddenly arrived and he saw his son, he began both to wail and to scold. His son Bo'orchu said, "What is the matter? A good friend came to me in trouble, I became his companion and went with him. Now I have come back." With this he rode off to fetch his leather bucket and pail which he had concealed in the grass. They killed a lamb fattened on the milk of two ewes and gave it to Temujin as provision for the road; they also prepared a leather bucket containing mare's milk which they loaded on the horse. In this way, they provided for his journey. Then Naqu Bayan said, "You two young men keep seeing each other, never abandon each other!"

Temujin left, and after traveling three days and three nights arrived at his tent on the Senggur stream. Mother Ho'elun, Qasar, and his younger brothers were worrying about him, and when they saw him they rejoiced.

Thereupon, Temujin left with Belgutei downstream along the Keluren River to look for Lady Borte, the daughter of Dei Sechen, from whom he had been separated since he had visited her at the age of nine.

Dei Sechen, the Onggirat, lived between Mount Chekcher and Mount Chiqurqu. When Dei Sechen saw Temujin he was very glad. He said, "I knew that your Tayichi'ut kinsmen were jealous of you, and I worried and despaired; and now at last I see you!" So saying he had him and Lady Borte united as man and wife, and then accompanied her to her new home.

Dei Sechen accompanied her, and, as they approached their destination and were still on the way, he turned back at the Uraq Chol Bend of the Keluren. His wife, the mother of Lady Borte, was called Chotan. Chotan escorted her daughter and took her to Temujin's home, which at that time was on the Senggur stream in the Gurelgu Mountains.

After Temujin had sent Chotan home, he sent Belgutei to invite Bo'orchu to join him as his companion. Bo'orchu after receiving Belgutei did not say a word to his father, but he jumped on his chestnut horse with the arched back. He tucked his grey woolen cloak behind him and came with Belgutei. This is how they became firm companions after first having joined in friendship.

20   Hayton: Temujin and the Rise of the Mongol Empire

INTRODUCTION

An Armenian monk and nephew of King Hethum I (r. 1226–70), Hayton hailed from the ancient Greek port city of Korykos (located in modern-day south-central Turkey). Exiled from Armenia by King Hethum II on charges of conspiracy, Hayton worked for a while in Cyprus and then in France in various pastoral duties. It was in France where he apparently advocated an alliance with the Mongols in order to recapture the Holy Land, an alliance that never materialized. Hayton traveled far and wide in the Mongol Empire. He composed a geography of Asia, as well as a history of the Mongols, dictated in Old French and translated into Latin, to be published later under the title La Flor des Estoires d'Orient *(The flower of the stories of the Orient). In the preface to his work, Hayton explains that he had based his account on three sources: the period up to the middle of the thirteenth century relied upon "Tartar" traditions; the second part (1251–65) relied upon the account of Hayton's uncle, King Hethum I; and the third part (from the debut of Abaqa Khan in Ilkhanid Iran) was his (Hayton's) own testimony. It is interesting to compare Hayton's account of the origins of the Mongols and Temujin's rise to prominence with that presented earlier in the* Secret History of the Mongols, *clearly meant to serve two very different audiences.*

How the Tartars Achieved Superiority

The land and country where the Tartars first lived is the great mountain Beljian. The histories of Alexander [the Great] speak of this mountain, where it is mentioned that he had encountered wild men. The Tartars dwelled first in that country like beasts, having neither faith nor law, wandering from place to place like grazing beasts, and living wretchedly under other nations whom they were serving. Diverse nations of the Tartars, who were called Mongols, assembled and proclaimed chieftains and governors among them. They became so numerous that they were divided into seven nations, and to this day these nations are considered nobler than the others. The first of these nations is called Tartar, the second Tangot, the third Eurach, the fourth Jalair, the fifth Sonit, the sixth Mengli, the seventh Tebet.

And so it happened that when these seven nations were still under the subjugation of their neighbors, as was described, there was a poor old man, an artisan [a blacksmith] named Cangius [Chinggis], who saw in a dream a vision; he saw a knight in armor upon a white horse who called him by his name and said to him, "Cangius, the will of the Immortal God is such that you should be governor and lord over the seven nations of the Tartars that have been called Mongols, and that through you they shall be delivered out of the servitude in which they had been for so long, and shall have lordship over their neighbors." Cangius woke up very joyfully, having heard the word of God, and recounted to all the vision that he saw. The nobles and the grandees would not believe him and scorned the old man. But it so happened that the following night, the chieftains of the seven nations saw the white horse and the vision just as Cangius had recounted, and were commanded by the Immortal God that they all should obey Cangius and that they should comply with his commandments.

Consequently, the seven said chieftains assembled the people of the Tartars and made them offer obeisance and reverence to Cangius, and they themselves did the same as to their natural lord.

How the Tartars First Made and Elected
Their Lord and Named Him Can

Then the Tartars set up a throne in their midst, and they spread a black felt on the ground and made Cangius sit upon it. And the chieftains of the seven nations raised him upon the felt, put him on the throne, and named him Can. And kneeling before him, they showed every honor and reverence befitting their lord. One should not be surprised about the solemnity which the Tartars show their lord under such circumstances, nor should one wonder about the felt which they use to elevate him to the throne, or whether, perchance, they did not know any better, or they did not have in their possession a nicer piece of cloth to seat their lord upon. One may well marvel why they did not wish to change their ancient practice, especially since they had conquered so many lands and realms and still keep their ancient practice. When they wish to elect their leader, and I have been twice at the election of the emperor of the Tartars, and seen how all the Tartars assemble in a great field and they seat their leader upon a black felt and set up a rich throne in their midst. After that, the great men and those of the lineage of Cangius, their first khan, come and raise him high and make him sit on the throne, and then they show him every honor and reverence befitting their precious lord as it should be. Not for rank, nor for the riches that they conquered, but because they did not wish to change their ancient practice.

Of the Commandments of the Emperor of the Tartars Named Can

After Cangius Can was made Emperor by the common will and consent of all Tartars, before he did anything else, he needed to know if all would obey him. Therefore, he proclaimed three Commandments. The First Commandment was that everyone should believe and worship the Immortal God, by whose wish he was made Emperor, and without delay all the Tartars began to believe and profess God's name in all their deeds. The Second Commandment was that they should count up and [divide into units of ten] all those who were able to bear arms; and that upon every unit of 10 should be a commander; and upon 10 units of 10 a commander; and upon 1,000 there was a commander, and upon 10 units of 1,000 a commander, and they called the company of 10,000 a Toman.

After that, the chieftains of the seven lineages of the Tartars were ordered to give up all their arms and positions and that they should pay whatever they are ordered to pay. The Third Commandment of Cangius Can seemed to be the cruelest, since he ordered the aforementioned seven great chieftains to each bring his eldest son before him. And when they had done so, he commanded every chieftain to behead his own son. And as much as this order seemed to all to be perfidious and cruel, none of the chieftains dared refuse his command because they knew that Cangius Can was made Emperor by the Immortal God's decree, and so each of the seven chieftains beheaded his own son. When Cangius Can knew the will of his people, and saw that all would obey him to the death, he commanded that they should appear in a knight's armor before him.

How Cangius Can Was Saved by a Bird

When Cangius Can had arranged well and wisely his battles, he entered into the lands of those who had long kept the Tartars in servitude, fought them and overcame them all and put their lands under his rule. After that, Cangius Can went forth, conquering lands and countries and all things as he pleased.

One day, as Cangius Can was riding with a small company of men, they met a great number of their enemies, who quickly set upon them. Cangius Can defended himself vigorously, but in the end his horse was slain under him. When Cangius Can's men saw their lord on the ground among the masses, they lost their courage and were put to flight, their enemies in pursuit, taking no heed of Emperor Cangius Can, who was on foot. When Cangius Can saw this, he hid himself in a little bush nearby. The enemies, who had victory, began to search for those who had escaped. And when they wanted to search that bush in which Cangius Can was hiding, a bird that is called a duke came and sat upon that bush, and when they saw the bird sitting upon that bush where Emperor Cangius Can was hiding, they left, saying that if anyone had been there that bird would not sit there. And thinking that no one was in that bush, they left without searching.

How the Tartars Wear upon Their Heads the Feather of the Bird Called Duke since It Saved Their Lord inside the Bush

When night fell, Cangius Can left his hiding place and took such actions that he came to his men and recounted to them all that had happened to him, and how the bird sat upon the bush where as he was hiding, and how because of that his enemies did not search for him. The Tartars rendered grace unto God, and since then they have great reverence for that bird which they call duke, that whoever is able to have a feather of that bird, wears it upon his head. I have made mention of this story so that people know why all the Tartars wear the feather upon their heads. Cangius Can rendered grace unto God that he was saved in such a manner.

How the White Knight Was Revealed to Cangius Can, Emperor of the Tartars, and of the News He Told Him How He Will Conquer Lands and Kingdoms of Diverse Nations

After that, he assembled his host together and battled his enemies and destroyed them and put them all to his servitude. And Cangius Can conquered all the lands that were on this side of Mt. Beljian, and held them so until he saw another vision, as shall be described hence:

When Cangius Can had conquered the sovereignty of all the countries that were on this side of Mt. Beljian, one night he saw once again in a vision the white knight. He said, "Cangius Can, the will of the Immortal God is that you pass Mt. Beljian to the west, and that you conquer the kingdoms and lands of diverse nations and reign over them. And so that you know that what I just told you is the will of the Immortal God, rise up and go to Mt. Beljian with all your men. And when you get [to the point] where the sea meets the mountain descend, you and your men, and kneel nine times toward the east, and pray to the Immortal God that he will show you where to go, and he will show you a path, and you and your men may pass."

How Our Lord Showed Cangius Can and His People How to Pass Mt. Belgian

When Cangius Can woke up, he strongly believed in the vision and immediately ordered his men to mount their horses, as he wished to pass Mt. Beljian. So they all mounted and rode forth until they came to the sea, but they could not pass because there was no passage, neither great nor small. And Cangius Can descended from his horse and made all his men descend as well, and bowed to the east nine times and prayed to the Omnipotent and Immortal God to show them the way to pass. All that night Cangius Can and his men spent in prayer, and on the morrow Cangius Can saw that the sea had distanced nine paces away from the mountain and left them a large and pleasant path. When Cangius Can and his men saw what had happened, they marveled, and they gave grace to Our Lord and passed toward the lands of the east.

And so, as it is told in the stories of the Tartars, after Cangius Can had passed Mt. Beljian he found the water bitter and the land abandoned, so much so that until he and his men came upon good land, they had suffered great malaise. After that, they found good lands, plentiful of all things, and they remained in that country many days and reposed. And, as it pleased God, a grave sickness took Cangius Can by surprise, so he summoned his twelve children and commanded them that they should always be all of one will and accord and gave them the following example: He commanded each of them to bring an arrow, and when the twelve arrows were put together, he commanded his eldest son to take all those arrows and break them with his hands. And so he [his first son] took them but could not break them with his hands. Then, he gave them to the second son, but he could not break them, and then he gave them to the third son, and then to all of them, and no one was able to break them. Then Cangius Can ordered to separate the arrows, and commanded the youngest of his sons to take each arrow and break it, and the child broke all twelve arrows. Cangius Can then turned towards his children and said to them, "Why could you not break the arrows as I had ordered you?" And they said, "Because they were all together." "And why has this little child broken them?" And they answered, "Because he broke them every one by itself." Then said Cangius Can, "It shall so happen that as long as you are all of one will and one accord, your lordship shall last forever, and when you are divided and at variance with one another, your lordship shall quickly turn to nothing and shall not endure." And Cangius Can gave his children and his men many other commandments and good examples which the Tartars hold in great reverence.

How Cangius Can, after He Reigned, Enthroned His Eldest Son

When Cangius Can had done that, realizing that he could not live much longer, he made his wisest son, indeed his best son, lord and emperor after him, and he made everyone obey him and serve him as their lord, and call him Octota Can [Ögedei Khan]. After all that, the good Emperor and first among the Tartars passed away from this world, and his son Octota Can held lordship after him. And before ending the story of Cangius Can, we shall relate how the Tartars hold the number nine in great esteem: in honor of the nine genuflections, and the nine paces that the sea distanced itself from the land and extended the path so that they could pass Mt. Beljian as ordained by God, the Tartars consider the number nine as good fortune. And if one should present anything to one's lord, it is best that one presents nine items if one wishes that one's present would be graciously received, and so is the practice of the Tartars unto this very day.

21   Nasawi: The Khorezmshah's Downfall

INTRODUCTION

Shihab al-Din Muhammad al-Nasawi was secretary and biographer of Jalal al-Din Mangubirti, eldest son of Sultan Muhammad Khorezmshah and the last ruler of the dynasty. Originally from the province of Nasa in Khurasan, Nasawi witnessed first-hand the Mongol advance on Khurasan, and even played a crucial role in convincing (i.e., bribing) the Mongols to spare his home town. He later became in charge of all the correspondence of Jalal al-Din Khorezmshah, served as his patron's ambassador to the Isma'ilis and Ayyubids, and continued to serve other Khorezmian generals in northern Iraq. He died, after many tribulations, in Aleppo in 1249–50.

His work, Sirat al-sultan Jalal al-Din Mangubirti, in Arabic, was completed in 1241–42. The text was published and translated into French by the renowned Arabist Octave Houdas in 1895. The text was studied by Bartol'd, and was also recently edited and translated into Russian by Buniiatov.

The following excerpt describes the events that led to the souring of relations between the Mongols and the Khorezmshah that concluded with open warfare and the annihilation of the Khorezmshah polity. Although Nasawi probably had intimate knowledge of some of these events, he also relies on other accounts authored before him, most particularly on the Arabic work al-Kamil fi'l-tarikh by the historian Ibn al-Athir (d. 1233).

Events that Occurred in Mawarannahr after the Sultan's Return

When the sultan returned from Iraq to Mawarannahr he received a visit from ambassadors from Chinggis Khan, Mahmud al-Khorezmi, 'Ali Khoja al-Bukhari, and Yusuf Kanaka al-Otrati, who had brought with them diverse products of the Turks, such as lumps of precious metals, rhinoceros horns, bags of musk, jasper stones, pieces of fabric known as *tarqu*, which are made with white camel wool, each piece of fabric was evaluated at fifty dinars. . . .

The aim of that embassy was to strike up relations of friendship, peace, and good neighbors. [The ambassadors] said, "The great khan sends you felicitations and entrusted us with the following words: 'I do not overlook neither the elevation of your rank nor the extent of your power. I am familiar with the magnificence of your empire, and I know that your authority is recognized in the majority of the countries of the world. Therefore, I consider it my duty to strike up friendly relations with you, whom I consider to be dearest and most beloved of my sons. On your part, you know equally well that I have seized the kingdom of China as well as the neighboring Turkic countries, and that all the tribes of these lands submit to me; and you know better than anyone that my provinces are nurseries for soldiers, of mines of silver, and that may produce an abundance of things. If you would agree that we open up, each from our own side, an easy access for negotiations between our countries, this will be an advantage for us all and we would both benefit.'"

Having heard the speech, the sultan summoned Mahmud al-Khorezmi to his quarters during the night without the other two ambassadors. He said, "You are a man of Khorezm and therefore you owe us your sympathy and allegiance." After promising to reward him if he answered his questions sincerely, the sultan detached a magnificent pearl from his bracelet, to be given to the ambassador as a token of his promises, and asked him to serve him [as a spy] at [the court of] Chinggis Khan.

Because of his respect and his fear, Mahmud accepted the proposition that was made to him. The sultan then said, "Answer me frankly. Chinggis Khan claims that he is the master of China, and that he has seized the city of Tomgach. Is it true or is it a deception?"

Mahmud said, "It is the very truth. Such an important event cannot remain secret, and the sultan will soon have evidence of that." The sultan said, "You know the grandeur of my countries and you also know how numerous are my armies. How then does this accursed dare call me his son in his speech? What can be the strength of the armies at his disposal?"

At that Mahmud began to feel irritated and saw that the conversation that had started amicably turned sour, so he decided to espouse wise advice and to flatter the sultan in order to escape death. He said, "Compared to your people and your innumerable troops, the army of Chinggis Khan has the consequence of a simple cavalier in the midst of a regiment, or that of a trickle of smoke through the night's shadows. . . ."

[The two countries continued to live in peace until the day when four negotiators came from Chinggis Khan]: 'Umar Khoja al-Otrari, al-Hammal al-Maraghi, Fakhr al-Din al-Danzaki al-Bukhari, and Amin al-Din al-Haravi came from [the lands conquered by Chinggis Khan] to Otrar. Inal Khan, son of the sultan's (maternal) uncle, was in the city at the head of 20,000 horsemen, and was governing it in the sultan's name. Motivated by the vilest sentiments, Inal Khan decided to seize the riches of the merchants. He wrote the sultan a letter of threats and treachery, in which he said, "These men came to Otrar under the guise of negotiators whereas in fact they are spies who meddle in affairs that are none of their business. When they are alone with simple people, they threaten them saying, 'you shouldn't doubt that war is upon you. It will arrive soon, and you will face things you won't be able to fight.' Based upon such a testimony, and others of its kind, it would be best if the sultan authorized the seizure of these negotiators, until he made a decision in this case." As soon as he was authorized to imprison them, Inal Khan became very aggressive and, using violence, he seized the negotiators and so they disappeared forever. Because of this trickery and treachery, he kept for himself all the riches that these men had brought with them and all the different objects in their possessions, but the consequences of this villainous act were disastrous.

Arrival of Ambassadors from Chinggis Khan after the Assassination of the Negotiators

Some time after that, Ibn Kafaraj Bughra, whose father had been one of the amirs of Sultan Tekesh, arrived accompanied by two Tatar envoys, sent as ambassadors from Chinggis Khan. They said to the sultan, "You have given a letter of safe conduct, written and signed by your own hand to the negotiators so that no one would harass them, but then you have treacherously betrayed your commitment. However, if treachery was itself an act of a villain, it became even more odious when it was conducted by a master of Islam. If you maintain that all that was done by Inal Khan was not a result of your own orders, deliver him to our hands. We will censure him for the act he had committed, and we will avoid spilling more blood so that the people can continue to live in peace. Otherwise, prepare yourself for war in which the most valorous souls will lose their worth, and the most well-directed lances will be diverted from their aim."

Despite the terror that enveloped his heart, and the fear that paralyzed his soul, the sultan refused to hand over Inal Khan. He could not, in reality, consent to such a demand, especially since many of his commanders belonged to the same tribe as Inal Khan. It was they who formed the embroidery whose sewing caused the end of his dynasty. . . . He also thought that if he would show too much cordiality in his response, he would only increase Chinggis Khan's desire, and therefore he appeared hard and uncompromising. He refused any reparations, and—his spirit troubled by fear—he ordered that the ambassadors be killed, an order that was executed at once. Alas, how much Muslim blood was spilled because of that murder! From all sides poured torrents of pure blood, and this movement of anger brought about the ruin and depopulation of the earth.

Measures Taken by the Sultan When He Realized that Chinggis Khan Marched against Him at the Head of His Armies

The first measure that the sultan took at that critical juncture and moment of dreadful danger was to surround, despite its size, the city of Samarqand with a wall whose circumference was 12 *farsakhs* and to install there a considerable garrison. In this manner, that city was to be a barrier from the Turks, and he would close before the enemy the path to the other parts of the kingdom. At the same time, he sent his agents and his tax collectors to all sections of his country, and they had to supply in advance the total tax for the year 615 (1218–19) to be able to finance the building of the Samarqand battlements. In reality, the Tatars did not permit him the time to execute his project, and he was unable to spend the sums collected for the construction of the city walls.

The second measure undertaken by the sultan was to send messengers to all his states with the order to deduct one third of the taxes for that year and to raise troops of archers and arm them. The number of men he was able to summon was fixed by the resources. Each man was to have a camel for a mount, provided with arms and provisions. This levy of men was executed with great diligence. From all corners of the realm arrived to predestined places to concentrate masses of men, hurrying like a rapid torrent, dashing forward like arrows shot from a bow. But, even at the moment when all troops were on the march to their destined meeting points, it turned out that the sultan himself had fled without battle and escaped on the Jayhun river. Had he stayed in his position until the reinforcements arrived the sultan would have been at the head of the most numerous army anyone had ever heard of, but nothing can resist the will of God, who, alone, can accomplish what He has decided and has the power to overturn or transform all things and to move empires from the hands of one leader to another.

Another fatal measure was that the sultan decided to disseminate his troops in the cities of Mawarannahr and Turkestan. Thus, he left Inal Khan in Otrar with 20,000 horsemen, Qutlugh Khan and another group in Shahrkent with 10,000 horsemen, and Amir Ikhtiyar al-Din Keshki and Aghil Hajib, known as Inanj Khan, with 30,000 men in Bukhara, Toghan Khan, his (maternal) uncle and the amirs of Ghur such as Jarmikh and Harur and Ibn Izz al-Din Kat and Husam al-Din Mas'ud and others with 40,000 in Samarqand, and Fakhr al-Din Habash, known as 'Inan al-Nasawi, with the troops of Sijistan in Tirmidh, and Balkhamur Khan in Wakhsh, and Ibn Muhammad, his father's (maternal) uncle, in Balkh, and Asrak Pahlavan in Khanderudh, and 'Aljaq Malik in Jilan, and al-Barthasi in Qunduz and Aslaba Khan in Ulaj, so that he did not leave any places in Mawarannahr without active troops. That was the main error, for had he offered to do battle with the Tatars before disseminating his troops, the sultan would have easily annihilated (them) and would have salvaged the land.

As soon as he arrived at the boundaries of the sultan's empire, Chinggis Khan went straight to Otrar. He attacked the place with intensity, fighting day and night, and seized the town. He made Inal Khan appear before him and ordered that the molten gold (he had stolen) be poured into his ears and eyes. This cruel death was the just punishment for Inal Khan, whose ignoble behavior, barbarous acts, and former cruelties were worth the condemnation of all.

Strategy with Which Chinggis Khan Was Able to Instill in the Sultan Suspicions against His Amirs and to Engage in Separating Them

As soon as he had settled the business in Otrar, Chinggis Khan received a visit from Badr al-Din al-'Amid, who was known in Otrar as Safi al-Aqra', minister of the sultan in the countries of the Turks, and had an interview with him. It so happened that, when the sultan had seized the principality of Otrar he had executed Badr al-Din's father, *qazi* al-'Amid Sa'd, his (paternal) uncle *qazi* Mansur, and a certain number of his cousins and brothers. He said to the khan, "You know that the sultan is the person I hate the most in this world because he executed many of my ancestors. If I had to sacrifice my life in order to take revenge on him, be sure I would do so voluntarily. In any case, I have to inform you that this is a very powerful sultan. Do not delude yourself as to the measures he had taken in disseminating his troops in every direction, because he still has with him a considerable number of troops who will give him the ability to abandon his other soldiers. If he so desires, he can still assemble an army twice as large in his vast empire and lands. I advise you then to devise a strategy of making him suspect his own military commanders."

Badr al-Din then proceeded to update Chinggis Khan in the matter of the hostility between the sultan and his mother. Having turned over the question from all sides, the two men decided upon the following course of action: Badr al-Din al-'Amid would write false letters in the name of commanders who were close to the sultan's mother. The letters said the following, "We have come from the lands of the Turks with our clients and vassals to make ourselves available to the sultan, because we wish to render service unto his mother. We have given him assistance against all the lords of the land so that he would be able to conquer, thanks to us, the lands, vanquish the pride of the princes, and subject the people to his judgment. But today, when the feelings of the sultan toward his mother have changed, when he is ungrateful and rebellious against her, she asks us to abandon her son. As a result, we await your arrival to tell us your instructions."

Chinggis Khan sent these letters through one of his courtesans, who pretended to be a deserter but was really accomplishing a mission. She showed the letters to the sultan, who before that threat already saw the world crumbling before his eyes. His zeal had weakened that he would be betrayed by those he had trusted. And he dispersed his troops as we had said earlier.

Chinggis Khan then sent one of his trusted men, Danishmand, to Turkan Khatun (the Khorezmshah's mother) to tell her the following: "you know how much your son has shown ingratitude for the cares you had bestowed upon him. In accordance with that, I wish to march against him with a number of amirs. If you accept this arrangement send me someone in whom you have complete confidence."

22 Chang Chun: A Daoist Monk in Central Asia

INTRODUCTION

Chang Chun (or, Qiu Chuji), a Daoist monk, was invited to meet Chinggis Khan following the latter's invasion of North China and after the great khan had learned of the high regard accorded to Chang Chun in the region; this esteem probably was bestowed upon him for his disciplined attempts to achieve immortality by "internal alchemy." The elderly monk, apparently already in his seventies, acknowledged the invitation and undertook the long journey to Central Asia. His travels there and back took three years, from 1221 to 1224. Chang Chun did not write the account of his travels himself. The author was one of his disciples, Li Chi Chang, and the work was published in 1228 by another of the monk's followers, named Sun Si, in a collection of Daoist works known as the Dao tsang tsi yao. In the 1860s, Chang Chun's travels drew some attention and were translated first into Russian in an extensive and acclaimed translation by Archimandrite Palladius (see also Secret History of the Mongols*). A year later, a rather poor and abridged French translation was published, and in the 1880s Emil Bretschneider published a partial English translation.*

The following excerpt, from the translation by the English Orientalist Arthur Waley, provides significant details not only about the desired representation of the monk for his immediate circle (after all, we are told that Chinggis Khan commanded that his pupils would be exempt from taxation), but also on conditions in Central Asia shortly after the initial phase of the Mongol conquest.

After a while we entered the city (Samarqand) by the northeast gate. The town is built along canals. As no rain falls during the summer and autumn, two rivers have been diverted so as to run along every street, thus giving a supply of water to all the inhabitants. Before the defeat of the Khorezmshah there was a fixed population here of more than 100,000 households; but now there is only about a quarter of this number, of whom a very large proportion are native Hui-ho (Muslims). But these people are quite unable to manage their fields and orchards for themselves, and they are obliged to call in Chinese, Khitai, and Tanguts. The administration of the town is also conducted by people of very various nationalities. Chinese craftsmen are found everywhere. Within the city is a mound about a hundred feet high on which stands the Khorezmshah's new palace. The Mongol Governor at first resided here. But the local population was exasperated by famine and there was perpetual brigandage. Fearing trouble, the Governor went to live on the north side of the river. The Master, however, consented to live in this palace. . . . We also saw (there) peacocks and large elephants which come from India, several thousand *li* to the south-east.

[After a long journey] we reached the Khan's camp. This was on the fifth day of the fourth month. When arrangements had been made for the Master's lodging, he at once presented himself to the Emperor, who expressed his gratitude, saying, "Other rulers summoned you, but you would not go to them. And now you have come ten thousand *li* to see me. I take this as a high compliment." The Master replied, "That I, a hermit of the mountains, should come at your Majesty's bidding was the will of Heaven." Chinggis was delighted, begged him to be seated, and ordered food to be served. Then he asked him, "Adept, what Medicine of Long Life have you brought me from afar?" The Master replied, "I have means of protecting life, but no elixir that will prolong it." The Emperor was pleased with his candor, and had two tents for the Master and his disciples set up to the east of his own.

The weather was becoming very hot, and the Emperor now moved to a high point on the Snow Mountains to escape the heat, and the Master accompanied him. The Emperor appointed the fourteenth of the fourth month (June 24th) as the day on which he would question the Master about the Way. This engagement was recorded by his state officers, Chinkhai, Liu Wen and A-li-hsien, as well as by three of his personal attendants. But just as the time was arriving, news came that the native mountain bandits were in insurrection. The Emperor was determined to deal with them himself, and put off the meeting till the first of the tenth month (November 5th). The Master begged that he might be allowed to return to his former quarters in the city. "Then," said the Khan, "you will have the fatigue of travelling all the way back here again." The Master said it was only a matter of twenty days journey, and when the Khan objected that he had no one whom he could give him as an escort the Master suggested the envoy Yang A-kou. Accordingly, three days later the Khan ordered Yang A-kou to take with him one of the native chieftains and about a thousand horsemen, with whom he was to escort the Master back (to Samarqand) by a different way.

We crossed a great mountain where there is a "stone gate," the pillars of which look like tapering candles. Lying across them at the top is a huge slab of rock, which forms a sort of bridge. The stream below is very swift, and our horsemen in goading the pack-asses across lost many of them by drowning. On the banks of the stream were the carcases of other animals that had perished in the same way. The place is a frontier pass, which the troops had quite recently stormed. When we got out of the defile, the Master wrote two poems.

On the road we met people coming back from the West, carrying a lot of coral. Some of the officers in our escort bought fifty branches for two bars of silver. The largest was over a foot long. But as they were on horseback it was impossible to prevent it getting broken. We now continually travelled by night, to take advantage of the cool, and thus after five or six days we got back to Samarqand. All the officials of the place came to welcome the Master in his rooms. It was the fifth of the fifth month (June 15th).

The Master was now back in his old quarters, which stood on the northern heights some hundred feet above a clear stream, the waters of which come from the Snow Mountains and are therefore very cold. In the fifth month, when the hot season began, he would lie in a verandah at the back of the house, with the wind blowing on him. At night he slept on a terrace at the top of the building. In the sixth month, when the hot season is at its height, he bathed in the lake; and thus, although he was so far from home, his existence was by no means disagreeable.

The arable land in the district is suitable for the cultivation of most kinds of corn [grain], but buckwheat and the soybean are not grown. Wheat ripens in the fourth month. The people here have their own way of harvesting it: they simply stack it in heaps and fetch a little to grind as they require it. By the sixth month the crops are all cut. Mr. Li, the attendant of the Governor, presented us with five acres of melon-field. The melons are extraordinarily sweet and fragrant; there are none quite like them in China. Some of them are as large as a peck-measure.

In the sixth month the second prince (Chaghatay) came back to Samarqand, and Liu Wen begged from us some of these melons to give as a present to the prince. Ten of them weighed a full *hod* [over fifty pounds?]. Fruit and vegetables are very abundant; the only sort lacking are the colocasia and chestnut. The aubergines are like huge coarse fingers, purple-black in color.

Both men and women plait their hair. The men's hats are often like *yuan-shan-mao* ("distant mountain caps") trimmed with all kinds of colored stuffs, which are embroidered with cloud-patterns, and from the hats hang tasseled pendants. They are worn by all holders of official rank, from the notables downwards. The common people merely wear round their heads a piece of white muslin about six feet long. The wives of rich or important people wind round their heads a piece of black or purple gauze some six or seven feet long. This sometimes has flowers embroidered on it or woven patterns. The hair is always worn hanging down. Some cover it in a bag of floss-silk which may be either plain or colored; others wear a bag of cloth or plain silk. Those who cover their heads with cotton or silk look just like Buddhist nuns. It is the women of the common people who do so. Their clothes are generally made of cotton, sewn like a straining-bag, narrow at the top and wide at the bottom, with sleeves sewn on. This is called the under robe and is worn by men and women alike. Their carriages, boats, and agricultural implements are made very differently from ours. Their vessels are usually of brass or copper; sometimes of porcelain. They have a kind of porcelain that is very like our Ting ware (delicate, white porcelain). For holding wire they use only glass. Their weapons are made of steel. In their markets they use gold coins without a hole in the middle. There are native written characters on both sides. The people are often very tall and strong, so much so that they can carry the heaviest load without a carrying-beam. If a woman marries and the husband becomes poor, she may go to another husband. If he goes on a journey and does not come back for three months, his wife is allowed to marry again. Oddly enough some of the women have beards and moustaches. There are certain persons called *dashman* (probably, danishmand) who understand the writing of the country and are in charge of records and documents.

At the end of the winter they have a great fast that goes on for a month (Ramadan). Every evening the head of the family himself slays a sheep and divides it among those present, the meal going on continuously until next morning. In the remaining months there are six other fasts. Again, from the top of a high building they project great logs of wood like flying eave-beams (that make a platform) some ten foot square, and on it they construct a small bare chamber hung round with tasseled pendants. Every morning and evening the leading man goes up there and bows to the west. This is called "addressing Heaven." They do not pray either to Buddha or to the Taoist divinities. He sings up there in a long drawn-out chant, and when they hear his voice all able-bodied men and women must at once run thither and bow down. This happens all over the country. Any one who disobeys is slain and his body cast into the market-place. The leader's clothes do not differ from those of his countrymen, save that his head is bound with a scarf of fine muslin thirty-two feet long, supported on a frame-work of bamboo.

In the seventh month, on the night of the new moon's first appearance, the Master sent A-li-hsien to remind the Khan that the time fixed for the Master's exposition of the Way had now arrived. A reply admitting this came on the seventh day of the eighth month (September 13th), and we set out immediately.

The Governor accompanied us for several tens of *li*. The Master said to him, "To the east of the native city two thousand households have lately broken into revolt. Every night the city is lit up with flames and there is great anxiety among the people. I would rather you went back and calmed them." "But if by any unlikely chance something should happen to you on the road," said the Governor, "what then?" "That," said the Master, "is none of your business," and persuaded him to return.

On the twelfth we passed through Kesh, and on the following day were joined by an escort of a thousand men on foot and three hundred horsemen. We entered the great mountains by a different road, which avoids the Iron Gates. We crossed a stream with red waters. It runs through a gorge with cliffs several *li* high. Following the stream south-eastwards we came to a salt-spring at the foot of a mountain. In the sun its brackish waters evaporate and turn into white salt. We took two pecks of it for our use on the journey. Mounting in a south-easterly direction we reached the watershed and saw to the west of us a high ravine filled with what seemed to be ice, but was in fact merely salt. On the top of the ridge were red stones also composed of salt. The Master tasted them himself, and was struck by the fact that in the east salt is only found on low ground, while in these parts it also occurs in the mountains. The natives are very fond of cakes, with which they eat a great deal of salt. This makes them thirsty, and they drink a lot of water. It is no uncommon sight even in the depths of winter to see poor people selling water in pitchers.

On the day of mid-autumn (fifteenth of the eighth month) we came to a river—the Amu—which reminded us of the Yellow River. It flows to the north-west. We crossed it in a boat and camped on the southern bank. To the west there is a frontier-fort called T'uan-pa-la; its situation in the mountains renders it very difficult to attack.

We now met on the road with Lord Cheng, the personal physician of the Khan's third son (Ögedei). The Master presented him with a poem.

We followed the river up-stream and then went south-east for thirty *li*. Lack of water now compelled us to travel by night. We passed the great city of Balkh. Its inhabitants had recently rebelled against the Khan and been removed; but we could still hear dogs barking in its streets.

At dawn we breakfasted and after going eastward for twenty or thirty *li* came to a river that ran to the north. We were just able to ford it on horseback, and on the far side rested and camped for the night. On the twenty-second (September 28th) Chinkai came to meet us, and we were soon in the Khan's camp.

Presently the Khan sent Chinkai to ask whether the Master wished to see him at once or to rest for a little first. The Master replied that he was ready. On this as on all subsequent occasions when Taoists interviewed the Emperor we did not kneel or bow down before him, but merely inclined the body and pressed the palms of the hands together on entering his tent. When the audience was over we were given kurmiss, and as soon as it was finished took our leave. The Emperor asked whether we were properly provided for at our lodging in Samarqand. The Master replied that previously the supplies received from the Mongols, the natives, and the Governor had been adequate, but that recently there had been some difficulties about food, the provision of which had fallen entirely upon the Governor. Next day the Emperor again sent his personal officers to our tent. He had asked him to suggest that the Adept should take all his meals with the Emperor. But the Master replied, "I am a mountain hermit and am only at my ease in quiet places." The Emperor said he was to be humored. On the twenty-seventh day the Emperor set out on his return to the north. On the way he sent us repeated presents of grape-wine, melons, and greens. On the first of the ninth month we crossed a bridge of boats and went on to the north. The Master now pointed out that the time for his discourse had arrived and suggested that the Governor A-hai should be summoned.

The Emperor was delighted with (the Master's) doctrine and on the nineteenth, when there was a bright night, sent for him again. On this occasion too he was much pleased by what he heard, and sent for the Master to his tent once more on the twenty-third (October 29th). He was here treated with the same regard as before, and the Emperor listened to him with evident satisfaction. He ordered that the Master's words should be recorded, and especially that they should be written down in Chinese characters, that they might be preserved from oblivion. During the remainder of the Imperial Progress to the east, the Master constantly discoursed to the Emperor concerning the mysteries of Tao.

On the twenty-sixth (December 30th) we set out. On the twenty-third of the twelfth month (January 26th, 1223) there was a snow-storm and such intense cold that many oxen and horses were frozen to death on the road. After three days we crossed the Khojand-muran from west to east and soon reached the Khan's camp. Here we learnt that on the twenty-eighth, in the middle of night, the bridge of boats had broken loose and been swept away. The Khan asked the reason of calamities such as earthquakes, thunder, and so on. The Master replied, "I have heard that in order to avoid the wrath of Heaven you forbid your countrymen to bathe in rivers during the summer, wash their clothes, make fresh felt, or gather mushrooms in the fields. But this is not the way to serve Heaven. It is said that of the three thousand sins the worst is ill-treatment of one's father and mother. Now in this respect I believe your subjects to be gravely at fault and it would be well if your Majesty would use your influence to reform them."

This pleased the Khan and he said, "Holy Immortal, your words are exceedingly true; such is indeed my own belief," and he bade those who were present write them down in Uyghur characters. The Master asked that what he had said might be made known to the Khan's subjects in general, and this was agreed to.

On the eighth (March 11th) the Khan went hunting in the mountains to the east. He shot a boar; but at this moment his horse tumbled and he fell to the ground. Instead of rushing upon him, the boar stood perfectly still, apparently afraid to approach. In a moment his followers brought him the horse, the hunt was stopped, and they all returned to the camp. Hearing of this incident the Master reproached the Emperor, telling him that in the eyes of Heaven life was a precious thing. The Khan was now well on in years and should go hunting as seldom as possible. His fall, the Master pointed out, had been a warning just as the failure of the boar to advance and gore him had been due to the intervention of Heaven. "I know quite well," replied the Emperor, "that your advice is extremely good. But unfortunately we Mongols are brought up from childhood to shoot arrows and ride. Such a habit is not easy to lay aside. However, this time I have taken your words to heart."

23   Juzjani: Chaghatay the Accursed!

INTRODUCTION

Minhaj al-Din Juzjani (1193–1265) was witness to the Mongol conquest of Central Asia in the 1220s. While he was fortunate enough to survive the Mongol onslaught, he was forced to flee his homeland of Ghur, in central Afghanistan, never to return. In 1226, he sought refuge in India and found employment in the Delhi Sultanate. It was there that Juzjani wrote the Tabaqat-i Nasiri, *his universal history of the Islamic world. This source comprises twenty-three sections, the more interesting of which detail historical events relating to the Saljuqs, the Khorezmshahs, the conquering Mongols, the Afghan Ghurids and their Shamsi slave-king successors, Juzjani's patrons in north India. In analyzing this source it should be stressed that Juzjani wrote in India, safely beyond the boundaries of the Mongol Empire, and his Delhi sultan patrons had no reason to protect the reputation of the enemy Mongols (one might argue that, if anything, the contrary would have been the case). Readers may therefore be inclined to endow his* Tabaqat-i Nasiri *with an additional measure of trust and reliability in this regard.*

Juzjani makes no effort to conceal his profound disdain for the Mongols, as evidenced in the title he chose for his chapter, reproduced here, on Chinggis Khan's second son, Chaghatay. He limits his compliments to discussions of the Mongols' extraordinary military efficiency—which, he suggests, they would use to cataclysmic effect in bringing about the end of the world. Additionally, his stinging description of the brutality and devastation associated with the Mongol conquests makes his account an ideal counterpoint to the more well-known Persian histories, penned by authors whose objectivity may be questioned on the grounds that either they did not witness the devastation or they were in one way or another employed by the Mongol state. It will be seen below that Juvaini's account, which he

completed in Baghdad in 1260, the same year that Juzjani finished the Tabaqat-i
Nasiri *in Delhi, privileges the Mongol achievements in the Middle East at the
expense of the magnitude and devastation of the conquests. An apologetic bias is
even more apparent in Rashid al-Din's later and considerably more sympathetic
treatment of his Mongol employers.*

Chaghatay, Son of the Chinggis Khan
May God's Curse Be upon Him!

Chaghatay, the accursed, was the second son of the Chinggis
Khan, the Mughal. He was a tyrannical man, cruel, sanguinary, and an evil-doer;
and among the Mughal rulers there was not one who was a greater enemy of the
Muslims. He used to require that no created being should, in his presence, take
the name of Muslim on his tongue, except with evil intent; and, throughout the
whole of his tribes [of which he was the head] it used not to be possible even to
slaughter a sheep according to the ordinances of Islam, and all [sheep] used to be
rendered [thereby] unclean. To say one's prayers [publicly] used to be impossible
for any Muslim. Chaghatay used constantly to urge upon Ögedei that it was necessary to massacre all Muslims and not let any of them remain; and no Muslim
used to dare to put himself in his sight.

He was older then Ögedei; and, as Chinggis Khan was aware that his nature
was excessively sanguinary, malevolent, and tyrannical, he did not bequeath the
sovereignty to him, and assigned it to his younger brother, Ögedei. Chaghatay's
place of residence likewise used to be the original Mughal locality, and that portion of the dominions of the Chinggis Khan which he held possession of [at his
father's death] was assigned to him as his portion. His troops were [located] in
different parts of Mawarannahr, Farghana, and Turkestan. For this reason, that
he had impeached the elder of his brothers, Jochi, before his father, [asserting]
that Jochi, in his mind, meditated killing the Chinggis Khan in some chase, when
this reached the father's hearing, the Chinggis Khan gave poison to his son Jochi,
and destroyed him.

This Chaghatay, the accursed, for some years, was at the head of his tribes
and forces; and, when the decree of his death arrived, Almighty God made a holy
man among His eminent saints the instrument of his death so that he went to
hell: and it was on this wise. There was a pious Dervish, of pure heart, from the
confines of Khurasan, whom they used to call Shaykh Mahmud Atash Kha'ar
[the Fire-eater], a Shaykh of much eminence, and a Dervish of great repute, who,
having cast off earthly wishes and desires, and, impressed with the aspiration
after Truth, had devoted his body to pain and affliction, and had gone out into the
world, and used to wander about in different countries. He reached, during his
wanderings, a place between two mountains through which lay the route between
the country of Turkestan and the territory of Chin, and between these two moun-

tains strong barriers were placed, and guards were there posted and overseers stationed, in order that they might examine every person who proceeded towards Chin, or who entered the territory of Turkestan from Chin, and have information respecting his condition.

When Shaykh Mahmud Atash Kha'ar arrived at that place, the guards beheld a person, a stranger to the usages of the world, and, in outward appearance, like a maniac; and they seized him, saying, "Thou are a *fida'i.*" Shaykh Mahmud replied: "Aye! I am a *fida'i*"; and, notwithstanding they importuned him, saying, "Who art thou? Say!" his reply was, "I am what ye have said, a *fida'i.*" As he had confessed this thing, they brought him before Chaghatay. Mas'ud Bek, who was the Minister of State of Chaghatay, recognized Shaykh Mahmud, but, through fear of Chaghatay, was unable to say anything, or mention Shaykh Mahmud's condition, or his eminence. Chaghatay demanded of Shaykh Mahmud, "Who art thou?" He replied, "That same *fida'i* I am." Chaghatay said, "What shall I do with thee? What doth it behove to do unto thee?" Shaykh Mahmud answered, "Command that they rain arrows upon me, that I may be freed from life." Chaghatay commanded so that they killed him with volleys of arrows.

Some days after Shaykh Mahmud was received into the Almighty's mercy, Chaghatay was in the act of discharging a recoiling arrow, in a hunting-ground, at the prey, when, verily, it entered the back of that accursed one, and he went to hell; and God's people, particularly the people of Islam, were delivered from his malevolence.

B | *Islamic Central Asia under Mongol Rule*

24   Rashid al-Din: In Defense of Chaghatay Khan

INTRODUCTION

Rashid al-Din (1247–1318) was born into a Jewish family in the city of Hamadan, in western Iran, just a few years before the Mongol prince Hülegü (r. 1256–65) led a conquering force into the Middle East. Rashid al-Din's father and grandfather were both employed at the Mongol court, and, after being trained as a physician, he too was awarded a position at the court of Abaqa (r. 1265–82), Hülegü's son and the second ruler of the Il-Khanate. During that time Rashid al-Din converted to Islam, and proved himself to be exceptionally bright and talented. He was later elevated to the position of grand vizier during the reign of Ghazan Khan (r. 1295–1304), also a convert to Islam.

It was Ghazan Khan who ordered Rashid al-Din to write the Jami' al-tav-arikh *(Collection of histories), a Persian history composed as the Mongols were near the peak of their power in the region. Rashid al-Din's efforts to complete this task were facilitated by his position as grand vizier under both Ghazan Khan and Öljeytü (r. 1304–16). In addition to enjoying unfettered access to the vast holdings of the Il-Khanate's Persian libraries and an array of Mongol and Chinese sources, Rashid al-Din had patrons who permitted him access to the information included in the* Altan Debter *(the "Golden Book"), a uniquely valuable Mongol chronicle that has since passed out of existence. As a Persian, Rashid al-Din was officially forbidden from reading this carefully guarded work—only Mongols were permitted access. But his il-khan patrons sidestepped this restriction by ordering Mongol research assistants to read the text of the Altan Debter and relay relevant information to Rashid al-Din. While this allowance may have stretched the spirit of the law, it has added immeasurable value to the Jami' al-tavarikh as a source for the history of the Mongols.*

The Jami' al-tavarikh presents a full and detailed account, and it is in some ways unsurpassed by any other Persian chronicle of the period. But one cannot overlook the fact that Rashid al-Din was clearly beholden to his Mongol patrons; indeed his occasionally obsequious treatment of Ghazan Khan and Öljeytü may leave critical readers wondering whether the work is anything more than sycophantic propaganda. However, while a pro-Mongol bias clearly runs throughout the Jami' al-tavarikh, the events discussed are frequently corroborated in other contemporary sources, and careful textual analysis suggests that Rashid al-Din's version of events is quite reliable. It is for this reason that his short essay on Chaghatay Khan proves so interesting—especially when compared against Juzjani's (no less biased) discussion presented in the previous reading.

Of the History of Chaghatay Khan

Chaghatay was a just, competent, and awe-inspiring ruler. His father, Chinggis Khan, said to the amirs, "Whoever wishes to learn the *yasa* and *yosun* of kingship should follow Chaghatay. Whoever love property, wealth, chivalrous manners, and comfort should walk in the footsteps of Ögedei. And whoever wishes to acquire politeness, good breeding, courage, and skill in the handling of weapons should wait in attendance on Tolui." And when he was sharing out the armies he gave him four thousand men, as is set forth in detail in his history in the section on the division of the armies. Of the amirs he gave him Qarachar of the Barulas people and Möge the father of Yesün Noyan, of the Jalayir people; and of the lands and *yurts* from the Altai, which is the *yurt* of the Nayman peoples [to the banks of the Oxus]. And, in accordance with the command of Chinggis Khan, he went forth with the armies, and carried out the operations with the utmost zeal and endeavor, and conquered the various countries in the manner already described. In the *qonin yil*, that is, the Year of the Sheep, corresponding to Sha'ban of 607 of the Hijra [January–February, 1211], when Chinggis Khan set out against the land of Khitai, Chaghatay together with Ögedei and Tolui captured five towns: Un-Ui, Tung-Cheng, Fu-Jiu, Suq-Jiu, and Fung-Jiu. Then, when they had besieged and taken the town of Jo-Jiu, he sent all three to the edge of a mountain and its environs, and they captured all the towns, provinces, and castles between the towns of Fu-Jiu and Khuming. From thence they went to the River Qara-Mören, and then, turning back, [they] captured and plundered the towns of Pung-Yang-Fu and Tai-Wang-Fu and their dependencies; and the plunder of Tai-Wang-Fu went to Chaghatay.

Thereafter, in the *lu yïl,* that is, the Year of the Dragon, of which the beginning corresponds to the Dhu'l-Hijja of the year 616 [February–March, 1220], when Chinggis Khan set out for the Tazik country and came to the town of Otrar, he left him with his brothers Ögedei and Tolui to lay siege to it. They took the town and thereafter captured Banakat and most of the towns of Turkestan and then joined their father in Samarqand after its fall. Then he sent him with Jochi and Ögedei to lay siege to Khorezm, and since he and Jochi did not agree, their father commanded Ögedei, though he was the youngest, to take command, and he, by his competence, brought about agreement between the brothers and together they took Khorezm. Then Jochi went to his heavy baggage, and the others, in the summer of the *morin yïl,* that is, the Year of the Horse, corresponding to the year 619/1222–1223 joined their father and were received in audience at Taleqan. Having passed the summer in that area Chaghatay, Ögedei, and Tolui all three together accompanied their father in pursuit of Sultan Jalal al-Din. They went to the banks of the Indus and defeated the Sultan's army, while [the Sultan] himself escaped across the river. That summer they were engaged in conquering the countries of those parts and then accompanied their father back to their original *yurt* and abode.

In the *daqïqu yïl,* that is, the Year of the Hen, corresponding to the year 622/1225–1226 when Chinggis Khan set out against the land of the Tangqut, who had risen in rebellion, he commanded Chaghatay to remain with the wing of the army behind the *ordos.* In accordance with this command, Chaghatay continued so occupied until his brothers Ögedei and Tolui, who had accompanied their father, returned: they then brought Chinggis Khan's coffin to the *ordos,* and, having jointly performed the mourning ceremonies, each departed to his own *yurt* and tents.

And since Chaghatay had a particular friendship for his brothers Ögedei and Tolui, he spared no efforts to seat Ögedei upon the throne of the Khanate and went to great pains to have him so enthroned in accordance with his father's command. Together with Tolui and the other kinsmen, he knelt nine times and made obeisance. And although he was the elder brother he used to treat Ögedei with the utmost respect and rigidly observe the niceties of etiquette, one example of which is the following. One day they were riding on easy-paced horses and Chaghatay, being drunk, said to Ögedei, "Let us race our horses for a bet." And having made a bet, they ran a race, and Chaghatay's horse, being a little faster, won by a head. At night in his tent, Chaghatay was reminded of this incident and he reflected, "How was it possible for me to make a bet with Qa'an and let my horse beat his? Such conduct was a great breach of etiquette. Judging by this we and the others are becoming insolent, and this will lead to harm." And before morning he summoned the amirs and said, "Yesterday I was guilty of a crime of committing such an action. Let us go to Ögedei so that he may convict me of my crime and carry whatever is a fitting punishment." And setting out with the amirs in a great throng he came to the audience-hall earlier than usual. The guards reported to Ögedei that Chaghatay had come with a great multitude, and Ögedei, although he had complete confidence in him, was apprehensive of the situation, wondering what his motive could be. He sent some persons to his brother to ask him. [Chaghatay] said, "We, all of us, *aqa* and *ini,* spoke great words in the *quriltai* and gave written undertakings that Ögedei was the Qa'an and that we should tread the path of loyalty and obedience and in no way oppose him. Yesterday I made a bet and raced my horse against his. What right have we to make a bet with the Qa'an. Therefore I am guilty and have come to confess my guilt and submit to punishment. Whether he puts me to death or beats me is for him to decide." Ögedei Qa'an was filled with shame at these words. He became more loving and tender and humbled himself before his brother, but though he sent someone to say, "What words are these? He is my *aqa.* Why pay attention to such trifles?" [Chaghatay] would not listen. However, in the end he agreed that the Qa'an should spare his life and made an offering of nine horses. The *bitikchis* proclaimed that the Qa'an had spared Chaghatay's life, so that everyone heard and knew that he was making the offering because he had been pardoned. He then entered the *ordo* and explained this to all present with the eloquence that he possessed.

On this account the concord between them increased, and the other kinsmen laid their heads upon the letters of the Qa'an's command and took the road of obedience to him. And those countries which had not been conquered in the age of Chinggis Khan were all subjugated during the reign of Ögedei Qa'an. And the sovereignty of his family and the state of his army were strengthened. And since Chaghatay lived after this manner with Ögedei Qa'an, the Qa'an made his son Güyük his attendant and placed him in his guard, where he used to serve him. And Chaghatay's greatness became such as cannot be described, and he ruled over his *ulus* and the army that Chinggis Khan had given to him; he was firmly established on the throne of his kingdom in the region of Besh-Balïq. And in all important affairs Ögedei Qa'an used to send messengers and consult Chaghatay and would undertake nothing without his advice and approval. He himself in all matters trod the path of agreement and co-operation and in every decision used to say whatever occurred to him. Whenever there was an important undertaking he would attend the *quriltai,* and all the princes and amirs would come to welcome him; he would then enter the Court of the Qa'an, make obeisance and go into the inner chamber. During the 13 years that Ögedei was established on the throne, Chaghatay agreed and co-operated with him in this fashion: he died 7 months before Ögedei Qa'an, in the year 638/1240–1241.

25   Juvaini: The Il-Khan Hülegü Captures the Castles of the Heretics

INTRODUCTION

'Ata Malik Juvaini (1226–83) was a younger contemporary of Minhaj al-Din Juzjani (1193–1265). Both authors completed their chronicles in the

year 1260 and both provide accounts of many of the same historical events. But their perspectives on those events could scarcely be more different. Unlike Juzjani, who was witness to the devastation brought on by the Mongol onslaught, the younger Juvaini was born into an environment in which the Mongols had already established themselves as the supreme power in the eastern Islamic lands. For him, the Mongol conquests represented divine punishment of Muslims for their sins, and the wisest course of action was to learn from past mistakes and accept Mongol authority. It was Juvaini who reported the famous words that Chinggis Khan announced from the pulpit in Bukhara:

> *O people, know that you have committed great sins, and that the great ones among you have committed these sins. If you ask me what proof I have for these words, I say it is because I am the punishment of God. If you had not committed great sins, God would not have sent a punishment like me upon you.*

It was at some point during his second visit to Mongolia, which lasted from May 1252 until September 1253, that Juvaini began work on the Tarikh-i Jahan Gusha, his "History of the World Conqueror," Chinggis Khan. Soon thereafter Möngke dispatched his younger brother Hülegü to Persia, and Juvaini was officially placed in his service. Juvaini's fortune rose with that of his patron, and in 1259, just one year after Hülegü brought an end to the 'Abbasid Caliphate (750–1258), the new il-khan appointed Juvaini governor of Baghdad. Given his firsthand experience in the Mongols' governing administration, Juvaini's richly detailed chronicle is arguably the most important source for the early history of the Mongol Empire in the Middle East.

Still, one must recognize that political expediency imposed limits on any efforts at objectivity. This is perhaps best illustrated in that, although Juvaini's narrative continues to 1260, it overlooks the execution of the final 'Abbasid caliph in 1258. Instead, Juvaini directs attention to what he perceives to be one of the Mongols' greatest achievements in the region: their defeat of the heretical Nizari Isma'ilis, reviled in the west as the Assassins. To Juvaini and his contemporaries, the followers of Hasan-i Sabbah (r. 1090–1124) were a greater threat to Sunni Islam than the Mongol infidels. The excerpt below is taken from the fath-nama that announces the Mongol victory over the ostensibly impenetrable fortress of Alamut, the Assassins' Eagle's Nest in northwestern Persia, and the fall of the last of the Nizari Isma'ili grand masters, Rukn al-Din Khurshah (d. 1256). The ornate style of the prose is indicative of much Persian literature produced in the period.

Copy of the *Fath-nama* of Alamut

Hülegü, the Buraq of whose lofty ambition touches the head of the Pleiades while the lightning of his considered intention tramples on the face of the earth. And because God Almighty hath said: *"Recollect God's favour upon you,"* the meanest slave of his daily-increasing fortune, 'Ata-Malik b. Muhammad al-Juvaini, the *mustaufi*, wishes to send these good tidings to all the climes of the world, far and near, and to utter the cry which the tongue of the Faith has caused to reach the souls of all orthodox Believers:

> The Truth has appeared with firm pillars, with a rising
> star and a lofty structure,
> While the wrongdoers and the wicked, the aberrant and the
> rebellious, have stretched out their hands after evil.

Of the details of these events, which will remain for ever on the face of the years, he will give some brief description and reduce a line or two to writing, causing it to reach the ears of high and low, the great and the noble, from the farthermost East to uttermost Syria (*may God let them bear the glad tidings!*) that ever since that *huma*, the heaven-residing parasol of the World-Conquering King, Hülegü, had cast its auspicious shadow over these regions and the pennants of the victory-proclaiming standards had been unfurled over these lands and countries, he had followed the divine law which says: *"We never punished until we had first sent an apostle"* and had dispatched messenger after messenger to Rukn al-Din both to encourage and to warn him, hoping that by politeness and civility he might [be induced to] come forward and make obedience and submission a shelter from the vicissitudes of Fortune. However, on each occasion because of his youthfulness he sent a reply which was wide of the mark of truth and remote from the direction of righteousness, its apparent differing from its real meaning and his words being inconsistent with his deeds. It was therefore decided by the King's judgement, which radiates like the sun and is the mirror of the essence of things and the elixir of wisdom, to overthrow the castles of Rukn al-Din, which rubbed horns with the Horn of the Bull. . . .

At the prompting of Prosperity and Good Fortune, in the middle of Shavval of the year 654 [November 1256], he dispatched *elchis* to the amirs and *noyans* who were stationed round the castles at a distance, like a belt round the waist of a wasp; and he ordered each to advance from his station. Suqunchaq, Noyan, and Tamgha he sent on in advance to reconnoitre with an army of Turks who had bidden farewell to sleep and rest and made a meal of the flashing sword. Behind them the Monarch himself, blessed in action and in counsel, the God-aided King of Kings, moved forward with an army in full array, of such great numbers that Gog and Magog themselves would have been destroyed by the waves of its battalions. . . . And the centre he adorned with men of experience who had tasted the sweet and bitter of life, men who consider the day of battle the wedding-night, and connect the blades of flashing swords with the cheeks of white-skinned women, and deem the pricks of lances to be the kisses of beautiful maidens. They set out by way of Taleqan with the speed of the wind, like a flood in their onrush and like a flame of fire in their ascent; and their horses' hooves kicked dust into the eyes of Time. And on the very day of departure they came midway upon a mountain ram. Some of the young men, eager for fame, at once filled it with their arrows. The King took this as an omen and knew that the butting ram would be a victim in the oven of calamity and the faith of Hasan-i-Sabbah would be without followers. . . .

Now the history of that castle is as follows. At the time when that people were at the height of their power, his father 'Ala al-Din, in accordance with [the words of Pharaoh:] *"O Haman, build for me a tower that I may reach the avenues, the avenues of the heavens,"* had instructed his officials and ministers to survey the heights and summits of those mountains for the space of 12 years until they chose that lofty peak which confided secrets to the star Capella; and on its summit, which had a spring of water on its top and three others on its side, they began to build the castle of Maymun-diz, making the ramparts out of plaster and gravel. And from a *parsang* away they brought a stream like the Juy-i Arziz and caused the water to flow into the castle. And because of the extreme cold it was impossible for beasts to find a home or live in that place from the beginning of autumn till the middle of spring. On this account Rukn al-Din thought it impossible for human beings to penetrate to the castle and lay siege to it, since the mountains intertwined and the very eagles shrank back from the passes whilst the game animals at the foot sought some other way around. Nay, because of its great elevation that lofty place applied to itself the words [of 'Ali]: *"The flood rusheth down from me, and the birds rise not up to me."*

And now the inmates of the castle saw how a people numerous as ants had, snake-like, formed seven coils around it and quickly contrived to make their abode upon hard rock. As in the *panja* they had joined rank to rank and laid hand in hand. In the day-time as far as their sight could reach the people of Maymun-diz could see nothing but men and standards, and at night, because of the great quantity of fires, they thought the earth a sky full of stars [and] a world full of swords and daggers, whereof neither middle nor edge was visible. . . .

However, the prudent King, though confident of his strength and power, wished to draw them into the net by the fairest of means without his army's having to suffer pain. He therefore dispatched an *elchi* to Rukn al-Din to announce the arrival of his standards; and he still sought to win him and his people over, saying that heretofore Rukn al-Din's best interests had been obscured to him by the evil suggestions of a group of *nasnas* (half-human creatures), and on account of the fewness of his years the eye of wisdom had not yet awakened from the slumber of neglect. . . . The King's magnanimity desired in all cases the pleasure of forgiveness and condonation.

From the castle he sent a reply saying: "As the saying is, the hyena is not in his hole, and he can do nothing that might entail their destruction until he has news," that is to say: "Rukn al-Din is absent and we cannot come out without his leave and permission."

The *elchi* returned and the next day, when from the breast of night the milk of the dawn-break gushed forth and the world was in turmoil from the roaring of the thunder-voiced men and lions the King proceeded by the road on the left to the highest summit, and having surveyed all the possibilities of entrance and egress and examined the various approaches returned to his encampment by the other route. On the next day, when the heralds of the heavenly Jamshid drew their glittering swords from the scabbard of the horizon and routed the black host of Night, with their morning draught [the Mongol army] struck the harp of war, and with intent to rend the veil of their adversaries they prepared to do battle with mangonels and stones. And they cut down and trimmed for these mangonels trees which those people had tended and watered for many years past, not realizing what purpose they would serve or what fruit they would ultimately bear. . . . And during these days they placed a group of athletes at every *amaj* to transport the heavy poles and pillars of the mangonels to the top of the hill.

The next day, when the lid of night was lifted from the oven of the earth and the loaf-like disc of the sun was pulled out of the paunch of the darkness, the King ordered his bodyguard to climb to the top of the highest peak and pitch the royal encampment there. . . .

Meanwhile, the garrison of the castle, having prepared by night for battle and entrusted the towers of their heaven-reposing castle to fellow ruffians, began the engagement; they set up the poles of their mangonels and in the middle of Shavval [November, 1256] commenced a brisk discharge of stones. . . . And on this side also the young men were splitting hairs with lance-like arrows and themselves flinching before neither stone nor arrow. Arrows, which were the shaft of Doom discharged by the Angel of Death, were let fly against those wretches, passing like hail through the sieve-like clouds.

> The arrow passed through coats of mail as the wind of
> early dawn through the petals of flowers.

When the sun drew the shield of shadow in front of him they ceased fighting, but on the fourth day, which was the crisis of their disease and the proof of the testimony of truth, when dawn began to break, cries and shouts rose up, and on both sides they set foot upon the road of battle. From the towers bows sent up swift-feathered shafts and a *kaman-i-gav*, which had been constructed by Khitaian craftsmen and had a range of 2,500 paces, was brought to bear on those fools, when no other remedy remained; and of the devil-like Heretics many soldiers were burnt by those meteoric shafts. From the castle also stones poured down like leaves, but no more than one person was hurt thereby.

Having that day experienced the force of the Mongols' arms they ceased fighting, and the garrison of the castle after the heat of war knocked at the door of peace. And Rukn al-Din sent a messenger with a message to this effect: "I had concealed myself hitherto because I was not certain of Your Majesty's arrival. The army will now cease fighting and to-day or tomorrow I will come out." With such trickery did that idle babbler cast water upon the fire so that that day they lifted their skirts from battle. On the following day he sent another messenger and asked for a *yarlïq* granting him safe-conduct. In compliance with their request the bearer of these good tidings wrote a *yarlïq*. . . . This *yarlïq* was sent to them and read out in public. Those who were not wanting in intelligence and valued their property and their lives rejoiced and exulted. And when the day drew to its close and light changed into darkness they promised he would come down the next day. When the morrow was born of dark Night and Rukn al-Din prepared to descend, some of the more fanatical *fida'is* went to every extreme in their opposition and would not allow him to go down. They even plotted to do away with those who had encouraged him to take that decision. Rukn al-Din again sent someone with the following message: "Before hastening to present myself I had prepared gifts [for your acceptance], but most of my followers were angry and agreed together to make away with me before this plan was carried out. On this account my intention was frustrated!"

When these words reached the august ear of the Il-Khan he gave no sign at all of his inner displeasure. He said that it was best for Rukn al-Din to guard his own person; and dismissed the messenger. . . .

Rukn al-Din now saw that he would be left with nothing but regret. He had been seeking to gain time with "perhaps" and "peradventure" and sending back messengers with unacceptable excuses, and was still procrastinating in the same manner in the hope that the cotton-dressers of winter might make cotton of the King's army. But now he saw that it was an illusion to look for winter and snow. . . . In these circumstances Rukn al-Din saw no refuge save in surrendering and seeking shelter under the shadow of the King's mercy; and in great fear and dread he resorted to supplication and intercession. . . . He dispatched a messenger and begged forgiveness for his past crimes. Accordingly the King's universal benefi-cence and utter compassion with the pen of power inscribed upon the pages of his and his people's actions the verse: *"Forgive with kindly forgiveness."*

Rukn al-Din first sent out the greater part of his notables and ministers to-gether with his son, and the next day, after being distinguished with the promised attentions, he came down himself. And this auspicious day was the last of Shavval of that year [19th of November, 1256], the last of the prosperity of the People of the Mountains, nay rather the first of the glad tidings of the Glorious Lord. . . . Having then hastened down with his family and followers Rukn al-Din sought refuge in the honour of kissing the threshold of the World-King's audience-place and, in an attitude of shame and contrition, confessed to the crimes and sins that he had committed in former days and in the preceding months. . . . The next day, Rukn al-Din took his brothers, children, domestics, and dependents and the inmates of the castle down on to the plain, and every one of the soldiers came out with his goods and belongings. Then the Mongol army entered and began to destroy the buildings, brushing away the dust thereof with the broom of annihilation. . . .

Apart from what was in the treasuries of Maymun-diz Rukn al-Din had nothing of any value to offer as a present to the King because at the time of the passing to and fro of the armies all his possessions had been distributed. [The King] scattered it all as largesse and offered it to the Pillars of State and the troops of the kingdom.

And to the other castles in that valley he sent his messengers and officers together with the *elchi*s of the Il-Kahn with orders for their destruction. And the King turned back, victorious and triumphant.

An elchi proceeded to the commander of Alamut to call on him to comply also and join his master in submission and allegiance. He hesitated to come down immediately, and Prince Balaghai was despatched with a large force of men to lay siege to the castle. Balaghai led his army to the foot of Alamut and invested it on every side. The garrison, having cast a glance at the consequences of the matter and the vagaries of Fate, sent a messenger to sue for quarter and beg for favourable treatment. Rukn al-Din intervened on their behalf, and the King was pleased to pass over their crimes. And at the end of Zu'l-Qa'da of that year [beginning of December 1256] all the inmates of that seminary of iniquity and nest of Satan came down with all their goods and belongings. Three days later the army climbed up to the castle and seized whatever those people had been unable to carry off. They quickly set fire to the various buildings and with the broom of destruction cast the dust thereof to the winds, levelling them with their foundations. . . .

On the night of their doom the decree [of God in the words:] *"We turned those cities upside down"* became as clear as broad daylight to those people. And yet when the time was not yet ripe, during the reign of Hasan-i-Sabbah, that same castle of Alamut, whose garrison and resources were then but small, had during a period of 11 years been several times besieged by Muhammad, son of Malik Shah, son of Alp Arslan, (as may be read in books of history), and all to no avail.

Now to the wise man it is clear and certain that every beginning has an end and every perfection a falling-off, which, when the time comes, there is no power which can prevent. *The Apostle of God (God bless him and give him peace!) hath said: "It is the right of God not to raise something without setting it down."*

During this week Shams al-Din, the governor of the castles of Kuhistan, arrived and asked for a *yarlïq*. He then set out with Rukn al-Din's officials in order that, beginning with Girdkuh, they might demolish all the castles, more than 50 of them, still remaining in the region of Kuhistan, castles which raised their hands against the heavenly spheres and assaulted the constellations; and in demolishing them turn the wine of their imaginings into a mirage.

And from Daylaman, Ashkavar, Tarum, and Kharkam came the governors. They were enrolled in the number of the King's obedient servants and having received *yarlïqs* destroyed their castles. . . .

By this victory which is on a par with the conquest of Khaibar,—and the obvious requires no exposition and seeing dispenses with hearing—the truth of God's secret intent by the rise of Chinggis Khan has become clear and the benefit afforded by the passing of dominion and sovereignty to the World-Emperor Mengü Qa'an plain to see. By this famous victory the keys to the lands of the world are placed ready for use in the hands of the [Mongols'] power, and the bolts of the remaining countries of the climes, which because of Fate's malevolence still hesitated, are now undone. The good call it the key to victories and the wicked the lantern for the morning draught. With these glad tidings the zephyr has begun to blow and the birds of the air to fly. And saints felicitate the souls of the prophets and the living send congratulations to the dead. . . .

In that breeding-ground of heresy in the Rudbar of Alamut, the home of the wicked adherents of Hasan-i-Sabbah and the evil followers of the practice of *ibaha*, there remains not one stone of the foundations upon another. . . . Their luckless womenfolk, like their empty religion, have been utterly destroyed. And the gold of those crazy, double-dealing counterfeiters which appeared to be unalloyed has proved to be base lead.

Today, thanks to the glorious fortune of the World-Illuminating King, if an assassin still lingers in a corner he plies a woman's trade; wherever there is a *da'i* there is an announcer of death; and every *rafiq* has become a thrall. The propagators of Isma'ilism have fallen victims to the swordsmen of Islam. . . . Their governors have lost their power and their rulers their honour. The greatest among them have become as vile as dogs. Every commander of a fortress has been deemed fit for the gallows and every warden of a castle has forfeited his head and his mace. . . .

The kings of the Greeks and Franks, who turned pale for fear of these accursed ones, and paid them tribute, and were not ashamed of that ignominy, now enjoy sweet slumber. And all the inhabitants of the world, and in particular the Faithful, have been relieved of their evil machinations and unclean beliefs. Nay, the whole of mankind, high and low, noble and base, share in this rejoicing. And compared with these histories that of Rustam the son of Dastan has become but an ancient fable. The perception of all ideas is through this manifest victory, and the light of the world-illuminating day is adorned thereby. *"And the uttermost part of that impious people was cut off. All praise be to God, the Lord of the Worlds!"*

26   Mirza Haydar Dughlat: The Conversion to Islam of Tughluq Timur Khan

INTRODUCTION

Mirza Haydar (1499–1551), a younger cousin of the Timurid prince and first Mughal emperor Babur (1483–1530), was born in Tashkent on the eve of the Uzbek invasions. As an established military commander and a ruler of Kashmir, Mirza Haydar constitutes an important historical figure in his own right. But our present concern is with him as the author of the Tarikh-i Rashidi, *a historical chronicle named after 'Abd al-Rashid Khan, ruler of Kashghar, 1533–60. The* Tarikh-i Rashidi *is an important source for the history of the Chaghatayd rulers of Moghulistan, in eastern Central Asia, from the reign of Tughluq Timur (r. 1347–63) to the mid-sixteenth century. A secondary point of interest is the source's discussions of the Dughlat family, a highly influential political force in eastern Turkestan until authority shifted to the Khojas, a local Naqshbandi religious lineage, in the seventeenth century.*

In the following excerpt Mirza Haydar repeats a tradition regarding the conversion to Islam of Tughluq Timur, the Chaghatay ruler of eastern Turkestan. From Mirza Haydar's perspective, Tughluq Timur's conversion was of monumental importance. With the notable exception of Tarmashirin (r. 1326–34), previous Chaghatay khans had determinedly clung to their ancestral religious traditions and pastoral-nomadic way of life, and they exhibited little (or no) interest in, or sympathy for, the customs and traditions of their conquered Muslim subjects. Tarmashirin's conversion to Islam illustrates this point, as his vehemently traditionalist followers executed him for forsaking Chinggisid tradition. Unlike under Tarmashirin, however, Tughluq Timur's conversion was a lasting one, and Mirza Haydar identifies it as the event that signaled a new religious identity for the Chaghatay Khanate. Rather than persecute their Muslim subjects, from this time the Chaghatay nobility began work returning Islam to an elevated position in the realm.

Mawlana Khoja Ahmad (may God sanctify his soul) was descended from Mawlana Arshad al-Din. He was exceedingly pious and much esteemed and revered. He belonged to the sect of *Khojas* (may God sanctify their spirits). For twenty years I was in his service, and worshipped at no other mosque than his. He led a retired life, devoting his time to religious contemplation, and he used to recite the traditions of his sect in a beautiful manner; so much so, that any stranger hearing him was sure to be much impressed.

From him I heard that it was written in the annals of his forefathers concerning Mawlana Shuja' al-Din Mahmud, the brother of Hafiz al-Din, an elder of Bukhara (who was the last of the Mujtahids, for after the death of Hafiz al-Din there was never another Mujtahid), that during his interregnum, Chinggis Khan assembled the Imams of Bukhara, according to his custom, put Hafiz al-Din to death, and banished Mawlana Shuja' al-Din Mahmud to Karakorum. [The ancestors of] Mawlana Khoja Ahmad also were sent there. At the time of a disaster in Karakorum, their sons went to Lob Katak, which is one of the most important towns between Turfan and Khotan, and there they were held in much honour and esteem. I was told many particulars concerning all of them, but I have forgotten them for the most part. The last of the sons was called Shaykh Jamal al-Din, an austere man who dwelt in Katak.

On a certain Friday, after the prayers, he preached to the people and said: "I have already, on many occasions, preached to you and given you good counsel, but no one of you has listened to me. It has now been revealed to me that God has sent down a great calamity on this town. A Divine ordinance permits me to escape and save myself from this disaster. This is the last sermon I shall preach to you. I take my leave of you, and remind you that our next meeting will be on the day of resurrection."

Having said this, the Shaykh came down from the pulpit. The *mu'azzin* followed him and begged that he might be allowed to accompany him. The Shaykh said he might do so. When they had journeyed three *farsakh*s they halted, and the *mu'azzin* asked permission to return to the town to attend to some business, saying he would come back again immediately. As he was passing the mosque, he said to himself, "For a last time, I will just go and call out the evening prayer." So he ascended the minaret and called the evening prayer. As he was doing so, he noticed that something was raining down from the sky; it was like snow, but dry. He finished his "call," and then stood praying for awhile. Then he descended, but found that the door of the minaret was blocked, and he could not get out. So he again ascended and, looking round, discovered that it was raining sand, and to such a degree that the whole town was covered; after a little while he noticed that the ground was rising, and at last only a part of the minaret was left free. So, with fear and trembling, he threw himself from the tower on to the sand; and at midnight he rejoined the Shaykh, and told him his story. The Shaykh immediately set out on his road, saying: "It is better to keep a distance from the wrath of God." They fled in great haste; and that city is, to this day, buried in sand. Sometimes a wind comes, and lays bare the minaret or the top of the dome. It often happens also, that a strong wind uncovers a house, and when any one enters it he finds everything in perfect order, though the master has become white bones. But no harm has come to the inanimate things.

In short, the Shaykh finally came to Bai Gul, which is in the vicinity of Aqsu. At that time Tughluq Timur Khan was in Aqsu. When he had first been brought there he was sixteen years of age. He was eighteen when he first met the Shaykh, and he met him in the following way. The Khan had organized a hunting-party, and had promulgated an order that no one should absent himself from the hunt. It was, however, remarked that some persons were seated in a retired spot. The Khan sent to fetch these people, and they were seized, bound, and brought before him, inasmuch as they had not presented themselves at the hunt. The Khan asked them, "Why have you disobeyed my commands?" The Shaykh replied, "We are strangers, who have fled from the ruined town of Katak. We know nothing about the hunt nor the ordinances of the hunt, and therefore we have not transgressed your orders." So the Khan ordered his men to set the Tajik free. He was, at that time, feeding some dogs with swine's flesh, and he asked the Shaykh angrily, "Are you better than this dog, or is the dog better than you?" The Shaykh replied, "If I have faith I am better than this dog; but if I have no faith, this dog is better than I am." On hearing these words, the Khan retired and sent one of his men, saying, "Go and place that Tajik upon your own horse, with all due respect, and bring him here to me."

The Moghul went and led his horse before the Shaykh. The Shaykh noticing that the saddle was stained with blood (of pig) said, "I will go on foot." But the Moghul insisted that the order was that he should mount the horse. The Shaykh then spread a clean handkerchief over the saddle and mounted. When he arrived before the Khan, he noticed that this latter was standing alone in a retired spot, and there were traces of sorrow on his countenance. The Khan asked the Shaykh, "What is this thing that renders man, if he possess it, better than a dog?" The Shaykh replied, "Faith," and he explained to him what Faith was, and the duties of a Musulman. The Khan wept thereat, and said, "If I ever become Khan, and obtain absolute authority, you must, without fail, come to me, and I promise you I will become a Musulman." He then sent the Shaykh away with the utmost respect and reverence. Soon after this the Shaykh died. He left a son of the name of Arshad al-Din, who was exceedingly pious. His father once dreamed that he carried a lamp up to the top of a hill, and that its light illumined the whole of the east. After that, he met Tughluq Timur Khan in Aqsu and said what has been mentioned above. Having related this to his son, he charged him, saying, "Since I may die at any moment, let it be your care, when the young man becomes Khan, to remind him of his promise to become a Muslim; thus this blessing may come about through your mediation and, through you, the world may be illumined."

Having completed his injunctions to his son, the Shaykh died. Soon afterwards Tughluq Timur became Khan. When news of this reached Mawlana Arshad al-Din, he left Aqsu and proceeded to Moghulistan, where the Khan was ruling in great pomp and splendour. But all his efforts to obtain an interview with him, that he might execute his charge, were in vain. Every morning, however, he used to call out the prayers near to the Khan's tent. One morning the Khan said to one of his followers, "Somebody has been calling out like this for several mornings now; go and bring him here." The Mawlana was in the middle of his call to prayer when the Moghul arrived, who, seizing him by the neck, dragged him before the Khan. The latter said to him, "Who are you that thus disturb my sleep every morning at an early hour?" He replied, "I am the son of the man to whom, on a certain occasion, you made the promise to become a Muslim." And he proceeded to recount the above related story. The Khan then said, "You are welcome, and where is your father?" He replied, "My father is dead, but he entrusted this mission to me." The Khan rejoined, "Ever since I ascended the throne I have had it on my mind that I made that promise, but the person to whom I gave the pledge never came. Now you are welcome. What must I do?" On that morn the sun of bounty rose out of the east of divine favour, and effaced the dark night of Unbelief. Mawlana ordained ablution for the Khan, who, having declared his faith, became a Muslim. They then decided that for the propagation of Islam, they should interview the princes one by one, and it should be well for those who accepted the faith, but those who refused should be slain as heathens and idolaters.

On the following morning, the first to come up to be examined alone was Amir Tulik, who was my great grand-uncle. When he entered the Khan's presence, he found him sitting with the Tajik, and he advanced and sat down with them also. Then the Khan began by asking, "Will you embrace Islam?" Amir Tulik burst into tears and said, "Three years ago I was converted by some holy men at Kashghar, and became a Musulman, but, from fear of you I did not openly declare it." Thereupon the Khan rose up and embraced him; then the three sat down again together. In this manner they examined the princes one by one. All accepted Islam, till it came to the turn of Jaras, who refused, but suggested two conditions, one of which was, "I have a man named Sataghni Buka, if this Tajik can overthrow him I will become a Believer." The Khan and the Amirs cried out, "What absurd condition is this!" Mawlana, however, said, "It is well, let it be so. If I do not throw him, I will not require you to become a Muslim." Jaras then said to the Mawlana, "I have seen this man lift up a two year old camel. He is an Infidel, and above the ordinary stature of men." Mawlana replied, "If it is God's wish that the Moghuls become honoured with the blessed state of Islam, He will doubtless give me sufficient power to overcome this man." The Khan and those who had become Musulmans were not pleased with these plans. However, a large crowd assembled, the infidel was brought in, and he and Mawlana advanced towards one another. The infidel, proud of his own strength, advanced with a conceited air. The Mawlana looked very small and weak beside him. When they came to blow, the Mawlana struck the infidel full in the chest, and he fell senseless. After a little, he came to again, and having raised himself, fell again at the feel of the Mawlana, crying and uttering words of Belief. The people raised loud shouts of applause, and on that day 160,000 persons cut off the hair of their heads and became Muslims. The Khan was circumcised, and the lights of Islam dispelled the shades of Unbelief. Islam was disseminated all through the country of Chaghatay Khan, and (thanks be to God) has continued fixed in it to the present time.

27   Ibn Battuta: Travels in Western Central Asia in the Fourteenth Century

INTRODUCTION

In the fourteenth century, a Muslim traveler from North Africa, Abu 'Abdallah Ibn Battuta, produced one of the greatest travel accounts ever written. Ibn Battuta was born in 1304, in Tangier, Morocco, into a family with a long tradition of judicial service. He too was trained in fiqh, the science of Islamic jurisprudence, and at a young age he achieved recognition as a specialist in the Maliki legal school. In 1325, at the age of twenty-one, Ibn Battuta left Morocco to participate in the annual pilgrimage to Mecca. But as he encountered new people and new places along the way he developed an overwhelming urge to explore the world. Over the next twenty-four years Ibn Battuta traveled over seventy thousand miles.

After multiple pilgrimages to Mecca and some time exploring the Middle East and East Africa, Ibn Battuta made his way to Anatolia and then sailed across the Black Sea to the Crimean peninsula, at that time the territory of Uzbek Khan (r. 1313–41), the Chinggisid ruler of the Golden Horde. Ibn Battuta spent three years gradually making his way southward through the Qipchaq Steppe, Khorezm, Transoxiana, and Afghanistan, until he finally entered India and spent the better part of a decade in the service of Sultan Muhammad ibn Tughluq (r. 1324–51). The extraordinary extent of his travels precludes even summation here—we can only mention the additional names of Bengal, the Maldives, Sumatra, Beijing, Granada, and Timbuktu.

According to the scribe Ibn Juzayy's introduction to Ibn Battuta's Rihla (Journey), soon after his return to North Africa, in the year 1354 the sultan of Fez ordered Ibn Battuta to record the full account of his experiences so that they might be retained for posterity. The product is a source that is at the same time a magnificent travel account, an introspective autobiography, and a historical ethnography.

One must note, however, that Ibn Battuta's account was compiled nearly thirty years after his initial departure from Tangier, and this explains the inclusion of an unknown number of errors in his account. Thus, as is the case with all primary sources, the Rihla *requires the reader to exercise caution in its use.*

The passage excerpted here begins with Ibn Battuta's arrival at the Crimean port of Caffa and his entrance into the land of Uzbek Khan, renowned for spreading Islam to the Turkic peoples of the Golden Horde. Ibn Battuta's observations reveal much about the lives of these recently converted Turkic nomads. The austere qazi *is especially surprised to find that these Muslims used millet, another grain, to make* buza, *an alcoholic beverage similar to beer that was permitted according to the Hanafi legal school. The passage leaves off with Ibn Battuta's account of Khorezm, Uzbek Khan's southernmost territory, which appears to have completely recovered in the century since the Mongol conquests, and adopted a strikingly orthodox Sunni-Muslim ethos.*

Asia Minor and South Russia

This place where we landed was in the wilderness known as Dasht-i Qïpchaq (*dasht* in the language of the Turks means "wilderness"). This wilderness is green and grassy, with no trees nor hills, high or low, nor narrow pass nor firewood. What they use for burning is animal dung (which they call *tazak*), and you can see even their men of rank gathering it up and putting it in the skirts of their robes. There is no means of travelling in this desert except in waggons, and it extends for six months' journey, three of them in the territories of the sultan Muhammad Uzbek, and three in those of other princes. On the day after our arrival at this roadstead, one of the merchants in our company went to some of the tribesmen known as Qïpchaq who inhabit this desert and profess the Christian religion, and hired from them a waggon drawn by horses. We rode in this, and came to the city of al-Kafa which is a great city along the sea coast inhabited by Christians, most of them Genoese, who have a governor called al-Damdir. We lodged there in the mosque of the Muslims. . . .

On the following day the governor came to visit us and prepared a banquet, which we ate in his residence. We made a circuit of the city and found it provided with fine bazars, but all the inhabitants are infidels. We went down to its port, where we saw a wonderful harbour with about two hundred vessels in it, both ships of war and trading vessels, small and large, for it is one of the world's celebrated ports.

We then hired a waggon and travelled to the city of al-Qiram, a large and fine city in the territories of the illustrious sultan Muhammad Uzbek Khan. There is an amir who governs it on his behalf, named Tuluqtemur. One of the subordinates of this amir, who had accompanied us on our journey, informed him of our arrival, and he sent me a horse by the hand of his imam, Sa'd al-Din. We lodged in a hospice, whose shaykh, Zada al-Khurasani, welcomed us and treated us honourably and generously. He is held in great veneration among them; I saw many persons come to salute him, of the rank of *qazi khatib,* doctor of law, etc. This shaykh Zada told me that outside this city there was a Christian monk living in a monastery, who devoted himself to ascetic exercises and used frequently to fast, and that he eventually reached the point of being able to fast for forty days at a stretch, after which he would break his fast with a single bean; also that he had the faculty of revealing secret things. He desired me to go with him to visit the man, but I refused, although afterwards I regretted not having seen him and found out the truth of what was said about him.

I met in this city its chief *qazi,* Shams al-Din al-Sayili, who is the *qazi* of the Hanafis, and the *qazi* of the Shafi'is, who is named Khidr, as well as the jurist and professor 'Ala al-Din al-Asi, the *khatib* of the Shafi'is, Abu Bakr (it is he who pronounces the *khutba* in the congregational mosque that al-Malik al-Nasir [God's mercy on him] erected in this City), the pious Shaykh and sage Muzaffar al-Din (he was a Greek who embraced Islam and became a sincere Muslim), and the pious and ascetic Shaykh Muzhir al-Din, who was a highly respected doctor of law. The amir Tuluqtemur was ill, but we visited him and he received us honourably and made gifts to us. He was on the point of setting out for the city of al-Sara, the capital of the sultan Muhammad Uzbek, so I planned to travel in his company and bought some waggons for that purpose.

Account of the waggons in which one journeys in this country. These people call a waggon 'araba. They are waggons with four large wheels, some of them drawn by two horses, and some drawn by more than two, and they are drawn also by oxen and camels, according to the weight or lightness of the waggon. The man who services the waggon rides on one of the horses that draw it, which has a saddle on it, and carries in his hand a whip with which he urges them to go and a large stick by which he brings them back to the right direction when they turn aside from it. There is placed upon the waggon a kind of cupola made of wooden laths tied together with thin strips of hide; this is light to carry, and covered with felt or blanket-cloth, and in it there are grilled windows. The person who is inside the tent can see [other] persons without their seeing him, and he can employ himself in it as he likes, sleeping or eating or reading or writing, while he is still journeying. Those of the waggons that carry the baggage, the provisions, and the chests of eatables are covered with a sort of tent much as we have described, with a lock on it. When I decided to make the journey, I prepared for my own conveyance a waggon covered with felt, taking with me in it a slavegirl of mine, another small waggon for my associate 'Afif al-Din al-Tuzari, and for the rest of my companions a large waggon drawn by three camels, one of which was ridden by the conductor of the waggon....

The habit of the Turks is to organize the journey through this desert in the same way as that of the pilgrims [to Mecca] on the Hijaz road. They set out after the dawn prayer and halt in the mid-forenoon, then set out again after noon and halt in the evening. When they halt they loose the horses, camels, and oxen from the waggons and drive them out to pasture at liberty, night and day. No one, whether sultan or any other, gives forage to his beast, for the peculiar property of this desert is that its herbage takes the place of barley for animals; this property belongs to no other land, and for that reason there are large numbers of animals in it. Their animals [pasture] without keepers or guards; this is due to the severity of their laws against theft. Their law in this matter is that any person found in possession of a stolen horse is obliged to restore it to its owner and to give him along with it nine like it; if he cannot do that, his sons are taken instead, and if he has no sons he is slaughtered just as a sheep is slaughtered.

These Turks do not eat bread nor any solid food, but they prepare a dish made from a thing in their country like millet, which they call *dugi*. They put water over a fire; when it boils they pour into it some of this *dugi*, and if they have any meat they cut it in small pieces and cook it along with the *dugi*. Then every man is given his portion in a dish, and they pour over it curdled milk and sup it. [Sometimes] they sup with it mares' milk, which they call *qumizz*. They are powerful and hardy men, with good constitutions. At certain times they make use of a dish that they call *burkhani*. It is a paste which they cut into very small pieces, making a hole in the middle of each, and put into a pot; when they are cooked, they pour over them curdled milk and sup them. They have also a fermented drink which they make from the grain of the *dugi* mentioned above. They regard the eating of sweetmeats as a disgrace. [To give an instance of this] I went one day to the audience of the sultan Uzbek during [the month of] Ramadan. There was served horse-flesh (this is the meat that they most often eat) and sheep's flesh, and *rishta*, which is a kind of macaroni cooked and supped with milk. I brought for him that night a plate of sweetmeats made by one of my companions, and when I presented them before him he touched them with his finger and put it to his mouth, and that was all he did. The amir Tuluqtemur told me of one of the high-ranking mamluks of this sultan, who had between sons and sons' sons about forty descendants, that the sultan said to him one day "Eat sweetmeats, and I free you all," but he refused, saying "If you were to kill me I would not eat them."

When we moved out of the city of al-Qiram we halted at the hospice of the amir Tuluqtemur, at a place known as Sajijan, and he sent for me to present myself before him. So I rode to him (for I had a horse ready for me to ride, which was led by the conductor of the waggon, and when I wanted to ride it I did so), came to the hospice, and found that the amir had prepared there a great banquet, including bread. They then brought in a white liquid in small bowls and those present drank of it. The Shaykh Muzaffar al-Din was next to the amir in the order of sitting and I was next to him, so I said to him, "What is this?" He replied, "This is *duhn* juice." I did not understand what he meant, so I tasted it and finding a bitter taste in it left it alone. When I went out I made enquiry about it and they said "It is *nabidh* [a fermented drink] which they make from *dugi* grain." These people are Hanafis and *nabidh* is permissible according to their doctrine. They call this *nabidh* which is made from *dugi* by the name of *buza*. What the Shaykh Muzaffar al-Din said to me was [meant to be] "*dukhn* juice" [i.e., millet juice], but since his [Arabic] speech was mispronounced, as commonly among foreigners, I thought he was saying "*duhn* juice" [i.e., oil juice]. . . .

The horses in this country are exceedingly numerous, and their price is negligible. A good horse costs fifty or sixty of their *dirhams*, which equals one dinar of our money or thereabouts. These are the horses known in Egypt as *akadish*, and it is from [the raising of] them that they make their living, horses in their country being like sheep in ours, or even more numerous, so that a single Turk will possess thousands of them. It is the custom of the Turks who live in this country and who raise horses to attach a piece of felt, a span in length, to a thin rod, a cubit in length, for every thousand horses [possessed by each man]. These rods are put on the waggons in which their women ride, each being fixed to a corner of the waggon, and I have seen some of them who have ten pieces [of felt] and some with less than that.

These horses are exported to India [in droves], each one numbering six thousand or more or less. Each trader has one or two hundred horses or less or more. For every fifty of them he hires a drover, who looks after them and their pasturage, like sheep; and this man is called by them *alqashi*. He rides on one of them, carrying in his hand a long stick with a rope on it, and when he wishes to catch any horse among them he gets opposite to it on the horse that he is riding, throws the rope over its neck and draws it to him, mounts it, and sets the other free to pasture. When they reach the land of Sind with their horses, they feed them with forage, because the vegetation of the land of Sind does not take the place of barley, and the greater part of the horses die or are stolen. They are taxed on them in the land of Sind [at the rate of] seven silver dinars a horse, at a place called Shashnaqar, and pay a further tax at Multan, the capital of the land of Sind. In former times they paid in duty the quarter of what they imported, but the king of India, the Sultan Muhammad, abolished this [practice] and ordered that there should be exacted from the Muslim traders the *zakat* and from the infidel traders the tenth. In spite of this, there remains a handsome profit for the traders in these horses, for they sell the cheapest of them in the land of India for a hundred silver dinars (the exchange value of which in Moroccan gold is twenty-five dinars), and often sell them for twice or three times as much. The good horses are worth five hundred [silver] dinars or more. The people of India do not buy them for [their qualities in] running or racing, because they themselves wear coats of mail in battle and they cover their horses with armour, and what they prize in these horses is strength and length of pace. The horses that they want for racing are brought to them from al-Yaman, 'Oman, and Fars, and each of these horses is sold at from one to four thousand dinars. . . .

Turkestan and Khurasan

After journeying through this desert and traversing it as we have described we arrived at Khorezm, which is the largest, greatest, most beautiful, and most important city of the Turks. It has fine bazars and broad streets, a great number of buildings and abundance of commodities; it shakes under the weight of its population, by reason of their multitude, and is agitated by them [in a manner resembling] the waves of the sea. I rode out one day on horseback and went into the bazar, but when I got halfway through it and reached the densest pressure of the crowd at a point called al-Shawr, I could not advance any further because of the multitude of the press, and when I tried to go back I was unable to do that either, because of the crowd of people. So I remained as I was, in perplexity, and only with great exertions did I manage to return. Some person told me that that bazar is much less crowded on Fridays, because [on that day] they close the Qaisariya and other bazars, so I rode [again] on the Friday and went to the cathedral mosque and the college.

This city is in the dominions of the sultan Uzbek, who is represented in it by a great amir called Qutludumur. It was he who built this college and the dependencies annexed to it. As for the mosque, it was built by his wife, the pious *khatun* Turabak. There is at Khorezm a hospital, which has a Syrian doctor called al-Sahyuni, after the town of Sahyun in Syria.

Never have I seen in all the lands of the world men more excellent in conduct than the Khorezmians, more generous in soul, or more friendly to strangers. They have a praiseworthy custom in regard to [the observance of] prayer services which I have not seen elsewhere, namely that each of the mu'azzins in their mosques goes round the houses of those persons neighbouring his mosque, giving them notice of the approaching hour of prayer. Any person who absents himself from the communal prayers is beaten by the imam [who leads the prayers] in the presence of the congregation, and in every mosque there is a whip hung up for this purpose. He is also fined five dinars, which go towards the expenses of upkeep of the mosque, or of supplying food to the poor and the destitute. They say that this custom has been an uninterrupted tradition amongst them from ancient times.

Outside Khorezm is the river Jayhun, one of the four rivers which [flow] from Paradise. It freezes over in the cold season in the same way as the river Itil freezes over, and people walk upon it. It remains frozen for the space of five months, and often they walk over it when it is beginning to melt and perish in consequence. It is navigable for ships in summer time as far as Tirmidh, from which they import wheat and barley, the journey downstream taking ten days....

Account of the melons of Khorezm. The melons of Khorezm have no equal in any country of the world, East or West, except it may be the melons of Bukhara, and next to them are the melons of Isfahan. Their rind is green, and the flesh is red, of extreme sweetness and firm texture. A remarkable thing is that they are cut into strips, dried in the sun, and packed in reed baskets, as is done in our country with dried figs and Malaga figs. They are exported from Khorezm to the remotest parts of India and China, and of all the dried fruits there are none which excel them in sweetness. During my stay at Dihli in India, whenever a party of travellers arrived, I used to send someone to buy sliced melon for me from them. The king of India, too, when any of it was brought to him, used to send it to me, knowing as he did my fondness for it. It was his way to give pleasure to the foreigners by sending to them the fruit of their own countries, and he used to give special attention to learning their desires and supplying them accordingly.

Part 4 | Timur and the Timurids

INTRODUCTION

In the middle of the fourteenth century, the Chaghatayids remained a significant power in Moghulistan but their influence had waned in the western stretches of the *ulus*. In Transoxiana political authority had gradually, and temporarily, shifted from the Chaghatayid Mongols to local Turkic Muslim tribal leaders. The first of the Turkic tribal nobility to usurp power from the Mongols was Amir Qazaghan (r. 1346–58) of the Qara'una. In 1346, Amir Qazaghan led a substantial force of Turkic manpower to occupy the Chaghatay Mongols' western capital of Qarshi, following which he executed his Chaghatay suzerain Qazan Khan (r. 1343–46) and placed a Chinggisid puppet on the throne. In 1351, Amir Qazaghan annexed Herat and appeared to be a new rising star in the eastern Islamic world. His reign was cut short, however, when the son of the former amir of the Qara'unas sought vengeance and killed him. For the next two decades, the political climate of Islamic Central Asia descended into near chaos as the Turkic nobility vied for power and territory among themselves and with the Chaghatay khans of Moghulistan, who several times invaded the region.

One of these Turkic nobles was Timur, a member of one of the more important families of the Barlas tribe. While historical records indicate that the Barlas (or Barulas) had been participants in the early Mongol invasion of Central Asia, over the course of the thirteenth century they had become a fully Turkic tribe dominant in the Central Asian region around the small city of Shahr-i Sabz, historically known as Kish, south of Samarqand. In the 1360s, Timur, also known as Timur-i Lang (Timur the Lame) because he walked with a limp due to a wound he received in his youth, managed to navigate this tumultuous political environment with Machiavellian skill to emerge first as the leader, or amir, of the Barlas tribe, and then the dominant power in all of Central Asia.

In 1370, Timur led an invasion of Balkh and overthrew his primary rival, Amir Husayn of the Qara'unas tribe. With that, Timur became the greatest of the Chaghatay amirs. As political legitimacy remained thoroughly entrenched in the Chinggisid lineage, Timur never reached beyond the title of amir to claim to rule as a khan. Rather, he appointed a puppet Chinggisid to legitimize his rule and further enhanced his prestige through marriage into the Mongol royal family, thereby adding to amir the relational title of *güregen,* or son-in-law. With that, Timur had effectively assumed authority over the western Chaghatay Khanate, and he began to establish his new capital at Samarqand.

Timur was rarely present at his capital to appreciate his grandiose monumental architecture and bazaars, bursting with people and merchandise from across Asia. Over the next thirty-five years, Timur's nearly incessant campaigning took him into the Qïpchaq Steppe, Moghulistan, India, Afghanistan, Persia, the Middle East, the Caucasus, and even Anatolia. Accounts describe the devastation Timur unleashed upon those whom he defeated as horrific, even when measured against the Mongol conquests. This was compounded by Timur's inability to maintain a firm hold over the conquered regions, which necessitated that he invade some locations—notably Khorezm, the Qïpchaq Steppe, Persia, and Moghulistan—on multiple occasions.

Timur's armies proved to be an incredibly destructive force, but trade flourished where there was peace. Thus, while Ibn 'Arabshah notes that Timur's campaigns against Toqtamïsh in the Qïpchaq Steppe devastated the main urban centers in the territory of the Golden Horde, this appears to have increased the commercial value of Timur's own urban centers to the south, especially his capital of Samarqand. Shortly after Timur defeated the Ottoman Sultan Bayazid (r. 1389–1402) at the battle of Ankara in 1402, the Spanish ambassador Ruy Gonzáles de Clavijo traveled to Samarqand for an audience with the infamous conqueror. Gonzáles's account describes Samarqand as the glimmering capital of Central Asia at the peak of its glory. The image Gonzáles presents contrasts harshly with those of other travelers who passed through the region just a few centuries later and characterize Samarqand as a much smaller and somewhat dilapidated city. One is left to ponder the extent to which this altered condition should be attributed to a regional "decline," or a natural correction following Timur's deliberate effort to inflate the city's population and commercial importance.

In 1405, when Timur was nearly seventy years old, he set out on what was to be his greatest campaign: the conquest of Ming China. The campaign never reached Chinese territory, as the terrible conqueror fell ill and died in his own frontier town of Otrar. After several years of civil war, the mantle passed to Timur's son Shahrukh (r. 1409–47), who transferred his capital to Herat and appointed his son Ulughbeg to serve as governor of Samarqand. The Timurids maintained a firm hold over Islamic Central Asia, Afghanistan, and Persia through Shahrukh's lengthy reign, although much of Persia slipped from their hands thereafter, especially following the untimely demise in 1449 of Shahrukh's son and heir, the "astronomer-king" Ulughbeg.

While Timur's descendants may have been less dynamic conquerors than their progenitor, they far surpassed him in other respects. First, patronage of the arts and sciences came to be considered as a defining feature of Timurid imperial high culture, and the cumulative effect of their sustained effort was to spark a period of cultural efflorescence that historians have come to refer to as the Timurid Renaissance. For centuries to come, the Timurid model of governance informed notions of political legitimacy in Uzbek Central Asia, Mughal India, Safavid Iran, and the Ottoman Middle East. This "renaissance" was exemplified in late fifteenth-century Herat, where the Timurid ruler Sultan Husayn Bayqara (r. 1469–1506) patronized such luminous figures as the poet and religious scholar

'Abd al-Rahman Jami (1414–92), the celebrated painter Kamal al-Din Bihzad (d. 1537), and the Chaghatay-language poet, recognized as the founder of the modern Uzbek language, Mir 'Ali Shir Nava'i (1441–1501).

Another defining feature of the Timurid era in Islamic Central Asia was the rise to a profoundly elevated social importance of the Naqshbandi Sufi *tariqa* in general, and several specific Sufi families in particular. This is partly attributable to the Naqshbandiya's emphasis on upholding the *shar'ia,* which earned Naqshbandi Sufis wide respect, and also to the Naqshbandiya's doctrinal support for "solitude within society," which enabled adherents to pursue their spiritual goals while remaining engaged in wider society. In considering the rise of particular Sufi families in Timurid Central Asia, one finds that that some Sufis shared a decidedly symbiotic relationship with the Timurid rulers. The Timurids found pious and influential Sufis to be an effective tool in reinforcing their legitimacy in a Perso-Islamic context. The Timurids therefore embraced the emerging Sufi leadership, and in exchange the Sufis publicly branded them the legitimate rulers of Islamic Central Asia.

In the fifteenth century, by far the most successful of these dynastic families were the Ahraris, a Sufi lineage which rose in power and prestige under the inspired leadership of Khoja 'Ubaydallah Ahrar (1404–90). As a young man, Ahrar moved from Tashkent to Samarqand for his education and, later, relocated there permanently to begin his own religious college. His ability and charisma attracted students, and his reputation brought him prestige in the political arena as well. During much of his long life Khoja Ahrar exerted considerable influence at the Timurid courts of Samarqand and Herat. His popularity and proximity to court proved beneficial, and over time his family supervised *waqf*s (religious endowments) that included thousands of acres of farmland, numerous villages, urban property, and a wide variety of other holdings across the region. From the fifteenth century, the Ahrari Khojas were in command of an extensive and extremely influential religious, political, and economic network that emanated from the Ahrari shrine in Samarqand.

The state that Timur carved out for himself and his heirs represents the last great nomadic empire and a period of remarkable efflorescence for Islamic Central Asia. Like the Mongols before him, Timur's military success rested upon his access to, and expert use of, pastoral-nomadic tribesmen whose mobility, equestrian mastery, and archery skills equipped them with a decided advantage over the standing armies of sedentary states. However, from the early decades of the sixteenth century, in the contest between nomadic and agricultural states the military advantage would shift, permanently, to favor the infantry armies of agricultural states. This process had begun centuries earlier with the invention of gunpowder weapons. The balance eventually tipped following their gradual improvement, which led to their mass production and successful incorporation into revolutionary new military strategies that ultimately undermined the age-old nomadic advantage.

The Timurid state in Central Asia and eastern Persia lasted to the beginning of the sixteenth century, when a conquering force of invading Uzbek tribesmen supplanted the final Timurids. This represents the end of the Timurid interregnum and the return of Chinggisid authority to the region, as it was a Chinggisid (more precisely a Jochid), Muhammad Shïbani Khan (r. 1500–1512), who led the Uzbeks to victory in Central Asia. However, both within Central Asia and elsewhere, the Timurid legacy would long outlast the dynasty's expulsion.

A | *Timur's Rise and Rule*

28 Ibn 'Arabshah: Timur and His Steppe Campaigns

INTRODUCTION

Ahmed ibn 'Arabshah (1392–1450) was born in Damascus, a magnificent city that had flourished as capital of the Dar al-Islam during the Umayyad Caliphate (661–750) and, at the time of Ibn 'Arabshah's birth, had enjoyed nearly a century and a half of peace and prosperity under the Mamluks. But while Ibn 'Arabshah was just a boy, Timur invaded Syria and laid Damascus to waste. The great Umayyad mosque burned to the ground, and the city was emptied of people and wealth. Young Ahmed ibn 'Arabshah and his family were among those that Timur had taken into captivity and marched to Samarqand. Ibn 'Arabshah eventually returned to the Middle East, where he earned a reputation as a respected hadith scholar and author of numerous works in Persian and Turkish. But he is best known for his Arabic-language biography of Timur, the 'Ajay'ib al-maqdur fi nawa'ib Timur, excerpted here from Sanders's English translation.

Readers of Ibn 'Arabshah's history encounter almost repetitive descriptions of Timur's widespread destruction and reports of astounding numbers of people killed in horrific ways. The author clearly has a bias. One must note, however, that Ibn 'Arabshah's account is corroborated by contemporary sources, including Timur's own court history. So while Ibn 'Arabshah certainly does not shy away from distasteful subject matter in his description of Timur's reign, his account should not be dismissed as hyperbolic overstatement—it is, in fact, generally reliable.

Ibn 'Arabshah's account is a valuable source for the several wars that Timur fought against Toqtamïsh, the Chinggisid ruler of the Qïpchaq Khanate (Golden Horde) whose installation Timur had earlier engineered. Having tired of his young protégé's duplicity, Timur resolved to settle the matter permanently. While Timur was with his army in Azerbaijan, Toqtamïsh made an aggressive move in the north Caucasus and Timur pounced. In late 1394, he crossed the Caucasus and pursued his rival, leaving a trail of destruction in his wake. In addition to demolishing the trading towns of the northern Caucasus, Timur ordered his army to lay waste to the Italian trading enclaves on the north coast of the Black Sea, evacuating the Muslim inhabitants and killing or enslaving the Christians. Timur and his forces then moved on and burned Astrakhan, a great commercial city at the mouth of the Volga River known at the time as Haji Tarkhan, and then reduced Saray, the Mongol capital on the lower Volga, to rubble. Several years later, in 1409–10, Ibn 'Arabshah traveled through the region and personally witnessed the devastation. Historians have connected this to the ultimate decline of the Golden Horde as a cohesive political force, a factor that contributed to the rise of Moscovy several decades later.

Of His Origins

His name was Timur; it is pronounced in this way and so also the form of the name implies; but foreign words are turned in a circle like a ball by the sporting cudgel of the Arabic tongue and revolve at pleasure in the field of speech; so they say sometimes Tamur, sometimes Tamarlang—which is not wrong; and *Tamar* in Turkish means iron, but *lang* means lame.

He was the son of Taragai, son of Abgai. The birthplace of this deceiver was a village of a lord named Ilgar in the territory of Kesh—may Allah remove him from the garden of Paradise! And Kesh is one of the cities of Transoxiana, about two days distant from Samarqand.

They say that on the night on which he was born something like a helmet appeared, seemed to flutter in the air, then fell into the middle of the plain and finally was scattered over the ground; thence also live coals flew about like glowing ashes and collected so that they filled the plain and the city: they also say that when that evil man saw the light, his palms were full of freshly shed blood.

They consulted the augurs and diviners about these portents and referred to seers and soothsayers about their meaning, of whom some replied that he would be a guardsman; others that he would grow up a brigand, while others said a blood-thirsty butcher, others finally that he would be an executioner, these opinions contending with each other, until events decided the issue. . . .

He and his fathers were shepherds, belonging to a mixed horde, lacking either reason or religion; others say that both belonged to a tribe accustomed to travel hither and thither, and courageous, who lived in Transoxiana and wintered within its borders. Others again say that his father was a poor smith, but that he himself from his youth excelled in keenness of intellect and strength; but because of poverty began to commit acts of brigandage and in the course of these exploits was wounded and mutilated; for when he wanted to carry off a sheep, which he had stolen one night, the shepherd cleft his shoulder with an arrow and maimed it, and shooting a second arrow at his hip, damaged the hip. So mutilation was added to his poverty and a blemish to his wickedness and fury, with which he went about with his hand against every man. . . .

Timur Returns from Diar-Bakr and Iraq, and Turns toward the Deserts of Qïpchaq

Then he [Timur] returned from Arabian and Persian Iraq, in which countries he had already firmly planted his footmark, and that after Shaykh Ibrahim [Shirvani] had come over to him and handed to him the keys of his dominions, who placing on his neck the yoke of his servitude and transferring himself to his sway, put himself among his slaves, but was treated by him like a son; soon, however, we shall relate how he went to him and in what way he gained his favour.

Then Timur made for the desert of Qïpchaq with great eagerness and haste.

This great kingdom contains vast deserts, whose Sultan was Toqtamïsh, the same who was the leader of the Sultans who fought against Timur, indeed the first who showed hostility to him, and met him in the regions of Turkestan and came against him and joined battle and there Said Barka overcame him as was told before.

The country is called Dasht-i Qïpchaq and Dasht Barka, and "Dasht" in the Persian language is the word for desert, and the special name of it Barka (namely Berke, son of Jochi, grandson of Chinggis Khan) who was the first Sultan, who after embracing Islam unfolded its standards through that country; for they were worshippers of idols and given to polytheism, ignorant of Islam and the true faith and the most of them have remained idolaters to this day.

He set out for these regions by way of Derbend, which was under the sway of Shaykh Ibrahim, Sultan of the Kingdom of Shirvan, whose family goes back to King Khosrow Anushirvan; and he had a *qazi* by name Abu Yazid, who of all the pillars of the state was in close touch with him, and this Yazid was a minister of the kingdom and the first in the sultanate; and when he consulted him about the matter of Timur and the action required of himself—whether he should submit to him or make preparations against him, whether he should take to flight or engage with him—Yazid replied, "In my opinion it is best to fly, and I think the safest and finest plan is to fortify yourself in the highest mountains."

The Sultan, however, said, "This does not seem to me well advised, that I should escape, but desert my subjects in time of danger, and what should I reply to Allah on the day of resurrection when I have directed their affairs and destroyed my subjects? Therefore I do not choose to attack him or engage with him, but as quickly as may be I shall hasten to him and make myself compliant to him, obeying his command, but if he restores me to my throne and confirms me in my kingdom, that is the very thing which I wish and the culmination of my prayers; but if he treats me ill or removes me from my province or throws me into bondage or kills me, at least my subjects will be defended from the evil of slaughter and rapine and captivity, and he will then set over them and over the kingdom whom he wishes."

Then he ordered that supplies should be collected and gave leave to the soldiers, who scattered and withdrew, and ordered that the cities of his territories should be decorated and beautified and that their inhabitants should carry on their work secure by land and sea and devote themselves to it and that orators should recite his name from platforms and that gold and silver money should be marked with his name and sign.

Then taking gifts and presents he started to meet him with good will and firm foot. And when he came near to him and stood in obeisance before him, he offered the gifts and presents and various rare and choice things. Now the custom of the Chaghatays in offering gifts of homage was to give nine of whatever kind, that in this way they might gain honours and higher dignity with the receiver; therefore Shaykh Ibrahim offered nine of every sort of various gifts, but of slaves eight; but when the men who received those gifts said to him, "Where is the ninth slave?" he replied, "I myself am the ninth," and Timur admired this saying, by which he won a place in his heart, and said to him, "Nay, you shall be my son and my deputy in this country and the support on which I shall lean," and he clad him in a precious mantle and restored him to his kingdom glad that he had gained his wish. And the supplies were divided and the fruits and foods distributed, out of which parts like mountains were left over by that army, which was itself in number like gravel and sand.

Then after dismissing Shaykh Ibrahim, Timur set out to the countries of the north and of the Tatars. But the other reason of invading that kingdom, though he needed it not, was Amir Idaku,[1] who was one of the chief leaders of Toqtamïsh on the left wing, and one of the ministers employed to ward off disasters and a counsellor, whose tribe was called Qomkomat; for the Turks have different tribes and names—like the Arabs. . . .

Then Timur prepared with the greatest haste to win for himself Dasht Barka, which is the proper country of the Tatars, filled with cattle of different kinds and tribes of Turks; fortified on the borders, it has well-tilled parts and wide tracts, healthy in water and air; its people nomads; its soldiers expert archers, most eloquent of speech among the Turks, pure in disposition, of charming features and perfect in beauty; their women seem suns, their men full moons; the kings are heads, the great men like chests; neither falsehood has place with them nor fraud, nor does cunning obtain among them nor sycophancy; it is the custom among them to move from place to place securely on wagons, where they are placed beyond fear; their cities are few and their settlements far apart.

---

1. More correctly, Edigü: a commander for Toqtamïsh of the Noghay confederation who would later rise up against him and usurp authority over the Golden Horde.

Dasht is bounded on the south by the Caspian Sea, violent and dangerous, and the Black Sea, which turns thither from the countries of Rum, and these two seas almost touch each other, but that the Jirkas Mountains (Caucasus) put a space between them to prevent their joining. On the east it has for boundaries the Kingdoms of Khorezm, Otrar, and Sïghnaq and other countries and tracts extending to Turkestan and the countries of the Jatas, going up to the borders of the Sin (Chinese), under the sway of the Moghuls and Khatas. On the north is Abir and Shabir (Siberia) and wastes, deserts, and hills of sand like mountains; for how many deserts are there, where birds and beasts roam! And it is, like the favour of the great, an end which cannot be reached and a limit which cannot be attained; on the west it borders on Russia and Bulgharia and the country of the Christians, and its confines extend to the dominions of the son of 'Uthman, Ruler of Rum.

There used to advance convoys of travellers from Khorezm making the journey in wagons, securely without terror or fear, as far as the Crimea—a journey of about three months; in width there is a sea of sand as broad as seven seas, through which the most skilful guide could not show the way nor the most crafty of experienced men make the journey, and those convoys did not take supplies or fodder or join to themselves companions—this because of the multitude of the people, and the abundance of security, food, and drink among the inhabitants, and did not set out except tribe by tribe or turn aside except to one who would receive his guest generously, so that they were well described by that verse:

> All the people of Mecca go round the hill of Okaz
> And their sons shout: "There comes a guest!"

But now through those places from Khorezm to the Crimea of those peoples and their followers none moves or rests and nothing ranges there but antelopes and camels.

The capital of Dasht is Saray, a city devoted to Islam and beautifully built, which I shall describe. It was founded by Sultan Barka (on whom be the mercy of Allah!) when he became a Muslim, and he made it his capital and chose it and drove in and invited the people of Dasht so that they might enter the protection of Islam, which faith having been received, the place became a resort of all good and happiness and was called Barka having before been named after Qïpchaq. . . .

And when Barka Khan had been exalted by the royal garb of Islam and had raised the standards of the religion of Hanifa in the country of Dasht, he called learned men from every side and doctors, to teach the people the doctrines of their religion and show them the ways of their profession of the Unity of God and the truth of the Faith, and he paid great rewards to them and poured forth on those who assembled seas of generosity and brought reverence to the Faith and the teachers and magnified the laws of Allah Almighty and the institutes of the Prophet, and he had with him at that time and afterwards Uzbek and Janibek Khan, Mawlana Qutb al-Din, the learned, of the city of Rei, and Shaykh Sa'd al-Din Taftazani and Sa'id Jalal, Commentator of the Hajabia, and other doctors of the sects of Hanifis and Shafeites; afterwards these were followed by Mawlana Hafiz al-Din Bazazi and Mawlana Ahmed of Khojend, on whom be the favour of Allah!

And thanks to these famous men Saray became a meeting-place of learning and a home of every sort of prosperity, and in a short time there gathered there of learned men and doctors and the cultured and able, all the most excellent, eminent, brilliant, and charming, and never a great city and its suburbs held so many.

Between the building of Saray and its devastation there passed sixty-three years, and it was among the greatest cities in extent and abounding in population. . . .

That Flood Comes and Sweeps over the Peoples of Dasht after Breaking Toqtamïsh

Then Timur came into those parts with a great army, nay, a turbid sea, whose soldiers carried flying arrows, sharp swords, and quivering spears and were ravening lions and furious leopards, all of warlike spirit, which takes vengeance on the enemy, stoutly defends its own flag and its allies and homes and its prey and its lairs and covers with the sea of war him who opposes its waves and breakers.

Therefore Toqtamïsh sent to the lords of his subjects and the magnates of his peoples and the dwellers in sandy places and inhabitants of the borders and chiefs who were his kinsmen and leaders of the right and left of his army, whom he summoned and called to meet the enemy and wage war, and they came clad in the long robe of obedience and hastening from every high mountain; and there assembled hosts and tribes of horse and foot and swordsmen and javelin-throwers and archers and attackers and defenders and warriors and slayers with the sabre and skilled archers and wielders of spears, who would not miss the mark compared with the sons of Tual, skilled spearmen. When they take their weapon and aim at what they need, they strike the mark whether sitting or flying.

Then Toqtamïsh rose to fight, ready for onslaught and battle, with an army numerous like the sands and heavy like the mountains. . . .

But Timur's army was not wanting in these things, since what each one had to do was decided and explored, and where to fight and where to stand was inscribed on the front of its standards. Then both armies, when they came in sight one of the other, were kindled and mingling with each other, became hot with the fire of war, and they joined battle and necks were extended for sword-blows and throats outstretched for spear thrusts and faces were drawn with sternness and fouled with dust; the wolves of war set their teeth and fierce leopards mingled and charged and the lions of the armies rushed upon each other and men's skins bristled, clad with the feathers of arrows, and the brows of the leaders drooped and the heads of the heads [captains] bent in the devotion of war and fell forward, and the dust was thickened and stood black, and the leaders and common soldiers alike plunged into seas of blood and arrows became in the darkness of black dust like stars placed to destroy the Princes of Satan, while swords glittering like fulminating stars in clouds of dust rushed on kings and sultans, nor did the horses of death cease to pass through and revolve and race against the squadrons which charged straight ahead or the dust of hooves to be borne into the air or the blood of swords to flow over the plain, until the earth was rent and the heavens like the eight seas; and this struggle and conflict lasted about three days; then dust appeared from the stricken army of Toqtamïsh, who turned his back, and his armies took to flight, but the soldiers of Timur were sent hither and thither in the kingdoms of Dasht and were stationed there, whose tribes he subdued and subjected all without exception to his will and collected cattle which he distributed and gold and silver, which he stored, and took booty and divided it, and let his men despoil and make prisoners and gave leave to use force and violence and wiped out their tribes and overturned their forts and changed the whole condition and took away with him all he could of wealth, prisoners, and goods; and his vanguard reached right to Azaq and laid waste Saray, and Saraychuq and Haji-Tarkhan and those parts . . . then he set out towards his Samarqand.

29   Ibn Khaldun: Personal Narrative of a Meeting with Timur

INTRODUCTION

Ibn Khaldun (1332–1406) is one of the most famous intellectuals of the medieval world. While he was not as prolific as some of the other scholars referenced in this volume, his contributions have been no less influential. His masterpiece is the Muqaddima, *his "Introduction" to the* Kitab al-'Ibar *(History of the world). This brilliant work lays out Ibn Khaldun's philosophy of history, which argues that scholars must approach sources critically and assess their reliability through both careful evidentiary analysis and an assessment of how closely the information they hold conforms to the natural laws of human society. His argument that these natural laws are rational, ordered, and capable of being understood has led some to label Ibn Khaldun the father of sociology. It is in determining these natural laws that Ibn Khaldun formulated his theory of 'asabiyya, a nuanced understanding of group loyalty, or solidarity, and its cyclical political implications that, one might suggest, presaged some modern theories of nationalism.*

Ibn Khaldun was born in Tunis, just a few decades after Ibn Battuta. Like his older contemporary, Ibn Khaldun also received an excellent education in the Islamic sciences. After some years of travel he moved to Cairo, where the Mamluk Sultan Barquq (r. 1382–89, and again 1390–99) appointed him chief qazi of the Maliki school of law. For Ibn Khaldun the Mamluk sultan was a generous patron, but for Timur the Mamluks represented a threat that he needed to neutralize. Specific concerns included the Mamluk alliance with the Golden Horde and their policy of supporting hostile groups in his conquered territories.

On the eve of Timur's invasion in the winter of 1400–1401, the young Mamluk Sultan Faraj (r. 1399–1405), Barquq's son and successor, was present in Damascus

with a sizable Mamluk army. The two forces never met: Faraj received word of
a rebellion in Cairo and he rushed to suppress it before Timur arrived, leav-
ing Damascus poorly defended and Ibn Khaldun stranded inside. Assessing the
situation, Ibn Khaldun dispatched a message to Timur requesting an audience.
His primary goal in arranging this meeting was to secure safe passage to depart
for Cairo, but the richness of his account suggests that he was also interested in
learning more about the infamous conqueror. Timur approved the request, but the
cautious city defenders refused to open the gate for Ibn Khaldun to exit the city.
Ibn Khaldun did exit, but in a manner much less dignified than he had intended:
early one morning he climbed into a basket and was lowered from the city walls
to the ground below. He was then led to Timur's tent, and the two figures had the
first of several meetings held during the thirty-five days that Ibn Khaldun spent in
Timur's camp. The following is Ibn Khaldun's personal memoir of his meeting with
Timur.

When my name was announced, the title "Maghribi Malikite
Cadi" was added to it; he summoned me, and as I entered the audience tent to
(approach) him he was reclining on his elbow while platters of food were passing
before him which he was sending one after the other to groups of Mongols sitting
in circles in front of his tent.

Upon entering, I spoke first, saying, "Peace be upon you," and I made a gesture of humility. Thereupon he raised his head and stretched out his hand to me,
which I kissed. He made a sign to me to sit down; I did so just where I was, and
he summoned from his retinue one of the erudite Hanifite jurists of Khorezm,
'Abd al-Jabbar ibn al-Nu'man, whom he bade sit there also to serve as interpreter
between us.

He asked me from where in the Maghrib I had come, and why I had come.
I replied, "I left my country in order to perform the pilgrimage. I came to it (i.e.,
to Egypt) by sea and arrived at the port of Alexandria on the day of the breaking
of the Fast in the year 4 (and 80) of this seventh century, while festivities were (in
progress) within their walls because al-Zahir (Barquq) was sitting (in audience)
on the royal throne during these ten days by count."

Timur asked me, "What did al-Zahir do for you?" I replied, "He was generous
in giving recognition to my position; he accorded me hospitable entertainment
and supplied me with provisions for the pilgrimage. Then, when I returned, he allotted me a large stipend, and I remained under his shelter and favor—may Allah
grant him mercy and recompense him." . . .

Then he gave a signal to his servants to bring from his tent some of the kind of
food which they call "rishta" and which they were most expert in preparing. Some
dishes of it were brought in, and he made a sign that they should be set before me.
I arose, took them, and drank, and liked it, and this impressed him favorably.

I then sat down and we remained silent, for I was overcome with fear on account of the misfortune which had befallen Sadr al-Din al-Munawi, chief *qazi* of
the Shafiites; he had been taken prisoner at Shaqhab by those who pursued the

Egyptian army, and was brought back and imprisoned by them with a demand for ransom for him. Because of this fear I composed in my mind some words to say to him (Timur) which, by exalting him and his government, would flatter him.

Before this, when I was in the Maghrib, I had heard many predictions concerning his appearance. Astrologers who used to discuss the conjunction of the two superior planets were awaiting the tenth conjunction in the trigon, which was expected to occur in the year 66 of the seventh [sic, eighth] century. One day, in the year 761, I met in Fez in the Mosque of al-Qarawiyin the preacher of Constantine, Abu 'Ali ibn Badis, who was an authority on this subject. I asked him about this conjunction which was to occur, and its implications. He answered me, "It points to a powerful one who would arise in the northeast region of a desert people, tent dwellers, who will triumph over kingdoms, overturn governments, and become the masters of most of the inhabited world." I asked, "When is it due?" He said, "In the year 784; accounts of it will be widespread."

Ibn Zarzar, the Jewish physician and astrologer of Ibn Alfonso, king of the Franks, wrote to me similarly; also my teacher, the authority on metaphysics Muhammad ibn Ibrahim al-Abili—may Allah have mercy on him,—said to me whenever I conversed with him or questioned him about it, "This event is approaching, and if you live, you will surely witness it."

We used to hear that the Sufis in the Maghrib also were expecting this occurrence. They believed, however, that the agent of this event would be the Fatimid to whom the prophetic traditions of the Shi'a and others refer. Yahya ibn 'Abdallah, grandson of Shaykh Abu Ya'qub al-Badisi, foremost among the saints of the Maghrib, told me that the shaykh had said to them one day as he came from morning prayer, "Today the Fatimid agent was born." That was in the fourth decade of the eighth century.

Because of all this I, too, had been watching for the event; so now, on account of my fears, it occurred to me to tell him something of it by which he would be diverted and might become kindly disposed toward me.

So I began by saying, "May Allah aid you—today it is thirty or forty years that I have longed to meet you." The interpreter 'Abd al-Jabbar, asked, "And what is the reason for this?"

I replied, "Two things: the first is that you are the sultan of the universe and the ruler of the world, and I do not believe that there has appeared among men from Adam until this epoch a ruler like you. I am not one of those who speak about matters by conjecture, for I am a scholar and I will explain this, and say: Sovereignty exists only because of group loyalty ('asabiyya), and the greater the number in the group, the greater is the extent of sovereignty. Scholars, first and last, have agreed that most of the peoples of the human race are of two groups, the Arabs and the Turks. You know how the power of the Arabs was established when they became united in their religion in following their Prophet. As for the Turks, their contest with the kings of Persia and the seizure of Khurasan from the hands of Afrasiyab is evidence of their origin from royalty; and in their group loyalty no king on earth can be compared with them, no Chosroes nor Caesar nor Alexander nor Nebuchadnezzar. Chosroes was the head of the Persians and their king, but what a difference between the Persians and the Turks! Caesar and Alexander were kings of the Greeks, and again what a difference between the Greeks and the Turks! As for Nebuchadnezzar, he was the head of the Babylonians and Nabateans, but what a difference between these and the Turks! This constitutes a clear proof of what I have maintained concerning this king (Timur).

"The second reason which has led me to desire to meet him is concerned with what the prognosticators and the Muslim saints in the Maghrib used to tell," and I mentioned what I have related above.

He then said to me, "I see that you have mentioned Nebuchadnezzar together with Chosroes and Caesar and Alexander, although he was not of their class; they were great kings, while he was only one of the Persian generals, just as I myself am only the representative of the sovereign of the throne. (As for the king himself,) here he is"—and he made a gesture toward the row (of men) standing behind him, among whom the one he meant had also been (standing). This was his stepson, whose mother . . . he had married after the death of his (the boy's) father, Satilmish. But he did not find him there, and those who were standing in that row explained that he had gone out. . . .

The news was brought to him that the gate of the city had been opened and the judges had gone out to fulfill their (promise of) surrender, for which, so they thought, he had generously granted them amnesty.

Then he was carried away from before us, because of the trouble with his knee, and was placed upon his horse; grasping the reins, he sat upright in his saddle while the bands played around him until the air shook with them; he rode toward Damascus and was left at the tomb of Manjak, near the Jabiya Gate.

There he sat in audience, and the judges and the notables of the city entered to him, and I entered among them. He then gave a signal to them that they should depart, and to Shah Malik, his viceroy, that he should give them robes of honor (confirming them) in their official positions, but to me he signaled to be seated, so I took a position in front of him.

He then summoned the emirs of his government who were in charge of building matters; they brought in the foremen of construction, the engineers, and discussed whether by leading off the water which flows round in the moat of the Citadel they could by this operation discover his ingress. They discussed this for a long time in his council, then left.

I, too, left for my home inside the city, after having asked and received permission to do so. I remained shut up at home, and began to work on the description of the Maghrib, as he had requested of me. I wrote it within a few days, and when I presented it to him he took it from my hands and ordered his secretary to have it translated into Mongolian.

Then he pressed the siege of the Citadel in earnest; he erected against it catapults, naphtha guns, ballistas, and breachers, and within a few days sixty catapults and other similar engines were set up. The siege pressed ever harder upon those within the Citadel, and its structure was destroyed on all sides. Therefore the men (defending it), among them a number of those who had been in the service of the Sultan, and those whom he had left behind, asked for peace. Timur granted them amnesty, and after they were brought before him the Citadel was destroyed and its vestiges completely effaced.

From the inhabitants of the town he confiscated under torture hundred-weights of money, which he seized after having taken all the property, mounts, and tents which the ruler of Egypt had left behind. Then he gave permission for the plunder of the houses of the people of the city, and they were despoiled of all their furniture and goods. The furnishings and utensils of no value which remained were set on fire, and the fire spread to the walls of the houses, which were supported on timbers. It continued to burn until it reached the Great [Umayyad] Mosque; the flames mounted to its roof, melting the lead in it, and the ceiling and walls collapsed. This was an absolutely dastardly and abominable deed, but the changes in affairs are in the hands of Allah—he does with his creatures as he wishes, and decides in his kingdom as he wills. . . .

Extract from the Report that Ibn Khaldun Submitted to His Mamluk Patron in Egypt

"This king Timur is one of the greatest and mightiest of kings. Some attribute to him knowledge, others attribute to him heresy because they note his preference for the 'members of the House' (of 'Ali); still others attribute to him the employment of magic and sorcery, but in all this there is nothing; it is simply that he is highly intelligent and very perspicacious, addicted to debate and argumentation about what he knows and also about what he does not know.

"He is between sixty and seventy years old. His right knee is lame from an arrow which struck him while raiding in his boyhood, as he told me; therefore he dragged it when he went on short walks, but when he would go long distances men carried him with their hands. He is one who is favored by Allah—the power is Allah's, and he grants it to whom he chooses of his creatures."

30   Ruy González de Clavijo: A Spanish Embassy to Timur's Capital

INTRODUCTION

Following his campaigns against Toqtamïsh in the steppe (1394–96), which Ibn 'Arabshah has described above, Timur returned his attention to Persia. While he was extending his control further to the west, a dispute broke out with the talented and charismatic Ottoman Sultan Bayazid (r. 1389–1402). Pointing to Bayazid's (highly effective) policy of employing Christian troops from his European territories to pacify Muslim subjects in Anatolia, Timur accused his Ottoman neighbor of contravening Islamic law. With this as his justification, in the summer of 1402, Timur invaded Anatolia and confronted an enormous Ottoman force at the battle of Ankara. At least partly because Timur promised the Turkish nobility greater independence, many Turkish beys abandoned their Ottoman suzerain. In the end, the Ottoman army was soundly defeated, Anatolia was pillaged, and Bayazid died in captivity a few months later.

The Spanish King Henry III of Castile-León (r. 1390–1406) had two ambassadors at Sultan Bayazid's court who were witness to Timur's victory at Ankara. These ambassadors reported that the Central Asian conqueror treated them well, and, not long after they returned to Spain, King Henry appointed Ruy González de Clavijo, a native of Madrid, his ambassador to Timur's court at Samarqand. On May 22, 1403, Clavijo and his entourage began what would be a nearly three-year journey to Samarqand and back.

What follows is Clavijo's description of Samarqand at the peak of its glory—a magnificent city, ornamented with beautiful and grandiose architecture, that had developed into an international entrepôt overflowing with people and all sorts of exotic merchandise from across Asia. Thus, while Timur's campaigns against the Qïpchaq Khanate dealt a crushing blow to the trans-Eurasian trade routes of the north, Clavijo's account suggests that they also brought commercial traffic and immeasurable value to his own commercial centers in the south. At the beginning of the fifteenth century, nobody in Europe or Asia doubted the "centrality" of Timurid Central Asia.

Every year to the city of Samarqand much merchandise of all kinds came from Cathay, India, Tartary, and from many other quarters besides, for in the countries round the Samarqand territory commerce is very flourishing; but there was as yet no place within the city where this merchandise might be suitably stored, displayed, and offered for sale. Timur therefore now gave orders that a street should be built to pass right through Samarqand, which should have shops opened on either side of it in which every kind of merchandise should be sold, and this new street was to go from one side of the city through to the other side, traversing the heart of the township. The accomplishment of his order he laid on two of the great lords of his court, letting them know at the same time that if they failed in diligence, for the work was to go on continuously by day as by night, their heads would pay the penalty. These nobles therefore began at speed, causing all the houses to be thrown down along the line that his Highness had indicated for the passage of the new street. No heed was paid to the complaint of persons to whom the property here might belong, and those whose houses thus were demolished suddenly had to quit with no warning, carrying away with them their goods and chattels as best they might.

No sooner had all the houses been thrown down than the master builders came and laid out the broad new street, erecting shops on the one side and opposite, placing before each a high stone bench that was topped with white slabs. Each shop had two chambers, front and back, and the street way was arched over with a domed roof in which were windows to let the light through. As soon as these shops were made ready, forthwith they were occupied by merchants selling goods of all sorts: and at intervals down the street were erected water fountains. The cost of all this work was charged to the town council, and workmen did not lack, as many coming forward as were wanted by the overseers. The masons who worked through the day at nightfall went home, their places being taken by as many as had gone, who worked throughout the night hours. Some would be pulling down the houses while others laid out the roadway, others again building anew, and the tumult was such day and night that it seemed all the devils of hell were at work here. Thus in the course of twenty days the whole new street was carried through: a wonder indeed to behold; but those whose houses had been thus demolished had good cause to complain.

Yet scarcely did they dare bring their case before his Highness: then however at last coming together they betook themselves for help to certain Sayyids, and these are the privileged favourites and courtiers of Timur who can talk as they please with him being, as is reputed the descendants of their Prophet Mahomet. These undertook the case, and one day therefore when certain of them were playing at chess with his Highness, they ventured to tell him that since he of his good will had ordered all the houses belonging to those poor people to be laid low, it were but right they should receive compensation for the lands this roadway passed through. It is reported that on hearing this Timur waxed wrathful, declaring that all the land of the city of Samarqand was his private property, for that he had bought the same with his own moneys, further that he had the title deeds in his possession, and indeed he would produce them for inspection on the morrow; adding that if aught had been wrongly taken he would compensate for the same forthwith. He spoke this with such command of his rights that those Sayyids were completely abashed. They were now but too thankful that the order had not been given for them all to lose their heads. Having thus fortunately escaped scathless, their answer to Timur was that whatsoever his Highness did must indeed be good, and that all he ordered should be carried into effect.

The Mosque which Timur had caused to be built in memory of the mother of his wife the Great Khanïm seemed to us the noblest of all those we visited in the city of Samarqand, but no sooner had it been completed than he began to find fault with its entrance gateway, which he now said was much too low and must forthwith be pulled down. Then the workmen began to dig pits to lay the new foundations, when in order that the piers might be rapidly rebuilt his Highness gave out that he himself would take charge to direct the labour for the one pier of the new gateway while he laid it on two of the lords of his court, his special favourites, to see to the foundations on the other part. Thus all should see whether it was he or those other two lords who first might bring this business to its proper conclusion. Now at this season Timur was already weak in health, he could no longer stand for long on his feet, or mount his horse, having always to be carried in a litter. It was therefore in his litter that every morning he had himself brought to the place, and he would stay there the best part of the day urging on the work. He would arrange for much meat to be cooked and brought, and then he would order them to throw portions of the same down to the workmen in the foundations, as though one should cast bones to dogs in a pit, and a wonder to all he even with his own hands did this. Thus he urged on their labour: and at times would have coins thrown to the masons when especially they worked to his satisfaction. Thus the building went on day and night until at last a time came when it had perforce to stop—as was also the case in the matter of making the street [for the new bazar]—on account of the winter snows which began now constantly to fall. . . .

Now therefore that I have narrated in detail all that befell us during our stay in Samarqand, I must describe that city for you, telling of all that is there to be seen in and round and about, and of all that Timur has accomplished there to embellish his capital. Samarqand stands in a plain, and is surrounded by a rampart or wall of earth, with a very deep ditch. The city itself is rather larger than Seville, but lying outside Samarqand are great numbers of houses which form extensive suburbs. These lie spread on all hands for indeed the township is surrounded by orchards and vineyards, extending in some cases to a league and a half or even two leagues beyond Samarqand, which stands in their centre. In between these orchards pass streets with open squares; these all are densely populated, and here all kinds of goods are on sale with bread stuffs and meat. Thus it is that the population without the city is more numerous than the population within the walls. Among these orchards outside Samarqand are found the most noble and beautiful houses, and here Timur has his many palaces and pleasure grounds. Round and about the great men of the government also here have their estates and country houses, each standing within its orchard: and so numerous are these gardens and vineyards surrounding Samarqand that a traveller who approaches the city sees only a great mountainous height of trees and the houses embowered among them remain invisible. Through the streets of Samarqand, as through its gardens outside and inside, pass many water-conduits, and in these gardens are the melon-beds and cotton-growing lands.

The melons of this countryside are abundant and very good, and at the season of Christmas there are so many melons and grapes to be had that it is indeed marvellous. Every day camels bring in their loads of melons from the country and it is a wonder how many are sold and eaten in the market. At all the outlying villages the melons being so abundant, at one season the people cure them, drying the same as is done with figs, which thus can be kept for use from one year's end to the next. The melons are cured after this fashion. They slice the fruit up into great pieces, removing the rind, when they are put to shrivel in the sun. As soon as these pieces are quite dry, they bind them one with the other, storing them in hampers and thus they keep good for a whole twelvemonth. Beyond the suburbs of Samarqand stretch the great plains where are situated many hamlets, these being all well populated, for here the immigrant folk are settled whom Timur has caused to be brought hither from all the foreign lands that he has conquered. The soil of the whole province of Samarqand is most fertile, producing great crops of wheat. There are abundant fruit-trees also with rich vineyards: the livestock is magnificent, beasts and poultry all of a fine breed. The sheep are famous for having those fat tails that weigh each some twenty pounds, in fact as much as a man can readily hold in the hand: and of these sheep the flocks are so abundant that even when Timur is in camp here with his armies, [and there is a scarcity] a couple of sheep can be had in the market for the price of a ducat [which is about six shillings]. The prices indeed are so low that for a Meri, which is a coin worth [about three pence] or half a real, you may have a bushel and a half of barley. Baked bread is everywhere plentiful, and rice can be had cheap in any quantity.

The richness and abundance of this great capital and its district is such as is indeed a wonder to behold: and it is for this reason that it bears the name of Samarqand: for this name would be more exactly written Semiz-kent, two words which signify "Rich-Town," for *Semiz* [in Turkish] is fat or rich and *Kent* means city or township: in time these two words having been corrupted into the name Samarqand. Further this land of Samarqand is not alone rich in food stuffs but also in manufactures, such as factories of silk both the kinds called Zaytumi and Kincobs, also crapes, taffetas, and the stuffs we call Tercenals in Spain, which are all produced here in great numbers. Further they make up special fur linings for silk garments, and manufacture stuffs in gold and blue with other colours of diverse tints dyed, and besides all these kinds of stuffs there are the spiceries. Thus trade has always been fostered by Timur with the view of making his capital the noblest of cities: and during all his conquests wheresoever he came he carried off the best men of the population to people Samarqand, bringing thither together the master-craftsmen of all nations. Thus from Damascus he carried away with him all the weavers of that city, those who worked at the silk looms. Further the bow-makers who produce those cross-bows which are so famous: likewise armourers: also the craftsmen in glass and porcelain, who are known to be the best in all the world. From Turkey he had brought their gun-smiths who make the arquebus, and all men of other crafts wheresoever he found them, such as the silver-smiths and the masons. These all were in very great numbers, indeed so many had been brought together of craftsmen of all sorts that of every denomination and kind you might find many master-workmen established in the capital. Again he had gathered to settle here in Samarqand artillery men, both engineers and bombardiers, besides those who make the ropes by which these engines work. Lastly hemp and flax had been sown and grown for the purpose in the Samarqand lands, where never before this crop had been cultivated.

So great therefore was the population now of all nationalities gathered together in Samarqand that of men with their families the number they said must amount to 150,000 souls. Of the nations brought here together there were to be seen Turks, Arabs, and Moors of diverse sects, with Christians who were Greeks and Armenians, Catholics, Jacobites, and Nestorians, besides those [Indian] folk who baptize with fire in the forehead, who are indeed Christians but of a faith that is peculiar to their nation. The population of Samarqand was so vast that lodging for them all could not be found in the city limits, nor in the streets and open spaces of the suburbs and villages outside, and hence they were to be found quartered temporarily for lodgment even in the caves and in tents under the trees of the gardens, which was a matter very wonderful to see. The markets of Samarqand further are amply stored with merchandise imported from distant and foreign countries. From Russia and Tartary come leathers and linens, from Cathay silk stuffs that are the finest in the whole world, and of these the best are those that are plain without embroideries. Thence too is brought musk, which is found in no other land but Cathay, with balas rubies and diamonds, which are more frequently to be met with in those parts than elsewhere, also pearls, lastly rhubarb with many other spiceries. The goods that are imported to Samarqand from Cathay indeed are of the richest, and most precious of all those brought thither from foreign parts, for the craftsmen of Cathay are reputed to be the most skilful by far beyond those of any other nation; and the saying is that they alone have two eyes, that the Franks indeed may have one, while the Muslims are but a blind folk. Thus the Franks and the Chinese in what they make have in the matter of eyes the advantage over the people of all other nationalities.

From India there are brought to Samarqand the lesser spiceries, which indeed are the most costly of the kind, such as nutmegs and cloves and mace with cinnamon both in the flower and as bark, with ginger and manna: all these with many other kinds that are never to be found in the markets of Alexandria. Throughout the city of Samarqand there are open squares where butchers' meat ready cooked, roasted or in stews, is sold, with fowls and game suitably prepared for eating, also bread and excellent fruit both are on sale. All these viands and victuals are there set out in a decent cleanly manner, namely in all those squares and open spaces of the town, and their traffic goes on all day and even all through the night time. Butchers' shops are numerous, also those booths where fowls, pheasants, and partridges are on sale: and these shops are kept open by night as by day. On the one part of Samarqand stands the Castle, which is not built on a height, but is protected by deep ravines on all its sides: and through these water flows which makes the position of the Castle impregnable. It is here that his Highness keeps his treasure, and none from the city without may enter save the governor of the Castle and his men. Within its walls however Timur holds in durance and captivity upwards of a thousand workmen; these labour at making plate-armour and helms, with bows and arrows, and to this business they are kept at work throughout the whole of their time in the service of his Highness.

Some [seven] years gone by, when Timur last left Samarqand and set forth on that campaign whereby he conquered Turkey and plundered Damascus, he gave orders that all the troops who should accompany him might carry along on the march their wives and children, unless indeed by preference any man might wish to leave his household behind at home, in which case he should do so. This order Timur had given because it was then of his intention to remain abroad from his capital for seven whole years, while he should conquer all his enemies: and he had sworn an oath that he would not re-enter this castle of his in Samarqand until that period of seven years had run out.

B | Central Asia in the Fifteenth Century

31 Khwandamir: Timur's Heirs: Shahrukh and Ulughbeg

Introduction

Ghiyath al-Din Khwandamir (1475–1535), a historian of the Timurids, owed much of his career to the political standing of his father, Khoja Humam al-Din Muhammad, a minister to the Timurid ruler of Samarqand. Thanks to the instruction given to him by his maternal uncle, the great historian Mirkhwand, and to the patronage of 'Ali Shir Nava'i (see below), Khwandamir was included in the official milieu in Herat. He became a diplomat in the service of Mirza Badi' al-Zaman, Sultan Husayn Bayqara's eldest son, and when the Uzbeks conquered Herat, Khwandamir was instrumental in the submission of the town to the new conquerors. He remained in the city after its occupation, first by the Uzbeks, later by the Safavids, and continued his service to his patron's family. He later traveled south and entered into Babur's service in the city of Agra in 1528, and soon after served his [Babur's] son Humayun until his death. He is buried in Dihli (Delhi). Khwandamir was a prolific author and poet, and his magnum opus is the Habib al-Siyar, written in the genre of a general history down to the year 1524, but also including biographies of eminent personalities in addition to the chronological narrative. The work was dedicated to the Safavid governor Karim al-Din Habib Allah, hence its title. The following excerpt details the fame earned by the two most prominent successors of Timur, his son Shahrukh and his grandson, Shahrukh's son, Ulughbeg. Shahrukh was particularly famous as a strict follower of the shar'ia, whereas Ulughbeg was also renowned for his advancement of the sciences, particularly astronomy.

His Majesty (Shahrukh), who was most particular in attending his religious duties and works of supererogation, spent all his free time in the performance of various acts of religious devotion, assisting most Fridays at the congregational mosque, where he rubbed the forehead of needfulness on the ground of devotion and raised the banner of intimate conversation with the deity to petition his needs.

On Friday the 23 of Rabi II 830 [February 21, 1427], having performed the prayer at the congregational mosque outside the city of Herat, he was mounting to leave the prayer-place when a man wearing a shepherd's cloak, Ahmad the Lur by name, a disciple of Mawlana Fazlullah Astarabadi, appeared on the roadside in the guise of a plaintiff holding a paper in his hand. His Majesty said to one of those nearby, "See what this person has to say." And Ahmad the Lur, seizing the opportunity, rushed fearlessly and plunged a knife into His Majesty's stomach. However, as the Omnipotent was protecting the blessed person of the auspicious emperor, the knife did not inflict a serious wound or touch the vital organs. 'Ali Sultan Qauchin obtained permission to kill that accursed one and immediately dispatched him.

Amir Alika and Amir Firozshah were waiting mounted at the mosque, and the naqarachis had begun the naqara as usual, when suddenly they heard the dreadful news and ceased what they were doing, at which the people were overcome by perplexity and astonishment. His majesty summoned Amir Firozshah, who rode posthaste to the mosque. When he realized that the wound was not serious, he loosened his tongue in thanksgiving to the Gracious Protector. His Majesty was inclined to sit in the litter, but Amir Firozshah objected, saying, "If the people do not see Your Majesty on horseback, they will wonder whether you are alive or dead, and grave sedition will ensue." Therefore the emperor mounted, the drums sounded, and the emperor proceeded through the marketplace to the Bagh-i Zaghan. The physicians and surgeons treated the wound, and within a few days it had healed completely. . . .

After this strange occurance, when Mirza Baysunghur and the amirs began an inquiry into the affairs of Ahmad the Lur, they regretted that he had been killed. Among his effects they found a key that opened a door in a commercial establishment. The people of the building said that a person fitting his description made felt caps there and many learned people came to him, among them Mawlana Ma'ruf the calligrapher.

This Mawlana Ma'ruf was possessed of great learning and skill, renowned for his calligraphy and wit, well spoken and, on account of his abundant talents, was sought out by the learned. He wore a felt cloak of the highest quality and on his head a tall cap of the same type. Formerly he had been in Sultan Ahmad Jalayir's retinue, but he had grown to despise Sultan Ahmad and gone to Shiraz, where Mirza Iskandar, then the governor of that region, held him in high esteem and offered him work copying in the princely library. Mawlana Ma'ruf had accepted to copy five hundred bayts a day. . . .

After the conquest of Shiraz, Shahrukh brought Mawlana Ma'ruf to Herat and employed him in the royal library. The people of Khurasan were glad to associate with him to learn calligraphy and for the sake of his company and conversation. He himself was so self-confident and lordly in his bearing that for over a year he kept some paper Mirza Baysunghur had given him for copying the *Khamsa* of Nizami before he returned it unwritten. For this reason Mawlana Ma'ruf was in ill favor with Mirza Baysunghur, and when he was accused of collusion with Ahmad the Lur, he was sentenced to death and was taken to the gallows several times. In the end he was imprisoned in the dungeon of Ikhtiyaruddin Fort. This line is of his own composition:

> Every arrow glance that has sailed straight from the quiver of your eyes
> has lodged in my breast, just as my heart desired.

. . . Mirza Ulughbeg, whose name was Muhammad Taraghay, was unique among His Imperial Majesty Shahrukh's sons for his great learning and patronage and among all his peers for his justice and equity. He united the wisdom of Galen with the magnificence of Kay-Kaus, and in all the arts, especially in mathematics and astronomy, there was no one like him. He memorized the Qur'an with all seven variant readings, and he constantly patronized people of learning and excellence. He was born on Sunday the 19th of Jumada I 796 [March 22, 1394] in Sultaniyya Fort. He was eleven years old when the *sahib-qiran* (namely, Timur) died.

Ulughbeg lived under his father's protection until 814, when he was given the rule of Transoxiana. After a short while that province flourished to such a degree that it surpassed the highest celestial sphere. In 824 [1421] the construction of a sublime *madrasa* and *khanqah* ordered by that peerless prince was completed, and many farms, villages, and free-holdings were endowed to those holy places. He also ordered expert master craftsmen to construct an observatory, the building of which was supervised by the second Ptolemy, Mawlana Ghiyas al-Din Jamshid, and the excellent Mawlana Mu'in al-Din Kashi. Among the results of the observatory are the astronomical tables known as the New Gurkanid Star Catalogue, which serves as a reference for most stellar coordinates these days.

Baraq Oghlan, a grandson of Urus Khan, left the Qïpchaq steppe in 823 [1420] for Samarqand and took refuge with Ulughbeg. The prince showed him great favor and sent him back to the steppe with all princely paraphernalia, and thanks to Ulughbeg's assistance he triumphed over Muhammad Khan, the *padishah* (king) of the Uzbeks, and became ruler.

At the beginning of 830 [November 1426] Baraq went to the borders of Sïghnaq and sent a messenger to Ulughbeg Mirza to say, "Now that my mind is at ease concerning the subduing of Jochi Khan's ulus, I have come here aided by your limitless bounty." But when Ulughbeg heard that Baraq Oghlan claimed the meadows of Sïghnaq by law and custom, he did not give the messenger an answer in agreement with this claim.

At the same time Arslan Khoja Tarkhan, the governor of Sïghnaq, reported that Baraq's marauders were wreaking havoc and that Baraq, thinking himself possessed of absolute power, was boasting of being a sultan. Therefore Ulughbeg sent a messenger to Herat to obtain permission to battle Baraq, but Shahrukh forbade any contention that would result in destruction, although he ordered a detachment led by Mirza Muhammad Juki to go to Transoxiana.

On the 17th of Rabi II [February 15, 1427], they left Herat for Samarqand, but before they arrived Mirza Ulughbeg had already set out for Sïghnaq, and so Mirza Muhammad Juki moved, without stopping, in his brother's wake. When they met they went together and pridefully provoked battle with Baraq. As the two sides met, Baraq put all his followers in the center and attacked the army of Transoxiana. Waves of battle crashed, swamping the ships of the lives of many, as blood flowed in rivers across the field and the sounds of drum and clarion rang out. Mirza Ulughbeg, deluded by his innumerable troops, belittled his enemy's small number, yet it was they who were favoured by victory and put the Transoxianans to flight. Stunned, Ulughbeg and Muhammad Juki wanted to enter the battle themselves, but some of their commanders kept them back and with guile managed to get them to safety and back to Samarqand as Baraq's men continued to maraud throughout Transoxiana and Turkestan. . . .

When Shahrukh entered the city [Samarqand] he instituted an investigation of the battle with Baraq and had a number of amirs and commanders executed, and Ulughbeg fell from grace for a few days. In the end, however, paternal feelings stirred, and the prince was reinstated in imperial favor and reconfirmed as governor of the *sahib-qiran*'s capital.

When Baraq learned of the emperor's arrival in Samarqand, he gave up hope of ruling Sïghnaq and took flight, and as a result the fire of strife he had caused in Turkestan died down.

32   Nava'i: A Comparison between Persian and Turkic

Introduction

Mir 'Ali Shir Nava'i (1441–1501) was a fifteenth-century poet, author, and official in Herat, working under Sultan Husayn Bayqara. Born into a family of chancellery scribes long in the service of a royal Timurid family, and having studied in Herat, Mashhad, and Samarqand, Mir 'Ali Shir returned to Herat in 1469 to find Sultan Husayn Bayqara firmly in power. He entered into the sultan's service—the sultan knew him well, as the two were actually educated together as children—and Bayqara became his greatest patron and admirer. Nava'i fulfilled several official positions in and outside the court, including the governor of Astarabad and special confidant of the sultan, but his fame is attributed to his unrivaled expertise in Chaghatay (or Turki), the Turkic literary language of Central Asia from the fifteenth to nineteenth centuries. The champion of Chaghatay poetry and literature, Nava'i not only composed dozens of works, but also enthusiastically promoted and supported literary compositions in Turkic, although he was well-versed in Persian poetry as well. Navai's influence on Turkic peoples' subsequent history and language continues to be celebrated today across Central Asia.

Of all languages Arabic possessed the most eloquence and grandeur, and there is no one who thinks or claims differently. For the glorious and sacred Qur'an descended [from Heaven] in that language and the blessed *hadiths* of the Prophet were spoken in it. Many of the true and wondrous secrets of God voiced by the great saints and religious leaders also have been clothed in the garb of this holy and blessed tongue. . . .

After Arabic there are three principal varieties of language, each having many arms and branches. These are Turkish, Persian, and Hindi, the origins of which go back to Yafith, Sam, and Ham, the three sons of the Prophet Nuh. These are the details: When the Prophet Nuh (May God bless him!) was delivered from the disasters of the Flood and he once again set foot upon the ground, no traces of mankind remained in the world. Then Nuh (upon whom be peace!) sent to the land of Khata [i.e., Khitai or Cathay] his son Yafith, whom historians call the father of the Turks. He [Nuh] made Sam, whom they call the Father of the Persians, the ruler of the lands of Iran and Turan, and he sent Ham, who is called the Father of the Hindus, to Hindustan. The children of these three sons of the Prophet spread and multiplied in the places named. The son of Yafith was the progenitor of the Turks. Historians all agree that he wore the crown of prophethood and was therefore superior to his brothers. The three languages—Turkish, Persian, and Hindi—thus spread among the children and the children's children of the three.

Because Ham was disrespectful to Nuh (upon whom be peace!), Nuh laid a curse in the blessed tongue [i.e., Arabic] on Ham's face. His white complexion darkened and his speech became corrupt and lost its purity and eloquence. The complexions of his children and his children's children, who inhabit the Land of Hind, have turned to the color of school children's slates, black as the night, and their speech has lost its ornaments of expression so that it sounds like pens with broken points. There is none among them whose skin is not as black as the black of ink and whose speech does not resemble the scratching of a broken pen. No one but themselves knows what is written in that paper and no one but one of those dark people can read and understand that writing, which suggests the footprint of a raven.

Since Arabic is a language of ideas and eloquences and Hindi one of exaggerations and corruptions, the one honored and sublime, the other utterly corrupt and base, no more need be said about them. There remain Turkish and Persian.

It is well known that Turkish is a more intelligent, more understandable, and more creative language than Persian, while Persian is more refined and profound than Turkish for the purpose of thought and science. That this is so is apparent from the rectitude, honesty, and generosity of the Turks and the arts, sciences, and philosophy of the Persians. But there are great differences of superiority and inferiority between the two languages. Turkish is much superior to Persian as regards the formation of words and expressions and contains nuances and eloquences which, God willing, shall be explained at the proper place.

There cannot be a cleaner and more brilliant proof of the superiority of the Turks than that social intercourse between the youth and elders, the notables and common people of these two nations is of the same degree. They do not differ in their ability to conduct trade and business and to ponder and resolve difficulties. There are more literates among the Persians. But although that is true, Turks from notables to commoners and from slaves to lords are acquainted with the Persian language and speak it according to their particular stations. Turkish poets even write beautiful poems in Persian. In contrast, not one member of the Persian nation, be he brigand or notable or scholar, can speak Turkish or understand anyone who does. If one in a hundred or even in a thousand learns and speaks this language, everyone who hears him knows that he is a Persian. With his own tongue he makes himself an object of ridicule.

There can be no better proof than this that Turkish is inherently superior to Persian, and no Persian can claim the contrary. The Persian language would be lost without Turkish expressions, for the Turks have created many words to express nuances and gradations of meanings which cannot be understood until explained by a knowledgeable person.

Turkish contains many nuances such as are made possible by these words and expressions, but they have remained unknown until the present day because on one ever studied the matter. Ignorant and affected youths have tried to compose facile poems with Persian words. But if anyone truly ponders and reflects sufficiently, he will realize the plentitude and scope of the Turkish vocabulary which facilitate the arts of eloquence and narrative style and versification and telling of fables. The superiority of the Turkish language has been demonstrated by many proofs. Therefore, Turkish poets and writers should have used their own tongue and not resorted to others. They erred in even attempting such a thing. If they were capable of composing in both tongues, they should have composed most in their own tongue and only rarely in another. When they indulged in hyperbole, they should have done so equally in both tongues.

Although it could not possibly happen, let us suppose that all the literati of the Turkish nation were to compose poetry in Persian and not in Turkish. They would not be able to compose very much, and what they did compose could never be compared with that written by eloquent Turks or by those who composed in both languages. If their works were read, a hundred errors would be found in their words and a hundred criticisms would be made about each of their works.

It is clear from the considerations which I have presented that there are many unique words and particles in the Turkish language, although it admittedly requires skill to combine them into harmonious and pleasing arrangements. The beginner, upon encountering difficulty in composing, shuns Turkish and changes to an easier road [i.e., Persian]. After this has happened several times it becomes habit; and after it has become habit the poet finds it difficult to abandon the habit in order to venture down a more difficult road. Later, other beginners, noting the conduct and the compositions of those who have preceded them, do not consider it proper to stray off that road. The result is that they too write their poems in Persian.

It is natural for a beginner to wish his works to be known to others. He wishes to submit them to scholars. But these are Persian-speakers who are not acquainted with Turkish, and this thought makes the poet shrink. Thus he is drawn to the use of Persian. He establishes relations with others and becomes one of them. This is how the present situation has come to be.

It is unfortunately true that the greater superiority, profundity, and breadth of Turkish as compared to Persian as a medium for poetry has not been realized by everyone. Ignorance settled over the house of mystery, and complete abandonment was drawing near. In the early days of my youth I began to perceive a few jewels from the inkwell of my mouth. These jewels had not yet become a string of verse, but jewels from the sea of consciousness which were worthy of being placed on a string of verse began to reach shore, thanks to the nature of the diver.

I reached the age of comprehension and God (whose praises I recite and who be extolled!) instilled in me sensitivity and attentiveness and a desire for the unique. I realized the necessity of giving thought to Turkish words. The world which came into view was more sublime than 18,000 worlds, and its adorned sky, which I came to know, was higher than nine skies. There I found a treasury of superiority and excellence in which the pearls were more lustrous than the stars. I entered the rose garden. Its roses were more splendid than the stars of heaven, its hallowed ground was untouched by hand or foot, and its myriad wonders were safe from the touch of other hands.

But the serpents of the treasury were cruel and the thorns of the garden were without number. It was like a dream—as if the deadly fangs of the serpents had prevented poetic-minded persons of learning from partaking of the treasure and had stabbed the heart . . . as if the sharp sting of the thorns had kept many collectors of roses from grasping in their hands the roses waiting to be plucked form this garden.

All effort on this road was sublime, and the poet was fearless and carefree. He did not cease trying, and he was not discouraged by what he saw. In the emptiness of that world he made predatory raids, and he saw in its sky the high-soaring falcon of his dreams. He took from among the jewels of that treasury rubies and pearls of inestimable value, and from among the fragrant herbs of that garden he gathered the eternally sweet aroma of roses and jasmine. Because of these gifts and riches and prizes he knew contentment; and as a result innumerable roses began to bloom for the people of the world and to spread spontaneously.

33   Khoja Ahrar: Letters

INTRODUCTION

*Khoja 'Ubaydallah Ahrar (1404–90) was a leader of the
Naqshbandi Sufi order and the de facto ruler of much of Mawarannahr in the
second half of the fifteenth century. Born in the vicinity of Tashkent, Ahrar soon
moved to Samarqand to pursue his education (which he never completed), and
then to Herat to continue his study of Sufism, particularly under Mawlana Ya'qub
Charkhi, a successor of Baha' al-Din Naqshband. Due to his connections with
the Timurid rulers of Mawarannahr, especially Sultan Abu Sa'id, Ahrar began to
occupy a powerful position in the region. He mediated conflicts among Timurid
princes, conducted negotiations with nomadic leaders, organized the defenses of
Samarqand, and became the most powerful landowner in the region and probably
the richest man in Mawarannahr. He helped to establish Naqshbandi supremacy
throughout Central Asia, and his disciples later carried his influence as far as
Turkey, East Turkestan, and India.*

*In his assortment of letters, Ahrar reveals his deep involvement in all matters
political, social, and economic, from his immediate associations with the Timurid
rulers to his ability to vouch for and safeguard the interests of different people
loyal to him. He also urges strongly for the implementation of the shar'ia and cau-
tions against a tolerant view toward unbelievers.*

*In one of his letters (no. 58), Khoja Ahrar tries to mediate for peace in light of
a recent rebellion in Balkh, attempting to prevent the success of the rebellion and
to guarantee that rumors of Samarqandi help for the rebels were false. In another
letter (no. 323), Ahrar calls upon the rulers to obey the shar'ia at all cost and stay
united in the faith to better be able to repel attacks from the outside. Finally, in
letter no. 535, probably addressed to the great poet and mystic 'Abd al-Rahman
Jami (d. 1492) in Herat, Ahrar solicits a tax exemption for his friend's family.*

Letter 58

After the statement of supplication it is reported that after Ahmad Mushtaq (Governor of Balkh who rebelled in 1471–72) sent someone here
[to Samarqand], many reports came [with him]. The sum of all the reports is that
these people should unite together and support one another because the appeals
for aid have become numerous. Although prior to the affair of Amir Ahmad
Mushtaq, there were appeals for help, these people nevertheless adhered to the
path of caution, even though externally they did not undertake to afflict those
who were seeking help. The reality is that they were not firm in giving help. After
the arrival of many rumors, most or all of which were lies, they could not calm
themselves. This *faqir* calmed them in a manner that may be ascertained from

the servitors of his Majesty [Sultan-Husayn Bayqara], (May the shadows of his kindness be extended over all the Muslims). [Even] if what is being heard here [in Samarqand], which I do not confirm and you [all] reject, is true, do not accept [such talk]. If what is heard is all false, one should hear it [but] not transgress the limits of servitude to the Almighty, and do not forget the Qur'anic *ayat, No, by your Lord, they have not truly believed until they make you the judge over that which they are disputing about among themselves*" (Qur'an, 4:65). Think of the next world. They too have agreed, but we could not prevent them from coming out [to help Ahmad Mushtaq].

Since his holiness the great descendant of 'Ali was setting out to obtain the honor of kissing the threshold, at this time [his] service [to you] is manifested in the presentation of this matter. I trust that, for the sake of the welfare of the Muslims, that which encompasses the good of both worlds, for all humanity, will also come to the noble mind of his Majesty. The honorable bearer of this letter of sincerity will bring whatever he knows to the attention of the servitors of the royal threshold. It is hoped that from the infinite kindness of the Almighty he will give whatever encompasses the good of the two worlds. To His grace and respect. Peace!

The needy one, 'Ubayd Allah.

Letter 323

He who humbles himself, God elevates him.
He who is for God, God is for him.

After the presentation of supplication, the petition is this: the request of this *faqir* is that, that, purely for God's sake, the blessing of sovereignty, which the Almighty bestowed out of His pure abundance of grace, and which is the best and strongest means of achieving the happiness of the two worlds, may [be] spent on that which brings the satisfaction of the God—that is, by exerting effort to ensure that the entire resolve of your Majesty, (May the shadows of your kindness be perpetuated), should be expended upon spreading the *shar'ia* of the Prophet Muhammad, (May the blessings of God be upon him), so that all may be light, and no darkness will have the power to withstand the light.

At this time when the enemies of the lives and faith of the Muslims have come close and are committing destruction, no worshipping is more complete and necessary for the kings, after the performance of *namaz*, than the engagement in the repulse of these oppressive man-eating [people]. Therefore, I am requesting that your Majesty and all the princes, and indeed all Muslims, set aside all other affairs and engage in warding off these oppressors. I am confident that if your Majesty would do all the things that you have taken upon yourself [to do] on that side [Khurasan] and also render help to the *makhdumzada* [Sultan Ahmad] so that some dignity may come to his Highness, the other *makhdumzadas* would also cooperate. With the grace of God, the warding off and cutting down of these ill-intentioned ones will soon be attained. Or perhaps if it is not done, it shall be no surprise. . . . [The interest of] the great family of your Majesty is also in this so that . . . [peace may be established] between the kinsmen. . . .

The needy one, 'Ubayd Allah

Letter 535

After the statement of supplication, it is reported that his holiness the great descendant of 'Ali, Sayyid Muhammad Qannad (a confectioner by trade), is the guest of this *faqir* here [in Samarqand]. The request is that his children may live peaceably in the shadow of protection of your honor [in Herat], and not be burdened because of the *ra'iyati* tax. During the time of his Royal Majesty, the late lamented martyr Sultan [Abu Sa'id], they had obtained consideration in some way. I trust that now as well, his Royal Majesty [Sultan-Husayn Bayqara], (May the shadows of his kindness be perpetuated), will also distinguish them with [his] kindness. Peace!

[No signature] In the handwriting of 'Ubayd Allah Ahrar

34   Five Readings on Sufi Orders in Central Asia: Competition, Practice, Politics

INTRODUCTION (ONE)

The famous Persian poet, Nur al-Din 'Abd al-Rahman Jami, wrote one of the most popular collective hagiographical works, the Nafahat aluns, *toward the end of the fifteenth century. The work covers Sufi masters from throughout the Muslim world down to the author's time, and much is thus based on other sources, but Jami gives eyewitness accounts of many shaykhs he knew himself from the region of Herat, including his own master in the Naqshbandiya, Sa'd al-Din Kashghari (d. ca. 1456). The following anecdote is taken from Jami's account of his master's life, and deals with Kashghari's relationship with his own master, Shaykh Nizam al-Din Khamush. The story involves the formal, organizational question of whether a Naqshbandi affiliate could also become a disciple of another master, in this case, another famous shaykh of Herat, Zayn al-Din Khwafi (d. 1435), the founder of a lesser-known Sufi order that spread outside Central Asia to the Ottoman world. The account suggests the reputation for communal jealousy and exclusivity increasingly demanded by Naqshbandi shaykhs—the "Khojagan"—during the fifteenth century; it also suggests that such jealousy was not shared by all Sufi shaykhs.*

He [Kashghari] used to say, "After several years in which I had been honored with the company of [Shaykh Nizam al-Din Khamush], I experienced a powerful urge to perform the pilgrimage to Mecca. . . . I requested permission from him, and he replied, 'No matter how much I look, I do not see you in a caravan of pilgrims this year.' Now before that, I had had dreams that caused me some doubt; but he had said not to worry so much. He said, 'When you go, tell those dreams to Mawlana Zayn al-Din, for he is a pious man and is firm on the path of the *sunna*.' He was referring to Shaykh Zayn al-Din Khwafi, who at that time was established in the position of spiritual guidance and shaykh-hood in Khurasan. When I came to Khurasan, going on the pilgrimage had to be postponed, as Mawlana Nizam al-Din had said, and was only accomplished many years afterwards.

"When I came to Shaykh Zayn al-Din and recounted those dreams, he said, 'Seal the pact with me and enter into discipleship with me.' I said, 'The saint from whom I received the Sufi path is still living. I trust you; if you know that this is permissible in the path of this community, I will do so.' He said, 'Seek guidance from God.' I said, 'I have no confidence in my own appeal for guidance; you seek guidance [on my behalf].' He said, 'You seek guidance, and I too will appeal for guidance.' When evening came, I appealed for divine guidance. I saw that the community of the Khojagan came into the Ziyaratgah of Herat, where Shaykh Zayn al-Din was at that time, and there uprooted the trees and broke down the walls; and the signs of anger and wrath were evident upon them. I understood that this was a sign to prevent me from entering another tariqa. My mind became at ease; I stretched out my legs and went to sleep in peace. When I came into the shaykh's assembly in the morning, even though I did not tell him of my vision, he said, "The Path is one, and everything returns to one; you should engage in that same Path of yours. If a vision or some difficulty should arise, tell me; to the extent that I can, I will help.'"

INTRODUCTION (TWO)

The best-known hagiographical work focused on Khoja Ahrar, the Rashahat-i 'ayn al-hayat, *includes the following anecdote involving two prominent Naqshbandi figures active in Herat: Sa'd al-Din Kashghari, mentioned above, and the latter's illustrious pupil, the poet Nur al-Din 'Abd al-Rahman Jami. The other figures named in the story are another of Kashghari's disciples, Mawlana Shams al-Din Muhammad Ruji, and Sadr al-Din Ravvasi, whom Ruji considered joining, as the account relates. Ravvasi was a disciple of the aforementioned Zayn al-Din Khwafi. The story deals with a common theme in hagiographical anecdotes, namely the meeting between a shaykh and a prospective disciple. In addition, it suggests something of the flavor of the etiquette expected among dervishes. Yet it also highlights competition between one Sufi community and the Naqshbandiya, as different groups sought to attract and hold on to affiliates, and in this case emphasizes an issue of Sufi practice on which various groups differed*

in this era: whether the Sufi "remembrance" (dhikr) of the divine name should be
performed aloud or in silence.

He [Ruji] used to say, "Already in my youth, when I was in the
village of Ruj, an inclination toward the Sufi path developed in me. I asked some
people whether there was a saint in Herat to whom I might go, and they mentioned the name of Shaykh Sadr al-Din Ravvasi; they said that he was among the
successors of Shaykh Zayn al-Din Khwafi and was then engaged in guiding Travelers [on the Sufi path] and training students. I set off at once for Herat, and from
the road I came to the shrine of the holy shaykh [Zayn al-Din], where Shaykh Sadr
al-Din was at that time; by chance just then he was performing the *dhikr* with his
companions. I stood for a time beside his *dhikr*-circle and observed their uproar;
it did not sit well with me, and so I headed for the city. On the way, Hafiz Isma'il
came up to me."

(Now this Hafiz Isma'il was a dervish, also from Ruj, who had entered the service of Mawlana Sa'd al-Din Kashghari before Mawlana Muhammad [Ruji] and
had been accepted by him; after [Kashghari's] death, he performed the pilgrimage
to Mecca in the company of my master, Mawlana Nur al-Din 'Abd al-Rahman
[Jami], and he was fully versed in this [Naqshbandi] path. [Ruji] continued,)

"Hafiz asked me, 'Where are you coming from, and what are you doing?' I
recounted the story to him, and he said, 'Go to the door of the Friday mosque.
There is a dervish there who sometimes holds gatherings with a group of disciples in the vestibule of the Friday mosque. Look to him; probably he will include
you in the gathering.' I went toward the mosque at once, and by chance his holiness the Mawlana [Jami] was seated in the hallway of the mosque with a group
of dervishes, in total silence. I stood outside and leaned against the wall; I was
watching them and observing their silence. I thought to myself, 'What was that
shouting and commotion about, compared with this silence and peace?' Suddenly
the holy Mawlana raised his head and said to me, 'Brother, come here.' Without
even thinking I went before him. He had me sit beside him and said, 'If a servant
or a retainer were to stand before Shahrukh Mirza and constantly keep saying,
in his presence, "Shahrukh, Shahrukh, Shahrukh," in a loud voice, it would be
extremely rude and offensive. The proper thing for a retainer in the presence of
a ruler, and for a servant in the presence of his master (khoja), is to be quiet and
attentive, not to shout and raise an uproar.'"

INTRODUCTION (THREE)

One of several hagiographies focused on Khoja Ahrar, compiled
by his son-in-law Mir 'Abd al-Avval Nishapuri at the end of the fifteenth century,
and known simply as his Malfuzat (Sayings), includes the following brief com-
ments by Khoja Ahrar reflecting his attitude regarding "political activism" and the
shaykh's duty to represent the interests of Muslims before rulers. The comments

are critical of two other prominent shaykhs he knew during the time he spent in Herat. He criticizes them for their timid and indirect approach to the political responsibilities of the shaykh, but also for their neglect of proper protocol in carrying out these responsibilities.

He [Khoja Ahrar] used to say, "Not once did Shaykh Baha' al-Din 'Umar go before Mirza Shahrukh in order to halt oppression or advance the *shar'ia;* he should have taken the *shar'ia* of the Prophet upon himself and gone, with all due protocol, before Mirza Shahrukh and his amirs. What indignity is there in this? Honor and dignity lie in honoring and respecting the *shar'ia.* Shaykh Zayn al-Din [Khwafi] did not go either. If at some point he had some important matter, then on a Wednesday—when Mirza Shahrukh would regularly come to [the shrine of] Khoja Abu'l-Valid—he would go in the morning to that shrine, he would perform the morning prayer there, and state his business. But he was never known to have gone in order to halt oppression or to remove something contrary to the law, and he was never known to have completely settled the matter. Shaykh Baha' al-Din 'Umar used to send someone else before the amirs regarding certain affairs, but there was no moderation in this fellow, and he did not pay any attention to protocol. He used to gallop his horse through the markets and streets of Herat. People used to call him 'the shaykh's ambassador.' For urgent matters and affairs of the people, it was that man who would go; [the shaykh himself] did not go."

INTRODUCTION (FOUR)

In 1578–79, Badr al-Din Kashmiri, who left his native land and came to Bukhara in the early 1550s, wrote a hagiographical work entitled Siraj al-salihin, *dedicated to 'Abdallah Khan and focused on the Sufi career of Yunus Muhammad Sufi of Merv (d. 1554), a disciple in the Naqshbandi order of Muhammad Islam Juybari (considered the founder of the lineage of the Juybari shaykhs in Bukhara). The work, which survives in a single manuscript, preserves important information on the Naqshbandi presence in Merv, and more generally on the region of Merv during the middle of the sixteenth century, when this region is only sparsely reflected in other sources. The following anecdote, however, is set in Bukhara, during the time of the Shïbanid ruler 'Ubaydallah Khan. It pits Yunus Muhammad Sufi against Shaykh Mirjan, who belonged to the Zayniya order, and casts the Naqshbandi shaykh as a harsh critic of 'Ubaydallah.*

When the holy [Yunus Muhammad] Sufi came from Shahr-i Sabz to Bukhara, he settled down in the quarter of Chah-i Zanjir. . . . He spent most of his time engaging in austerities and acts of worship in the mosque of Shaykh Mirjan, and one day, in his cell at the mosque, he was immersed in a mystical state ... and missed the Friday prayer. When Shaykh Mirjan came back from the Friday mosque, he criticized and rebuked [Yunus Muhammad] Sufi, saying, "You are an ignorant man and do not remember matters of ritual obligation and the *sunna*! The fact is that the Friday mosque is not more than ten steps away. You have missed the Friday prayer with no excuse!"

After all Shaykh [Mirjan's] talk, [Yunus Muhammad] Sufi raised his head and said, "With regard to a person who follows a prayer-leader who speaks falsehoods, is that person's prayer legitimate or not?" Shaykh [Mirjan] said, "It is not." [Yunus Muhammad] Sufi said, "Well, then, the person you have given the sermon sings the praises and good qualities of 'Ubaydallah Khan from atop the pulpit, and counts him among just rulers. We have seen the 'justice' of 'Ubaydallah Khan, for each year he leads an enormous army, with innumerable troops, into Khurasan, in order to make war; yet before he fights and struggles against the Qizil-bash, as soon as he crosses to the other side of the Syr Darya, his burdensome army inflicts so much oppression and injustice upon Muslims who are people of the Sunna and the Community that it cannot be considered just. They kill a great many Muslims on suspicion of heresy or infidelity; 'Ubaydallah Khan sees and knows with the eye of certainty, and seeks no witness or testimony regarding the sins of those who are slain. We have seen with our own eyes a body of his troops strip naked and expose and take captive the women and children among the people there. They brought them before 'Ubaydallah Khan: he saw their condition; he averted his eyes; he did not hear their cries; he did not answer them!"

... When the "question" of Shaykh [Mirjan] and the "answer" of [Yunus Muhammad] Sufi had transpired in this fashion in the mosque of the quarter of Chah-i Zanjir, Shaykh [Mirjan] went to his home. Then, in the morning before dawn, Shaykh Mirjan, like a disciple of pure sincerity and distinction, [took several pieces of clothing as gifts] and came to the cell of [Yunus Muhammad] Sufi; he apologized and sought pardon for the preceding exchange, and behaved humbly. [Yunus Muhammad] Sufi said, "Shaykh, what happened? Tell me." He replied, "Because of the discourtesy and insolence I showed with regard to you, the pure spirits destroyed me during the night. Forgive me; those words were spoken from ignorance. If you do not pardon me in this way, my children will be left orphans." After that, [Yunus Muhammad] Sufi softened and recited a blessing; he and the Shaykh [became friends].

INTRODUCTION (FIVE)

The following story again highlights the reputation for "jealousy" among Naqshbandi shaykhs; in this case the rival is a Kubravi shaykh, 'Abd al-Latif, who established himself in Khorezm, but is here shown as attempting to expand his appeal south to Merv. The expansion he attempted follows the pattern of the Khorezmian Uzbek dynasty during the middle of the sixteenth century, as its members campaigned against the Safavids in Khurasan and succeeded in establishing what amounted to a second power-base for the 'Arabshahid clan far

to the south of Khorezm, in towns such as Durun, Abivard, Nasa, and Merv. The
chief figure in these campaigns was Din Muhammad b. Avanish, who remained
active in the affairs of Khorezm despite his southern base (the specific instance of
dynastic discord alluded to in the story may be dated to the late 1550s).

Close disciples and devotees have related that at first, Din Muhammad Khan had full confidence in Shaykh Yunus Muhammad and was his
earnest disciple. When Shaykh 'Abd al-Latif came from Mecca the exalted to
Khorezm, and set off from Khorezm toward the region of Merv, Din Muhammad
Khan heard the news that the shaykh was coming, built a *khanqah* for him in the
city [of Merv], and went out to welcome him. He met the shaykh in the vicinity of
Nasa, and became his disciple with the utmost sincerity and devotion. . . .

When Amir [Yunus Muhammad] heard of this, he declared, "Two lions will
not fit together in a single forest." . . . He said, "Shaykh 'Abd al-Latif and I have an
understanding; he cannot come to Merv, or if perhaps he should come, he cannot
stay." However much people sent him constant reports, that the shaykh reached
such-and-such a place on such-and-such a day, and from there was heading for
Merv, his holiness [Yunus Muhammad] did not at all believe these accounts. After
several days, he said to his companions, "Last night I saw the shaykh in a dream;
he came before me, brought two *tanga*s as an offering, recited a blessing, and then
got up and left."

After several more days, news came that serious strife had broken out among
the sultans and kings of the province of Khorezm. Shaykh 'Abd al-Latif had taken
Din Muhammad Khan with him to Khorezm in order to make peace among the
sultans of that country, to show the way to a cessation of hostilities, and to remove
the dust of enmity and strife from among the sultans. As it turned out, when they
arrived in Khorezm, the strife had intensified, and the fire of battle and warfare
had been kindled, to the point that a great many people were killed in the fighting.
They say that one night, Payanda Muhammad Sultan, the son of Din Muhammad Khan, had a frightening dream in which the city walls of Khorezm collapsed
upon the father and son; suddenly the holy Amir [Yunus Muhammad] appeared
and brought the son out of danger, but left the father. When he awoke, he understood: "My father has adopted the path of opposition; he left the noble *silsila* of
the Naqshbandiya and entered into the silsila of the Kubraviya. He became the
disciple of Shaykh ['Abd al-Latif], and this is the result of that, and a sign of it."
And God most high knows best. The holy Khoja Baha' al-Din Naqshband said,
"Whoever turns away from our *tariqa* endangers his religion."

[The author then notes that six months later, Din Muhammad Khan came
back to Merv "in a state of ruin, without having made peace with his brothers";
he "repented" of his disloyalty to the Naqshbandiya, and Yunus Muhammad accepted it. Nevertheless, the khan fell seriously ill within a week; his wife sent an
offering of food to Yunus Muhammad's *khanqah*, and asked for a blessing as well
as for some object blessed by the shaykh that might bring about a cure. The author

then adds a personal note, in a short passage that brings the story to its conclusion, but also hints at some of the psychological subtleties of the hagiographical genre.]

The writer of these words declares that at that moment [when he received the request of Din Muhammad Khan's wife], the holy Amir [Yunus Muhammad] was holding a quince. He raised it and recited something ever so softly; then he blew his breath upon the quince one time. I thought I saw a spark of fire come out of his mouth and settle down upon the quince. Did anyone aside from me, among those present at the gathering, see that fiery breath, or not? In any case, he gave the quince to the steward to take to the sick man; he ate it, but did not get better, and the following week, he set out from the transitory world toward the eternal realm.

Part 5 | Central Asia in the Sixteenth and Seventeenth Centuries

INTRODUCTION

The sixteenth century witnessed the last great nomadic migration in Central Asia as much of the steppe population, referred to by the designation "Uzbek," made its way to the sedentary regions. Led by descendants of Chinggis Khan, the new-comers conquered the lands of Khorezm and Mawarannahr and established their control over much of Central Asia. On the way, they also separated into several groups, the most famous of which were the Qazaqs, who had settled in the areas of Moghulistan. The reasons for what became known as the "Uzbek Conquest" are varied, and contributing factors include internal conditions in the Dasht-i Qïpchaq, changing natural conditions in that region, the weakening of the Timu-rid states, and the appearance of a successful and charismatic leader in Muham-mad Shïbani Khan.

Following the Uzbek leader Abu'l-Khayr Khan's death in 1467, the steppes were thrown into a vicious cycle of wars and feuds with domestic and outside enemies (Moghuls, Uzbek-Qazaqs, and Oirats), which led to highly unstable con-ditions: anxiety and an economic crisis as a result of the loss of livestock—the nomad's main capital—led the steppe inhabitants to look elsewhere for security and fortune. In addition, some argue that the steppe was suffering from growing aridization, mainly in its western parts, a process that would have reduced the amount of land available for grazing. Meanwhile, the ultimate destination for the nomads, the Timurid domains, was concomitantly suffering from a long period of political decline. The Uzbeks were aware of the Timurid position through trade and travel, and also because they were led by a new leader, Muhammad Shïba-ni Khan, who had considerable experience in Timurid service. Furthermore, whether in rhetoric or conviction, at the end of the fifteenth century the Uzbeks advanced toward the Timurid state as the protectors of Sunni Islam against the emerging Shi'a in Safavid Persia.

The full consequences of the Uzbek conquest are difficult to assess, but it clearly altered the ethnic composition of Central Asia by adding a substantial increase in the Turkic population, which advanced the gradual process of Tur-kicization of Tajiks and Sarts (the sedentary population) and the spread of bi-lingualism. At the same time, the region experienced an increase in the signifi-cance of Sufi orders, and the growing importance of *sayyid*s (descendants of the Prophet). Although some have compared the Uzbek conquest to previous major conquests in the history of Central Asia, most notably by Arabs and the Mongols, it seems clear that under the Uzbeks the countryside suffered much more than the urban environment. The Uzbeks did not systematically destroy cities, but they did pillage and occupy key supply areas in the countryside. The nomads who had inhabited those lands, particularly the Chaghatays, were pushed aside to mountain valleys and dispersed. Furthermore, the Uzbeks were not completely alien to the local communities in the sedentary areas: they already identified with the religion (Islam) of most of the inhabitants, their leaders were educated in Persian, and a large portion of the population was already Turkic. The conquest drove away or destroyed the last remnants of Timurid rule in Central Asia, and most Timurids were either vanquished or fled, like Babur, to India. The new Uzbek ruling elites built upon several Timurid principles of administration, while endeavoring to transcend the memory of their predecessors.

After the conquest, the Uzbek ruling elite governed through a loose confederation of autonomous appanages. The authority of the central khan was symbolically recognized in the capital—until the middle of the sixteenth century Samarqand, and later Bukhara. This was further complicated as, in most cases, Turkic tribes did not occupy one single tribal territory, although there were areas that were referred to as the tribe's "yurt." Additionally, the appanage system was not stable, particularly due to the lack of a well-established mechanism for dynastic succession, which caused tension among the aspirants to the throne. In addition, princes became attached to their temporary appanages and often refused to leave them. Wars often continued until the elimination of a branch of the dynasty. In the second half of the sixteenth century, after a rather lengthy "civil" war of sorts, a powerful alliance between 'Abdallah Khan II and the influential Juybari family won the day. Their rule thrived, but as the sixteenth century came to an end internal conflict in 'Abdallah Khan's house left it depleted of potential successors, and a new dynasty—the Janids—assumed control over the area.

Following the conquest, the Uzbeks did not forsake many of their steppe-based political and social structures. The ruling elites continued to be members of the Chinggisid dynasty, generally referred to as khans, khaqans, or occasionally sultans. The nomads valued making decisions by consensus, if they could reach one. This included selecting the identity of the next ruler, although custom decreed that succession would go to the eldest member of the clan. The steppe was perceived as the possession of the ruling dynasty, and every member of the ruling house enjoyed the right to a certain portion of land to govern. By right of birth, the Chinggisids enjoyed considerable privileges and were distinct from the rest of the population. The "commoners" were organized in small pastoral communities known as *aul* or *avul,* which usually consisted of several extended families. Such political units were sometimes connected on a patrilineal basis, having a common eponym ancestor by whose name the group was called, although the tribe would also include adopted groups. Tribal leaders were known as *biy* (similar to "beg" or "bek"). Their functions included settling disputes, leading the group during seasonal migrations, and commanding the militia. Tribal elders known as *aq saqals* (lit., white beards), fulfilled similar functions, but on a much smaller and more localized level. The *biys* enjoyed access to the khans and sultans, and were often highly influential as they both supplied their khans with troops and managed the tribe's internal affairs.

In addition to social and political developments, the sixteenth century also witnessed the expansion of original Central Asian historiography on a much larger scale than before—indeed, the so-called Uzbek conquest contributed to an extensive growth in both Persian and Chaghatay Turkic literature. Whereas most of the official historical works in Central Asia before the sixteenth century were written outside the region, from this period there was a surge in the production of chronicles, family histories, biographies, and hagiographies in the region, above all in the city of Bukhara. Most of these new materials were written in Persian, but a significant amount was authored in Turkic. Historiography in Khorezm, considered the most "Turkified" region in Central Asia, was written exclusively in Turkic. To this wealth of materials we may add the extensive reports authored by visitors from elsewhere, as the region experienced a renewed interest from travelers and merchants, as well as numerous diplomatic exchanges, particularly with Russia.

A | *The Shïbanids and Central Asian Society in the Sixteenth Century*

35 *Zubdat al-athar:* The Beginnings of the Shïbanid State

INTRODUCTION

This source is a general history from the Creation down to the year 1525, written in Turkic by 'Abdallah b. Muhammad b. Ali Nasrallahi for the ruler of Tashkent, Sultan Muhammad, who was a cousin of Shïbani Khan and a son of Söyünch Khoja (Söyünjük) Khan. The author, of whom we have little information, seems to have been an official serving the Timurids in the city of Balkh, and following the Uzbek conquest may have fled to Herat, only to enter into the service of the new rulers some time after that, as was done by many Timurid officials and intellectuals.

The passage begins by explaining the circumstances of the writing of the work, including an interesting observation on the state of historical production in Turkic at the time, and the reasons for accomplishing a historical chronicle in Turkic. The author then recounts the history of the formation of the Uzbek state, beginning with Chinggis Khan's eldest son, Jochi, the ruler of the area that became known as the Golden Horde, where the ancestors of the Chinggisid elite and their Uzbek subjects emerged.

His [Sultan Muhammad's] noble assembly passed its time in commentary on the words of the All-knowing King (i.e., the Qur'an), and the sayings of the Lord of Mankind (i.e., Muhammad)—peace be upon him—and in telling stories of the great shaykhs. And in his presence histories were presented, and their meaning became apparent through his noble reading. Clearly, the praised qualities stored in his noble mind emerged through his wisdom and dignity.

Until in the year 933 (1526) a sublime order was bestowed upon this humble and poor slave of the court, 'Abdallah, saying, "It is necessary to compile a history." However much non-existence of perfection and insufficiency of virtue the Sultan knew I had, upon his order I was occupied with writing this history and I have made this rough draft, but on account of predestination in the meantime a strong illness afflicted my body, and at times it reached such a degree that the hope of living was over. But God most high gave a remedy from his treasure of mercy, and despite the fact that the disease overwhelmed me for two years at this time it became much easier. I made an effort and managed to end this task in full.

At the time, His Highness the Sultan of Sultans pronounced those blessed words, that it is a surprise that although the descendants of Chinggis Khan who ruled these countries and the descendants of Timur Bek were all Turks, the histories which were written in their name were all in the Persian language. Since they were all Turks, it is necessary that histories will also be written in Turkic. Then I was ordered to write our history in the following words, "Compose this history in Turkic!" Consequently, according to the order of His Highness, these scattered parts (i.e., this work) were written in Turkic. And since before this time no history was written in Turkic under any king in his time, at the time of His Highness the Sultan of Sultans this has happened. This book, therefore, should be considered the invention of His Majesty.

Whenever I came before him, requesting His Majesty for materials for this rough draft, he would show such care and attention in his words and his style and his stories, so that no uncertainty remained. Consequently, these scattered parts were written with good illustrations and splendid traditions.

> Effortlessness emerged from his improvement,
> Eloquence was found from his name.

It should not remain concealed that in this draft one can see the results of His Majesty's efforts.

Since the Sultan of Sultans' genealogy continues through Shïbani Khan, descendant of Jochi Khan son of Chinggis Khan, in this chapter were written the circumstances of Shïbani Khan, concluding with the deeds of the Sultan of Sultans. May it be clear to the people of the world that the sultans of the Turks are from two *sahib-qiran*s: One is Chinggis Khan, and the other Timur Bek, and since the origin of His Majesty, the Sultan of Sultans, reaches back to those two *sahib-qiran*s, it is necessary to write about His Majesty's ancestors. Reaching back to his ancestors on Chinggis Khan's side, His Majesty the Sultan of Sultans Sultan Muhammad, son of His Majesty the late Khaqan Söyünch Khoja Khan, son of Abu'l-Khayr Khan, son of Dawlat Shaykh Sultan, son of Ibrahim Oghlan, son of Fulad Sultan, son of Mengu Timur Khan, son of Bad Oghul Sultan, son of Jochi Buqa Khan, son of Bahadur, [son of] Shïban, son of Jochi Khan, son of Chinggis Khan. The Sultan of Sultans' genealogy to Timur Bek: His Majesty the Sultan of Sultans Sultan Muhammad, son of Söyünch Khoja Khan, son of the high-born,

Queen of Sheba of the age, Rabi'a Sultan Bigum, daughter of Ulughbeg Gurgan, that is, the greatest khaqan of the time and the most learned scholar of the age, son of the fortunate Khaqan Shahrukh Mirza, who illuminated the people of his age . . . and he was the son of Amir Timur Gurgan. And the origin of these two *sahib-qiran*s reached the ascendance of heaven and was conceived of light. It is hoped that since the Imperial Sultan is heir to these two *sahib-qiran*s, God most high will apportion their countries to him.

But, with the Lord's guidance, let us return to the subject at hand.

Concerning the rise of Shïbani Khan, it should be clear to the scholars of the age and to celebrated wise men and to the scribes of affairs and transformations, that whatever fortune and felicity is allotted to one family, as long as they keep themselves and their possessions in a shelter of faith, justice, modesty, and protection—*Allah guides whom He will unto a straight path* (Qur'an 2:142)—from day to day their fortunes shall increase, and their time shall be free from trouble. But, when too much delight and wealth reach them as to exceed the limits of perfection, and when pride and arrogance find their way into their minds, they rise up to acts of rebellion and they forget the commands of the Lord (may his greatness be exalted). Consequently, as it is proper for their rebellions, retaliation will ensue and their fortunes will perish. Even if the mind is adorned with brilliance and learning, every thought or good intention would result in punishment because of their arrogance, and fortune will pass from them to another family. The affairs of the Chaghatay kings serve as confirmation for these words. During their later rule, the pillars of their state were proud and marked by conceit; they would not implement the Lord's commands, and this rendered the kings weak and poor. Then, the Glorious Lord took away their fortune and gave it to Shïban Khan's descendants who were heirs to their property. . . .

Jochi Khan passed away six months before his father, Chinggis Khan, so Chinggis Khan appointed Ögedei Khan in his stead and then bid farewell to this world. According to his will, brothers, children, allies, aids, pillars of state, and the dignitaries of His Highness, all together placed Ögedei Khan on the throne, and the reigns of his authority decided the affairs of the state. He appointed princes and begs to positions in the country and among the people, and has made Batu Khan—Jochi Khan's eldest son and famous as Sa'in Khan—king of Jochi Khan's *ulus*. He ordered his own children and princes and *biy*s to attack and bring in the possessions of the courts of the Rus and Cherkes, and Bulghar, and Europe. In these military campaigns, Shïban Khan, who was the wisest and bravest of the brothers, fought valiantly and destroyed the enemies with his effort. These kingdoms were conquered for Batu Khan, and many victories took place. While he [Batu] was sitting firmly on the throne, he distinguished Shïban Khan among his relatives, and he apportioned to him [to Shïban] some of the people and the country and the state. And from among the beks, four *qarachi*s and their followers entered into his service as follows: Qushji, Nayman, Buyrak, and Qarluq.

Whoever became king over Jochi Khan's *ulus,* his children followed: When Shïban Khan died, his son Bahadur Oghul became ruler among the people, and when he passed away, his son, Jochi Buqa became sovereign. After him, Bad

Oghul, and after him, Mengu Timur Oghlan, and when he died, his son, Fulad Oghul was chosen among the people, and then Ibrahim Sultan, and then his son, Dawlat Shaykh Oghlan, became sovereign. When he passed away, his son, Abu'l-Khayr Khan became ruler and leader of the people, but since he was a zealous man, he did not follow anyone.

Mention of Abu'l-Khayr Khan

Because Abu'l-Khayr Khan was zealous in his core, he did not submit to any king in the Dasht-i Qïpchaq. He took the hem of the dress (and put it in his belt) and because of his self-reliance he said, boasting, "Victory and triumph will come from the Lord, the opener of the gates." After all, *help from Allah and victory is near* (Qur'an 61:13), so why should he submit to a person like himself?

Consequently, he set out with a few men, and within a short while he made the people look up to him. Leading an army, he fell upon Khorezm, liberated it from Ibrahim Sultan, son of Shah Malik Bek, and occupied it. The greatest spiritual leader, Mawlana Kamal al-Din Husayn Khorezmi, composed in Turkic a commentary on the *Qasida-i Burda,* and dedicated it to the khan. And he (Abu'l-Khayr Khan) conquered most cities and towns from the area of (the city of) Turkestan, and when the banner of fortune was hoisted from the sky, Sultan Abu Sa'id Mirza, who was a descendant of Timur Bek, was put to flight by 'Abdallah Mirza, and came to Yasï (that is, the city of Turkestan). When he learned that 'Abdallah Mirza intended to repulse him, Abu'l-Khayr Khan gave him shelter in his court, and also led an army and set out to the kingdoms of Mawarannahr. When he reached Shiraz (not the city, but one of the gates to Samarqand), four *yighach* from Samarqand, 'Abdallah Mirza came opposite him and a hard battle was fought. In the end, the wind of victory blew Abu'l-Khayr Khan's banner of victory, 'Abdallah Mirza was slain, and he annexed all the provinces of Mawarannahr. By lofty design, that Khan entrusted Abu Sai'd Mirza to rule over these kingdoms, and he (Abu'l-Khayr) married the noble-born Rabi'a Sultan Bigum, Ulughbeg's fourth daughter and mother of the greatest Khaqan [i.e., Söyünch Khan].

It should be evident to people of sound judgment that, in this history, whenever Shah Bakht Khan is mentioned, we mean Muhammad Shïbani, and whenever the aforementioned great Khaqan appears, it means Söyünch Khoja Khan, and wherever the Sultan of Sultans is described, we refer to His Highness, Sultan Muhammad Sultan. And this history has reached its conclusion with his (i.e., the sultan's) listening, and was adorned with his noble name.

> It was ornamented with his name
> It was made accurate with his finest stories

In short, after several years of absolute authority over the people and the land, in accordance with the Qur'anic verse *every soul shall taste death* (Qur'an 3:185), the cup-bearer of doom tasted from the bowl of death. The khan's enemies gained the upper hand, disagreement arose among his sons, adversaries attacked from every direction, and the khan's children dispersed. Among them was Muhammad Shïbani, who was known as Shah Bakht Khan. Together with a few sons, the great Khaqan [Söyünch Khoja Khan] came to Mawarannahr. Because of the generosity showed to his father by Abu'l-Khayr Khan, Sultan Ahmad Mirza b. Abu Sa'id Mirza generally observed respect toward them. Finally, several rebels with the idea of instigation would become hostile toward them. The sagacious khan and his men, out of necessity—as life is something dear—left . . . and Shah Bakht Khan, with thirty or forty men, went in the direction of Turkestan. When they reached the town of Arquq good fortune became their guide and at once they took over the city. The subjects became obedient, and they were exalted to great fortune. After that, Otrar province was occupied, and then they came upon Yasï. Mazid Tarkhan was key to the conquest of the cities of Turkestan. His people became obedient and submissive. Shah Bakht Khan then came upon Tashkent. Having captured Muhammad Sultan when Turkestan was conquered, the khan and his men raided and sought possessions in every direction in the manner of Qazaqs. Having reached Tashkent, they plundered its surroundings, and they moved off several tribes and sent them to Turkestan. When the victorious troops were returning again and again, they scattered to every side. Muhammad Sultan, who was born with Shah Bakht Khan, was taken by surprise while passing from Sayram, and was made prisoner (of the Moghuls). The Moghul khan, Sultan Mahmud Khan, out of farsightedness, did not advance his murder, and after several days, with his generous honor, he sent him to the khans. The result was that this goodness benefited him.

> God said that doing good,
> rewards you ten times more

When that Moghul Khan sent back Muhammad Sultan, being one among several khans, they became convinced that they did not have to worry about attacks from that side (Moghulistan). The subjugation of Mawarannahr continued, as they raided several provinces several times. Opposition grew toward the sultans of Mawarannahr. Their beks were rebellious and became disobedient, and they made helpless people with property. When these circumstances became known to the khan, he resolved to conquer Mawarannahr. Leading an army upon Mawarannahr, he battled Baqi Tarkhan (the Timurid governor of Bukhara) in order to conquer Bukhara. When he reached Soghd province, news reached him that Baqi Tarkhan set out against him with thirty thousand men, with the intention of defending (his city) and fighting (him). The khan realized that he had to repel him first. He turned to face him from the direction of Samarqand, and when he reached the town of Dabus, he [Baqi Tarkhan] drew the battle order and set up the right and left wings. Shah Bakht Khan said, "Let us encounter each other at the break of dawn." The great khan [Söyünch Khan] didn't like these words and said, "Whether we are few or many, we have to march this very day." Upon hearing those words, the warriors charged, and in one moment defeated and scattered Baqi Tarkhan's troops, and he himself fled and entered the town of Dabus. At that time, the great khan [Söyünch Khan] and the sultans consulted the council. Shah Bakht Khan went to Bukhara, and the grandees and most notable of the city came to meet him and surrendered themselves to his mercy and thus remained safe from slaughter. This great victory occurred in the year AH 906.

Muhammad Shïbani Khan and the great khan and the Shïbanid sultans now turned toward Samarqand in order to conquer it. They gloriously stopped at a station on the road to Qanaqul. On that occasion, the governor, Sultan Mahmud Mirza, Ali Mirza, and fifty beks became so predominant in the city that of the sultanate remained only its name. Indeed, it was heard from knowledgeable people that that prince was receiving as salary only five *sir* [1 *sir* = 500 grams] of meat per day (probably for himself and his close attendants), and even this was not easily obtained. Consequently, he got sick and tired from this sort of governance, and his soul was tormented from the predominance of the beks.

One day, a group assembled in the Ustu Mahal (in Samarqand) and, leaving on horseback the Firuza gates they met with Shah Bakht Khan at Bagh Midan (outside of the city). The khan and sultans and *biys* conquered the Shiraz gate without battle and then the troops, glorious as heaven, raided Kash and Nakhshab and went in different directions and took into possession the provinces with no opposition. . . .

In the meantime, news reached that Khusraw Shah Bek with an army of fifty thousand men had gathered on the bank of the Wakhsh River. The khan, together with ten thousand men passed from Darband but was yet to reach the river Wakhsh when Khusraw Shah Bek and Vali Bek realized that they could not make a battle stand despite the fact that there were fifty thousand men in their encampment. The decision to flee entered their mind, and so their armies dispersed. Seeking shelter, they joined Badi' al-Zaman Mirza (son of Sultan Husayn Bayqara) in Arhang. The khan and his men reached the river Wakhsh and saw what had happened, and many weapons and equipment fell into the hands of the troops, exalted as heaven. And there Shah Bakht Khan recited the following verse:

> They fled, without seeing the dust raised by the troops,
> Much like when one mentions a slave fleeing from a beating

36   Babur: Description of the Farghana Valley and Babur's Ejection from Samarqand

INTRODUCTION

While Babur (1483–1530) is most famous for his achievements in India, he was born in the Central Asian city of Andijan, in the Farghana Valley. His father was 'Umar Shaykh, great-great grandson of Timur and ruler of the valley, and his mother was a descendant of Chinggis Khan. Babur therefore

carried Chinggisid blood, but he was not a Mongol. He proudly identified himself
as a Timurid, and ethnically he was a Chaghatay Turk, a group that had become
more culturally "refined" and distinct from the nomadic Mongols, or "Moghuls,"
of Moghulistan.

After 'Umar Shaykh died in 1494, Babur was elevated as his father's heir, and
soon thereafter he began his quest to capture Samarqand, the Timurid ancestral
capital. He had several successes in this effort, but all were fleeting. The invad-
ing Uzbeks overpowered Babur's defenses, pushed him from Samarqand and,
ultimately, from Central Asia entirely. After years of hardship, Babur established
himself as ruler of Kabul and then, in 1526, he orchestrated a sweeping victory
over the Delhi Sultan Ibrahim Lodi. By the time of his death in 1530, Babur had
laid the groundwork for a new Timurid state in north India: the Mughal Empire.

The Baburnama, *literally the "letters" or memoirs of Babur, is a remark-*
able historical source. It provides a unique insight into the societies of Islamic
Central Asia, Afghanistan, and north India at the turn of the sixteenth century.
Yet it is also at times an intensely personal autobiographical memoir, in which the
reader confronts the innermost thoughts, feelings, aspirations, and doubts of an
introspective, self-critical, and important historical figure. Still, one should not
overlook that the Baburnama *is by design a subjective source. Babur intended for*
it to serve as a pedagogical guide for his sons and also as a (perhaps exaggerated)
record of his military victories, which, alongside his Timurid ancestry, were used
to bolster his claims to legitimacy as ruler of Kabul and north India.

Babur begins his memoirs with a sentimental description of the Farghana
Valley, his beloved homeland. This is followed with Babur's account of his defeat
at the hands of the Uzbek Muhammad Shïbani Khan (1451–1510), and his flight
into exile.

Description of Farghana

In the month of Ramadan of the year 899 (June 1494) and in the twelfth year of my age, I became ruler in the country of Farghana.

Farghana is situated in the fifth climate and at the limit of settled habitation. On the east it has Kashghar; on the west, Samarqand; on the south, the mountains of the Badakhshan border; on the north, though in former times there must have been towns such as Almalïq, Almatï, and Yangi which in books they write Taraz, at the present time all is desolate, no settled population whatever remaining, because of the Mughuls and the Uzbeks.

Farghana is a small country, abounding in grain and fruits. It is girt round by mountains except on the west, i.e., towards Khojend and Samarqand, and in winter an enemy can enter only on that side.

The Seyhun River (Syr Darya) commonly known as the Water of Khojend, comes into the country from the north-east, flows westward through it and after passing along the north of Khojend and the south of Fanakat, now known as

Shahrukhiya, turns directly north and goes to Turkestan. It does not join any sea but sinks into the sands, a considerable distance below [the town of] Turkestan.

Farghana has seven separate townships, five on the south and two on the north of the Seyhun.

Of those on the south, one is Andijan. It has a central position and is the capital of the Farghana country. It produces much grain, fruits in abundance, excellent grapes and melons. In the melon season, it is not customary to sell them out at the beds. Better than the Andijan *nashpati* (pear), there is none. After Samarqand and Kesh, the fort of Andijan is the largest in Mawarannahr. It has three gates. Its citadel (*ark*) is on its south side. Into it water goes by nine channels, out of it, it is strange that none comes at even a single place. Round the outer edge of the ditch runs a gravelled highway; the width of this highway divides the fort from the suburbs surrounding it.

Andijan has good hunting and fowling; its pheasants grow so surprisingly fat that rumour has it four people could not finish one they were eating with its stew.

Andijanis are all Turks; not a man in town or bazar but knows Turki. The speech of the people is correct for the pen; hence the writings of Mir 'Ali-shir Nava'i, though he was bred and grew up in Herat, are one with their dialect. Good looks are common amongst them. The famous musician, Khoja Yusuf, was an Andijani. The climate is malarious; in autumn people generally get fever.

Again, there is Osh, to the south-east inclining to the east of Andijan and a distance from it four *yighach* by road (33 miles). It has a fine climate, an abundance of running waters, and a most beautiful spring season. Many traditions have their rise in its excellencies. To the south-east of the walled town lies a symmetrical mountain, known as the Bara Koh; on the top of this, Sultan Mahmud Khan built a retreat and lower down, on its shoulder, I, in 902 AH (1496 AD), built another, having a porch. Though his lies the higher, mine is the better placed, the whole of the town and the suburbs being at its foot.

The Andijan torrent goes to Andijan after having traversed the suburbs of Osh. Orchards lie along both its banks; all the Osh gardens overlook it. Their violets are very fine; they have running waters and in spring are most beautiful with the blossoming of many tulips and roses.

On the skirt of the Bara Koh is a mosque called the Jauza Masjid (Twin Mosque). Between this mosque and the town, a great main canal flows from the direction of the hill. Below the outer court of the mosque lies a shady and delightful clover-meadow where every passing traveller takes a rest. It is the joke of the ragamuffins of Osh to let out water from the canal on anyone happening to fall asleep in the meadow. A very beautiful stone, waved red and white, was found in the Bara Koh in 'Umar Shaykh Mirza's latter days; of it are made knife handles, clasps for belts, and many other things. For climate and for pleasantness, no township in all Farghana equals Osh.

Again there is Marghinan; seven *yighach* (about 47 miles) by road to the west of Andijan,—a fine township full of good things. Its apricots and pomegranates are most excellent. One sort of pomegranate, they call the Great Seed; its sweetness has a little of the pleasant flavour of the small apricot and it may be thought better than the Semnan pomegranate. Another kind of apricot they dry after stoning it and putting [an almond in it]. They call it *subhani;* it is very palatable. The hunting and fowling of Marghinan are good. . . . Its people are Sarts, boxers, noisy and turbulent. Most of the noted bullies of Samarqand and Bukhara are Marghinanis. The author of the *Hidayat* was from Rashdan, one of the villages of Marghinan.

Again there is Isfara, in the hill-country and nine *yighach* (about 65 miles) by road southwest of Marghinan. It has running waters, beautiful little gardens, and many fruit-trees but almonds for the most part in its orchards. Its people are all Persian-speaking Sarts. In the hills some two miles to the south of the town, is a piece of rock, known as the Mirror Stone. It is some 10 arm-lengths long, as high as a man in parts, up to his waist in others. Everything is reflected by it as by a mirror. The Isfara district is in four subdivisions, one Isfara, one Warukh, one Sukh, and one Hushyar. When Muhammad Shïbani Khan defeated Sultan Mahmud Khan and Alacha Khan and took Tashkent and Shahrukhiya, I went into the Sukh and Hushyar hill-country and from there, after about a year spent in great misery, I set out for Kabul.

Again there is Khojend, twenty-five *yighach* (187 miles) by road to the west of Andijan and twenty-five *yighach* (154 miles) east of Samarqand. Khojend is one of the ancient towns; of it were Shaykh Maslahat and Khoja Kamal. Fruit grows there well; its pomegranates are renowned for their excellence. People talk of a Khojend pomegranate as they do of a Samarqand apple; just now however, Marghinan pomegranates are much met with. The walled town of Khojend stands on high ground; the Seyhun River flows past it on the north at the distance, maybe, of an arrow's flight. To the north of both the town and the river lies a mountain range called Munughul; people say there are turquoise and other mines in it, and there are many snakes. The hunting and fowling-grounds of Khojend are first-rate. . . . The climate is very malarious; in autumn there is much fever; people rumour it about that the very sparrows get fever and say that the cause of the malaria is the mountain range on the north (i.e., Munughul).

Kand-i-badam (Village of the Almond) is a dependency of Khojend; though it is not a township, it is rather a good approach to one. Its almonds are excellent, hence its name; they all go to Hormuz or to Hindustan. It is five or six *yighach* (18 miles) east of Khojend.

Between Kand-i-badam and Khojend lies the waste known as Ha Darwesh. In this there is always wind; from it wind goes always to Marghinan on its east; from it wind comes continually to Khojend on its west. People say that some darweshes (dervishes), encountering a whirlwind in this desert, lost one another and kept crying, "Hay Darwesh! Hay Darwesh!" till all had perished, and that the waste has been called Ha Darwesh ever since.

One of the townships on the north of the Seyhun River one is Akhsi. In books they write it Akhsikit, and for this reason the poet Asir al-Din is known as Akhsikiti. After Andijan, no township in Farghana is larger than Akhsi. It is nine *yighach* (about 50 miles) by road to the west of Andijan. 'Umar Shaykh Mirza made it his capital. The Seyhun River flows below its walled town. This stands above a great ravine and it has deep ravines in place of a moat. When 'Umar Shaykh Mirza made it his capital, he once or twice cut other ravines from the outer ones. In all Farghana no fort is so strong as Akhsi. Its suburbs extend some two miles further than the walled town. People seem to have made of Akhsi the saying, "Where is the village? Where are the trees?" Its melons are excellent; they call one kind Mir Timuri; whether in the world there is another to equal it is not known. The melons of Bukhara are famous; when I took Samarqand, I had some brought from there and some from Akhsi. They were cut up at an entertainment and those from Bukhara could not compare with those from Akhsi. The fowling and hunting of Akhsi are very good indeed. . . .

Again there is Kasan, rather a small township to the north of Akhsi. From Kasan the Akhsi water comes in the same way as the Andijan water comes from Osh. Kasan has excellent air and beautiful little gardens. As these gardens all lie along the bed of the torrent people call them the "fine front of the coat." Between Kasanis and Oshis there is rivalry about the beauty and climate of their townships.

In the mountains round Farghana are excellent summer-pastures. There, and nowhere else, the *tabalghu* [the red willow] grows, a tree with red bark; they make staves of it; they make bird-cages of it; they scrape it into arrows; it is an excellent wood and is carried as a rarity to distant places. Some books write that the mandrake is found in these mountains, but for this long time past nothing has been heard of it . . . There are turquoise and iron mines in these mountains.

If people do justly, three or four thousand men may be maintained by the revenues of Farghana.

Babur in Samarqand

On taking Samarqand, envoys and summoners were sent off at once, and sent again and again, with reiterated requests for aid and reinforcement to the khans and sultans and begs and marchers on every side. Some, though experienced men, made foolish refusal; others whose relations towards our family had been discourteous and unpleasant, were afraid for themselves and took no notice; others again, though they sent help, sent insufficient. Each such case will be duly mentioned.

When Samarqand was taken this second time, 'Ali Shir Beg ('Ali Shir Nava'i) was alive. We exchanged letters once; on the back of mine to him I wrote one of my Turki couplets. Before his reply reached me, separations and disturbances happened. Mulla Bina'i had been taken into Shaibaq (Shibani) Khan's service when the latter took possession of Samarqand; he stayed with him until a few days after I took the place, when he came into the town to me. Qasim Beg had his suspicions about him and consequently dismissed him towards Shahr-i Sabz but, as he was a man of parts, and as no fault of his came to light, I had him fetched back. He constantly presented me with odes. He brought me a song in the Nawa mode composed to my name and at the same time the following quatrain. . . .

Babur Besieged in Samarqand

One day Shaibaq Khan attacked between the Iron Gate and the Shaykh-zada's. I, as the reserve, went to the spot, without anxiety about the Bleaching-ground and Needle-makers' Gates. That day, in a shooting wager, I made a good shot with a slur-bow, at a Centurion's horse. It died at once with the arrow. They made such a vigorous attack this time that they got close under the ramparts. Busy with the fighting and the stress near the Iron Gate, we were entirely off our guard about the other side of the town. There, opposite the space between the Needlemakers' and Bleaching-ground Gates, the enemy had posted 700 or 800 good men in ambush, having with them 24 or 25 ladders so wide that two or three could mount abreast. These men came from their ambush when the attack near the Iron Gate, by occupying all our men, had left those other posts empty, and quickly set up their ladders between the two Gates, just where a road leads from the ramparts to Muhammad Mazid Tarkhan's houses. . . . As attack was being made on the other side of the town, the men attached to these posts were not on guard but had scattered to their quarters or to the bazar for necessary matters of service and servants' work. Only the begs were at their posts, with one or two of the populace. . . . Some Uzbeks were on the ramparts, some were coming up, when these four men arrived at a run, dealt them blow upon blow, and, by energetic drubbing, forced them all down and put them to flight. Quch Beg did best; this was his out-standing and approved good deed; twice during this siege, he got his hand into the work. Qara Barlas had been left alone in the Needle-makers' Gate; he also held out well to the end. Qutluqh Khoja and Qul-Nazar Mirza were also at their posts in the Bleaching-ground Gate; they held out well too, and charged the foe in his rear.

Another time Qasim Beg led his braves out through the Needle-makers' Gate, pursued the Uzbeks as far as Khoja Kafsher, unhorsed some and returned with a few heads.

It was now the time of ripening rain but no-one brought new corn into the town. The long siege caused great privation to the towns-people; it went so far that the poor and destitute began to eat the flesh of dogs and asses and, as there was little grain for the horses, people fed them on leaves. Experience shewed that the leaves best suiting were those of the mulberry and elm. Some people scraped dry wood and gave the shavings, damped, to their horses.

For three or four months Shaibaq Khan did not come near the fort but had it invested at some distance and himself moved round it from post to post. Once when our men were off their guard, at mid-night, the enemy came near to the Turquoise Gate, beat his drums and flung his war-cry out. I was in the College, undressed. There was great trepidation and anxiety. After that they came night after night, disturbing us by drumming and shouting their war-cry.

Although envoys and messengers had been sent repeatedly to all sides and quarters, no help and reinforcement arrived from any-one. No-one had helped or reinforced me when I was in strength and power and had suffered no sort of defeat or loss; on what score would any-one help me now? No hope in any-one whatever recommended us to prolong the siege. The old saying was that to hold a fort there must be a head, two hands, and two legs, that is to say, the Commandant is the head; help and reinforcement coming from two quarters are the two arms, and the food and water in the fort are the two legs. While we looked for help from those round about, their thoughts were elsewhere. That brave and experienced ruler, Sultan Husayn Mirza, gave us not even the help of an encouraging message, but none-the-less he sent Kamalu'd-din Husayn Gazur-gahi as an envoy to Shaibaq Khan.

Surrender of Samarqand to Shïbani

The siege drew on to great length; no provisions and supplies came in from any quarter, no succour and reinforcement from any side. The soldiers and peasantry lost hope and, by ones and twos, began to let themselves down outside the walls and flee. . . . Trusted men of my close circle began to let themselves down from the ramparts and get away; begs of known name and old family servants were amongst them. . . . Of help from any side we utterly despaired; no hope was left in any quarter; our supplies and provisions were wretched, what there was, was coming to an end; no more came in. Meantime Shaibaq Khan interjected talk of peace. Little ear would have been given to his talk of peace, if there had been hope or food from any side. It had to be! A sort of peace was made and we took our departure from the town, by the Shaykh-zada's Gate, somewhere about midnight.

Babur Leaves Samarqand

I took my mother, Khanïm, out with me, . . . At this exodus, my elder sister, Khan-zada Begim, fell into Shaibaq Khan's hands. In the darkness of that night we lost our way and wandered about amongst the main irrigation channels of Soghd. . . . On the road I raced with Qasim Beg and Qambar-'ali (the Skinner); my horse was leading when I, thinking to look back at theirs behind, twisted myself round; the girth may have slackened, for my saddle turned and I was thrown on my head to the ground. Although I at once got up and remounted, my brain did not steady till the evening; till then this world and what went on appeared to me like things felt and seen in a dream or fancy. Towards afternoon we dismounted in Yilan-auti, there killed a horse, spitted and roasted its flesh, rested our horses awhile and rode on. Very weary, we reached Khalila-village before the dawn and dismounted. From there the route went to Jizak.

In Jizak just then was Hafiz Muhammad Duldai's son, Tahir. There, in Jizak, were fat meats, loaves of fine flour, plenty of sweet melons, and an abundance of excellent grapes. From what privation we came to such plenty! From what stress to what repose!

> From fear and hunger rest we won
> A fresh world's new-born life we won

From out our minds, death's dread was chased
From our men the hunger-pang kept back

Never in all our lives had we felt such relief! Never in the whole course of them have we appreciated security and plenty so highly. Joy is best and more delightful when it follows sorrow, ease after toil. I have been transported four or five times from toil to rest and from hardship to ease. This was the first. We were set free from the affliction of such a foe and from the pangs of hunger and had reached the repose of security and the relief of abundance.

37 Anthony Jenkinson: An English Merchant in Central Asia

INTRODUCTION

In the year 1498, the Portuguese Captain Vasco da Gama became the first European to sail into the Indian Ocean and land on the southwest coast of India. The Portuguese ships of his day, caravels, were smaller than those used by other countries, but they were comparatively light and fast. Their lateen (triangular) sails greatly facilitated navigation, and their revolutionary use of cannons gave the Portuguese a considerable military advantage over other ships sailing the Indian Ocean. Within a few years the Portuguese took control of a number of trading posts, and by the middle of the sixteenth century, the Portuguese Estado da India nearly monopolized the growing European trade with Asia. Other European powers tried—and failed—to challenge the Portuguese by gaining access to Asian markets through other routes.

It was with this intention that the English merchant Anthony Jenkinson (1530–1609) joined the Muscovy Company, an English joint-stock company that was chartered in 1555 to expand England's trade with Russia and, through Russia, with Asia. The Russian Empire had recently expanded considerably under Tsar Ivan IV ("the Terrible," r. 1547–84) with the conquest of the khanates of Kazan in 1552 and Astrakhan in 1556, both successor states to the Mongol Golden Horde. Soon thereafter Queen Elizabeth (r. 1558–1603), a founding stockholder in the Muscovy Company, appointed Jenkinson to serve as her ambassador to Moscow.

Hoping to extend the company's trade to Asian markets, Jenkinson left Moscow in April of 1558 and sailed down the Volga River to Astrakhan with a Tatar interpreter, two other company employees, and a supply of kersey (English wool), a commodity which, at that time, amounted to roughly 90 percent of England's exports. The party then sailed across the Caspian Sea and traveled overland to Bukhara, which they reached in December of that same year. Jenkinson was poorly informed of events in the region prior to his arrival, and he had the ill fortune to arrive near the end of a two-decade period of crisis and civil war.

Patently unhappy with the commercial prospects in Bukhara, Jenkinson returned to Russia. It was there, in 1560, that he wrote his account as a report to his employers, the stockholders in the Muscovy Company, in England.

The following excerpt from Jenkinson's account describes his experiences as he traveled from Urgench (modern Kunia-Urgench, in Turkmenistan) southward to Bukhara. It includes revealing observations regarding the difficulties associated with caravan travel in the region, especially for foreign non-Muslims, and the nomadic communities he encountered. Jenkinson's almost casual comment about the advantage that he drew from his use of handguns in his conflict with a group of local bandits, and the interest with which the ruler of Bukhara viewed this technology, will prove particularly prescient in discussions of the end of the "nomadic advantage" in centuries to come.

Thus proceeding in our journey, the tenth day at night being at rest, and our watch set, there came unto us four horsemen, which we took as spies, from whom we took their weapons and bound them, and having well examined them, they confessed that they had seen the tract of many horsemen, and no footing of camels, & gave us to understand, that there were rovers and thieves abroad: for there travel few people that are true and peaceable in the country, but in company of caravan, where there be many camels: and horse-feeting new without camels were to be doubted. Where upon we consulted & determined amongst ourselves, and sent a post to the said sultan of Kait, who immediately came himself with 300 men, and met these four suspected men which we sent unto him and examined them so straightly, and threatened them in such sort, that they confessed, there was a banished prince with 40 men, 3 days journey forward, who lay in wait to destroy us, if he could, and that they themselves were of his company.

The sultan therefore understanding, that the thieves were not many, appointed us 80 men well armed with a captain to go with us, and conduct us in our way. And the sultan himself returned back again, taking the four thieves with him. These soldiers traveled with us two days, consuming much of our victuals. And the 3rd day in the morning very early they set out before our caravan, and having ranged the wilderness for the space of four hours, they met us, coming towards us as fast as their horse[s] could run, and declared that they had found the tract of horses not far from us, perceiving well that we should meet with enemies, and therefore willed us to appoint ourselves for them, and asked us what we would give them to conduct us further, or else they would return. To whom we offered as we thought good, but they refused our offer, and would have more, and so we not agreeing they departed from us, and went back to their sultan, who (as we conjectured) was privy to the conspiracy. But they being gone, certain Tartars of our company called holy men, (because they had been at Mecca) caused the whole caravan to stay, and would make their prayers, and divine how we should prosper in our journey and whether we should meet with any ill company or no? To which, our whole caravan did agree. And they took certain sheep and killed them, and took the blade bones of the same, and first sawed them, and them burnt them, and took of the blood of the said sheep, and mingled it with the powder of the said bones, and wrote certain characters with the said blood, using many other ceremonies and words, and by the same divined and found, that we should meet with enemies and thieves (to our great trouble) but should overcome them, to which sorcery, I and my company gave no credit, but we found it true: for within 3 hours after that the soldiers departed from us, which was the 15th day of December, in the morning, we escried far off divers horsemen which made towards us, and we (perceiving them to be rovers) gathered ourselves together, being 40 of us well appointed, and able to fight, and we made our prayers together every one after his law, professing to live and die one with another, and so prepared ourselves. When the thieves were nigh unto us, we perceived them to be in number 37 men well armed, and appointed with bows, arrows, and swords, and the captain a prince banished from his country. They willed us to yield ourselves, or else to be slain, but we defied them, wherewith they shot at us all at once, and we at them very hotly, and so continued our fight from morning until two hours within night, divers men, horses, and camels being wounded and slain on both parts: and had it not been for 4 handguns which I and my company had and used, we [would have] been overcome and destroyed: for the thieves were better armed, and were also better archers then we; but after we had slain divers of their men and horses with our guns, they durst not approach so nigh, which caused them to come to a truce with us until the next morning, which we accepted, and encamped ourselves upon a hill, and made the fashion of [a] castle, walling it about with packs of wares, and laid our horses and camels within the same to save them from the shot of arrows: and the thieves also encamped within an arrow shot of us, but they were betwixt us and the water, which was to out great discomfort, because neither we nor our camels had drunk in 2 days.

Thus keeping good watch, when half the night was spent, the prince of the thieves sent a messenger half way unto us, requiring to talk with our captain, in their tongue, the caravan basha, who answered the messenger, I will not depart from my company to go into the half way to talk with thee: but if that thy prince with all his company will swear by our law to keep the truce, then will I send a man to talk with thee, or else not. Which the prince understanding as well himself as his company, swore so loud that we might all hear. And then we sent one of our company (reputed a holy man) to talk with the same messenger. The message was pronounced aloud in this order: Our prince demandeth of the caravan basha, and of all you that be bussarmans (that is to say circumcised) not desiring your bloods, that you deliver into his hands as many caphars, that is, unbelievers (meaning us the Christians) as are among you with their goods, and in so doing, he will suffer you to depart with your goods in quietness, and on the contrary, you shall be handled with no less cruelty then the caphars, if he overcome you, as he doubteth not. To the which our caravan basha answered, that he had no Christians in his company, nor other strangers, but two Turks which were of their law, and although he had, he would rather die then deliver them, and that we were not afraid of his threatenings, and that should he know when day appeared. And so passing in talk, the thieves (contrary to their oath) carried our holy man away to their prince, crying with a loud voice in token of victory, Ollo, ollo. Where with we were much discomforted, fearing that that holy man would betray us: but he being cruelly handled and much examined, would not to death confess any thing which was to us prejudicial, neither touching us, nor yet what men they had slain and wounded of ours the day before. When the night was spent, in the morning we prepared our selves to battle again: which the thieves perceiving, required to fall to agreement & asked much of us: and to be brief, the most part of our company being loath to go to battle again, and having little to loose, & safe-conduct to pass, we were compelled to agree, and to give the thieves 20 ninths (that is to say) 20 times 9 several things, and a camel to carry away the same, which being received, the thieves departed into the wilderness to their old habitation, and we went on our way forward. And that night came to the river Oxus, where we refreshed our selves, having been 3 days without water and drink, and tarried there all the next day, making merry with our slain horses and camels, and then departed from that place, & for fear of meeting with the said thieves again or such like, we left the high way which went along the said river, and passed through a wilderness of sand, traveled 4 days in the same before we came to water: and then came to a well, the water being very brackish, and we then as before were in need of water, and of other victuals, being forced to kill our horses and camels to eat. . . .

So upon the 23rd day of December we arrived at the city of Boghar [Bukhara] in the land of Bactria. This Boghar is situated in the lowest part of all the land, walled about with a high wall of earth, with divers gates into the same: it is divided into 3 partitions, whereof two parts are the king's, and the 3rd part is for the merchants and markets, and every science hath their dwelling and market by themselves. The city is very great, and the houses for the most part of earth, but there are also many houses, temples, and monuments of stone sumptuously built, and gilt, and specially bathstoves so artificially built, that the like thereof is not in the world: the manner where of is too long to rehearse. There is a little river running through the midst of the said city, but the water thereof is most unwholesome, for it breedeth sometimes in men that drink thereof, and especially in them that be not there born, a worm of an ell long, which lieth commonly in the leg betwixt the flesh and the skin, and is plucked out about the ankle with great art and cunning, the surgeons being much practiced there, and if she break in plucking out, the party dieth, and every day she commeth out about an inch, which is rolled up, and so worketh till she be all out. And yet it is there forbidden to drink any other thing then water, & mares milk, and whosoever is found to break that law is whipped and beaten most cruelly through the open markets, and there are officers appointed for the same, who have authority to go into any man's house, to search if he have either aquavitae, wine, or brage, and finding the same, do break the vessels, spoil the drink, and punish the masters of the house most cruelly, yea, and many times if they perceive but by the breath of a man that he hath drunk, without further examination he shall not escape their hands.

There is a metropolitan in this Boghar, who causeth this law to be so straightly kept: and he is more obeyed then the king, and will depose the king, and place another at his will and pleasure, as he did by this king that reigned at our being there, and his predecessor, by the means of the said metropolitan: for he betrayed him, and in the night slew him in his chamber, who was a prince that loved all Christians well.

This country of Boghar was sometime subject to the Persians, & do now speak the Persian tongue, but yet now it is a kingdom of itself, and hath most cruel wars continually with the said Persians about their religion, although they be all Mahometists. One occasion of their wars is, for that the Persians will not cut the hair of their upper lips, as the Bogharians and all other Tartars do, which they accompt great sin, and call them caphars, that is, unbelievers, as they do the Christians.

The king of Boghar hath no great power or riches, his revenues are but small and he is most maintained by the city: for he taketh the tenth penny of all things that are there sold, as well by the craftsmen as by the merchants, to the great impoverishment of the people, whom he keepeth in great subjection, and when he lacketh money, he sendeth his officers to the shops of the said merchants to take their wares to pay his debts, and will have credit of force, as the like he did to pay me certain money that he owed me for 19 pieces of kersey. Their money is silver and copper, for gold there is none current: they have but one piece of silver, & that is worth 12 pence English, and the copper money are called Pooles, and 120 of them goeth the value of the said 12 pence, and is more common payment then the silver, which the king causeth to rise and fall to his most advantage every other month, and sometimes twice a month, not caring to oppress his people, for that he looketh not to reign above 2 or 3 years before he be either slain or driven away, to the great destruction of the country and merchants.

The 26th day of the month I was commanded to come before the said king, to whom I presented the Emperor of Russia his letters, who entertained us most gently, and caused us to eat in his presence, and divers times he sent for me, and devised with me familiarly in his secret chamber, as well of the power of the Emperor, and the Great Turk, as also of our countries, laws, and religion, and caused us to shoot in handguns before him, and did himself practice the use thereof. But after all this great entertainment before my departure he showed himself a very Tartar: for he went to the wars owing me money, and saw me not paid before his departure. And although indeed he gave order for the same, yet was I very ill satisfied, and forced to rebate part, and to take wares as payment for the rest contrary to my expectation: but of a beggar better payment I could not have, and glad I was so to be paid and dispatched.

But yet I must needs praise and commend this barbarous king, who immediately after my arrival at Boghar, having understood our trouble with the thieves, sent 100 men well armed, and gave them great charge not to return before they had either slain or taken the said thieves. Who according to their commission ranged the wilderness in such sort, that they met with the said company of thieves, and slew part, and part fled, and four they took and brought unto the king, and two of them were sore wounded in our skirmish with our guns: And after the king had sent for me to come to them, he caused them all 4 to be hanged at his palace gate, because they were gentlemen, to the example of others. And of such goods as were gotten again, I had part restored me, and this good justice I found at his hands.

The Bukharan Merchant Fair

There is yearly great resort of merchants to this city of Boghar, which travel in great caravans from the countries thereabout adjoining, as India, Persia, Balkh, Russia, with divers others, and in times past from Cathay, when there was passage: but these merchants are so beggarly and poor, and bring so little quantity of wares lying two or three years to sell the same, that there is no hope of any good trade there to be had worthy the following.

The chief commodities that are brought thither out of these aforesaid countries, are these following.

The Indians do bring fine whites, which the Tartars do all roll about their heads, & all other kinds of whites, which serve for apparel made of cotton wool and crasko, but gold, silver, precious stones, and spices they bring none. I inquired and perceived that all such trade passeth to the Ocean sea, and the veins where all such things are gotten are in the subjection of the Portingals [Portuguese]. The Indians carry from Boghar again wrought silks, red hides, slaves, and horses, with such like, but of kersies and other cloth, they make little accompt. I offered to barter with merchants of those countries, which came from the furthest parts of India, even from the country of Bengala, & the river Ganges, to give them kersies for their commodities, but they would not barter for such commodity as cloth.

The Persians do bring thither craska, woolen cloth, linen cloth, divers kinds of wrought pied silks, argomacks, with such like, and do carry from thence red hides with other Russe wares, and slaves, which are of divers countries, but cloth they will buy none, for that they bring thither themselves, and is brought unto them as I have inquired from Aleppo in Syria, and the parts of Turkey. They Russes do carry unto Boghar, red hides, sheepskins, woolen cloth of divers sorts, wooden vessels, bridles, saddles, with such like, and do carry away from thence divers kinds of wares made of cotton wool, divers kinds of silks, crasca, with other things, but there is but small utterance. From the countries of Cathay are brought thither in time of peace, and when the way is open, musk, rhubarb, satin, damask, with divers other things. At my being at Boghar, there came caravans out of all these aforesaid countries, except from Cathay: and the cause why there came none from thence was the great wars that had dured 3 years before my coming thither, and yet dured betwixt 2 great countries & cities of Tartars, that are directly in the way betwixt the said Boghar and the said Cathay, and certain barbarous field people, as well Gentiles and Mahometists bordering to the said cities. The cities are called Taskent and Caskar [Kashghar], and the people that war against Taskent are called Cassaks [Qazaqs] of the law of Mahomet, and they which war with the said country of Caskar are called Kings, Gentiles, & idolaters. These 2 barbarous nations are of great force living in the fields without house or town, & have almost subdued the aforesaid cities, & so stopped up the way, that it is impossible for any caravan to pass unspoiled: so that 3 years before our being there, no caravan had gone, or used trade betwixt the countries of Cathay and Boghar, and when the way is clear, it is 9 months journey. To speak of the said country of Cathay, and of such news as I have heard thereof, I have though it best to reserve it to our meeting. . . .

38   Juybari Archives: A Sixteenth-Century Bukharan Deed of Sale

INTRODUCTION

The Juybari shaykhs (or khojas, as they are sometimes referred to), were a prominent dynastic family who played an important role in the political and economic life of Central Asia from the sixteenth through the nineteenth centuries. They emerged in the sixteenth century as a very influential family with enormous wealth, largely acquired through their successful association with the Jani-Begid branch of the Shïbanids, most particularly with 'Abdallah Khan. Enjoying the rulers' patronage while acting as mediators, advisors, and businessmen, the Juybaris occupied the highest positions in the religious establishment. Their family name, Juybari, came from the quarter in the city of Bukhara where they lived. They claimed descent from the Imam Abu Bakr Ahmad ibn Sa'd, a tenth-century scholar, and were entrusted to maintain his shrine with all its lands.

The Juybari "archives" provide important information on the social and economic history of Central Asia in the sixteenth century and include the documentation of 385 property transactions of the Juybari family—mostly by Khoja Islam Juybari (d. 1563) and his son, Khoja Sa'd Juybari—in Mawarannahr. The documents were assembled and prepared for publication (with an introduction and Russian translation) by E. E. Bertel's and P. P. Ivanov in 1938 (and finally published in 1954).

On the 11th of the great month of Sha'ban, in the year 966, a just, honored, and legal agreement was made willingly between Bibi Khani, daughter of Khoja 'Abdallah b. Yar Muhammad, to the implementation of the following: that I [Bibi Khani], being legally authorized to deal in my own property, have sold in a definitive, faithful, legal, irreversible, correct, and effective sale to His Holiness, the spiritual guide, axis of heaven, leader of the circle of sainthood, restorer of all the lords of the Path, refuge of the masters of truth, cream of the house of sainthood and miracle working, pillar of the abode of sayyidship and naqibship, resolver of doubts and subtleties, revealer of difficulties and truths . . . His Holiness Khoja Muhammad Islam, the *wakif* [donor of religious endowment] . . . known as Khoja Juybari, noble son of His Holiness . . . the late Khojagi Ahmad . . . wholly and fully, a small caravansary comprising ten buildings and three vestibules and an *aiwan* [probably an open area]—all are my property—whose size is approximately 251 *gaz* according to Bukharan measurement [1 *gaz* equaled between half a meter and one meter], on Masjid Mulla Amiri Street, outside the old citadel of the above-mentioned city. One boundary of the property adjoins partly the houses and shops of Mawlana Mir Kalan, son of Khoja Mir Moghul, and partly toward the public road and partly toward the houses of Mir Faraj, son of Mir Sayyid Muhammad Naqash. Another borders several of the stores of Khoja Mir Shaykh, son of His Holiness, Shaykh Nur al-Din Muhammad al-Purani, and some in the shop of the aforementioned Khoja Mir Kalan. And yet another boundary are the abandoned houses of Khojaberdi, son of Khoja Muhammad, and another limit is the house of Shams al-Din b. Mir Laghari and in part the house of Bibi Khani, the aforementioned seller. At each border there are clear marks. . . . Overall, the sum [of the sale] is 250 *tanga* of the current mint of the khan, in a reciprocal transaction, and with legal guarantee for its fulfillment, according to the proper estimate of the assets, devoid of deceit and deception and faulty conditions . . . and I explained the meaning [of this transaction] with the agreement of His Holiness [the buyer], and that was on the aforementioned date in the presence of trusted confidants. [Here follows a list of witnesses].

39   Akbar, Emperor of India: A Letter to 'Abdallah Khan Uzbek, King of Turan

INTRODUCTION

Briefly stepping outside of Central Asia, we note that Babur, the Timurid heir and founder of the Mughal Empire, died in the year 1530 and that the Timurid mantle then passed to his son, Humayun. Twenty-six years later, in 1556, regal authority passed to Humayun's thirteen-year-old son, Jalal al-Din Muhammad Akbar (r. 1556–1605), renowned in Indian history as the first truly great Mughal emperor. During his forty-nine-year reign, Akbar transformed his grandfather's legacy into a vast, prosperous, and powerful empire that stretched across much of the Indian subcontinent.

Considered as a whole, the period during which Akbar ruled in India would later represent the golden age of the early modern Islamic dynasties of the Indian Ocean. Akbar's lengthy reign overlapped with those of two other highly successful and celebrated Muslim monarchs: his senior contemporary, the Ottoman Sultan Suleyman Qanuni ("the Lawgiver," r. 1520–66), commonly referred to in Europe as "the Magnificent" due to the grandeur of his court; and the younger ruler of Persia, Shah 'Abbas (r. 1587–1629). A third Muslim ruler, perhaps less well known

but still highly successful in the Central Asian milieu, was the Shïbanid-Uzbek
ruler of the Bukharan Khanate, 'Abdallah Khan II (r. 1583–98).

The following text is drawn from an official diplomatic letter that Emperor
Akbar entrusted to an ambassador and dispatched to 'Abdallah Khan on June
15, 1596, near the end of both of their regal careers. It represents the first such
letter that Akbar had sent to 'Abdallah Khan for ten years, since the two had a
sharp exchange regarding Akbar's permissive and, to 'Abdallah, questionable
religious policies in India. The purpose of this letter is to move away from points
of debate, strike a harmonious tone, and explain away any misunderstandings
that may have arisen following Akbar's territorial acquisitions in Afghanistan and
Kashmir. Specifically, Akbar suggests that the Hindu Kush mountain range should
serve as the firm boundary between their realms. He hopes to convince 'Abdallah
that he has no designs on Badakhshan, and that he is committed to maintaining
a peaceful relationship with his respected neighbors to the benefit of all. Given
the elaborate strategies involved in imperial politics, and Akbar's fear of losing
his Afghan territories to a potential Perso-Uzbek alliance, one may, of course, be
inclined to question the veracity of such diplomatic discourse.

At the time of enjoyment when the season was auspicious and
our heart glad and we were in the pleasant country of Kabul, we read with delight
those choice pages of friendship, which were the masterpiece of the pinacothek
of concord . . .

What you have written with a pen perfumed with brotherhood on the subject
of our mutually exerting ourselves to strengthen the foundations of Peace, and
to purify the fountains of concord, and of making this Hindu Koh the boundary between us, has most fully commended itself to us. Clearly there is no nobler
thing in the outward universe and social state than Love and Harmony, for the
due ordering of the classes of human beings is linked and bound up therewith.
Whenever this idea is manifested in the ranks of sovereigns—who are pillars of
the courts of Majesty—it shall assuredly be fruitful of blessings, and procreant of
beauties here and hereafter. By it thousands of souls and tribes shall take their rest
in the cradles of safety! It would have been fitting for us to begin the exposition of
the ways of peace, and the demonstration of the rights of friendship, seeing that
since the commencement of the unfolding of the morning of auspiciousness, the
whole of our righteous practice has been—contrary to the ways of most of former
rulers—to follow the path of amity and association with the various nations of
mankind. As your Highness has entered upon this subject, it is proper that this
time you should give your attention to instances of such conduct. For example,
when at this time the ruler of Iran, relying upon former ties, sent Yadgar Sultan
Shamlu to us and asked for help, we did not consent. Also, when Shahrukh Mirza
petitioned that he might have a fief in Kabul, or Kashmir, or Sawad, Bajaur, and
Tirah—which are cold countries—we did not grant his request, having taken into
consideration the proximity (of 'Abdullah), but gave him a fief in the province of
Malwa. Also we summoned the Mirzas of Qandahar to court and committed the

charge of that country—which belonged from of old to the imperial territories—
to old servants of ours, lest the Turan troops should attack that quarter under
the idea that it appertained to Persia, and also that there might be a great com-
mingling of your territories and ours. Also a wicked vagabond raised the head of
disturbance in the hill-country of Badakhshan and claimed to be the son of Shahrukh Mirza and was joined by the landholders there. Though he sent petitions
and asked for help, we did not attend to him, and at last he became a vagabond in
the desert of ruin.

As the keeping of one's word is indispensable to a great mind, we desired that
when proposals of peace had once been made, they should be carried into effect.
In fact, if the cordial expressions conveyed by messengers and letters be acted
upon, what could be better? Or let a place be fixed and let us there have a feast
of concord, and let us there discuss, without the intervention of any go-between,
matters of religion and state, and things temporal and spiritual! It has come to
our hearing that a number of fly-like creatures have made our being in the Panjab
their text and have spoken things contrary to the foundations of friendship. Alas,
that things which never entered into our minds, should have been mentioned!
or that actions should be contrary to one's avowals! Although the climate and
the hunting in this country are agreeable to us, we have determined to proceed
to Agra the capital, in order that the mouths of praters may be closed. What you
have written about there being a cloud on your heart with reference to the matters
of Shahrukh Mirza is a thing which gives rise to meditation, for if in the souls of
great rulers who are the contemplators of divine lights, and the exponents of the
ways of purity, the dust of rivalry settle, what can be the case with other classes
of Mankind? Especially when the cause of them is his (Shahrukh's) youth and
ignorance. Why should these not be obliterated by the waters of pardon? He by
his self-will had committed faults against our family, and in retribution therefore
became a bewildered one in the desert of exile. When he took refuge with us, and
signs of repentance were visible on his forehead we passed over (his offenses).
As to what you have hinted, seeing that the coming of Shahrukh Mirza and the
sons of Muhammad Hakim to our court are merely instances of our love for the
noble family, why should you regard their approach in this light? What, on account of love and friendship, you have detailed about your victories has pleased
us for we have considered these successes as the result of your good qualities. As
to what you have written in the letter brought by Mawlana Husayni to the effect
that your son in consequence of tender years had made improper requests, and
about your being vexed at this lest it should cast dust on the skirt of our friendship, and with reference to your lengthy apologizing on his account—the courier
was drowned on the way before his arrival and so the purport of the letter did not
become known. We were sorry for the catastrophe. The ties of ancient relationship and the associations of renewed love are not such that, if it be granted that
something should occur, any dust of vexation should settle on the skirt of friendship. Children are sportive with their real fathers, especially with your Majesty;
if they behave in the same way to those who stand towards them in a similar relation, what marvel is it? Auspicious children who make the pleasing of their father

their object, exert themselves to preserve the relationship. The glorious compacts and agreements—which have been ratified by skilful ambassadors, one after the other, are fixed in our mind. In the code of Islam and the rules of generosity one-hundredth part of them would be sufficient for making permanent the pillars of friendship and concord, and still more in the case of the liberal and the choosers of truth. What you have written about certain expeditions having been postponed till the arrival of Ahmad 'Ali Ataliq has been understood. You will have heard of his death, which occurred after we had given him leave to return. He was intelligent and active-minded. If he had returned to you, you would have heard from him many secrets of affection. May every desire of your heart be accomplished! Every assistance that is due from friendship shall be shown (by us), so that praiseworthy endeavours may be manifested.

God be praised that from the beginning of our ascending the throne of rule till now, which is the tenth year of the second cycle [i.e., fourth decade], and is the dawning of the morning of fortune, and the opening smile of the spring of dominion and glory, the whole righteous aim of this suppliant at the Divine court has been to disregard his own interests, and to work always for the healing and ordering of mankind. By the blessing of God, [I have ruled] the vast territory of Hindustan. . . .

B | *Central Asia in the Seventeenth Century*

40 Abu'l-Ghazi: Reasons for Writing the Genealogies of the Turks and Turkmens

INTRODUCTION

Abu'l-Ghazi Bahadur Khan, ruler of Khiva from 1644–66, was the son of 'Arab Muhammad Khan and a descendant of Chinggis Khan. Having quarreled with his brother Isfandiyar, Abu'l-Ghazi fled to Tashkent, where he lived with the Qazaqs for two years, before attempting to retake Khiva for himself. His effort failed, and he spent the next ten years in exile, in Persia, where he acquired a thorough knowledge of Persian and Persian sources, and later dwelled with Qalmaqs for several years. He finally returned to Khiva after his brother's death and became not only a powerful khan, but also a prolific author. Abu'l-Ghazi is unusual in the literary landscape of Central Asia at the time, in that he was a khan who wrote the chronicles himself without commissioning other authors and scribes to do so. He gives the reasons for it below. The following excerpts are taken from the author's introductions to his two main works, the Shajara-yi tarakima (Genealogy of the Turkmens) and the Shajara-yi turk (Genealogy of the Turks), both written in Chaghatay. They represent attempts to make order and sense of pre-existing oral and literary traditions in the middle of the seventeenth century, authored with unusual authority by one versed in Persian, Turkic, and Mongolian, as well as enjoying thorough acquaintance with both written and oral sources.

The Shajara-yi tarakima, *completed in 1660–61, tries to settle the disparities between the many different versions of the* Oghuz-nama, *the folkloric—some say epic—story of the early Turks, as well as the history of the Turks presented in other sources, mainly in Rashid al-Din's work. The work has received several editions and translations into modern Turkish, as well as Russian (by A. N. Kononov).*

The Shajara-yi turk *was written in the genre of a general history, from Creation to the author's time, and still serves as the most important source for the history of Khorezm in the sixteenth and seventeenth centuries. The work reached the West in the eighteenth century, when a Swedish prisoner of war in Siberia somehow obtained a manuscript and brought it back with him to Europe upon his release. The* Shajara *was edited and translated several times in the eighteenth and nineteenth centuries, the most famous publication (with a French translation) by Baron Desmaisons in 1874.*

From the *Shajara-yi tarakima*

Here are the words of Abu'l-Ghazi Khan, of the descendants of Chinggis Khan and son of Urganchi 'Arab Muhammad Khan: Having seen many tribulations, at the age of thirty-nine, in the year 1051, in the year of the snake, I have sat on my father's throne in the Kingdom of Khorezm and was engaged in the business of the country. At that time, the Turkmens were living in Manghish-laq and in Abu'l-Khan and on the bank of the river Tajan [Tezhen]. Having heard of our arrival, those of them who had lived in Khorezm escaped to those three aforementioned places. After that, some by way of nomadizing and some by road, migrated, and in the three yurts not one household remained.

And so, some of them came to Khorezm and became subjects: nobles, commoners, and military men. Since then many years passed. Turkmen *mullas* and shaykhs and beks heard that I knew history well. One day, they all came and petitioned me, "Among us there are many *Oghuz-namas*, but none of them is good. Some have mistakes in them, and do not agree with one another. Each one is of its own kind. It would be good if there was one correct history to rely on." They made their request. I then accepted their request and the reason for which this book was written is that, seventeen years before that, all the Turkmens were our enemies. For that reason we fought them a great deal. In Khurasan, near Durun, we drew up our ranks and battled them on the banks of the river Burma.

God came to our aid. From then until the end our cause was virtuous, and from the nobles and commoners twenty thousand people died, among them were guilty and innocent, just as the Prophet's words [in Arabic], "Said the Prophet—Peace be upon Him—when joy enters the heart of a believer it is better than all creatures." The meaning of this saying is that, if someone makes one Muslim happy, his reward will be greater than all of Adam's children, and all the *jinn*'s servitude to God. Thus, the words that I will say (or write) may turn the hearts of several thousand men. By the grace of God, I hope that this would be a reward if killing (that I had mentioned) counts as a sin. And if someday, someone reads this book, may he know what he didn't know and may he offer benediction for our soul.

This book is called *Shajara-yi tarakima*. Before us, many words in Arabic and Persian were added to the Turkic histories, and the Turkic was written in rhymed prose in order to show their own skill and mastery to the people. We have done nothing of the sort because the readers and listeners to this book will certainly be Turks and it is necessary to tell the Turk in the Turkic way so that all of them understand. If they do not know the words we have told what is the profit in that? If among them there are one or two knowledgeable readers, they may be able to teach those many who don't know; it is necessary to speak to both nobles and commoners so that it may be acceptable to their hearts. Now, let us write, to the extent of our knowledge, and remedy what we don't know, from Adam's time until the present about the Turkmens and those who assumed the Turkmen name, and those who joined the Turkmens.

*   *   *

From the *Shajara-yi turk*

The reason for writing this book: The son of 'Arab Muhammad Khan, Abu'l-Ghazi Bahadur Khan Chinggizi, and Khorezmi says that the historians wrote in Turkic and Persian the history of good and bad deeds of Chinggis Khan's fathers and ancestors and descendants, who became rulers in every kingdom. One wise man would write one book in the name of one king, and a few years later a wise historian would appear before one of the king's descendants who became king, and would say, "I will write better than the other historian." He would write a history in the name of that king. In this manner, gradually, wherever Chinggis Khan's descendants lived, in the name of the kings that wrote ten or twenty, and some say thirty histories.

Now, before me there are eighteen [historical] works written for descendants of Chinggis Khan in Iran and Turan. However, because of our forefathers' lack of ability and the lack of knowledge of the people of Khorezm, no one has written the history of our society since 'Abdallah Khan's ancestors had separated from our own. I offered one person to write this history. However much I thought about it, I could not find a suitable person [for the job]. For this reason, it became necessary for me to write it myself, as the Turkic proverb goes, *An orphan cuts its own umbilical cord.* From Adam's time until this day, histories were written whose number God only knows. No king and amir and no governor or sage could write their own history themselves. From this desire of our yurt and the incapacity of the people of Khorezm in no time the work was done.

41   Ivan Khokhlov: A Russian Envoy to Central Asia

INTRODUCTION

Seventeenth-century Russian relations with the Uzbek khanates were not characterized by sustained diplomatic exchange. Rather, Uzbek khans and Russian tsars dispatched diplomatic missions with specific concerns: protection for merchant and pilgrim caravans from nomads and corrupt border officials; the right of merchants to trade in Russia and Central Asia respectively; and specific requests made by the rulers for luxury goods. Added to this was the ongoing matter of Russian slaves held by Central Asians, and the Russian desire to impress upon the Central Asian rulers an image of Russia's strength and grandeur. All of these ideas found their way into the diplomatic instructions given to Tsar Mikhail's envoy to Bukhara, Ivan Danilovich Khokhlov. The latter was dispatched in 1620 in answer to a request made by the Bukharan ruler Imam-Quli Khan (r. 1611–41) for both a Russian diplomatic mission and expensive Russian hunting birds. Khokhlov, member of a family of Russian frontier military officers, had served in the North Caucasus and already had diplomatic experience, having spent two years at the Safavid court and accompanying a Safavid diplomat to and from Moscow.

Khokhlov's party consisted of Russians, Tatars, and Central Asians: diplomats, translators, soldiers, merchants, and, on the return trip, freed Russian slaves. Overcoming the misfortune of having his boat crash on the eastern shore of the Caspian, and having defended himself against Turkmen attacks, Khokhlov eventually managed to reach Khiva, where the local princes and officials extorted bribes and threatened him with death. Khokhlov was still able to leave the khanate and cross into Bukharan territory, arriving in Samarqand in the summer of 1621, to experience further thorny negotiations. Despite all obstacles, Khokhlov and party, with the addition of freed Russian slaves and a Khivan exiled prince, managed to return to Astrakhan, in Russian territory, on October 22, 1622.

Khokhlov's account provides an excellent example of the numerous hardships encountered by diplomats, merchants, and travelers in Central Asia, and an insight into the ingenious strategies they had to develop for their survival and the success of their mission. The following excerpt presents two such encounters, first with the Turkmens on the Mangishlaq Peninsula, and the second in the khanate of Bukhara.

Encounter with the Turkmens

The place is called Tüparagan, and the people who live there are nomadic Turkmens. . . . No one obeys a sovereign. Bordering on the Urgenchian Arab Khan ('Arab Muhammad Khan ruler of Khiva, 1603–22), they give him a tribute of sheep, but in nothing else do they obey him. Because of those rogues, Ivan raised a fortification on the beach, ringed it with stone, and made a fight. The next day, at one in the afternoon, many of the local Tüparaganis . . . came and wanted to attack them. He commanded for them to be fired upon using the arquebuses. They, having seen the arquebus fuselage, did not press the assault but asked what kind of people they were and whence did they come?

The Urgenchian envoy, speaking with them, said that he is a high-level envoy of Mikhail Fedorovich, the Great Sovereign Tsar and Grand Prince of all Russia, on his way to the Urgenchian Arab Khan, and with him is going an envoy of the great sovereign Arab Khan. But the Turkmens did not believe this, and seeing that he had a gyrfalcon, said that the high-level envoy of the sovereign is going to their enemy, to the Qizil-bash (Safavid) Shah. The Urgenchian envoy said again to them that they were going to Arab Khan and not to the Shah; furthermore, he spoke to them about Arab Khan, and his children and all the Urgenchian customs. Thus those people realized that they were dealing with Urgenchians. Then they talked about customs duties. Ivan refused to give them duties, since he was sent from Mikhail Fedorovich to Arab Khan on state business, and was not a merchant; he would give them nothing by way of duties. Concerning this they were in negotiations for two days. Those people, seeing that they couldn't take anything, started to talk about trade, and had horses and camels brought over to sell. But Ivan did not trust them and spoke with them in order that they would swear according to their Muslim law that they would neither kill him nor rob him. Of the Turkmens, thirteen good persons swore to him that they would not injure him or rob him. Then Ivan and his companions traded with them. They bought horses and camels.

Thus they left for a hill, about thirty-three miles from the sea. . . . Those thieves wanted to injure and rob them so they hid from them. Riding ten *versts* away, the mission camped by the White Mosques. They [the Turkmens] rustled all the horses and camels which they had purchased and received from them and they killed one of the men of the Urgenchian high-level envoy. They wanted to attack them for the third time, but one of the Turkmens was acquainted with the Urgenchian high-level envoy and he warned them. . . . The party purchased three horses, paying twenty rubles, and they hired that same Turkmen fellow who was acquainted with the Urgenchian envoy, giving him two pieces of worked leather, a mantle, a shirt, pants, and a knife; they secretly sent an Urgenchian *tezik* with him to Arab Khan with news in order that he would send for them and order that they be conducted safely from among the Turkmens. This was because those Turkmens obeyed no one except Arab Khan.

After that, however, they were besieged by the Turkmens for twenty days. Then they were reconciled with them. Fifty persons were faithful . . . and they conducted them up to Urgench, and they did not injure or rob them, and crossing the desert, at no place did they abandon them. After that, the Turkmens once again rode against them. . . . Ivan commanded them to be fired on . . . and someone (from the embassy) killed one of their fellows. Because of that they had a fight with them, and they besieged them for seven weeks; then those Turkmens asked of them, in recompense for the killed man, the Urgenchian envoy and the translator Ivan Tyrkov. Sensing that there was no getting past them . . . the mission gave them cloth, fancy leather, knives, fancy dishes, and other small goods that they had. They gave them all that merchandise unwillingly because they no longer had food supplies and to remain there was impossible. The closest water was two *verst*s away. At night, half of the people would stand guard on the fortifications, and the other half would go for water. But this was not feasible; they were perishing with hunger and lack of water. Having taken the goods, those Turkmens swore that they would conduct them as far as the domains of the princes. They purchased and rented horses and camels, and travelled for three days towards the royal princes' domain, and on the road those Turkmens recognized the high-level envoy of the Bukharan khan and robbed him of all his belongings. And thus they were conducted to the princes' domains; there the sentry, who was Arab Khan's officer and also the officer of Habash (the khan's son), met them. All the merchandise that the Turkmen had of Ivan: cloth, and leather, and great goods, they [the Turkmens] divided in half with them [the officials] and they took those goods . . . to the Khan Arab and to the royal princes. In the princes' domains Ivan was given neither provisions nor a cart; rather, he rode on those horses and camels that he had purchased and rented. To the officer, who had come from the khan and met them, they gave as presents two lengths of woolen cloth, three pieces of leather, and two rubles.

In Samarqand

After that, Ivan sent to the khan's uncle to speak about the captives, in order that he would, per the tsar's order, command them to be given a *laisser passer,* stating that the captives who wanted to go to Rus could travel without trouble.

The khan's uncle, Nadir Divanbegi, commanded Ivan to come to an audience with him, with presents. But Ivan did not go to him; rather he sent the translator Ivan Tyrkov and the interpreter Semeika Garasimov. In gratitude for freeing the captives he sent to him presents: two woolens, three leather *yufts* (high-quality hides), two squirrel pelts, and ten fancy plates; the translator and the interpreter brought the presents to him, but he ordered that Ivan come to see him; he had words for Ivan.

Thus Ivan came to the residence of Nadir Divanbegi. The khan's uncle conversed with him concerning the Noghay, asking if the Noghay obey Mikhail Fedorovich, the Sovereign Tsar and Grand Prince of all Russia, or do they nomadize independently? Ivan answered that the Noghay obeyed the Great Sovereign Tsar from a very early time, but in the turbulent and kingless time the Noghay Ishterek Bey and the princes were independent of the Muscovite Government and for a long time nomadized independently on the plains. No one, however, became a sovereign over them; but according to the will and desire of God, and according to the desires of Mikhail Fedorovich, Sovereign Tsar and Grand Prince of all Rus . . . the Noghay Ishterek Bey and all the princes have given homage to the great sovereign and obey the sovereign at all times with joy.

Nadir Divanbegi asked why, then, do the Noghay go to war against the sovereign's cities and raid them? Ivan said that during the turbulent and kingless time, when Ishterek Bey and the nobles nomadized independently, and were not subjects of the Muscovite Sovereign, at that time the Noghay people went against the Muscovite frontiers and raided villages and took villagers into captivity. But when Mikhail Fedorovich, the Great Sovereign Tsar and Grand Prince of all Russia, was made tsar of all the lands, the Noghay Ishterek Bey showed deference to the [Russian] sovereign. From that time the Noghay do not ride against the Sovereign's frontiers. Concerning the longtime captives, who were amongst the Noghay, Ivan said that many have been located and brought to the Astrakhan kingdom.

Nadir Divanbegi said that they already knew for a long time that the Noghay raided villages and all their captives were villagers, but there were no captives from the cities; they knew this already from the captives. Nadir Divanbegi said, "Imam-Quli Khan commanded me to speak to those Russian people of your sovereign, who were in his possession and in his kingdom in captivity. Now he has ordered all the captives to be released. But of those long-time captives, who have come to his attention in the kingdom, God has given them in order that he can deal with his rebellious subject Tursun Sultan (a powerful Qazaq prince). Having located those captives he will release them to your sovereign. But for now, he said, they [the Qazaqs] have sinfully gone against their sovereign Imam-Quli Khan and taken from the sovereign his slaves. Tursun Sultan, by raiding, has killed many and taken many into captivity. Imam-Quli Khan with various measures will send those subjects to the sovereign of your land. Because your sovereign would have it so, having located those people, he will release them to their sovereign." Ivan said that he would inform the advisors of Mikhail Fedorovich, Great Sovereign Tsar and Grand Prince of all Russia, of this speech.

After that, Nadir Divanbegi, [speaking] about their *laisser passer* and concerning the captives, said, "their sovereign had sent written commands concerning the captives to the authorities in Bukhara. Furthermore, their sovereign Imam-Quli Khan had given the diplomatic mission four thousand *khanlyk*s (about 240 rubles) for provisions on the road; the orders concerning this were in the possession of Nazar the Shiqavul, with whom you have been placed." Saying this, Nadir Divanbegi released Khokhlov back to his quarters and ordered that he be allowed to travel to Bukhara. They traveled from Samarqand to Bukhara for three days up to the fasting season of *Gospozhina* (Feast of the Assumption of the Virgin Mary) and they arrived in Bukhara on August 6th.

42   Sayyeda-ye Nasafi: A Visit to the Shrine of Baha' al-Din Naqshband

INTRODUCTION

Sayyeda of Nasaf (d. 1707 or 1711) is perhaps the best-known representative of the flourishing literary scene in Bukhara in the second half of the seventeenth century. Despite his efforts to obtain a position at the Ashtarkhanid court, Sayyeda apparently spent most of his life as a common laborer. The following passage is the first section of a narrative poem of unknown date that leads the reader on a walking tour of the major landmarks of the city of Bukhara. Sayyeda begins this tour with a visit to the shrine of Baha' al-Din Naqshband in the suburbs of the city. This passage begins by praising the "patron saint" of the shrine and the city, and celestial imagery is used throughout the description of the shrine to underline its spiritual significance. At the same time, as Sayyeda enters the shrine, he draws on the images of lyrical poetry to give a human face to the buildings. The scene is further animated by a swirl of pilgrims, mendicants, religious shaykhs and elders, and the vendors who at the end offer visitors a bite to eat.

At dawn, the world-adorning sun
disclosed paths to enjoyment everywhere.
My mind cleared of vapors, I set out
to make the rounds of the shrines.
A garden rose up before my eyes from afar,
renowned as the tomb of Shah-i Naqshband.
Did I say "garden"? It is a garden like Medina,[1]
where tomb vaults thrust forth their proud chests.
Immaculate pilgrims surround it in pure white,
their robes like crying towels cinched at the neck.
The Prophet called Baha' al-Din's spirit "son"
and placed him in the cradle as the axis of the age.
His miracles are as plain as full dawn.
His prayers expect an answer, like lovers' eyes.
His heart is aware of the secrets of divine truth;
he has united religious law with the mystic path.
The heads of the proud are his way-markers.
The heads of kings are beggars at his threshold.
Chain mail rends its collar making vows to him.
Knotty problems are undone by the key of his hand.
The haughty bend like polo sticks as his mendicants.
His beggars have no need of this world.
Like the morning candle, his elders rise at dawn.
Those who chant his name pour sweat like dew.
Eye and heart are enlightened by his dust.
His door needs mendicants day and night.
Did I say "door"? His blessed threshold!
The gates of paradise are its buttresses.
Painted like a sky full of stars,

---

1. Medina is the city on the Arabian Peninsula where the Prophet Muhammad and his followers are buried.

the door beam is a staff for the Milky Way.
Its chain is a ringleader of the light,
like a lock of hair fallen across an angel's face.
Purposes are made manifest by its archway,
and problems flee from his name.
To become renowned on all horizons, heaven
sits upon its veranda, rests its chest on its vault.
The vault of the veranda is adorned with fine lines,
looking like a youth whose beard just shows.
The arch captivates tall men of proud bearing.
The tresses of beauties gird its spiral columns.
Upon its benches, leading elders
are seated like the Prophet's companions.
Heaven is an attendant at its threshold.
Kings are travelers beneath its portico.
Did I say "portico"? The sky is obliterated within it.
The stones on which its columns stand are Mt. Sinai's.
Its prayer niche is arched like idols' eyebrows.
Onlookers yearn for its ceiling.
Its face opens on the garden—
in amazement, it turns its back to Mecca.
The imam there is as immaculate as the rose.
The *mu'azzin* teaches the nightingales to sing.
Behind the imam, the people line up as at the resurrection.
Above the roof, the whiffs of smoke are the angels.
The carpets are the veils on angels' faces.
The prayer rugs are curtains of light.
Its lanterns have wicks of hyacinth stalks,
their spouts slick and smooth with the attar of roses.
Heaven is buffeted by the breezes of its air.
Earth is trampled by the impression of its mats.
Whenever its doves take flight,
they perch like the glance on the eye's roof.
Clawing kinks have released their wings,
and they fly like the spirit-birds of the mystics.
Each one has made itself at home on a certain column,
like wise owls atop the cypress boughs.
They cast their shade everywhere,
and the blood of kings is made luminous.
In grief over this, the *homā* seeks a cage-weaver,
and Simorgh on Mt. Qaf is roast dripping blood.[2]

---

2. The *homā* is a kind of eagle whose shadow was supposed to bestow kingship on whomever it
fell; the Simorgh is a legendary bird who nests on Mt. Qāf at the edge of the world and would sometimes come to rescue the heroes of Iranian epic in their hour of need. Here both birds are used to
give the shrine dominion over temporal, secular power.

The pool at the shrine gives the pearl its luster,
and the heart of the sea melts with envy.
When the heavens cover this pool,
the milk of mercy wells up into clouds.
The fountain of youth seems but its mirage.
Thirsty Khezr needs its sparkling splendor.[3]
Whoever moistens his lips with its waters
will not thirst on the arid plain of the Resurrection.
Whoever performs ablutions with its waters
will be granted forgiveness on Judgment Day.
The earth is honored by the waters of the shrine.
The musk of China is exalted by its dust.
Trees, living and steadfast, surround it,
forever busy sawing litanies.
Like shaykhs, the trees swing their heads to and fro,
tongues lush and verdant chanting His praises.
Like the sky, their leaves have spread wide their skirts.
Just like tree of life, they shade the earth.
Their branches have passed beyond the heavens.
In the end, they reach the trees of paradise.
His tomb tablet is Moses's white hand.[4]
The sun plants roses on its thorny granite.
The torch of Mt. Sinai shines from its lamps,
and their brackets are fountains of light.
Their rays illuminate the heavens.
Whose eyes have beheld such a torch on the earth?
A banner has been raised from his dust.
Its shadow gives flight to the homā.
The red rose stole its scent from his tomb.
Delicate leaves drink from its dust.
The heads of the cherubim sweep its path.
The burning bush provides the candles for his hermitage.
The shrine's dome has no like:
Within it, heaven is a mere magic lantern show.
Bakeries surround the whole courtyard.
Their shops are open to the poor.
Did I say "bread"? Loaves rosy-cheeked as the dawn
are pulled out from the oven of heaven.
White and warm like the disk of the sun,
the eye of hope is sated just looking at them.

---

3. Khezr, who discovered the waters of eternal life, is the legendary guide of lost travelers.
4. When tested before the pharaoh, Moses pulled his hand from the folds of his cloak, and it shone a brilliant white, as though illuminated by divine light.

The sweet-sellers are singing to one side,
like parrots at the edge of a sugar cane field.
Did I say "sweets"? The sweet soul is their lover.
The customers are like Mahmud, and they are Ayaz.[5]
To the other side the grocers have their stalls
decorated for the sake of their guests.
Did I say "shops"? Their counters are like slivers of the moon.
Their broad trays are stars imprinted on the sky.
From the hubbub of people, the grounds of the shrine
seem to the eyes a sky, full of stars.
Every night, the young men make their faces
votive candles for the elders' spirits.

43   Churas: Erke Bek, a Turkestani in the Service of the Oirats

INTRODUCTION

Fazil Mahmud Churas, an official in the service of the Chaghatayids in East Turkestan, was instructed to write the history of the rulers of the region by his patron Erke Bek, apparently during the reign of Isma'il Khan, ruler of Kashghar, some time in the 1670s. The work, authored in Persian, begins with what seems to be a reproduction of the Tarikh-i Rashidi *by Mirza Haydar Dughlat (see chapter 26) and follows with its own unique account where Dughlat left off. This part of the text was edited and translated into Russian by Oleg Akimushkin in 1976. Churas's* History *is a rare portrayal of the history of the region during a time of scarce historical production in East Turkestan.*

The excerpt before you is a short biography of Erke Bek, the patron of the work, a Turkic commander fighting in the service of the Oirat confederation (Oirat being the designation of the Qalmuqs by Mongols and Oirats, and referred to as Qalmaq by Turkic and Persian speakers, as well as Russians). Erke's biography reveals the Oirats' deep involvement in the affairs of their neighbors, whether Mongols, Russians, Chinese, or Central Asians. The fighting against the Mongols described in this excerpt probably occurred in the year 1646, during a rebellion against the Qing of Prince Tenggis of the Sönid Mongols, who was allied with the Khalkha, and consequently, with the Oirat noble Sengge. The Oirats took advantage of the fact that the Chakhar, settled in central Inner Mongolia, did not join the rebellion, and plundered them. Eventually, peace was reached between the

---

5. Mahmud of Ghazna and his page Ayaz became prototypes of ideal lovers in the poetic romances of medieval Persian literature.

Khalkha and the Qing in 1655. Despite these border conflicts, tribute missions between the Zünghars and the Qing were common up to 1683, and Turkestani merchants in large numbers joined these tribute missions in order to take advantage of the duty-free subsidized trade.

Mention of the Lineage of Erke Bek and His Circumstances

It was reported that the exalted ancestor of Erke Bek, at the time of Sultan Yunus Khan (1462–87), was the honored amir of the Arlat tribe and he became the master of the people of Sayram. His offspring grew and increased there as follows: Erke Bek, son of Tahir Bek, son of Darvish Bek, son of Sadiq Bek, son of Shukur Bek. When he was twenty years old, Erke Bek left Sayram and when he arrived at the Horde of the Khung-Taiji (r. 1634–53) and Sengge (Baatur Khung-Taiji's son) he was twenty-one, and was becoming honored and celebrated.

Sengge gathered his followers and kinsmen and set out to wage war on the Chakhar. After many stops on their way, [which took] close to six months, they fell upon the Chakhar. The Chakhar too had assembled an army and prepared it to confront Sengge. In that war, Erke Bek displayed such bravery, that even Rustam Dastan and Iraj Nujavan (two *Shah-nama* heroes) did not do battle in such a manner. . . . Erke Bek's courage put to flight the Chakhar troops and reduced them to become one with the black dust. Sengge elevated him from obscurity to prominence. Sengge retuned from fighting the Chakhar. The Qalmaq heroes and warriors commended Erke Bek's courage and valor to such a degree that when a difficult and dreadful task presented itself, it sufficed to charge Erke Bek with the matter. When his skill and bravery became known and clear to Sengge, he assembled three hundred men and sent Erke Bek to the Russians (probably Russian settlements in Siberia). When they reached that territory, the Russian men, having heard the news, gathered approximately six hundred men, armed them, and set out to face Erke Bek. His companions had fallen sound asleep, but God most high filled Erke Bek's heart with vigilance. Without delay, he mounted his horse and set out with twenty men, and as they rummaged around they saw the Russian troops, all armed and wearing armor and ready to shed blood.

Erke Bek, trusting in the protection of the Glorious Lord, brought ruin upon the heads of his enemies. Having gained victory, he continued to raid and pillage. Several foes had surrendered before him, but the remaining were killed. Erke Bek's companions went to the Russian castle, while he set out in pursuit, on foot, of those who had fled, and having gained on them, made them one with the black dust. He then followed the Qalmaqs to the fortress, and saw that they were standing at a distance. He reprimanded and scolded them and, assaulting the castle, reduced its inhabitants to naught.

Among the Russians were several followers of Sengge, and they brought forth countless gifts. Erke Bek had returned from that campaign having profited immeasurable spoils. He divided the spoils and arms and horses, and of each portion sent one-ninth to Sengge.

Sengge saw the portion of the spoils sent to him by his trustworthy amir, and he sent a share to Daima Khan, to China, with [Erke Bek as] an envoy. Erke Bek, placing himself at the service of the Judge of the needs of mankind [i.e., God], performed the embassy, and returned safely and in full honor.

At the time when Sengge set out and fought the Chakhar, Erke Bek displayed such courageous acts that even Rustam Dastan and Iraj Nujavan did not do battle in such a manner. Sengge elevated Erke Bek to the highest rank. And God most High enthused light in Erke Bek's heart, so that at all times he strove to build the lands of Islam. In the year 1080 [1669–70], as he was rebuilding the lands of Islam, the amir attained his greatest reputation. With praiseworthy and laborious good work, he repaired the way stations and the reservoirs and bridges and mosques that had fallen into ruin. And in this manner he renovated the kingdom. May the vestiges of that amir's good deeds remain for ever and ever, if it pleases God.

Part 6 | Central Asia in the Eighteenth and Nineteenth Centuries

Part 6

INTRODUCTION

The people of Central Asia have long benefited from their position at the center of the Eurasian landmass. Throughout much of their history, Central Asians have enjoyed bilateral commercial relations with the neighboring civilizations of China, Russia, the Middle East, and India. And Central Asia's location, beyond the frontiers of the larger agrarian civilizations, has also made it an infrequent target for military conquest. Indeed, in those instances when military conflicts did occur, geographic obstacles and a virtually unlimited supply of horses and nomadic manpower generally placed the advantage in the Central Asians' favor. But in the rapidly changing world of the eighteenth and nineteenth centuries, Central Asia's geographical position proved to be far less advantageous than it had in the past.

This transition was underway well before 1758–59, when the armies of the Manchu Qing dynasty (1644–1911) established Chinese control over East Turkestan, later designated as Xinjiang (New Province). This victory extended Qing authority further to the west than any Chinese dynasty had achieved since the Tang era (618–907), and for those in Central Asia it represented a traumatic event. Several million Muslim Turks found themselves subjects of the distant non-Muslim Qing emperor, and many more were left wondering how such an unfortunate development could come about. This was compounded as the Russian Empire concomitantly encroached from the north and subsumed the steppe. The legendary biographies of Timur, included here in original translation, illustrate some of the ways that Central Asians grappled with their altered position in eighteenth-century Eurasia.

From the Central Asian perspective, the emergence of China and Russia as expansive colonial powers was disturbing, but at the same time it also provided some with valuable opportunities. In the eighteenth century, groups of Qazaqs, Qïrghïz, and Uzbeks willingly accepted positions subordinate to the Qing in exchange for improved commercial privileges in Qing territories. Russian diplomatic interests in the region date even earlier: already in 1620, Ivan Khokhlov was placed in charge of an embassy and sent to Bukhara and Khiva. The Khokhlov embassy was only one of many Russian missions to Central Asia in the seventeenth century, and many more were sent in later years. In 1715, the Khivan Khanate considered establishing an alliance with Russia against the neighboring Turkmen tribes. Tsar Peter the Great (1672–1725) embraced the idea, and he sent a Russian expedition to Khiva, ostensibly to help the Khivans but also hoping to expand Russian interests in the area and eventually open a direct line of trade with India. After a long and difficult journey the Russian troops arrived at Khiva, but distrust and speculations regarding Russia's long-term motivations in the region led the new Khivan Khan to order their execution.

Peter's expedition to Khiva was an especially ill-fated one, but few of the early Russian missions to Central Asia produced any significant results. Still, these initial failures did eventually make several things clear to the Russians; not the least of these was that advancing an imperial agenda in Central Asia would first require establishing a defensive position against predatory nomadic tribes in the vast and unprotected steppe. Shortly after suffering the terrible massacre at Khiva, the Russian Empire began establishing a network of militarized commercial fortresses on its southern frontier. By the mid-eighteenth century, Russia boasted a network of outposts that stretched across the steppe. This eventually came to be known as the Orenburg Line because of the central importance of the fortress at Orenburg as a commercial outpost, regional political and military center, and staging ground for diplomatic missions to the sedentary states in the south.

As these events unfolded, Central Asians were left to consider their considerably less elevated place in the changing Eurasian political arena. A long series of defeats to China and Russia made it clear that the Chinggisid bloodline, which had been the key to political legitimacy in the region for some six centuries, had grown thin—Central Asians were ready to look elsewhere for capable and inspired leadership. Tribal nobility turned away from their Chinggisid khans and instead embraced a growing network of Muslim elite, both 'ulama' and Sufis, who offered legitimacy in exchange for support for their pious endeavors and religious institutions. Religious endowments from rulers, government officials, merchants, and other sources financed thousands of mosques, madrasas, Sufi khanqahs, and other Islamic institutions, reinforcing and further expanding the Islamic cultural landscape across the region.

Nadir Shah's invasions of Central Asia in 1737 and 1740 dramatically upset the political balance in Bukhara and Khiva, and served as another catalyst for Central Asia's eighteenth-century transformation. Subsequent years witnessed the rise of three new states, each governed by ruling dynasties belonging to three different Uzbek tribes: the Qongrat in Khorezm, the Manghït in Bukhara, and the Ming in the Farghana Valley. The sources excerpted here represent only a small sampling of the rich literary traditions of these states, much of which remains poorly explored in general and virtually unknown to western scholarship.

In Bukhara, at the beginning of the eighteenth century, the Manghït tribe had risen to an elevated position under the Chinggisid Janid dynasty (1599–1747). The Manghït aristocracy gradually usurped power from the deflating Chinggisid leadership, and at the time of Nadir Shah's invasion in 1740, Bukhara was under the dual authority of the last Janid ruler, Abu'l-Fayz Khan (r. 1711–47), and his Manghït atalïq (chief minister) Muhammad Hakim Biy. In 1747, the atalïq's son Muhammad Rahim ran a coup in Bukhara; he killed Abu'l-Fayz Khan and his son, thereby ending the Janid dynasty and Chinggisid rule in Bukhara along with it. The Manghït maintained puppet khans until 1785, when Shah Murad (r. 1785–1800) disposed of the tradition and assumed the title of amir (commander). Just a short while later the Qongrat *inaqs* of Khorezm similarly discarded the practice of ruling through Chinggisid puppets. They governed for themselves from 1804 until 1873, when the region was made a protectorate of Russia. Both the Qongrat *inaqs* and the Manghït amirs worked to centralize their authority by limiting the power of ambitious tribal chieftains, relying instead on loyal slaves and the influential Islamic elite.

A similar process unfolded further to the east, in the Farghana Valley. As the seventeenth century drew to a close, Bukharan control over the Farghana Valley weakened, and in the eighteenth century, the valley became an independent locus of political power in Islamic Central Asia. This was a decades-long process that began in 1709 with the rise to power of Shahrukh Biy (r. 1709–21), the progenitor of the Uzbek Ming ruling dynasty that would eventually govern the khanate of Qoqand (1799–1876). Although contemporary accounts of his rise to power are lacking, later reports found in the Qoqand chronicles indicate that Shahrukh led a confederation of Uzbek tribes to overcome a group of theocratic Naqshbandi Sufi Khojas and establish Uzbek tribal authority in the Valley. In subsequent decades, Shahrukh's descendants established a new capital at Qoqand (c. 1740), from where they worked to consolidate their power and gradually expand their authority across the valley.

Shortly after the Qing conquest of Xinjiang, the Uzbek Ming ruler of Qoqand, Irdana Biy (r. 1751/2–63), a grandson of Shahrukh, accepted a subordinate position to the Qing emperor and began sending embassies to China. Qoqand's political relationship with the Qing remained a shaky one, partly because Naqshbandi Khojas several times used Qoqand as a staging ground for their efforts to force the Qing to withdraw from Xinjiang. But Qoqand's commercial relationship with China was lucrative: merchants from the Farghana Valley enjoyed trading privileges in Qing territory, and the Ming aristocracy used the proceeds to strengthen their military and expand irrigation agriculture in the Valley. By the end of the eighteenth century, Qoqand was the capital of a new Khanate that governed the entire Farghana Valley and, soon thereafter, beyond. As Tsarist Russia pushed its frontier further into the steppe, the khans of Qoqand sent their armies to the north and west, first seizing Tashkent and then further to the north, garrisoning troops at key locations to protect their caravan trade with Russian markets along the Orenburg Line.

Qoqand's golden age was a short one. As the Qing expanded westward and the Russian Empire pushed southward into the region, Central Asia was also attracting increased attention from the British colonial administration in India. The Great Game began in the early nineteenth century as an Anglo-Russian contest for influence in Persia. Soon thereafter, Britain became alarmed by Russian territorial gains in Transcaucasia, and it did not take long for Central Asia, including especially Afghanistan, to become enmeshed in Great Game politics. From the British perspective, there was widespread concern that Russia intended to advance through Central Asia in order to invade India, or, more realistically, to establish alliances of their own and promote anti-colonial movements that would undermine British colonial interests in the region. Russian concerns in the region were perhaps more tangible, primarily stemming from a perceived need to establish a secure frontier along Russia's lengthy southern border. Additionally, both the Russians and British had clear economic motivations to expand their empires into Central Asia; both exhibited a persistent demand for raw materials to support their growing industrial enterprises, and both considered Central Asia to be a viable supply source for those materials. And finally, following Russia's decisive defeat in the Crimean War (1853–56), Russian politicians and generals redirected their ambitions and expansionist agendas eastward, away from Europe and toward Central Asia. As the nineteenth century wore on, Russia was established as a growing force with an industrializing economy and a strong interest in Central Asia. It became increasingly clear that even the most dynamic Central Asian state would be unable to withstand the rising tide of Russian imperialism.

The Great Game literature of the Russian, British, and other Western travelers through the region differs substantially from the contemporary indigenous sources—waqf-namas, chronicles, poetry, hagiographies, popular literature, and more. Still, it represents a valuable genre for the study of Central Asian history. Of course the European accounts provide unique insights into the competing imperialist agendas in the region on the eve of Russian colonization. But the Russian and British agents dispatched to Central Asia were also educated and observant, and in addition to their political discussions, their accounts provide valuable ethnographic details that indigenous sources generally lack.

A | *The Age of Transition*

44. Timur's Legendary Biographies

Introduction

In the beginning of the eighteenth century, a corpus of extensive fictional biographies of Timur emerged and began circulating in the oasis realms of Central Asia. These manuscripts, written in prose in Persian and in Chaghatay Turkic, survived in numerous renderings in manuscript form, retelling a fantastic life story of Timur, chronologically from his birth to his death, in several dozen long and complex chapters. The author, or authors, of these works remained anonymous, and provided no direct explanation for the circumstances of the composition of these literary creations. However, it is clear that the biographies surfaced during a time of crisis in Central Asia, perhaps as one of the responses to that crisis.

These works quickly became one of the most popular literary productions in the region, and were probably considered by many to be the popular history of Central Asia. Their message was not only entertaining but also didactic, instructing the Muslim community how to behave in times of need and strife, and also outlying for the region a vision of the relationship between state and religion, emphasizing the need for a strong leader guided, at it were, by representatives of the Sufi community. The story presented here begins with Timur as a young boy detached from his family, and, following a vision, he is instructed by a Sufi shaykh to seek his fortune in the city of Bukhara. When he arrives in the city, he discovers the manifestations of the aforementioned crisis: oppression, corrupt and ineffective bureaucracy, hooliganism, drunkenness, and a general sense of collapse. However, there is still some hope in certain quarters.

Timur headed for Bukhara. He walked much of the way and became tired. He entered through one of the gates of Bukhara and came into one of the buildings, found a room, and settled there. By chance, someone had left a bag in that room that contained one ruby from Badakhshan (considered to be the most precious of rubies). There was nothing else there. He decided to take the ruby and try to sell it in the bazaar. Suddenly, a few men emerged from behind a wooden beam. They were running away, and Timur tried to ask them, but they would not answer and dispersed in every direction. A young, drunk bully emerged, carrying a dagger. Someone shouted, "Hey, Turk-boy, run away!" Timur stayed put. After all, he was tall and strong. That youth struck Timur with his dagger. Timur evaded the blow, but then the ruby fell to the ground. The thug picked up the ruby and started to run away. Timur gave chase. One man shouted at him, "Turk-boy, stop chasing this tyrant! He will kill you! He is the beloved of Baraq Khan." Baraq Khan was Bayan-Quli Khan's son [namely, the khan's son and a prince]. He set fire to the houses of many Muslims for his own enjoyment, but out of fear no one ever complained about him to his father. [At that time] Bayan-Quli Khan was becoming old and had no other son. If Baraq Khan were to be disposed of, no other person would be able to inherit Chaghatay's throne!

Although the 'ulama' managed to endure this hardship, order was needed. Sahib-qiran [i.e., Timur] was very young when he stepped into the caravansary; he had nothing and was hungry and thirsty. He thought that he would petition the dadkhah [the official in charge of receiving petitions]. At that time the dadkhah was Amir Yadgarshah Arlat. Timur explained the circumstances to him, but he said, "Go to the tumanbashi, he will take care of you." Timur went to him but he said, "Go to Amir Jalayir the mingbashi." He [Amir Jalayir] sent him to Amir Bayan Sulduz, who was of the noyans, but among the Chaghatays there was no man of strength or courage. He said to Timur, "This is a matter for the shar'ia, go see a qazi." The qazi was Imam Sa'd, who said, "I have no respect for the khan. I am a man of the shar'ia first. Go bring a witness [who will testify for you]." Timur went to the jewelers' market to look for a witness, but all the people said, "We are simple men. We cannot be your witnesses. We want to live." The amir went into a mosque and collapsed out of hunger.

In the middle of the night, a dervish came in carrying a torch. He saw Timur and asked him how he was doing. Timur explained the events that had happened. The dervish said, "Yes, it is unfortunate that we have such tyranny in Bukhara." He then said, "Tomorrow after the morning prayer, go to the minaret and you will find Malham Paradoz sitting there. Explain your situation to him. Maybe he could help. Do whatever he tells you."

The next morning Timur went to the minaret. There was a small shop in which an old man was sitting, sewing some old clothes. Timur became upset, [thinking] "How could this old man help with my misfortune?" He stepped forward anyway and greeted the man. The old man returned his greetings, but remained busy with what he was doing. He did not say a word. After a while, Timur decided to explain his situation to him. He listened to Timur's words and asked,

"Didn't you speak to the *'ulama'* about it?" "I did," said Timur, "but they sent me to Yadgarshah."

Timur thought that nothing could come out of this, but then suddenly Amir Yadgarshah himself appeared and greeted the old man with much respect. The old man seemed not to notice him and continued his sewing. After a while he said, "You impious tyrant, why didn't you help this poor young man?" Yadgarshah said fearfully, "I sent him to Amir Mu'ayyad, so that he would help him. He is my superior."

The old man sent an apprentice to bring Amir Mu'ayyad. Mu'ayyad explained that it was on account of his superior, Bayazid. Then Bayazid was summoned, and he blamed Bayan Sulduz, who arrived with his retinue, all wearing their fine brocade robes with their royal emblems. The old man paid no attention to them, and they just stood there in sheer reverence.

Timur was shocked. He felt like as if he were drowning and put his finger in his mouth [as a sign of puzzlement]. After a while, the old man said, "Hey, Bayan Sulduz, if you are of Qarachar Noyan, how come you never heard the request of this visitor?" He said, "I did, and I directed him to the *qazi* of our noble *shar'ia*." So they brought *qazi* Sa'd. Timur was astonished to see the respect which the *qazi* showed the old man. The latter, still sitting in his place, said to the *qazi*, "Why did you not implement the judgment of the *shar'ia*?" The *qazi* said, "I was looking for a witness. This young man just left and never returned."

Timur said, "I went to the Jewelers Market, but they just said that they were simple people and did not want to be witnesses. I asked them about the ruby, but they said that they would not want to deal with the *qazi*. They said that Baraq Khan is a tyrant and that they are afraid of him." Upon hearing these words the old man became bitter and enraged. He commanded that they bring Baraq Khan.

Timur could not keep silent any more. He said, "Baba, why do all these people show you such respect?" The old man said, "Sit quietly and I will tell you." But he was still busy doing his work [sewing]. Everyone kept silent and uttered no word waiting for the old man to speak.

Suddenly the sound of carriages was heard. Baraq Khan was entering with much pomp and splendor. All the amirs and townsfolk were standing in their places; everyone assembled to see the glory of His Majesty. The old man remained seated in silence. Baraq Khan and his entourage approached the old man. Then he said, "O Tyrant, for a while I was guilty of praising you, but now I will tell your father to destroy you." Baraq Khan said, "Baba, what have I done wrong?" Then he explained to him what had happened. Baraq Khan said, "I had no news of that." He sent for his close servant. As it so happened, his beloved was there. He said, "I don't know how the ruby got here. I must have been drunk." Baraq Khan placed his hand on his heart and with much reverence said, "Baba, with your permission, let this young man come to me tomorrow, and I will give him the price of two rubies." A jeweler said, "The price is one thousand gold." The Khan said, "I will give him two thousand gold."

"Young man," the old man said to Timur, "Stand up. You will take your money from Baraq Khan."

Timur said, "My claim is settled. Now explain what has just happened."

The man said, "First go and recover your money. Then return here and I will explain." Timur went to Baraq Khan's headquarters and saw him there, sitting on a sofa, entertained by dancers. He averted his eyes. Rising from his seat, Baraq Khan saw Timur and sent his servants to bring two thousand gold coins. Then he came to Timur and began to apologize profusely. He also asked him to convey his apologies to the old man. Timur gathered the gold and went back to the old man. The old man asked, "Did you take it?" Timur said, "Yes, I did." Then he placed the gold before them, divided the pile in half and gave one part to the old man. The man became irritated and said, "Hey, stupid kid. I have no need for anything in this world. Use it yourself for your own expenses." Sahib-qiran said, "Baba, tell me your secret. Make my poor soul happy."

The old man said, "Ah, charming young man, listen to my words. For the last forty years I have been making clothes. I never coveted anything from anyone. I have been calling the morning prayer from this minaret. Ten years ago during the time of the evening prayer, rain began to fall. At that time, a woman was passing. A man, a drunk of the Chaghatay, was following her and caught her by the hand, and forced her into a house. The woman wailed and cried, 'My hand, my hand, stop it! O good Muslims, I am pure. My husband said that if I'm not home tonight he will divorce me, take pity on me.' So I went to that Turk's house to help her, but his servants were there. They beat me up and I fled. I thought to myself, 'How could the woman stay with her husband?' And then I had an idea. I went up to the minaret and sounded the call for prayer, but not in its usual form. It seems that Bayan-Quli Khan was in the citadel, reciting a prayer from the Qur'an. His retainers alerted him, and he asked who was calling for prayer at this time. They told him, 'It must be a madman or a fool.' The khan sent someone to check, and he came and brought me before the khan. The khan asked, 'Are you crazy or are you sane?' I said, 'I am sane.' And I proceeded to explain to him what had happened. The khan sent for the Turk and the poor woman, and they were brought before him. He then searched for the woman's husband and brought him too. He tied a rope around the Turk's neck and strangled him to death. Nothing was revealed to the husband of the woman's sin. Then he called me Ata [lit., father]. He said, Ata, help me and let me know of whatever happens in the city.' Thanks to God Almighty I pledged to make another late call to prayer if this serves justice. And I have kept my word for the last ten years. And this is why the amirs fear me." (Today they call him Baba Paradoz, and his grave is on the south side of Bukhara near the South Gate.)

One night Bayan-Quli Khan saw Shaykh al-'Alam [namely, Shakh Sayf al-Din Bakharzi, a famous thirteenth-century Sufi] in a dream. He said, "Do not behave contrary to the *shar'ia*. Rise and give your daughters in marriage." Bayan-Quli Khan had nine daughters. He rose from his sleep, assembled his daughters, and told them, "My daughters, it is time for you to choose a man to marry." They all agreed. The youngest daughter was Saray Mulk. She said to her father, "Father,

I do not wish to depart from your fortunate shadow and I am not going to marry." Then Bayan-Quli Khan gave one daughter to Amir Chaku, one to Amir Jahanshah, one to Amir Öljei. He married off all his daughters [except for Saray Mulk] with much celebration and merriment. One day Shaykh al-'Alam appeared before him again in a dream and said, "Marry your daughter!" When he woke up he called his youngest daughter and said, "You have to get married." She said, "I am not going to choose a husband." Again Shaykh al-'Alam appeared before him in a dream and in a warning voice said, "Marry off your daughter!" Again he summoned his daughter and told her, "O my daughter, heed to my wishes and choose a husband." She said, "Do you care about my wishes? If so, give me Taraghay Bahadur's son [namely, Timur]." Since the khan was upset with Taraghay Bahadur, he did not consent. Again his daughter said, "My wish is that whoever beats me in chess, I will accept him, even if he is a shepherd." The khan was upset and said, "How can I deal with your disrespect?" She said, "I will marry even your slave boy if he is of worthy quality. Whoever wins in chess, I will become his wife." The khan agreed.

The next morning the rumor spread and many chess players gathered at the palace. The princess beat them all. At the same time, Shaykh al-'Alam appeared again in his dream and told him to give his daughter to whomever she wishes. She told him, "My beloved father, tell your messengers to tell every chess player, wherever he is found, to come." The messengers spread throughout the markets, announcing and summoning all the chess players in the realm. Timur heard the call, stepped outside, and the messenger explained to him what it was all about. Since Timur had no equal in chess, he decided to go.

The khan saw a Turk-boy, wearing a robe, on his head a fur hat. The khan said, "What does this kid want?" The messenger said, "As much as I tried to discourage him, he insisted on coming along." Sahib-qiran said nothing. The khan commanded that they bring a slave boy to him (this was Saray Mulk in disguise). They brought her. Timur knew that although the clothes were those of a slave boy, the person before him was a girl. As soon as they saw each other, they fell in love. They set the chess board between them. Sahib-qiran said, "I am going to play on one condition." The khan said, "The condition is that if you win, this slave boy is yours." He said, "And what happens if I lose?" The khan said, "Nothing is required of you if you lose." He said, "If I lose, I will become the slave of this slave boy." They played three times. Each game lasted one night and one day. Timur emerged as the winner. Finally, the princess loosened her robe, and rising, went into the house. The khan became upset. Timur did not reveal his true origin. The reason was that the khan was upset with his father. Therefore, Timur was afraid to reveal his true identity. The khan said, "Leave now! Come back tomorrow. The slave-boy is yours." Timur returned to the caravansary. The khan came back to the house and summoned his daughter. She said, "Stay loyal to your oath. Give me to him, even if he is a slave." The khan was upset. He placed a guard at the door, so that when the Turk boy came he would not be allowed to enter.

The next morning, when Sahib-qiran came to the palace, the guards at the gate would not let him pass. He returned to his room at the caravansary. The next day a maid came to the Sahib-qiran from the palace, carrying a letter: "Praise be to God. Know that the slave-boy who played chess with you is actually me, Saray Mulk, daughter of the khan. If the anxiety of love has kindled your heart, please petition the khan on our behalf. My father is a just man and will surely give me to you. If he gives you another slave, do not accept him." Timur honored the maid and sent her back. The next morning the khan went hunting. As he was riding Timur appeared before him on the road and said, "O, just king. Please keep your promise." The khan became upset that he could not go on the hunt on time and returned. The next day he sent to Timur a number of slaves, but Timur would not accept them, saying, "These are not the slaves I played chess with." The khan became agitated and appointed Siraj Qamari, his vizier, to talk to Timur. The vizier came to him and said, "Young man, that is the khan's own daughter. Go, accept something else instead." He was holding a box in his hands that contained much gold. The vizier said, "Go ahead, take it." But Timur refused, and for the next three days he was weeping for his love.

Then he decided to visit the shrine of His Holiness Shaykh al-'Alam. He covered his head and began to wail, "O Lord Creator, do not put my heart in such a state of love, and sustain me through this separation." Timur cried himself to sleep. Shaykh al-'Alam appeared before him in a dream and said, "O Amir Timur, rise! God most High will show you the way." Timur immediately woke up and headed back to the city. He soon saw something on the road that turned out to be a box. He came close and saw that it was the same box that the vizier had offered him earlier. He picked up the box and returned to town. He saw that many people gathered and were speaking anxiously amongst themselves. Timur asked one of them what had happened, but no one would answer. Suddenly the vizier Siraj Qamari came rushing. Timur greeted the vizier. The vizier spotted the box under Timur's arm, and commanded, "Arrest the thief!" They put shackles on his legs, chains on his hands. [It turned out that the previous night, a thief entered the khan's quarters, and managed to injure the khan, steal the box, and escape.]

Timur asked, "What wrong have I done?" But people simply cursed at him. The vizier brought Timur before the khan. The khan was sitting on his throne as the amirs and begs were sitting on his left and right flanks. Baraq Khan, the khan's son, was also sitting at his side. The vizier entered saying, "I found the thief." The khan said, "Was it you who came in search of my daughter?" Timur said, "Yes." The khan said, "And you injured me?" Then Sahib-qiran explained everything that had happened, but the khan showed no interest in his words. They took Timur and put him in prison. The khan's condition had worsened and soon his soul returned to his creator in the month of Ramadan. His son, Baraq Khan, took his place. The khan was buried next to Shaykh al-'Alam.

So Baraq Khan was installed upon the seat of kingship and was carefully watching Siraj Qamari. He soon executed Qamari, but after the latter's death the land fell into chaos, and Baraq Khan began to lose his mind. He was humiliating all the begs to the point that Amir Chaku, Amir Bayan Sulduz, and Amir Yadgarshah, as well as others, dropped out of his government and distanced themselves from him. Amir Timur was still in prison, as Baraq Khan seemed to have lost his memory and completely forgot about him.

The weather was very hot. It was the time of summer. Seeing no solution, Timur was sitting in his cell, weeping. In the middle of the night someone came and called to Timur, "Young man, stand up! I will help you." Timur asked him for his name, but he said, "It's no concern of yours." And he smuggled Timur out of prison. The jailor awoke from his sleep, and immediately raised the alarm. The people of Bukhara began to give chase, but Timur ran into the Friday Mosque [the mosque had six gates]. They all gathered at the gates, but no one dared to go inside. Timur climbed to the top of the minaret and waited there. He struck with a stick those who tried to climb after him. Outside, a hundred men gathered. Day passed and night descended. A little after midnight, the black-dressed man [who had saved him from prison] climbed up. Timur tried to hit him, but he said, "I am your friend." They descended the minaret when everyone around them had already fallen asleep. Two other men dressed in black joined them from the shadows. They led Timur directly to the citadel. The gate was opened before them and they stepped into the citadel. Timur asked, "Where are you leading me? I am going to face too many hardships this way." They laughed. He was led into an interior hall decorated with carpets and gold, and one of them said, "Let us play chess together. I am Saray Mulk." Timur said, "My queen, I have suffered a lot because of my love for you. Praise the Lord that we finally succeeded in meeting." Timur told her about his true origins, and the princess realized that he was indeed Taraghay Bahadur's son. The two spent the next few days together in utter delight.

One night Baraq Khan was walking on the roof, when he saw a light coming out of his young sister's room. This surprised him so he went over to check. He glanced through the crack in the door and saw the two lovers engaged in prayer. He immediately summoned ten of his strongest slaves. The princess heard their footsteps, looked outside and saw that the men had gathered outside her door. She immediately cried to Timur to stop his prayer. Timur tried to get up from his place but he was injured and collapsed. They entered, made him stand, beat him up, and carried him to the field outside of Shaykh Hasan Bakharzi's shrine, where they threw him to the ground and left him to die. Then Baraq Khan sent for one of his slaves to take the princess out of town and kill her secretly without anyone knowing about it, for "she shamed me."

The slave put the princess on a horse and rode out of town to the steppe. The princess realized that, for sure, she was about to die. She slowly took out a dagger from the side-saddle and struck the man's neck with such force that his head rolled—like an apple—to the ground. She then jumped off the horse. She took the slave's clothes and put them on, climbed back on the saddle, and headed to the town of Qarshi. In two days she reached Qarshi and from there went to Shahr-i Sabz. Her horse grew tired and she was forced to walk until she reached a place called Yighachlïq. There she saw a yellow-skinned man waiting for the shepherds and watching many sheep. That man was Taraghay Bahadur. As she approached him she fell, and her hat rolled off her head, uncovering her hair. Amir Taraghay Bahadur asked, "Who are you? Where are you from?" And she answered, "I am Taraghay Bahadur's daughter-in-law." Bahadur became upset. She explained to him all that had happened. Then Taraghay Bahadur wept, "O my dear child, Timur is my son, but I haven't been able to find him for the last two years." Then he showed his new daughter-in-law every kind of reverence and respect and assigned to her a few maids. Next, he wrote a letter to Baraq Khan detailing how Timur went to Bukhara, played chess with the khan's daughter, and how devoted the two were to each other. He included Saray Mulk's regards to her father and concluded the letter with an implied threat. The letter reached Baraq Khan. As soon as he became aware of the letter's contents he became confused. He said, "I did not know that Timur was Taraghay Bahadur's son. Does anyone know whether Timur is dead or alive?"

That very night, as the devotees of Shaykh Hasan Bakharzi were visiting the shrine, they saw something lying in the field outside [the shrine]. They came near and saw a young man moving very slowly, several of his limbs broken. Two of them carried him into the shrine to treat his wounds. He spent forty days in the shrine before he was entrusted into the care of Shaykh Hasan Bakharzi himself.

45   Thompson and Hogg: British Trade East of the Caspian

Introduction

Two English merchants, George Thompson and Reynold Hogg, traveled from Russia to Central Asia in the year 1740 attempting to identify avenues for profitable trade in the region. This was part of a growing and more concentrated British effort to explore commercial opportunities around the Caspian Sea. These merchants' account is particularly interesting as they explore the possibilities to access Central Asia from the north and northeast, overcoming a host of obstacles with skillful negotiations and considerable luck. Their portrayal of the route itself, their encounters with nomadic protectors, middlemen, and brigands, and their description of goods and commerce help us understand Central Asia during an era of crisis. Thompson and Hogg arrived in the oasis realms of Khiva and Bukhara shortly before the invasion of Nadir Shah, the Turkmen ruler of Persia, and their account should be understood also within that context. Their account was supplemented to the volume "Attempts made to open a trade to Khiva and Bukhara."

On the 26th of February 1740, we set out from St. Petersburg with a small quantity of goods, expecting to return by the end of the ensuing winter. Our intention was to learn if any trade could be carried on amongst the Tartars, particularly those of Khiva and Bukhara. Passing through the cities of Moscow, Vladimir, Murom, and Arsamas, April the 6th we arrived at Samara, which is situated on the east side of the Volga, at the distance of 1800 *versts* from St. Petersburg. Samara being the last place in Russia in our route, we procured the necessary dispatches of the governor, who had the command of the Tartar expedition. The 12th of June we proceeded on our journey under a convoy, and travelling south-east in a beaten road through a desert 300 *versts* we arrived the 17th at Yayïq, a town belonging to the Cossacks, who are subjects of Russia. Here we changed our European for Tartar habits, and providing ourselves with camels, horses, and other necessaries, we discharged our Russian attendants. It was not without the utmost difficulty that we persuaded some Khalmucks (Qalmaqs) and Tartars to engage in our service: the Cossacks of the Yayïq absolutely refused, giving us many instances of the distresses of their own people, who had been plundered and made slaves in attempting to go to Khiva; but we were resolved to encounter all difficulties. A chief of the Kirghiz [Qazaq] Tartars had sent us two persons as guides; and we flattered ourselves that the authority of their chief would be an inducement to their fidelity in our defense.

Finding other Kirghiz, who were returning home from Yayïq with merchandize, we joined them, making in all about twenty persons on horseback; our goods were loaden on camels. The 26th of June we set out on our journey, and travelled due east about 60 *versts* every day, through a desert without any road or path; the Tartars directing their course by remarkable hills and rivulets, well known to them. We were obliged to keep watch night and day, knowing that when parties meet, the weakest, even if they are of the same horda, are subject to many inconveniencies, and if they are of different hordas, they kill those who are advanced in age, and make slaves of the young people.

On the 7th of July we perceived a party at a distance, and our companions pursued, and took three Qalmaqs, with seven horses. This was esteemed a legal, and a valuable prize, and was attended with this further advantage, that we procured intelligence of the horda we were in quest of.

July the 11th, We fell in with a party of Kirghiz, with whom most of our company remained; so that we were constrained to continue our journey with our two guides only. We proceeded north-east till the 16th, when we arrived near the horda of our friend, Jani Bek Bahadur; he made us the compliment of sending his son, with several other relations, to meet us, who conducted us the next day to his *kibitka*. On reckoning our distance, we found it 800 *versts* from the river Yayïq. This Tartar-chief was sitting on a carpet in his tent; he rose, and bid us welcome, and making us sit down with him, he took a large dish of kumiss, which he drank, and made us do the same. We gave him some small presents, which he immediately divided amongst the company. Some days after we made him a more valuable present, telling him that our design in going to Khiva was to fix and carry on a trade there; in which, if we succeeded, we should bring much larger cargoes; and then it would be more in our power to requite him for all his favours: in answer to which he assured us, that we might command all the service in his power, to forward our design; and insisted that we should continue with him till the extreme heat was abated, and refresh our cattle, which, from hard travelling, were in a very weak condition.

The Kirghiz Tartars possess a very extensive tract of land, having the Bashkir Tartars to the north, the black Qalmaqs, with the city of Tashkent to the east, the Qaraqalpaq Tartars and the Aral lake to the south, and the river Yayïq to the west. They are divided into three hordas, under the government of a khan. That part which borders on the Russian dominions, was under the authority of Jani Bek, whose name on all occasions was honoured with the title of Bahadur.

They live in tents made of wooden slakes, and covered with a felt of camel's hair; this they fix or remove with great ease, whenever they change their quarters, and they never stay above two or three days in a place. They feed on horse-flesh, mutton, and venison, and drink fermented mare's milk to excess; so that they often intoxicate themselves with it. They have no grain, nor any kind of bread. When they go upon an expedition they take a small quantity of cheese, which they call crute; this being dissolved in water, is their chief sustenance during their journey. Money is hardly known among them; their riches consist in cattle, fox, and wolf furrs, which they exchange with their neighbours for cloaths, and other necessaries. What little religion they have, is Mahomedanism, and their language has a great affinity with that of the Turks. They are a strong robust people, but rude, ignorant, and treacherous. They are very civil to strangers, whilst these continue under their protection; for they esteem it the greatest dishonour to affront a guest: but no sooner is he departed, than his professed friend and protector will sometimes be the first person to rob him, and happy if he escapes without being made a slave.

These Kirghiz Tartars have very little sense of many atrocious crimes, particularly robbery. Their ordinary punishment in this case, is only restitution to the person robbed; and for murder the loss of their goods: sometimes indeed for the latter, the criminal and his whole family are delivered up into slavery to the relations of the deceased.

We remained with Jani Bek, and travelled in his company till the 8th of August, when we found ourselves in the latitude of 51½, five days journey to the east south-east of Orenburg. This city was lately built by the Russians, as a barrier against the Kirghiz and Qaraqalpaq Tartars, and likewise with a view of opening a trade with them for furrs, gold-dust, and rhubarb.

Having received directions from Jani Bek, and taking one of his relations for our guide, we joined a caravan of Kirghiz and Turkmen Tartars, about sixty in number. With these we travelled south west near 50 *versts* a day for eight days: we met several parties, but received no harm from them; although several Turkmens joined us, who, after having been robbed of their effects, had with great difficulty escaped with their lives.

August the 6th, we reached the Aral lake, which is reckoned 22 days journey from Orenburg, and 12 from the river Yayïq. We travelled south along a very high and rocky shore, where we were scarce able to get any water once in two days; and this was so bitter and salt, that necessity only obliged us to drink of it.

The Qaraqalpaqs inhabit the east shore of this lake, where the river Syr falls into it, and the Aral Tartars the south shore, where it receives the great river Amo. The latter use only small fishing boats, and never venture far from the shore. It is said that a person cannot conveniently ride round this lake in less than 35 days, being computed above 1000 English miles. There are abundance of wild horses, asses, antelopes, and wolves; here is also a very fierce creature, called *jolbars,* not unlike a tiger, which the Tartars say is of such prodigious strength as to carry off a horse.

September the 3d, we left the lake, and arrived at a valley full of brush-wood, and almost knee deep of stagnated water. We were informed that this was the channel of the river Oxus, which had run betwixt the Aral lake and the Caspian sea; but was stopped up by the Tartars many ages since.

The 5th, we came to the city Urgench, which appeared to have been a large place; but now was entirely in ruins, no other building remaining than a mosque. Here our company were very devout; they offered their prayers to heaven for their safe journey, and then went in search of gold, which they said, they had frequently found washed out by the rains from amongst the ruins of this city. We travelled on south-east till the 8th, when we arrived at some villages belonging to the Tartars of Khiva. On the 9th, our company left us, and with our guide only we proceeded due west 9 hours, and reached the city of Khiva, which is 17 days journey distant from the Caspian sea, and from Orenburg 33, computing a day's journey to be 40 Russian *versts.*

We took our lodgings in a caravanserai, which was a very mean building. Here our goods and baggage were immediately searched and valued, for which we paid duty 5 percent. We had then full liberty to sell them, but we could not dispose of a sufficient value to maintain ourselves and our cattle: for Nadir Shah, who was then on his return from India, was expected to make this place a visit; so that it was our misfortune to arrive when the state began to be in great confusion. The people were so infatuated as to think themselves a match for the Persians; but when they heard that the Shah was with them in person, they were greatly terrified.

A few days after our arrival; one of the Kirghiz came to us by night from our guide, and informed us, that if we consulted our own safety, we must return immediately; that the company we had parted with on the 9th, had been plundered by the Turkmens, and several of them killed; that they durst not stay longer in these parts; but were resolved to make up their loss on the road by reprisals. Finding he made no impression on us, he took his leave, promising to return in the spring, in company with our guide; if the country was in peace. Khiva lies in the latitude of 38½, and is the residence of a khan. It is situated on a rising ground, has three gates, and is defended by a strong wall of earth, very thick, and much higher than the houses: it has turrets at small distances, and a broad deep ditch full of water. The place is large, but the houses are low, the greater part of them being built with mud; the roofs are flat, and covered with earth. It commands a pleasant prospect of the adjacent plains, which, by the industry of the inhabitants, are rendered very fertile.

The dominions of Khiva are of so small extent, that a person may ride round them in three days; it has five walled cities, all within half a day's journey of each other. The khan is absolute, and entirely independent of any other power, except the Mulla Bashi, or high-priest, by whom he is controled. The Khivan Tartars differ very little from the Kirghiz; but surpass them in cunning and treachery. Their manners are the same, only that the Kirghiz live in tents, whilst the others inhabit cities and villages. Their only trade is with Bukhara and Persia, whither they carry cattle, furrs, and hides, all which they have from the Kirghiz and Turkmen Tartars, who often prove very troublesome neighbours to them. The place itself produces little more than cotton, lamb-furrs, of a very mean quality; and a small quantity of raw silk, some of which they manufacture.

The consumption of European cloth, and other commodities, is inconsiderable, as is the whole trade of this place; so that no profit can be expected any ways proportioned to the risque. The duty on all goods belonging to Christians is 5 percent, and to all others who are not of the Mahommedan faith: but on the goods of Mahommedans only 2½ percent. The whole revenue arising to the khan does not amount to 100 ducats yearly. Their coin is ducats of gold, each weighing one *mithqal*, or 3 penny-weight English; also *tanga*s, a small piece of copper, of which 1500 are equal to a ducat. Their weights are the great *batman* equal to 18 lb. Russian, and the lesser *batman* 9½, which they divide into halves, quarters, and smaller parts. Their measure is called *gaz*, equal to 12 inches English. . . .

Mr. Thompson, whom we left proceeding to Bukhara, gave the following account of the remainder of his journey: "I went to Hazarasp, the last city in the dominions of Khiva, and the caravan which I had joined, crossed the Amu in boats: we travelled five days along the eastern banks of that river; then we provided a supply of water, and entered a sandy desert, taking very little rest till our arrival at Bukhara.

This is a large and populous city, lying in the latitude 39½ three days journey to the northward of the river Amu: it is the residence of the khan, who is entirely absolute, though his power extends very little beyond the city. The adjacent country is called Turkestan, and is governed by several Beks, or chiefs, who are wholly independent of each other, as well as of the khan of Bukhara.

The town is situated on a rising ground, with a slender wall of earth, and a dry ditch: the houses are low, and mostly built of mud: but the caravanserais and the mosques, which are numerous, are all of brick: the bazars, or market-places, have been stately buildings, but are now the greatest part of them in ruins; these are generally built of brick and stone. Here is also a stately building of the same materials, appropriated for the education of priests, who receive very considerable profits by their public discourses on the different points of their religion, which is the same as that of the Turks. They differ from the Persians, not only in regard to Muhammad's successor, but in particular ceremonies: their hatred to the Persians is much greater than to the Christians, and they esteem themselves equally unclean by touching either of them; never omitting to wash themselves immediately after leaving their company.

The place is not esteemed unhealthy as to the air and soil; but the water is so very bad, that many of the inhabitants are confined several months in the summer by worms in their flesh, which they call Rishtas: some of these, when taken out of their bodies, prove to be above 40 inches long. There are also serpents and scorpions which infest their houses, and are very venomous; the sting of the scorpion causes great pain, and sometimes death: the most effectual remedy they find for the immediate cure of this distemper is to bruise the scorpion, and apply it to the wound.

The inhabitants of this city are more civilized and polite than those of Khiva; but they are also cowardly, cruel, effeminate, and extremely perfidious. Great numbers of Jews and Arabians frequent this place; though they are much oppressed, and often deprived of their whole possessions by the khan, or his attendants, who seize them at their pleasure and notwithstanding they pay most heavy taxes, it is criminal in them to be rich.

The trade of Bukhara is much declined from what it was formerly: their product is cotton, lamb-furrs, down, rice, and cattle; and they manufacture soap, cotton-yarn, and callicoe, which, they carry to Persia, and receive returns in all sorts of manufactures of that country; such as velvet, silk, cloth, and sashes: woollen-cloth is also brought hither from Persia, as likewise shalloons, indigo, coral, and cochineal. They have rhubarb, musk, and castorium, and many other valuable drugs from the black Qalmaqs and Tashkent. Formerly they received lapis-lazuli, and other precious stones, from Badakhshan, the capital of the country of that name, which is computed sixteen days journey from Bukhara. But the late wars, and the frequent robberies on the roads make it difficult to procure any of these commodities; so that they are carried through another channel. The khan and his officers are possessed of very rich jewels; but never dispose of them, unless in cases of the greatest necessity, and even then they are jealous of their being carried out of the country.

They make very little consumption of European commodities: as to cloth, they use it mostly in caps; but no foreign commodity bears a price proportionable to the risque of bringing it to market.

Their money is ducats of gold, weighing a *mithqal,* or 3 penny-weight English, also a piece of copper, which they call *tanga*s, that pass at 50 to 80 to a ducat, according to their size. They have no silver money of their own coin; but since Nadir Shah took this place, the Persian and Indian silver coin is very current amongst them.

The measure in Bukhara is *gaz,* equal to 31 inches English; but they always measure cloth by the Persian measure of 40 inches. Their weights are the *batman*s, containing 16 *drumser*s; which last they divide into halves, quarters, etc., each *drumser* containing 1375 *mithqal*s, of which 85½ are equal to a Russian pound; so that the Bokharian *batman* is above 16 pounds.

The duty, on all imported goods, belonging either to natives or foreigners, is 1 percent, and on goods exported 10 percent. The revenue from this duty is reckoned 1000 ducats yearly in time of peace, which but seldom happens. The Persian and Tartar languages are both spoken here; but all their writings are in the Persian tongue.

46   'Abd al-Karim Kashmiri: Nadir Shah's Campaign in Central Asia

INTRODUCTION

'Abd al-Karim Kashmiri (d. 1784), a historian of India, was living in Delhi when it was sacked by Nadir Shah in 1739. He then joined the Turkmen ruler as a fiscal officer, and perhaps also as one of his secretaries, and accompanied him throughout his campaigns. Kashmiri was able to observe many of the events he describes firsthand, or base some of his accounts on personages close to the ruler himself.

Although his account sheds light on the mechanics of conquest in Central Asia, implemented by Nadir Shah, Kashmiri also details the conditions of Central Asia shortly after Nadir Shah's campaign, as well as several observations regarding the circumstances of both Central and South Asia in the middle of the eighteenth century.

Nadir Shah Marches from Herat on an Expedition against Turan

Having appointed Nasrallah Mirza, his second son, to govern in Iran during his absence, he (Nadir Shah) set out upon his expedition against Turan, accompanied by Riza-Quli Khan Mirza his eldest son; and by quick marches arrived at Maruchaq. This town is well inhabited, but all the water in its neighbourhood is very bad. Nadir Shah has compelled some people of the tribe of Shahun to settle here. Throughout Iran, and the bordering territories, are an infinite number of *aylat*s, or wandering tribes, and of whom the Persian army is chiefly composed. The most numerous of these tribes, are the Akrad, or Kurds, the Aqsar, the Jalaru, the Qarachlu, the Fardad 'Ali, the Shamlu, and the Bekhtyari. Like the Arabs of the desert, they wander about in quest of good pasturage and water, which when they have found, they pitch their tents and remain till their cattle have eaten up all the grass on that spot, when they remove in search of more. Amongst these people, riches and property signify flocks and herds of camels, horses, oxen, sheep, and goats. Some of them, however, settle in towns, and apply themselves to agriculture. These customs prevail also throughout Turan.

From the borders of Maruchaq to the town of Andkhuy, dependent upon Balkh, there are very few buildings; and the country being unfrequented, abounds with game and wild beasts. The soldiers killed such numbers of deer, that nobody would eat mutton. Tahmas Khan Jalayir, an officer of high rank, having gone into the jungle with a small party of chosen men to hunt, a wild boar issued suddenly from amongst the reeds, and his horse taking fright, threw him. The boar then attacked him, when Ghulam Khan shot the tremendous beast with an arrow, and also cut him with his sword, upon which he quitted Tahmas Khan, and seizing Ghulam Khan killed him. He now returned to Tahmas Khan, but he was again fortunately delivered from his clutches by another servant coming up, and killing the boar with a matchlock. Tahmas Khan being very short and thick, and of a dark complexion, Nadir Shah laughed heartily at the relation of his adventure, and told him, that his little brother had used him very uncivilly.

Between Herat and Balkh is a sandy desert, entirely destitute of water, three days journey in length; the exact breadth I was not able to learn; but it extends to the borders of Khorezm, and to Qaraqalpaq, the entrance into the Dasht-i Qïpchaq. It also marks the boundary between Bukhara and Merv Shayjan. Rustam, the son of Zal, marched by this road from Iran to Turan. Nadir Shah went to Turan through Maruchaq, Andkhuy, and Balkh, and returned by Merv Shayjan; so that either way you must cross this frightful desert. In passing it this time, many men and great numbers of horses perished.

From Herat to Balkh our route lay chiefly west. As Balkh had been some time in the possession of Nadir Shah, the army did not meet with any molestation on the march to that city. Yar Muhammed Khan, the governor of that territory, obtained Nadir Shah's permission to go to Mecca, and was furnished, at his expence, with everything necessary for the journey. I afterwards met with this nobleman at Damascus, where he had been waiting a long time for the caravan; and again on the road, and at Mecca I had frequently the pleasure of seeing him. After performing the pilgrimage of Mecca, he went to Surat, and from thence into the Dekhan, where he was received with great respect by Nizam al-Mulk, who allowed him an establishment of one thousand rupees per mensum (per month); which at the death of Nizam al-Mulk was continued to him by the sons of that nobleman.

Balkh must have been a fine city before the rapacity of its governors had reduced the inhabitants to their present state of indigence. The city is gone to decay but there are some beautiful seats in the neighbourhood.

Nadir Shah Marches from Balkh to Bukhara

At the time that the Persian army were employed in plundering Dehly, Nadir Shah turned his thoughts to the conquest of Turan; and for that purpose sent a great number of workmen from Dehly and other places to Balkh, to get ready a thousand boats against his arrival in that quarter, some for the construction of bridges, and others for the transportation of grain. Had he not taken this precaution, he must have failed in this expedition, for the King of Turan had destroyed all the boats on the river Jayhun (the Amu Darya); and without carrying grain from Charjuy to the borders of Khorezm, being twelve days journey, it would have been impossible to have subsisted his army. He had long before determined upon this conquest, and when he marched into Hindustan, directed the governor of Balkh to form granaries against his return. What a wonderful exertion of mind, what resolution and foresight must this man have possessed, to have been able to form distant designs, whilst he was only entering upon the conquest of a mighty kingdom. To return from this digression. After he had made his arrangements at Balkh, and loaded the boats with all the necessary supplies, he detached 'Ali-Quli Khan, and Tahmas Khan, to guard the eastern bank of the river Jayhun, whilst he marched with the army along the western side to protect the boats upon which alone they had now to depend for supplies. After passing the twelve stages through the desert, he arrived at Charjuy, where he threw over the river a bridge of boats. The next day Hakim Ataliq, the prime minister of Abu'l-Fayz Khan, King of Bukhara, was introduced to Nadir Shah in public, but delivered his embassy in such a low tone that not one of the byestanders could hear a word of it. But Nadir Shah answered with a loud voice, "Unless he comes himself, the operations of the army must proceed." He bestowed upon the ambassador a donation of a thousand *mohurs* of Hindustan, twenty-five pieces of Yazdi brocade, a rich dress, and a horse with silver harness; after which he told him he might depart. The King of Turan, unwilling to make the submission in person, prepared for resistance. The Persian army crossed the bridge, and a detachment under the command of Tahmas Khan was ordered to scour the country about the city, to create alarms. The nobles of Turan, sensible of the impossibility of withstanding the arms of the conqueror of Hindustan, prevailed upon Abu'l-Fayz to submit in the manner required; and accordingly an ambassador was sent to make the offer, and carried with him valuable presents. After a long conference, it was settled that Abu'l-Fayz Khan should wait upon Nadir Shah, and that hostilities should immediately cease. The ambassador received a dress and other presents.

The Nussukchi Bashi was ordered to station people, to protect the suburbs from violence; and to prohibit all persons from entering the city. By this precaution, the city of Bukhara was not only preserved from plunder, but the soldiers paid the tradesmen the full value for everything that they got; but the distant parts of the country were ravaged by the Qizil-bash. Nadir Shah exacted from the city nothing but provisions and absolute necessaries; for being master of all the wealth of Hindustan he looked with contempt upon the humble possessions of the natives of Turan.

The Interview of Nadir Shah with the King of Turan

The day being fixed for the interview with Abu'l-Fayz Khan King of Turan, Nadir Shah directed all his officers to appear in their most magnificient attire, in order to impress the unfortunate Prince with astonishment and awe. The Princes Riza-Quli Mirza and 'Ali-Quli Khan were on this occasion permitted to be seated, whilst the nobility stood as usual.

Abu'l-Fayz, attended by only a few of his courtiers, came on horseback from the city; but he was obliged to alight before he arrived at the royal quarters, and was conducted to the tent of Nadir Shah by Tahmas Khan. When he entered the tent, Riza-Quli Mirza and 'Ali-Quli Khan stood up and paid him their compliments; whilst Nadir Shah only answered his salutation verbally without deigning to rise from his throne. The different reception which he gave to Muhammad

Shah (ruler of India), may be ascribed to his being awed by the splendour and magnificence of the court of Hindustan; or to his not being then so far intoxicated with success, as to have forgotten the forms of respect due from one monarch to another. It is even possible that his breast was not yet bereft of every generous sentiment, and that he felt the double sensation of respect and of compassion. After sitting in this manner for near two hours, the King of Turan was conducted to a tent, pitched at some distance from Nadir Shah's quarters. Mirza Muhammad Ibrahim Isfahani was appointed his *mehmandar*, or host.

The third day after the interview, Nadir Shah concluded a double marriage. Himself took to wife the sister of Abu'l-Fayz Khan; and his nephew 'Ali-Quli Khan wedded the daughter of that monarch. After the conclusion of these ceremonies, Abu'l-Fayz Khan, in token of his entire submission, sent to Nadir Shah, by Hakim Ataliq, the diadem which he had himself worn, together with three hundred camels, two hundred horses, and twenty Persian manuscripts most beautifully written. Nadir Shah returned the crown to Abu'l-Fayz Khan with a message that he was to consider himself King of Mawarannahr. The cattle were sent to the stables; and the books were divided amongst Mahdi Khan the *munshi al-mamalik* (the secretary), Mirza Zuki, and others. It seemed as if the books had been sent to exemplify the following verse of the Qur'an, *Those who possess learning, and do not practise what it teaches, resemble asses loaded with books.* These were the only fruits of Nadir Shah's conquest of Turan, in making which he had nothing in view, but to show the irresistible force of his arms. He gave away upwards of three lacks of rupees (300,000 rupees) in presents, and his military expences amounted to an immense sum.

Bukhara, from being the residence of the monarch, is the finest city in Turan. As I was the deputy of Mirza Muhammad Ibrahim, the *divan* of the household, who was ordered to entertain the King of Turan, I had the best opportunities of seeing everything that is curious in the country, amongst which are the tombs of the holy men celebrated at full length by Jami, in his poem entitled *Rashahat.* Also on account of my office I had a share of every kind of provisions and fruits that were sent to Nadir Shah by the governors of different places. The inhabitants of Turan, when compared with those of Turkey, Persia, and Hindustan, may be said to be poor in point of money and the luxuries of life, but in lieu thereof the Almighty has given them abundance of most exquisite fruits; with robust forms, and healthy constitutions, the greatest of earthly blessings.

In reflecting upon the poverty of Turan and Arabia, I was at first at a loss to assign a reason why those countries had never been able to retain wealth, whilst, on the contrary, it is daily encreasing in Hindustan. Timur carried into Turan the riches of Turkey, Persia, and Hindustan, but they are all dissipated; and during the reigns of the four first Caliphs, Turkey, Persia, part of Arabia, Ethiopia, Egypt, and Spain, were their tributaries; but still they were not rich. It is evident that this dissipation of the riches of a state must have happened either from some extraordinary drains, or from some defect in the government. Hindustan has been frequently plundered by foreign invaders, and not one of its Kings ever gained for it any acquisition of wealth; neither has the country many mines of gold and silver, and yet Hindustan abounds in money and every other kind of wealth. The abundance of species is undoubtedly owing to the large importation of gold and silver in the ships of Europe and other nations, many of whom bring ready money in exchange for the manufactures and natural productions of the country. If this is not the cause of the prosperous state of Hindustan, it must be owing to the peculiar blessing of God.

B | *The Uzbek Tribal Dynasties*

47 *Tuhfat al-khani:* The Inauguration of Muhammad Rahim Khan Manghït

Introduction

Tuhfat al-khani *(The khan's gift), also known as the* Tarikh-i Muhammad Rahim Khani, *describes the growing influence of the Manghïts on the Ashtarkhanid court and their official seizure of power in the year 1756. Under Muhammad Rahim Khan the Manghïts became the rulers of the khanate de jure and not only de facto. The work was written by Muhammad Vafa Karminagi (1685–1769), whereas a later addition (up to the year 1769 or 1782, depending on the manuscript) was added by 'Alim Bek Ishan Nasafi. Although the work contains valuable information on the Manghïts, it has never been edited or published. This is perhaps one of the reasons why it has been so underutilized by scholars.*

Muhammad Rahim Atalïq, a Manghït tribal chieftain and the strong man in the khanate, assumed the title khan and became the first ruler of the Manghït dynasty in Bukhara, a dynasty that survived well into the Russian conquest. In the portion of the manuscript presented here, we learn how he asserted his authority and legitimation in an elaborate ceremony that followed a tradition that the Muslim authors attributed to Chinggis Khan but that had been practiced—with variations—since at least the fifth century AD.

Account of the Installation of His Blessed Majesty upon the Seat of the Caliphate and the Throne of Kingship by the Graces of the Lord

When the secretary of fate inscribed upon the tablet of destiny with the pen of the divine decree the esteemed verse *We have made you the ruler of the earth* (Qur'an 38:26) . . . and [when] the blessing-laden divine essence made him worthy of the bejeweled crown and the diadem and the girdle and parasol and diadem, [then] the endless bounty of the divine made his star of felicity sit upon the royal throne, in order to attend to the needs of the people and provide sustenance for all mankind. . . .

Upon the surface of the mighty empire, the victorious and triumphant armies of the khan of nobility and benevolence, growing bit by bit and gathering little by little, exceeded by all accounts 12,000 soldiers, and each of the soldiers was supported by a few men, and from morning to night they bound the belt of service to act for the glory and dignity of the state.

In these times, the guardians of the *shar'ia* and the community, and the men of instruction and legal opinions, whether in private or publicly, announced and explained to the court [sublime] as Saturn that whenever the Generous Lord shows approval (by means of such benevolence) to someone who has glory, the most correct traditions and the decisions based upon them [require] that he imitate the exemplar of mankind, the greatest leader (i.e., Muhammad) thus: [that] it is proper for the sovereignty of the kingdom and worthy governance to have the *khutba* of the world-monarch recited in the pulpits of Islam adorning his imperial titles, and [that] the face of *dirhams* and *dinars* will be engraved with his royal die . . . and according to the will of God, from the first days of the month of Rabi' al-awwal, which corresponds to the beginning of Qaws (Sagittarius) and the last parts of the month of Tir (of the old Iranian calendar), in the year 1170 (AH) [AD 1756], a binding decree, a decree which is to be obeyed, was issued to the state attendants and to the officials of the royal treasury of His Highness, that they prepare the sums of cash and abundant goods, and they make ready the implements of spreading justice and [everything] required for the royal rank. . . .

On Saturday, the 21st of the aforementioned month, the elite of the amirs and the best of the nobles were granted an audience in the private assembly. In keeping with the verse *And take counsel with them in the affairs* (Qur'an 3:150), the sovereign, the patron of religion and state, brought [the inauguration procedure] before them, and explained the right-guided opinion of the people of guidance and prudence about attending to the royal accession and performing the affairs and royal decrees. And he made his eloquent tongue issue the sweet words of the following statement:

> The reins of the affairs of mankind in arranging the affairs of the times must be in the palms of ability and in the grip of authority of a mighty monarch, so that heroes of his blood-spilling sword will every moment tear the root of life from the enemies of the kingdom and the Muslim community with an assault *wherein is great might* (Qur'an 37:25) and [so that] the guards

of his venomous sword will pour the wine of death into the mouths of those who rebel against religion and state. From the beginning of the state and the rise of the star of felicity of Muhammad Khan Shïbani, the past sultans and khaqans established this praiseworthy tradition, and displayed noble zeal, and demonstrated miraculous power in arranging the affairs of the kingdom and securing its borders. For undertaking this exertion and effort, they earned fame in both worlds and won out over their peers and equals. When the will of the Almighty God resolved upon the expiration of the rule of their dynasty and the destruction of Mawarannahr, for an [entire] generation they recited a worthless *khutba* in the name of Abu'l-Fayz Khan. During his reign all kinds of corruption appeared from every corner of the kingdom, to the extent that in most of the regions and cities and areas of this country not a soul was to be found. [But] in accordance with the words *He eradicated the people who were tyrannical* (Qur'an 6:45), not a single one of the rebels or of the people of enmity and malice has now been left in our fortunate state.

It has been eleven years since one blow of the royal sword hamstrung the unbroken steed of wickedness and the piebald horse of corruption, and the hand of effort uprooted the tree of oppression and tyranny from its roots and foundations.[1] The ailing health of the kingdom was approaching its recovery, and the four pillars of the building of prosperity were being erected. Now it is proper for the state counselors to adorn the royal throne with the person of the monarch, so that the flame of his fortunate glory will be the beginning of the rise of the star of Canopus of the new state.

On Monday, the 23rd of Rabi' al-awwal, which corresponds to the beginning of Toqsan[2] and the middle of the month of Qaws and the last days of the Year of the Mouse, in the year 1170 AH [December 16, 1756], the chamberlains of the royal court, having brightened and polished the floors of the audience hall of the imperial palace with the broom of service, spread out multicolored carpets. They adorned the throne of the monarch with brocade and silk, embroidered cloth and satin. The astrologers chose for the hour of the imperial enthronement the [rise of the] planet Jupiter, which, according to the rules of those who observe the astronomical tables, was on the third hour of the aforementioned day.

The expanse of the hall of audience was filled with the crowd of the great men and amirs, and great numbers of nobles and commoners, and the multitude of the army and the subjects of the kingdom, and the vast number of commanders of the victorious army swayed the secured posts, and the crowds of attendants were waiting for the appearance of the felicitous monarch and expecting his fortunate footsteps.

At that time, when the morning of his rule and the time of accession to the imperial throne became imminent, the king, as magnificent as Darius of great majesty, with the power of 'Alamgir and adorned like Awrangzib, and with the

---

1. A reference to the year 1158/1745, when the city of Bukhara was sacked by rebellious Uzbek tribes and Muhammad Rahim was sent by Nadir Shah to help restore order in the city.
2. The ninety days of the cold season according to traditional local calculation.

royal crown upon his head and the bejeweled robe upon his chest, from head to toe studded with pearls and jewels, and with generous thought and strong heart, and relying upon the aid of the Lord, set his foot outside of the royal palace with the aim of establishing his rule and arranging the foundation of religion and state. Together with the servants of the palace he came to the entrance of the court and summoned his close servants to come there. And he dignified each one with honorable tasks and stationed his bodyguards. In the manner and custom of the khaqans and the principles of the Chinggisids and the Qa'ans, he went toward the public hall of audience and the venerable throne.

When the green sapling of the fortune of the king of praiseworthy qualities appeared in the assembly of the people of God, the great amirs and the notables, distinguished by their power and knowledge, in perfect joy and gladness, gathered at the foot of the throne of the caliphate. They brought forth and spread out the white felt of good omen, which was among the customs of the royal method of accession. And His Highness, having placed his blessed foot upon the noble carpet, sat upon it, as was the royal custom, facing the *qibla* of felicity.

Although the ancient custom and the longstanding rule of the Chinggisid sultans is that in completing the affair of the khanship (i.e., the inauguration ceremony) and in executing the business of placing [someone] on the throne of successorship, the amirs of the four clans raise the felt at its corners—and they do not allow others [to do it]—[now] the great *naqib*s and the most honored judges and sayyids and the exalted amirs, out of their loyalty, sincerity, and utter enthusiasm, came rushing and dashing forward and grasped that piece of felt from all sides. For example, the *ishan*, spiritual guide of His Felicitous Majesty, Ishaq Khoja Makhdum-i A'zami, and Muhammad Amin Khoja *naqib* Sayyid Atayi, and the chief *qazi* Amir Nizam al-Din Husayni, and *qazi* Mir Abu Tahir Samarqandi, and 'Abdallah Khoja *shaykh al-islam* Juybari, and Shihab al-Din Khoja *shaykh al-islam* Ahrari, and *qazi* Mahmud Shah Samarqandi, and the pillar of amirs, Khojam Yar Biy Utarchi, and *amir al-umara* Daniyal Biy Manghït, and Ghayballah Biy *divanbegi* Bahrin, and Jahangir Biy *divanbegi* Saray, and Imam-Qul Biy *parvanachi* Manghït, and Dawlat Biy *parvanachi* Manghït, and several of the *dadkhah*s and *toqsaba*s and many of the commanders of the army.[3] [And] they began to praise God, and they raised the imperial khaqan above the throne, like the rising of the sun and the moon. The cry of joy and the sound of felicitations and the praise of the people with the meaning of the words of the glorious Qur'an, *Such is the grace of God, He bestows it on whom He will* (Qur'an 57:21), reached the zenith of the Pleiades. The royal throne of command became, by being honored with the khan's august person, the rising-point of fortune, and the imperial throne found beauty and elegance from the ascension of the benevolent and magnificent khaqan. . . .

The great amirs and most reverend judges and *sayyid*s, having come from the right and left wings of the court, sat in their places. And the *toqsaba*s and mas-

---

3. The *divanbegi* was the head of the civil administration, the *parvanachi* issued decrees for important people, the *dadkhah* was in charge of correspondence with foreign rulers, and the *toqsaba* was a military rank.

ters of ceremony and the chiefs of the *yasauls*, ready for service, lined up at the end of the royal assembly, arranging [themselves] in rows for the reception. The bodyguards and the close retainers placed themselves in appropriate places to the right and the left at the back of the royal throne. The cooks and the cupbearers of the royal kitchen unfolded the generous tablecloth. They brought so many sweets, and so much food and drink that the eye of greed could not be kept open, because of the sweet wine, and became sated with the abundance of food.

In spite of his young age, Mir Zayn al-Din Khoja, son of the chief *qazi*, wrote a learned treatise about the imamate, appropriate for the occasion. And he was shown kindness and given a robe of honor. And the poets of the age composed splendid poems in praise of the king of all time, and they pledged their allegiance before the royal assembly. And they became distinguished among their peers through kindness and royal gifts and glorious honors. The kingly will so demanded that the commanders of the army with their retinues, and the amirs of the right and left wings, and the dignitaries and elders, be favored and honored with proper robes of honor, and therefore, the blessed pillar of the state, Dawlat Qoshbegi, who was in charge of the royal treasury, exalted all the judges and *sayyids* and army generals, the commanders of thousands and hundreds and tens, with [the grant of] splendid robes of honor and royal garments. That day, the floor of the court was made so colorful by various kinds of fabrics that the people were wearing—brocade, and silk, and embroidered cloth, and silk with gold threads, and thick, smooth woolen cloth, and warm woolen cloth, and other dresses of many colors—that in looking upon them, the eye of curiosity was bewildered.

Since the weather was cold, they set up the throne in the hall of audience, which had been recently renovated, wherein the authority of the king served as an architect. And a wise mind composed this verse concerning it:

> Heaven has not seen such an august edifice with its [own] eyes;
> No one can recall such an exalted building.

On Thursday, the *muharrir-i awraq* [the writer of (these) pages, i.e., the author] presented a poem in the hall of the king of the horizons, and was ennobled through the grace of His Imperial Majesty.

On Friday, the fifth day of the king's reign, His Majesty mounted his horse in his ever-increasing glory, and with the army commanders and servants and attendants at the bridle of the horse of felicity, turned to the mosque of the high citadel (*ark*) in order to perform the obligatory prayers and to complete their devotion and benediction. That day, the preachers of the age recited the fortunate *khutba* and the imperial titles in the blessed name of the king of the age from the pulpits of Islam, from Bukhara to Samarqand and Miyankal and Shahr-i Sabz and Qarshi and Khuzar and Qaraqul, to the banks of the Amu Darya and the rest of the villages and roads and paths of the kingdom. And they praised the noble and prosperous king. At the time of the public prayer, His Majesty, as great as Jamshid, sat upon the imperial throne. The amirs of the right and the left wings were arranged in their places. The deputies of His Majesty and the governors divided up the duties of governance in accordance with the [khan's] obligatory command. The secretaries, distinguished by their eloquence, wrote the diplomas and royal orders and the headings of *yarlïqs* and decrees [with the name of] Abu'l-Muzaffar wa'l-Mansur Muhammad Rahim Bahadur Khan.

48   *Majma' al-arqam*: An Administrative Manual from Bukhara

INTRODUCTION

The administrative manual Majma' al-arqam *by Mirza Badi' Divan, was apparently written in Bukhara in 1798, with an appendix (whose authorship and provenance are still debated) added around 1800–1801. The author is mentioned in a list of officials in a contemporary Bukharan chronicle as one of the highest-ranking administrators, appointed or reappointed, shortly after the enthronement of Amir Haydar (r. 1800–1825), to the position of "vizier of the supreme divan" and apparently was in charge of the treasury.*

The list of ranks in the Bukharan administration that is presented in the Majma' al-arqam *should be treated with some caution, as it tends to present the different positions in an overly formulaic manner, disregarding contradictory information from other sources. Be that as it may, the work still provides a detailed and comprehensive register that serves as a testimony to the complexity of Bukharan bureaucracy. Only a handful of examples of the numerous positions listed in the* Majma' al-arqam *are provided here.*

The manual begins by asserting that the rulers of Mawarannahr have traditionally divided their administration based on the number four, an auspicious number on which so many things were based. In the words of the manual, there are four established forms of physical geography; the first rightly guided caliphs were four in number; there are four elements (earth, water, wind, and fire), four human tempers (phlegm, yellow bile, black bile, and blood), four seasons of the year, four cardinal directions, four types of precipitation (snow, rain, dew, and hail), and so forth.

[In agreement with the principle of four], the rulers of Mawarannahr, in accordance with the brilliant *shar'ia* set up four [types] of high positions for the esteemed learned men:

First among them, the judges, highest among them is the *Shaykh al-Islam*. To him appeals the Supreme Judge (*qazi al-quzzat*) and conforms with him. Consequently, the position of *Shaykh al-Islam* is highest above all the other judges. Next, the Supreme Judge (*qazi al-quzzat*), to whom appeal such distinguished personages as the Military Judge (*qazi askar*), of whom he (the Supreme Judge) is higher, and he commands over all the troops and common people. Next, the Military Judge (*qazi askar*), to whom appeal the troops and he is in charge over them.

The second position is occupied by the *mufti*s; highest among them are called *a'lam.* They issue *fatwas* for the people. Next are the military *muftis* (*mufti askar*), who issue *fatwas* for the military, especially during times of military gatherings, or during the travels of the amir to adjacent lands.

The third position is that of the *mukhtasibs.* If there is no *mukhtasib* from among the *sayyids,* they allow someone from among the non-*sayyids* to supervise the people's observance of the *shar'ia.*

The fourth are positions of the teachers . . . who spend much of their time instructing students.

There are four other positions in His Majesty's court. . . .

The first—the highest position—is entrusted to special representatives of the Juybari administration from inside and outside the city walls. Sometimes *sayyids* are appointed to the position.

The second is the *naqib,* who looks after the conditions, equipment, and allocation of troops during campaigns, movements, and battles.

Third is the *uraq,* who has the duties of the *mukhtasib* in the military.

The fourth is the *naqshbandi,* who is in charge of the administration, irrigation, and grounds of the resplendent shrine [of Baha' al-Din Naqshband].

Four other positions, the administrators of which are chosen from among the learned, the *sayyids,* the Uzbeks, or others, whoever is found suitable [are as follows]: the *mir-i asad,* the *faizi,* the *sadr,* and the *sudur.* The *faizi,* if he is a scholar or a *sayyid,* is charged with the duties of the *mukhtasib* outside the city of Bukhara. The *mir-i asad* too, if he is a scholar or a *sayyid,* is charged with the duties of the *mukhtasib* among the *sayyids* inside Bukhara. The *sadr* manages registration of *waqf* inside Bukhara, and the *sudur* handles *waqf* registration outside the city.

There are four other positions of bureaucracy: First, the high divan (*divan-i kalan*), who manages the documentation of *tankha, tilgu,* and so forth. The second is the *mushrif,* who in charge of recording government inventory such as shields, clothes, and assorted gifts.

The third is the *daftardar,* who decides on affairs of the highest registrars, repeals or approves *tankha* or *soyurgal.* The fourth, the *divan tanabana,* handles land tax.

There are four other positions: First among them is the secretary (*munshi*), who writes the *yarliqs* and official documents. The second is the *arbab,* who looks after the cleaning of canals . . . the third is the *divan* for the affairs of Arabs . . . and the fourth consists of different *divans,* handling bookkeeping and accounts.

There are four other, more minor positions: The librarian keeps treaties and looks after books. The second is the *bakhshi,* who is in charge of expenditures of building activities; the third is the *divan sayis khana,* who is in charge of horses and stables; and the fourth, the *divan tushak-khana,* manages the store room and supplies.

The next four positions are those who support the amir: First among them is the *ataliq,* which means "fatherhood" and so they call the [amir's] guardian. The *ataliq* has to have the kind of relations with the sovereign as a father has with his son, and also has to treat the rest of the subjects in a similar manner. He also handles water management of the rivers of Bukhara and sees that water is distributed fairly as far as Samarqand and Qaraqul. . . . The second is the *divanbegi,* who manages the *kharaj* lands *mu'azaf,* and is in charge of revenues from all types of lands, and is also in charge of the officials of the chancellery. The third is the *parvanachi,* who issues the *yarliqs* for people of significance. The fourth is the *dadkhah,* who receives all complaints and petitions, and the government's response to said petitions. He is also in charge of correspondence with foreign rulers.

49   A Collection of Royal Decrees from Khiva

INTRODUCTION

Documentary evidence from Central Asia is varied and extensive and includes, among other things, numerous types of yarliqs *(decrees) issued by the rulers, now kept in (mostly) Central Asian archives. Such documents typically followed similar practices in other parts of the Muslim world, particularly in Iran. The three following examples from the khanate of Khiva, typically written in Turkic, provide a glimpse into the complex world of Central Asian chancellery practice. The first is a decree granting land for military service. The second is known as* tarkhan yarliq, *namely, granting the status of* tarkhan *or the right to be exempt from duties and taxes to certain individuals. A typical yarliq begins with the invocation of God and the attestation of the khan's command, whereas the main body of the text first states the people concerned with the content of the document, then addresses the special status of the recipients of the decree, then explains the khan's decision, and finally warns against attempts to ignore or dispute the khan's decision. The third example is a yarliq announcing the appointment of an official.*

1. Land grant for military service.
Decree of Abu'l-Ghazi Khan, 1206/1791–92

Abu'l-Muzaffar va'l-Mansur Sayyid Abu'l-Ghazi Muhammad Bahadur Khan. Our word:

Having distinguished and exalted with our endless royal favors the refuge of the amir's rank, the tool of governance Shah Niyaz Ataliq, we gave him two plots of land in the locality Kinik, out of crown land, as a salary for *nukers* (soldiers), in exchange for thirty *tilla* and a copy of the Qur'an, having made them tax exempt private property. The first plot is approximately 10 *tanaps* (1 *tanap* equaled approximately 4,000 square meters), with the following borders: in the east—*waqf* land cultivated by the heirs of Nur Allah Sufi; in the north—the wall of the mosque, and partly *waqf* land on lease to Mulla Dawlat and partly a water escape canal; in the west—*waqf* land cultivated by the heirs of Fathallah Makhdum and the land leased by Qara Qilich, and in the south—canal Aq Yap. And the second plot is also approximately 10 *tanaps*, [with the borders] from the east—*waqf* land held by *tushakchi* (the khan's official in charge of his bedding), from the north— canal Aq Yap, from the west—*waqf* land cultivated by Hasan Shigavul, and from the south—along the entire length the old [canal] Aq Yap. Now, as soon as the contents of this royal decree become known, the above mentioned two plots [of land] whose borders are known should be considered as purchased private property, and no one, by any means, should trespass and disturb him (the grantee). And after himself it should be a hereditary property of his descendants, from generation to generation, for ever and ever. And, if they wish, in case of need, [to sell it], it should be, the same way, the tax exempt private property of the buyer. And we also granted one *qulaq* (a measure of water for irrigation) of water from the khan's canal. At the time of watering may the *mushrif* (a tax collector and/or supervisor of the khan's estates), and the crown officials give one *qulaq* of water without hindrance. And whether it is during an *aspak* or not during an *aspak* (a condition of water shortage in one portion of the canal), they should not throw .. . to the aforementioned. From now on, any one, who, out of greed, takes away this land or helps to take it away, may be cursed by God and detested by all the angels and may remain without the intercession of the Lord most merciful, abhorred and destitute. *"And if any man changes it after hearing it, the sin shall rest upon those who change it."* The royal decree was written [in the year of] 1206.

2. *Tarkhan yarlïq*.
Decree of Muhammad Rahim Khan, 1224/1810

[This document relates to the testimony of nine khojas from the descendants of 'Ali asking for the renewal of privileges they had received from former rulers. Having learned their genealogy, the khan decided to grant them the status of *tarkhan*.]

Now, as soon as they learn the contents of this august royal decree [all the officials] should know that the aforementioned group are *tarkhan*s and exempt from taxes. Understanding that they are exempt from all state taxes and royal dues, all the officials should withdraw their feet and the scribes should withdraw their pen. Wherever they sow grain and plant trees, [the officials] should not demand [that they pay] *jarib* and *tanabana* (two types of land tax) and should not collect tax from their silk. Envoys and travelers, those who come and go, should not descend on their homes and seize their animals as *ulagh* (the duty to supply animals to the khan's envoys). Custom officials, boatsmen, *qorughban*s (special guards), *daravazaban*s (gate-keeprs), *tarazuban*s (officials in charge of the bazar scales), biys [of?] *qaravul*s (small military detachments), and *katavul*s (officials with unclear duties) should not covet and exact from them a single *habba* (symbolic of low value) and a single *dinar* (symbolic of a high value), and they should by no means cause them harm and damage and make them vexed. [The officials] should not demand a new decree every year, so that the aforementioned group, in peace and quiet, after saying the five [obligatory] prayers, be busy with the prayers for our everlasting kingdom. The decree bearing [the royal] seal was in the mouth of Jumadi II 1224 of Hijra.

3. Appointment of Officials.
Decree of Muhammad Amin Khan, 1271/1854

He [is God.] Abu'l-Muzaffar va'l-Mansur 'Abd'l-Ghazi Muhammad Amin Bahadur Khan. Our word:

Since the abundant fairness and honesty of Mulla Muhammad Musa have
become clear and evident to our mind, illuminating like sun, we exalted and distinguished him with our royal favors and kingly largesses and appointed him to
the town of Hazarasp, with its dependencies and appurtenancies, to replace Mulla
Muhammad Nazar Akhund, to be jointly as *ra'is* (public supervisor of the *shar'ia*)
with Mulla Ya'qub Khoja, and to be jointly a *mufti* with Mulla Sayyid Nazar, and
granted him [this] royal decree, in the order that he, as befits his impartiality and
fairness, instruct the Muslims on the religion and rites, inspects the *mullas*, the
imams, and the *mu'azzins*, have the boys sent to the school, orders those who are
negligent with their prayers to perform them, censures those who are acting contrary to the *shar'ia*, and, when the Muslims need it, writes [for them] testimonies
and legal opinions. Now, as soon as the people of the above mentioned town learn
the contents of this royal decree, they should recognize the aforementioned, the
same way as his associates, as an associate *ra'is* and *mufti;* and when they have
their marriages, they should register it with them and hand over [to them] the
marriage contracts and, when needed, receive from them testimonies and legal
opinions. And in the matters of the rules of the *shar'ia*, they (i.e., the people of the
town) should consider the commands [issued] by them as orders [to be followed]
and their prohibitions as prohibition [to be observed], and they should understand that doing [anything] contrary to the meaning of this sublime decree will
inflict upon them royal punishment. And both aforementioned *ra'is* and *mufti*
should treat the people in such a way that they will be able to give a righteous response should tomorrow bring "the Day when the Reckoning will be established."
The royal decree was written in [the year of] Hijra 1271, in the royal capital of
Khorezm, the place of paradise-like assemblies, on the 22nd of the month of Rabi'
I, Monday, corresponding to the year of the Leopard.

50   *Muntakhab al-tavarikh:*
On the Relations between
Qoqand and Kashghar

INTRODUCTION

*The Muntakhab al-tavarikh, written by Haji Muhammad
Hakim Khan (born in the Farghana Valley circa 1803), provides a fascinating narrative of events relating to the early history of the khanate of Qoqand (1799–1876).
Because Hakim Khan was a member of Qoqand's ruling family and he spent much
of his life at court, the source offers a unique and detailed "insider" analysis of the*

political history of the khanate from the mid-eighteenth century to 1843, when he
completed work on the text.

Further to the east, in Kashghar, political authority had long since shifted
from Chinggisid hands to the leaders of two rival clans of Naqshbandi Khojas,
both descended from Makhdum-i A'zam (1461/2–1542/3), a famous Sufi and
a sayyid (i.e., a descendent of the Prophet Muhammad) from Samarqand. It
remained that way until the armies of the Manchu Qing dynasty (1644–1911) con-
quered the region in 1758–59, and several million Muslim Turks became subjects
of the Qing emperor.

The following excerpt from the Muntakhab al-tavarikh *describes a jihad led*
by Jahangir Khoja (1790–1828), a descendent of the Afaqi Khojas who aimed to
oust the Chinese and reassert Khoja authority over Altishahr, the "Six Cities" (or,
as referred to by Hakim Khan, Yetishahr, the "Seven Cities") region in what is
today China's westernmost province of Xinjiang.[4] *This was neither the first nor the*
last of the Khojas' efforts to reclaim their ancestral territory, but this particular
jihad is notable in that Jahangir Khoja actually managed to defeat the Qing army
and, for a short while in 1826–27, successfully reinstitute Khoja rule in Altishahr.

Hakim Khan's account also provides valuable insight into the tense relation-
ship between the charismatic and influential Khojas on the one hand and their
patrons in Qoqand on the other. The Khojas were immensely popular in both re-
gions, and the rulers in Qoqand respected them and valued their support. But one
finds that the Khojas' political ambitions also posed a serious threat to Qoqand—
if not directly, then out of fear that their efforts to retake their ancestral lands
might provoke a potentially disastrous Qing response. In the end, Hakim Khan
concludes that Jahangir Khoja's theocratic revival was doomed to failure. While he
attributes this to Jahangir's poor leadership and personal shortcomings, one might
also point to the overwhelming force of Chinese troops that invaded Altishahr in
the spring of 1827, charged with recovering the territory that the emperor had so
humiliatingly lost to Jahangir the previous year.

During his reign, Amir 'Umar Khan had given refuge and sup-
port to Jahangir Khoja, *siadat panah,* in the *ark* (fortress) of Qoqand. But when
Madali (Muhammad 'Ali Khan) took power, he had no interest in following in
his father's footsteps. Because of this, Jahangir Khoja suffered difficult times and
resolved to make an alliance with his brother, Mahmud Khan, Turä Khan, and
a few other people and flee the Farghana Valley to Kashghar. They left, but soon
after their departure Madali received word of this and sent a company of soldiers
to stop them before they could leave his territory. The soldiers quickly closed the
roads and, after three days, they caught up with Jahangir Khoja and captured him
in mountains near Andijan. The soldiers brought Jahangir Khoja to Qoqand in

---

4. The six cities of Altishahr are: Kashghar, Yarkend, and Khotan in the west, and Aqsu, Kucha, and Uchturfan in the east. The "seventh city" of Yetishahr is Yangi Hisar, located to the south
of Kashghar.

humiliation and disgrace, and Madali had the renegades cast into prison. After three days, Madali issued an order freeing Turä Khan, but not Jahangir Khoja.

That was in the beginning of year 1238 (autumn 1822). Also in that year, there was a terrible earthquake the likes of which nobody had ever heard or seen before. Many people were trapped in their houses and died, and many houses were damaged. In the mountains near Qoqand, a few families were even pulled underground. Black ash was visible from underground, and water bubbled from below like a fountain and covered the earth. Tremors recurred for some six months.

It did not take long for Jahangir Khoja to develop a desire to return to Kashghar. Through trickery and deceit, he managed to escape from prison, secure a horse, and flee. Moving as quickly as he could, in three days he passed beyond the boundaries of Qoqand. He reached Alay (Kyrgyzstan) and then entered the fortress of Tashqurghan and claimed the state as his own. News spread quickly that Jahangir Khoja had returned to rid Kashghar of the *kafir*s, and many Qïrghïz joined forces with him. At that time, Issa Dadkhah, the ruler in Andijan, and Khudayar Mirza, a noble of Qoqand, abandoned Madali to join Jahangir Khoja. They spent one year in Tashqurghan and then took a large number of troops to Kashghar. The journey through narrow mountain passes was extraordinarily difficult, and many Qïrghïz quit to return home. Finally, Jahangir Khoja and a few of his companions reached the *mazar* (tomb) of Sultan Satuq Bughra Khan (near Artush), one of the seven sultans, and also the tomb of his ancestor, Afaq Khoja, and Jahangir Khoja prayed, asking them for help.

Learning that Jahangir Khoja had returned to the region, the Chinese sent a force of 4,000 troops from their citadel at Gulbagh toward the tombs. When the Chinese arrived, they surrounded the place and began to attack. Jahangir Khoja fought back, but his troops abandoned him. Still, he kept fighting until only seventeen of his soldiers remained. Then, Jahangir Khoja sent one of his companions, Hasan Khoja, to Qizil Su, a large Muslim settlement, to let them know that Jahangir Khoja had returned and needed their assistance. While Hasan Khoja was en route, the *kafir*s prevailed and entered the tomb. Many people died, but Jahangir Khoja, Issa Dadkhah, and another follower managed to escape. That night, while the Chinese troops were searching in the dark for Jahangir Khoja, he entrusted his freedom from this predicament in the hands of God. With that thought in mind, he and his two companions hid in a grave and waited for death to come. Jahangir Khoja had resigned himself to the fact that he would soon be dead, but God saw fit to release him from that miserable condition.

Two days before the Chinese troops captured the tomb, Jahangir Khoja had sent word to Jamayeh Chum Baghish informing him that he would be coming and inviting him to join his *jihad* against the Chinese. Upon hearing Jahangir Khoja's name, 6,000 brave *ghazis*, great fighters, took up their swords and rushed to his aid. They reached the tomb at dawn to find that the enemy Chinese had taken it, and Jahangir Khoja was nowhere to be seen. The Muslims fought the *kafir*s with everything they had. It was such a fight that a stream of Muslim blood flowed toward paradise and a stream of *kafir* blood descended to hell. Finally, the breeze of victory began blowing from the Muslims' side and the *kafir*s began to lose. Not one of the 4,000 Chinese troops remained. They all either fled or were sent to hell.

When the army of Islam had finished with the *kafirs*, they began to search for Jahangir Khoja. While the search was underway, Hasan Khoja arrived with another 12,000 *ghazis* from Qizil Su. Even with everyone looking there was still no sign of Jahangir Khoja. But one of Jahangir Khoja's companions had exited the grave, and, while he was wandering about, some of the *ghazis* captured him and interrogated him about Jahangir Khoja. At first, because he did not know whether they were friends or in league with the Chinese, he denied having any knowledge of Jahangir Khoja's whereabouts. But he quickly realized that they were all slaves and servants of Jahangir Khoja and, with great joy, he led the *ghazis* to him. As soon as they learned that Jahangir Khoja was healthy they all praised God and rushed to greet him. The entire army of Islam, weeping, approached Jahangir Khoja at the graveyard and fell to their knees before him. Then with great respect and honor, they put Jahangir Khoja on a fast and noble horse. As people heard this news, everyone, young and alike, came out to welcome Jahangir Khoja as he was on his way toward Kashghar. Amirs, *'ulama'*, and dervishes all welcomed him with respect. Even the governor of Kashghar, who had been appointed by the Chinese, saw no alternative but to welcome Jahangir Khoja.

The governor tried to explain away his error in working on behalf of the Chinese and beg forgiveness, but Jahangir Khoja had him executed. Then, with respect and glory, Jahangir Khoja sat on the throne of Kashghar.

Jahangir Khoja's Rule in Kashghar

Everybody, including Madali, learned the wonderful news that Jahangir Khoja had assumed power over the seven cities of Kashghar. Madali became very envious, and he regularly sent ambassadors to Jahangir Khoja so that they might establish an official relationship. Jahangir Khoja responded in kind, and his ambassadors reported to Madali that the Chinese fortress of Gulbagh remained unconquered and that if Madali were to lead a force to Kashghar, he would agree to an alliance and they would take Gulbagh together.

Fear of the Chinese made Madali tremble at just hearing the name "Gulbagh." But Madali's subordinates informed him that the Chinese treasure inside the fortress at Gulbagh included many gold bricks and that, if he would agree to the mission, victory would be easy and the treasure would be his. Madali broke out laughing like a monkey, and, wasting no time, he gathered the army of Farghana and marched toward Kashghar. At the time, the brother of Muhammad Rahim Divanbegi, 'Abd al-Rahman Bek, came from Ura Teppe with 300 soldiers and the son of Muhammad Sadiq Divanbegi, Ulughbeg, came from Shahr-i Sabz with 200 soldiers.

Madali reached Kashghar, but Jahangir Khoja prepared no welcome for him. Cautious and afraid, Madali sent a small company to visit Jahangir Khoja, who exhibited no interest in establishing any sort of agreement. Madali became concerned that he was deceived and that there would be no alliance, so he sent another company to Jahangir Khoja. This one consisted of Sultan Khan Khoja, Haqq Quli Dadkhah, and Bahadur Khoja. Sultan Khan Khoja was an especially high-ranking and influential figure, and Madali knew that Jahangir Khoja respected him. This company was welcomed appropriately.

Sultan Khan Khoja suggested to Jahangir Khoja that he should go to meet Madali, and Jahangir Khoja answered, "I will agree to do it out of respect for you (Sultan Khan Khoja), but only seated in horses' saddles (i.e., on equal footing and in the presence of the military). If you agree this condition I will do it, otherwise you will have to think about another solution." Sultan Khan agreed. He further reported that, during that visit, he was witness to the fact that Jahangir Khoja's court was more splendid than any ruler of Mawarannahr and that he had more wealth than any other king. He saw people from throughout the region bring him gifts of gold and jewels, but Jahangir Khoja was already so wealthy that he hardly took notice.

Another person reported (to Hakim Khan) that a merchant from Khotan came to Jahangir Khoja and delivered a box of treasure. Jahangir Khoja gathered together the merchants of his state and asked them to determine the treasure's value, and they found it to be beyond estimation. After a long discussion, they decided to have a twelve-year-old old boy stand in front of them, and they began pouring treasure around him until his head disappeared under a pile of gold. Another person reported that a woman from a noble family in Yarkend bought 600 slaves, had them dressed and prepared with weapons for battle, and delivered them to Jahangir Khoja to aid in his *jihad*. Jahangir Khoja's government was wealthy and respected. There is no need for more description.

Meeting of Jahangir Khoja and Madali Khan

Jahangir Khoja was in command of an army of 300,000 well-armed troops. At no era of any kings had anyone seen or heard of such a military with such rank and splendor. Madali and his troops were surprised and stunned by this army, and such a panic seized Madali's heart that it trembled like a church bell. With no other options, he came forward toward Jahangir Khoja and the two armies reached each other. Jahangir Khoja and Sultan Khan met with Madali and Haqq Quli and they embraced each other. Jahangir Khoja then welcomed Madali, and suggested that he alone should orchestrate the capture of the Gulbagh fortress. Jahangir Khoja went back to his palace and Madali blockaded Gulbagh.

The army of Farghana struggled against Gulbagh for five days, but no wind of victory blew to them from any direction, and during the siege many Muslims became martyrs. Having made no progress, one night the troops began to flee, Madali panicked and began to look for a way out of the conflict. Confused and demoralized, Madali sat down and did nothing, like a dead cow. Realizing that they were losing time, Madali's commanders put him on a horse and rushed him to Qoqand. But instead of making the long journey back to Qoqand, many of Madali's commanders abandoned him to remain in Kashghar; Jahangir Khoja welcomed them and honored them with gifts. Madali suffered much difficulty and hardship during his return journey to Qoqand, and, when he finally arrived, he took to drinking *buza* (millet beer) and playing with pigeons.

Back in Kashghar, after Madali's departure, Jahangir Khoja surrounded Gulbagh with his enormous army and put the fortress under siege. After some time, Jahangir Khoja had made no progress, so he decided to return to his palace. At that time, the 12,000 Chinese soldiers in Gulbagh had run short of food, so one night they gathered and left Gulbagh castle by foot. Jahangir Khoja heard the news and quickly rode toward the fortress. His lion-hearted *ghazis* arrived quickly and began fighting, and the huge Muslim army began killing the *kafirs*. As they lost hope, the *kafirs* began killing each other, and before long not one of the 12,000 Chinese soldiers remained. Everyone in the seven cities heard that the Chinese were run out of the region.

Jahangir Khoja made Mahmud Khan Turä Khoja governor of Khotan, he made his brother, Muhammad Khan, governor of Yarkend, and he made 'Umar 'Ali Khoja b. Khan Khoja governor of Aqsu. When Jahangir Khoja ruled all seven cities he directed his attention to his acquaintances. He did not know that the wise said: "You must not have sympathy for a weak enemy, for if he gains strength he will not spare you."

The Chinese Expel Jahangir Khoja from Kashghar and Make Him a Martyr

Jahangir Khoja did not appreciate his rule, and he dedicated little effort to the state's affair. He kept company with people of questionable character and avoided those who would be good companions. He spent his time as ruler drinking wine with the beautiful women of Kashghar, not conferring with his military commanders. His people were shocked by his behavior, and they grew unhappy, and his advisors told him that, after spending a life without rule, he should appreciate the state that God had provided to him.

The advice was good, but it proved to be of no benefit. Jahangir Khoja continued to spend his time engaged in immoral activities.[5] It did not take long for this news to reach people in Khotan, and then it reached the *kafir* rulers in China, who concluded that the clothes of a king would not fit on Jahangir Khoja. The Chinese amassed an enormous army and, in just three days, reached Kashghar by an isolated route.

When Jahangir Khoja heard that the Chinese had returned he lost himself in a torrent of sadness. He placed Turä Khan and Bek Murad in command of his army and sent them to battle against the *kafirs*. The army of *kafirs* came from the other direction, and when the two armies met there was such a battle that the land was stained red with blood. Finally, the breeze of victory began blowing in the favor of the *kafirs*; the Muslims retreated and the *kafirs* pursued. The Chinese army was like fire in a cane field, burning and turning to ash everything in its path. The

---

5. Hakim Khan elsewhere suggests that Jahangir Khoja suffered from an addiction to opium.

kafirs entered Kashghar and martyred all of the Muslims who did not flee. Turä Khan, Turä Khoja ibn Mahmud Khan, and Musa Khan ibn Sultan Khan were all captured and sent to China, and Kashghar was once again in Chinese hands. At that time, in the month of Rajab, 1241 (1826), Jahangir Khoja and a few of his friends fled, taking the difficult road to Alay.

The emperor of China sent a letter to his commanders ordering them to capture Jahangir Khoja. The Chinese commanders received help from several Muslims, who "sold their religion" very cheaply. They managed to get a letter to Jahangir Khoja promising him that the Chinese would return Kashghar to him if he would return. When the news reached Jahangir Khoja, he and a few of his friends made their way back to Kashghar. But it was a trick; the Chinese ambushed them in the mountains outside of Kashghar. Jahangir Khoja fled up the mountain, and the Chinese army surrounded the mountain and followed him in pursuit. Before long Jahangir Khoja gave up; the Chinese captured him and took him to Kashghar. When the Muslims saw that Jahangir Khoja had been captured, they all began to cry. The Chinese put him in a carriage and sent him to the emperor in Khanbaliq (Beijing).

Jahangir Khoja ruled for nine months, and he was thirty-eight years old when he died. Many of the troops and noblemen of Qoqand who had left Madali to join Jahangir Khoja then returned to Qoqand, where Madali welcomed them back. The Khojas, however, were not so welcome. Madali had their beards shaved off, and he ordered many of them to be put in prison, where they were given mush instead of bread.

C | *The "Great Game" to Russian Rule*

51 Alexander Burnes: The Importance of Bukhara in Great Game Politics

INTRODUCTION

Alexander Burnes (1805–41) traveled from India to Bukhara in 1832, as the Anglo-Russian colonial contest for Central Asia (the "Great Game") was gaining momentum. In Bukhara, Burnes attended numerous official meetings, and he appears to have gotten along quite well with the Qoshbegi (grand vizier). This can at least partly be attributed to Burnes's excellent language faculties and his appreciation for the niceties of official discourse, which impressed his hosts and greatly facilitated his mission. While some have questioned Burnes's political acumen and the value of his military advice, his mission to Bukhara was hailed a great success; he was promoted in rank and celebrated as a hero in both Calcutta and London.

From Bukhara, Burnes and his small company crossed Turkmen territory to Mashhad, before he made his way westward to Tehran and then the Persian Gulf. Burnes embarked a ship at Bushire and sailed to Bombay; after reporting to the governor-general in Calcutta, he was ordered to embark another ship and sail immediately for England. It was on that voyage that Burnes drafted the majority of his lengthy travel account, which he augmented with several chapters that survey the political climate and strategic value of various states across the region.

The following reading is extracted from one of these essays, in which Burnes expresses his views on the political and military strength of the Bukharan state. Burnes characterizes Bukhara at the time of his visit as a pale and weakened version of its former self, but he argues that Britain should work to foster a closer relationship with Bukhara both for commercial incentives and also to stem Russia's southward advances. Burnes recognized that the Russians had a clear advantage in the region, but it was his opinion that the Central Asians' hostility toward Russia and the obstacles involved in subjugating the pastoral-nomadic peoples of the region would make further Russian advances in Central Asia unlikely.

Burnes was, of course, wrong about this, but he did not live to realize it. After returning to India, in 1836 the young celebrity was put in charge of a diplomatic mission to Kabul. In 1839, he was appointed political resident, and soon thereafter he became caught up in the First Afghan War (1839–42). On November 2, 1841, as the British occupation toppled, a mob on the city streets of Kabul hacked him to death.[6]

On the Political and Military Power of Bukhara

The importance of Bukhara does not arise from the extent of its territories, but the position in which they stand. The fame which it enjoys as a kingdom is to be traced to the days of the Chaghatays. It then included all Mawarannahr, or the country *between* the rivers Oxus and Jaxartes, extended to Khorezm and the Caspian, and far into Khurasan. That age of splendour has long since passed; but the favourable site of the capital still invests it with a great influence among the natives of Transoxiana. Situated between the richest regions of Europe and Asia, and in a tract surrounded by steppes and deserts, Bukhara becomes the resting place of the merchant and the traveller, and the centre of an extensive commerce. Viewed either in a military or political light, its situation is commanding and in the highest degree valuable. Blessed with an exuberance of the productions of the soil, in a land of barrenness it arrests the attention of remote and neighbouring nations. In former times, it attracted the cupidity of the Greeks and the Arabian Caliphs. It was overrun by the hordes of the North; and from it, as a base, the renowned Timur led his legions victorious to the remote countries of Asia. In modern days, it has received ambassadors from the emperors of China and Russia, the Sultan of Constantinople, and the monarchs of Persia and Kabul. It likewise holds a supremacy among the surrounding Uzbek nations, who look up to it as the capital of their tribe, and render a voluntary, though nominal, homage to the ruler.

The King of Bukhara rules, as in other Asiatic nations, a sovereign despot; nevertheless, he is controlled in every action by the authority of the *mullah*s, or

---

6. The memoir of his years of service in Afghanistan was published posthumously. See Alexander Burnes, *Kabul: Being a Personal Narrative of a Journey to, and Residence in that City in the Years 1836, 7, and 8* (London: John Murray, 1842).

priests. This arises from no inability on his own part to assert his power, but from the constitution of the monarchy, which is exclusively based on the laws of the Qur'an, here more strictly enforced perhaps than in any other Mahommedan country. The reigning King of Bukhara, Nasrallah, or, as he is styled, Bahadur Khan, is a young man of twenty-seven years of age. He takes the title of *Amir al-Mu'minin*, or Commander of the Faithful, and is always addressed by the name of Hazrat; which is only used by the Mahommedans of Turkestan in speaking of their prophets. The name of King is seldom mentioned in official documents; that of Amir is preferred, which without the affix of *"al-Mu'minin,"* was the title by which Timur and his successors were designated, down to the days of Babur. It has a religious signification, which particularly unites it to the King of Bukhara. He looks upon himself as one of the heads of the Mahommedan religion. A respect is, nevertheless, paid to the Sultan of Constantinople, as he is here styled the Caliph of Rome; and the King of Bukhara is proud to hold the title of his bow-bearer.

The reigning King succeeded to the throne seven years since. He is naturally just and liberal, and very strict in the observances of religion. He appears, indeed, to be gradually sinking into the bigoted habits of his father; which the nature of his government renders it difficult to avoid. On his accession he divested himself of all his own and his father's wealth; which has gained him a high reputation among his countrymen. In all his acts he is guided by the law; and the people pretend that his private expenses are defrayed from the capitation tax; which he exacts from Jews and Hindus, since it would be sinful to so appropriate the money of true believers. He is of an ambitious and warlike disposition, and employs his revenues in the conciliation of his army; to whom he has endeared himself by profuse largesses.

His minister, the *qoshbegi,* possesses great influence over him; and, though chiefly indebted to him for his throne, the King entertains no dread of his power. He never leaves the citadel till his Vizier is present to take charge of it. His Majesty will not receive his food at any other hands but those of his minister. This person is of an advanced age; upwards of sixty. He is an Uzbek, of the tribe of Manghït, possessed of talent and acquirements; and unremitting in his attentions to business. He also trades to a great extent, and is fond of money, but strictly just in levying the taxes on commerce. The high office of Vizier may be considered hereditary in his family: his father enjoyed it; his brothers hold two of the governments; and his sons, of whom he has thirteen, are employed in different districts or provinces. He has fixed on one of these as his successor. There is a great mixture of cunning in the minister's character; but he is a liberal-minded man, and favourably disposed to Europeans, and, in particular, the English. The whole wealth and power of the kingdom is at his command; since he receives the revenues, and is able to sway the priesthood, to whom he is ever respectful and conciliatory.

Nothing is more remarkable to a traveller in Turkestan than the entire want of chiefs, or Sirdars, among the people, as in India and Kabul. Here there are no great men, no Khans, or nobles, and no one of consequence, but the court and the priesthood. The whole of the governments are either held by slaves or dependents of the minister; and every town and village is ruled by the *mulla*s or Khojas, the descendants of the first Caliphs. As the base of the government of Bukhara is the Qur'an, and the whole community are, or desire to be, considered spiritual, it will fully account for the exception in favour of the church. That engine and the state go heart in hand in Turkestan, and give mutual support to each other. There is no shadow of popular government; but still, there is no evidence of discontent under such a system of rule, though people could not be more thoroughly enslaved than the Uzbeks. We must attribute this universal contentment of the community to the protection which is derived from a strict enforcement of the laws of the Qur'an. That book, at best, appears but a poor Magna Carta; yet it fixes on a settled basis the principles of jurisprudence; which, no doubt, leads the people to consider the clergy as their best protection against the ambitious power of the government. Their rigid adherence to the written law entitles these doctors to the share of gratitude which they enjoy. No measures of state are ever entered upon without their sanction; and a great portion of the revenues are alienated for the support of the national religion and the colleges which teach it. The surplus revenues of the capital are even divided after this manner; and the whole plan of administration bears a nearer resemblance to a hierarchy than any other government. If a murder be committed; if a robbery occur; if a dispute arise on any subject, it is immediately referred to the priesthood, since the King does not take upon himself to judge of the merits of a case without them. I am assured that this system has existed at Bukhara from the earliest ages of Mahommedanism, and is not coeval with the invasion of the Uzbeks, though it was more firmly established in the reign of the last King, Haydar Shah, who held his creed in bigoted veneration. Whatever may be the opinions entertained of the religion of Muhammad, it is productive of great advantages in the administration of a kingdom, when its laws are rigidly enforced. The police of the city and kingdom of Bukhara is strict and efficient: the largest bales of goods, as I have already stated, are left in open stalls at night without danger, and the roads of the country are free from either robbers or thieves. The uncompromising manner in which offenders are treated, and the summary justice inflicted upon them, instil a salutary terror into the minds of the ill-disposed. The most trivial offences are punished with death: fines, and imprisonment in horrid dungeons, are also employed, but more rarely. The laws of Muhammad are as much enforced as they ever were under his own eye; and the legislation that united the wandering Arabs of the desert has been transferred, without a single improvement or alteration, to a people differing in manners, habits, and languages, and considerably advanced in some points of civilization. . . .

The military force of Bukhara is levied from the different districts of the kingdom, and has no discipline. It consists of about 20,000 horse and 4,000 infantry, with forty-one pieces of artillery. There are likewise a description of troops, called "eeljaree," or militia, which are formed of the dependents and servants of the government, and amount to about 50,000 horse, 10,000 of which are from Balkh and the countries south of the Oxus. It might be further increased by levies among the Turkmens; but the services of that tribe can only be commanded by the individual who can enforce them. This is no great number, where almost every individual, rich and poor, has a horse of some description. These troops are seldom or ever called upon to serve, and. when embodied, receive no pay. The registered, or "duftur," troops are paid in grain, and the chiefs have assignments of land. Each soldier receives yearly eight Bukhara maunds of grain, each of which is equal to 256 lbs. English. It consists of wheat, barley, juwaree, and urzun. The infantry receive the same allowances as the cavalry, and, what is singular, they come into field on horseback, and then dismount. They arm with matchlocks, and are called "khusa burdar." The horsemen have swords; sometimes long knives, and heavy spears, about twenty feet long, with a short blade. These lances are constructed of different pieces of wood (generally of willow), and have an unwieldy appearance; they never break at the joinings. The Uzbeks have few fire-arms, and use them indifferently. An Indian or an Afghan never sets out on a journey but he bristles with arms. The Uzbek, on the other hand, contents himself with a lance, or the knife which he usually wears in his girdle. From what I hear, the Uzbeks are not much to be dreaded as enemies. Their manner of fighting wants spirit and courage; they vociferate loudly, and the fate of the advanced guard decides the conquest. They are a superior description of irregular cavalry, but poor soldiers. The park of cannon lies neglected in the citadel, for the Uzbeks do not properly appreciate the value of artillery, and the King has only to contend with horse. There are no native artillerymen, and the guns lie separated from their carriages, which, as may be imagined, are by no means efficient. The train could, however, be easily put in order by some of the Russian slaves. All the cannon are brass; three-fourths of them appeared to be small field-pieces, four and six pounders. There are four mortars; the rest are large guns. The powder of the country is serviceable. . . .

Bukhara possesses a much higher influence, both physical and moral, than any of the states around it; but its affairs were left in a most embarrassed state by the late King, who bestowed more attention on religion than politics. The Khan of Urgench or Khiva waged a continual war with him. The Khan of Qoqand was also his declared enemy. The chiefs of Shahr-i Sabz and Hisar acknowledged no allegiance, and the Mir of Qunduz plundered and even seized Balkh. The affairs of the kingdom are at present more prosperous, and the designs and power of the reigning King bid fair to keep pace with one another. He has this year chastised the chief of Shahr-i Sabz, and seized upon six of his villages. That town, which is famed as the birth-place of Timur, is considered the strongest in Turkestan, from the marshy nature of the country which surrounds it. The power of Qoqand has been also broken, and one of its frontier districts, that of Jizak, which formed one half of Ura-Tübe, has been annexed to Bukhara within these four years. Hisar might be also overcome, though it is mountainous, since the chief is dead, and his country has been divided among four brothers. The most powerful enemy of the kingdom is the chief of Qunduz; and if the city of Balkh has been wrested from him, he has conceded it to policy, and not to fear. He retains the name of that ancient city on his coin, and there is little amity between the states. The King of Bukhara entertains designs on Qunduz; but the country is distant, and it is very doubtful if he could make an impression upon it, though his formidable title of Commander of the Faithful would secure to Bukhara the aid of the *mullas* and a large army. The enmity of the Khan of Khiva terminated with the death of Muhammad Rahim Khan, the late chief, who sent an ambassador on his death-bed to ask forgiveness. The sons of the two parents, who were ever at war with one another, are now united. The injuries which Khiva inflicted on the kingdom determines its influence over the destinies of Bukhara. With an inferior power, the chief of that state plundered its caravans, robbed its subjects, obstructed its commerce, and laid waste its territories. The intervening deserts protected him from reprisal, though a vigorous monarch might successfully invade his territories from the Oxus. If the Khan of Khiva continues friendly, the King will be able to extend his power to the eastward, where he has long meditated an expedition.

The connexion of Bukhara with China, Kabul, and Turkey, is friendly; and all of them have sent ambassadors. Last year an envoy from China was deputed to solicit the assistance of the King, in maintaining the peace of the western frontier of China, from the inroads of the Khan of Qoqand. His majesty wisely declined all interference, but the chastisement which the Chinese inflicted on the inhabitants of that state some years ago may relieve the emperor at Pekin from any alarm regarding his frontiers. The commercial relations between Bukhara and China are on a footing favourable to both states; but the Uzbeks are not permitted, more than other nations, to pass beyond Yarkend, Kashghar, and their tributary towns. While the monarchy existed in Kabul, the intercourse between that kingdom and Turkestan was friendly and frequent, for the Afghans possessed the province of Balkh. The number of Afghans in Bukhara is considerable, and the whole Indian trade is carried on by their intervention. There is, however, no intercourse between the King of Bukhara and the chiefs who have risen on the ruins of the Kabul monarchy: the Uzbeks despise the friendship of Persia, from the hatred which they have for the heretical doctrines entertained by that people. Their only intercourse is commercial, and but few of them engage in trade, which is left to the Persians or Mervees, who are of the Shi'a creed. The liberality of the present minister of Bukhara has contributed to soften the asperity of feeling between the Persians and Uzbeks, but it is difficult to say on which side the greatest animosity subsists. The Persians have far the greatest cause, since they are constantly seized and sold into slavery. The fame of the Ottoman empire has extended to Bukhara, but the people have very imperfect notions of the weakness of the Porte. They believe the sultan to be the most potent monarch of the globe, and I have been frequently interrogated as to the extent of tribute which the different European nations rendered to him. We can comprehend the reasons for this assiduous attention of Bukhara, even on religious grounds; but the countries are far apart, and their intercourse is limited to empty expressions of devotion and attachment to one another.

From the time of Peter the Great, there has subsisted a continued communication between Bukhara and Russia, and it has been based on the reciprocal advantages of commerce. The land route between the countries was first opened in the reign of that monarch, and, during the last seventy years, the transit has been uninterrupted. In the reign of Alexander, and about the year 1820, the Russians endeavoured to cultivate a closer connexion, and despatched an embassy to Bukhara. They had failed in the preceding year to open the road between the Caspian and Khiva. It is but fair to believe, that some of the views of this mission were commercial, but they were likewise connected with political ends. The embassy was well received at the capital. A mission was sent in return to St. Petersburg, and several others have since followed it. From that period, the subjects of Russia have ceased to be sold into slavery in Bukhara; it is supposed that these missions have had reference to the affairs of Khiva, but Russia will require no foreign aid to coerce that chiefship. The Russians have also established a friendly feeling with the chief of Qoqand: they have impressed the whole of the Uzbeks with high notions of their power, to the detriment of all other European nations; but they have yet to eradicate, by their future conduct, other opinions, which have been as universally adopted, that they want truth and honour in their diplomacy. Setting aside the physical obstacles which present themselves to the Russians making a conquest of Bukhara, the people are generally inimical to them. It is even probable that Bukhara, with all her pretended amity, would succour Khiva, if attacked by the Tsar. Should these countries ever be subdued from that quarter, it would be found most difficult to retain them, or control the wandering tribes around. Regular troops would be useless, and irregulars could not subdue a race who had no fixed places of abode. It is not, however, to be concealed, that the court of St. Petersburg have long cherished designs in this quarter of Asia.

52 Mohan Lal: A Journey among the Turkmens

INTRODUCTION

Mohan Lal was a native of Kashmir whose father, Rai Budh Singh, had served as an administrator for the late Mughal emperors and a secretary for the famed Mountstuart Elphinstone (1779–1859), governor of Bombay. Benefiting from his father's position, Mohan Lal was among the first Indians enrolled at Delhi College. He received an education in English language and literature, and as a young man he developed a profound admiration for British civilization; one might even characterize him as an unapologetic anglophile.

It was in Delhi that Mohan Lal first met Alexander Burnes, who was sufficiently impressed by Mohan Lal's comportment and ability that he invited the young Kashmiri to join his mission to Central Asia so that he might serve as an interpreter, and an educated and trustworthy companion who could help Burnes navigate the delicate intricacies of elite discourse in the regions they would visit. In December of 1831, Mohan Lal left Delhi to begin the long trek to Bukhara.

The section of Mohan Lal's account excerpted here discusses the company's travels from Bukhara to Mashhad, as they made their way through Turkmen territory. In addition to his observations of local conditions among the Turkmen tribes, Mohan Lal focuses on the Turkmen slave raiders as a defining feature of the countryside. He characterizes these "Alamans" (raiders) as cruel and benighted predators whose very existence is indicative of a despotism that, he forecasts, would soon be replaced by a more enlightened conquering power. One should note that slavery has an ancient history in Central Asia as it does in much of the world, including India. Mohan Lal's sensitivity to this issue is a product of his British education and his awareness of, and sympathies for, the growing abolitionist movement in Great Britain at the time.

Mohan Lal published the first edition of his travel account in 1834, shortly after his return to India. He later joined Alexander Burnes in Kabul and, unlike Burnes, survived the First Afghan War by taking refuge in the house of an Indian merchant. Mohan Lal later wrote a history of the Afghan ruler Dost Muhammad Khan that includes his astute observations of events surrounding the war, made all the more valuable as he was one of very few survivors.[7] Once an unabashed anglophile, he grew disenchanted by the British imperial arrogance that led to so much death and destruction. Shortly after the war he retired from British service and withdrew from the public eye.

August 15 [1832].—A few days before our leaving Mirabad, rumours reached us of the approach of a Russian embassy to Bukhara, and that the whole population of that city was in terror and confusion. These reports appear to have been premature, as nothing further has been heard of it. An Envoy, however, was expected at Bukhara, and sooner or later may arrive. The last mission from the court of St. Petersburg, I believe, was in 1820, and, as far as I could learn, it was not received with any conspicuous favour. The people of Bukhara are evidently timid, and having an interest in the trade with Russia, they do not discourage intercourse with that nation, but they greatly fear her power. The Russians, on the other hand, treat the Uzbeks with contempt, which tends to create a mutual dislike.

If the English Government would come forward, and establish relations with Bukhara, either commercial or political, it would acquire the good-will and confidence of those remote nations, which, in case of war with Russia, would become our allies. There is no other power likely to anticipate our intentions at present; but no time ought to be lost. The Qoshbegi, the minister, behaved to us in a manner that leaves no room to doubt his sincerity. He said that English chintzes [cotton cloth] would be very acceptable articles of trade.

August 16.—We set out for Mashhad, in company with a caravan which consisted of fifty camels. Our course lay till eve over a country which was naturally dry, but improved a good deal by the industry and skill of the husbandmen. The productions of these cultivated places are not, however, sufficient to supply the neighbouring towns, when they suffer a dearth. The deserts now came in sight, and we were surprised to see the sandy hills shifting their situation by the violence of the wind. Near sunset we reached Ardal, a barren village, thinly peopled. Here there was a mud fort, beautifully constructed, which indicated the existence of military art among this savage tribe. . . .

---

7. Mohan Lal, *Life of the Amir Dost Muhammad Khan, of Kabul: With His Political Proceedings towards the English, Russian, and Persian Governments, including Victory and Disasters of the British Army in Afghanistan* (London: Longman, 1846).

August 21.—We left Charjuy in the afternoon, and passed through a rich country. We were amused at the sight of horses used (instead of bullocks) for tilling and watering the fields. We passed a few rivulets, and afterwards fell into the dry mouth of a perfect *dasht* (desert). We halted in a waterless place, or *chul,* nine miles distant.

On our route we happened to meet seven miserable individuals, who had been made slaves by Turkmens, and were on their way to the market of Bukhara for sale. Two of them were young and beautiful boys, and others had long beards. The poor souls were forced by the cruel Turkmens to walk on foot, without shoes, in such a fiery desert. Their hands and necks were fastened together in a line with a long iron chain, which was very heavy and troublesome to their bare necks. They were crying, and appeared to be exhausted with hunger and thirst, while their oppressive drivers were deaf to their entreaties. They were Shi'as, and inhabitants of Qayan, a place in Persia. They saluted us, shedding a flood of tears at the same time. Mr. Burnes gave them a melon, which quenched their thirst a little. It was a dreadful sight indeed and I was astonished to think how hard were the hearts of the Turkmens.

I am proud of the customs and laws of the English Government, which is an enemy to slavery. In my humble opinion, the enslaving of people will soon bring an enlightened nation to rule in this country, where the laws savour of nothing but despotism, and are framed according to the will of a despot.

August 24.—We took our departure about midnight, and traveled through a sandy desert, where we did not see a single bird. All the road was destitute of water, and we were now among a barbarous race of Turkmens, and were obliged to take great precaution in concealing our real character. We hid our cooking-pots, which would have appeared very strange to their eyes, and satisfied ourselves with dry and stale victuals, which made me very unwell. We put up in a *chul,* eighteen miles, where there was a scarcity of water.

August 25.—A march in the night of eighteen miles brought us to a *dasht* (or desert), called Sairab, which contained three wells of salt-water. The road continued as yesterday. We saw two dead camels on the way, which perhaps fell a sacrifice to thirst.

August 26.—We journeyed at night over a level ground, which seemed to be fruitful. On our route we passed by a well which contained tolerably good water, and after eight hours we reached Uzkhu, a distance of eighteen miles. There were two tents of Turkmens, who came to see our caravan, and laughed at us.

August 27.—We moved at night over a table-land; our road was betwixt the wells inclosed by walled villages, which presented nothing but a heap of ruins and dust. We encamped on the right bank of the Merv river, in a place called Shahrukh, a distance of sixteen miles. Here were about sixty tents of Turkmens, regularly formed, which had a beautiful appearance. All the Turkmens, with their little ones, came to see the *qafila* [caravan], but we hid ourselves in our camel-baskets. This part of the country is known by the name of Merv, which was once a very populous town. It was formerly under the Persian yoke, and latterly has been governed by Bukhara; but the weakness of the latter city invited the barbarous

ruler of Khiva over to invade and to command that ancient place. The first inhabitants of Merv were all Qizil-bash, who live now in Bukhara.

The city of Merv, which was surrounded by numerous tents of Turkmens, is
ruined by the negligence of the present ruler.

August 29.—We continued at Shahrukh: here the officers of the Khiva cus-
tom-house came and took duties from the merchants, who gladly paid six and
a half rupees, or a tila, upon goods of 265 rupees value. They are very simple in
their searching, and even in their laws, as they neither examine the merchandise
nor count the loads of the camels. They believed what the merchants said to them,
and took what they gave them. We were told by our companions to hide ourselves
from their eyes, as they were foes to Europeans. In the territory of Khiva, travelers
are often deprived of their property, and even of their life.

August 29.—We set out early in the morning, and passed over rich ground.
The huts of the Turkmens extended as far as our eyes reached. They do not cultivate more than suffices for their own wants. The productions are wheat, maki
javar, melons &c. The females are very handsome, fair, and of good size. Their
dress, and even their bonnets, which resembled that of European ladies, added
splendour to their beauty. We were ascending very high on the right bank of the
river, expecting to have a place to ford over, as there was no boat on the stream.
Along our route were green bushes, in which we saw herds of camels, horses, and
sheep feeding. Their drivers were slaves, burnt with the sun, and suffering both
hunger and thirst.

A good breed of smart horses cover the face of this country, and are fed with
great care. We crossed the river at noon on camels, and let our horses swim up the
current. The river may be crossed on a bridge, constructed of two small boats; it
is not rapid, but deep in many places. This water bears also the name of the Tajan
[Tezhen] river, when it reaches that country, and then falls into the Oxus. We
halted on the left bank (thirteen miles distant), which was overrun by a jangal of
Jahu trees.

August 30.—We followed the left bank of the Merv river, and journeyed
through a jangal. Our route began gradually to be agreeable: we passed through a
flourishing tract, adorned with green crops and the tents of the Turkmens, whose
labours in cultivation, with which they are familiar, were productive. The brooks
of water branching from the river enriched the fields. The Turkmens have not
much money, but possess a considerable number of fat dumbas (sheep), fine horses, and strong camels, which they call treasure: every family is furnished with
about 200 or 300 quadrupeds.

We reached Merv, a distance of sixteen miles, where we were surrounded
by a swarm of savage Turkmens, who looked at us with wondering eyes. We met
three taking a slave to Bukhara for sale. He was indulgently allowed to ride on
horseback behind one of the Turkmens; the other two were stationed one on each
side, lest he might run away.

August 31.—We recommenced our journey towards Sarakhs, and passed
on our road two dry, large roofed wells, dug by 'Abdallah Khan. One of them
was placed before the door of a handsome structure, which had fallen into decay.
There was lying on the ground the corpse of a man cut in two pieces, supposed to

be a Turkmen, killed, perhaps, when asleep, by his slave, who escaped to his native country with the horse and arms belonging to his master.

We saw nine wells on the way, which were filled with dirt. We had loaded two camels with water at our last station, with which we allayed our thirst in this parched desert. We put up in a *chul,* called Bacha Bagh, eighteen miles distant. . . .

Sept. 3, 4—We remained at Sarakhs, which is a very large place, inhabited by Turkmens, who live now independent; they have been occasionally subject to the ruler of Khiva, and very rarely to that of Mashhad. They have elected among themselves a jury of twelve persons, and have consented to be guided by their advice, and that justice should be administered in their name. They are called *aqsaqal,* which means, in Turki, "silver beard." There are very few houses, which are of mud, irregularly built. The Turkmens occupy small and fine reed tents, which are beautifully adorned inside with silken flowers; they stretched over an extensive plain, and numbered about 3,000. The Turkmens make the doors of their tents opposite each other, by which means they generally have an open square between them. Sarakhs contains fifty Jews and one Hindu, who are employed in traffic. There are about 1,500 Qizil-bash slaves, a great number of whom are chained, like criminals. The beauty of the slave-girls (who are not less than a thousand) exposes them to the brutality of the Turkmens and their guests.

Sarakhs contains two mud forts, neatly built, one of which is situated upon a rising ground; it sends 4,000 horsemen in time of war, but they make no great stand, even against an inferior enemy. They have no large guns. Mr. Wolff, the missionary, was taken prisoner by the people of Sarakhs, and released after two days, not being considered of much value, as he told us, in Kabul. . . .

Sept. 8, 9.—We were in Sarakhs, upon the return of the Alamans from Mashhad: their booty consisted of 115 slaves. Our pity was excited by the shrieks of the poor children, some of whom were deprived of their clothes. What a weak spirit the Persian ruler shews, in not checking this cruel practice of the Turkmens, who, after several days' journey, make inroads into the heart of the Mashhad territory, and always return with impunity! . . .

Sept. 11.—We moved from Sarakhs early in the morning, and having traversed an extensive plain, halted in a desert, destitute of water, at twenty miles' distance. At eve we were joined by some horsemen of Sarakhs, who came to convey us as far as Derbend Muzdaran, a range of high hills, which run between Khurasan and Persia. The robbers generally conceal themselves in the cavities of this mountain, and attack the caravans suddenly. To guard against an incident of this kind, all the people of the *qafila* loaded their guns, and drew sharp-edged swords, and thus we began to travel. We passed the dry bed of a large stream, which, in spring, rises from Herat, and washes the base of the Mashhad hills. Jahu plants covered the ground, which are used as fuel.

Sept. 13.—We traveled all night through the barren hills, and the dawn of the day was anxiously expected by the whole party, who appeared tired of the dark. We reached a fertile spot, a distance of thirty miles, where we rested till evening, and then passed on our road through many villages spoiled by Turkmens.

Tibris, a fine walled village, contains very few inhabitants, who are harassed by the Tartars. Some time ago it was destroyed by the Alamans, and most of the residents made slaves. On our approach, the villagers ran up to us, shedding a flood of tears, and called at once *"Agha, Salam Alaykum!"* One was inquiring about his daughter, son, and wife; and another, about his brother, sister, and father, in the hope of receiving a satisfactory answer, which we could not give, respecting their relations detained in slavery.

About midnight, when winding our way along the bank of a small stream, amongst long grass, and in a dreary valley, we were suddenly alarmed by the cry of "Alamans," upon which the caravan quickened its pace, and collected together in a compact circle: all the camels were sitting down, trembling, as if aware of the danger. We expected to be attacked by Turkmens: our horsemen, consequently, formed themselves into a line in front; but after waiting a short time, we were agreeably surprised to find that there were no robbers, and the people we suspected were families returning home, who were also afraid of us. The spot where this occurred was very wild, and fitted for a *chapaw*, or attack; and as a large body of Alamans had lately been plundering near Mashhad, we had some opportunity of seeing the manner in which the preparations for the defense of a caravan were made. The scene was rather interesting than otherwise, as several of our party had pistols without powder, and blunt swords, without courage to fight; so that, had we been really attacked, much confusion and noise must have arisen from those foolish would-be heroes.

Sept. 14.—A journey in the night brought us to the holy city of Mashhad, where we found the gates shut up till eight o'clock in the morning. This custom continued for a long time, on account of the great fear of the Alamans, who generally attack the place the very moment the sun rises.

On our approach to the city, the people came to visit the caravan; they were all beautifully shaped and dressed, which put us in mind of the showy people in India. We got first into an Uzbek saray; but having no room there, we were obliged to go to another, which was next to it. Though the saray was very small, yet it was thickly peopled by cloth-merchants.

I attempted to examine the bath at Mashhad, where none but Muhammadans are allowed to enter. I nearly risked my character, as the merchants, who suspected me to be a Christian, in the late journey, were present; but, luckily for me, they could not recognize me in the Persian attire, which I had purposely put on. I bathed, and was rubbed with a hairy bag by a barber so swiftly, that I felt my body very light and healthy.

53   Levshin: Observations on the Qazaqs

INTRODUCTION

Aleksei Levshin (1797–1879) was a prolific author and administrator who spent two years (1821–22) in Orenburg, a border town that had long served as the headquarters for Russian interaction with the Qazaqs. In 1832,

Levshin's extensive monograph on the Qazaqs was published in St. Petersburg. A product of his long acquaintance with the Qazaqs, the book quickly became one of the most distinguished sources on the life of the nomads. It was translated into French already in 1840, and remains highly regarded in modern-day Kazakhstan. Levshin's attitude toward the subjects of his observation was generally one of ambivalence. Careful not to plunge into the pitfall of romanticism, as did so many of his contemporaries and later visitors to nomadic lands, Levshin treated the Qazaqs both sympatheticly and harshly. He sheds light on numerous facets of Qazaq culture, although even he was unable to solve some of the riddles that surrounded, and still do, certain aspects of Qazaq history: for example, in trying to find out the underlying reason behind the Qazaq division into three hordes (zhuz), Levshin could only conclude that the matter was clouded in secrecy. Throughout this excerpt, Levshin refers to the Qazaqs as Kirgiz, or Kirgiz-Kazak, in the fashion customary among Russians at that time.

Their Manner of Life. The Kirgiz manner of life is a living picture of the age of the Patriarchs. The life of the entire population is pastoral, and it is possible to say that they live almost solely for their herds; their settlements or *auls* instantly disappearing only to reappear in other places; the simplicity and closeness to nature of such conditions is fascinating and captivating to the eye of the romantic and the poet. People with fervent imagination, while gazing upon the Kirgiz, may fancy themselves in the carefree and happy pasture lands of Arcadia, or as the tranquil contemporaries of Abraham; they may dream of imaginary blissful people, ignorant of vices, governing great cities. . . . But the composed traveler sees in them (the Kirgiz) only half-savages and compares them with the Scythians of Herodotus, the Mongol-Tatars of Chinggis, today's Bedouins, the Kurds, the peoples who live on the banks of the Yenisei, the Hottentots, and other similar rudimentary tribes of Asia and Africa. And, in reality, the Kirgiz hordes are very similar to those peoples, partly for their manners and their nomadic way of life, necessary for sustenance of their numerous herds, and the way they move from place to place with their portable homes.

The constant movements or migrations from place to place of the Kirgiz-Kazaks do not weigh heavily upon them; quite the contrary, they find in them one of the greatest sources for pleasure, and they are happy not to tie themselves to the land. During the summer, nomadic life is actually very pleasant, but it is horrendous during the winter. During that season, surrounded from all sides by heaps of snow, the steppe Kirgiz almost never leave their tents: sitting huddled around the fire, they suffer almost equally from the heat and the cold. The force of the wind blows enormous flakes of snow through the door and the high covers into the tent, and sometimes, turning into a violent storm, topples the felt structure on all its inhabitants. The children, naked, crawl out from under the felt and sheepskins in which they are habitually covered, and, too close to the hot ashes, they burn their feet or their hands. In order to protect themselves from winter's calamities the Kirgiz choose for their winter abode the setting of groves, the cover of reeds, hills, or the sands of the southern part of the steppes.

During the summer, they spend most of their days sleeping or drinking kumiss (fermented mare's milk), and they hardly eat any meat, but at night they gather together, celebrate, tell stories to each other, or listen to the musicians who play the *chibizga* (*sybyzgy,* a wind instrument), the *kobyz* (a string instrument), or the *balalaika.* Autumn is their best time of the year. It is during this period that they make their longest journeys, and hold their primary festivals.

Language. Their language is a corrupt Turkic dialect in which there are numerous words, unintelligible not only for a Turk, but also for the Tatar of the Crimea, Kazan, and sometimes even for the Orenburg (Tatar). Moreover, where the Turks and Tatars write *sh,* the Kirgiz say *s,* where the (Turks and Tatars) have *ia, u, ii, io, iu,* they pronounce them *dja, dje, dji, djo, dju.* Instead of *g* they make use of *h.* They pronounce the majority of vowels indistinguishably, and the letters *a* and *e* often sound so similar that they never tell the difference.

Reading and Writing. A Kirgiz who understands the Qur'an and, consequently, knows Arabic, is considered a marvel of wisdom. Being able to read and write his own language (i.e., the Tatar language) is considered a sign of a learned man. In general, they cannot read or write.

Poetry and Music. Despite the ignorance and coarseness of the Kirgiz people, we find sometimes among them the beginnings of music and poetry. Moses, David, Homer, Polybius, Plato, and Aristotle spoke of the arts' existence during a period when the world was still in a shroud; modern travelers have found them (the arts) even among most of the half-savages. The Kirgiz, who in many ways are close to these latter (half-savages), prove that Man is born a musician and a poet.

Naturally, their poetry is not subordinate to the laws of science, and they do not compose verses based on poetic principles, but let no cultured reader fail to recognize that, similar to the most ancient peoples of the world they (the Kirgiz) have songs in which they celebrate the feats of their heroes, describe nature, and chant of love.

The words of the songs almost never pass without variation from one to another, each re-composing them, so that every Kirgiz is himself an improviser retelling events, thoughts, and sentiments in his own way, mixing into his portrayals objects under his own eyes.

One can easily imagine that such sudden products are, for the most part, incoherent and distorted, especially when making comparisons to, as is known, the majority of (inflated) rhetoric of (other) Asians; but often one can find merit among these songs; some even offer certain harmonious movements in their verses, and even in their rhythms.

The songs of the Kirgiz are sometimes accompanied by music, sometimes as duets, trios, and quartets, where the singers sing alone or together, one or more stanzas. The topics of such concerts include either simple tales, or debates among lovers, or the praises for some distinguished guest whom they wish to honor.

The epic poem is replaced among the Kirgiz with tales full of marvels, battles, and murders. Their heroes almost resemble the European knights of the twelfth and thirteenth centuries, journeying across the steppe looking for adventure, fighting sorcerers, other *bogatyrs* (*bahadurs,* or heroes), and the most famous knights, forming relations with women, often the daughters of their enemies, rescuing the unfortunate victims from their tyrannical husbands, receiving their (the ladies') charms, celebrating them in song, pillaging and destroying the *auls* for them, kidnapping them, and finally leading them to their homes to accord them the fourth or fifth place in their hearts (since they're already married to three or four wives). The very idea of such a prize would distress the heart of a European woman, but a Kirgiz woman, born and raised into slavery, receives her prize perhaps not calmly, but at least obediently and with no astonishment.

54 Nikolai Ignatiev: Russia's Agenda in Central Asia

INTRODUCTION

Count Nikolai Ignatiev (1832–1908) is most well known to English-speaking audiences as a semi-historical villain in the widely read Flashman series.[8] Digging beneath the historical fiction, one finds that Nikolai Ignatiev had a long career as an actual Russian diplomat. In 1856, he was a member of the Russian delegation at the Paris Conference, which ended the disastrous Crimean War (1853–56). A coalition of forces that included Great Britain, France, and the Ottoman Empire had just issued a decisive and humiliating defeat to Russia, demonstrating that Istanbul's European allies were too strong for Russia to advance an imperial agenda in the west. Exploring other theaters for Russian expansion, Ignatiev plotted to make advances further to the east. He consulted with the foreign minister, Prince Gorchakov, who was, like Ignatiev, an opponent of the Crimean War and an advocate for more active involvement in Central Asia. Tsar Alexander II (r. 1855–81) agreed to their plan, and he placed Ignatiev in charge of a mission to Khiva and Bukhara.

Ignatiev's mission had several objectives. Most immediately, he was to gather intelligence about the military capabilities and political climates of Khiva and Bukhara, and to negotiate for an improved Russian diplomatic and commercial position in the region. He was also to determine whether there were any sympathies for the British and, if so, figure out ways to undermine them.

On May 15, 1858, Ignatiev led a party of more than one hundred Russian soldiers and Cossacks from Orenburg. After several weeks and more than 700 miles of difficult travel, Ignatiev arrived to a lukewarm welcome in Khiva. This was partly because the Khivans were suspicious of Russia's motivations in the region and partly, it seems, because many of the valuable items that he carried as gifts for Sayyid Muhammad Khan (r. 1856–65) were damaged beyond repair during the

---

8. Ignatiev is presented as Flashman's nemesis, and he tortures and several times tries to kill the fictional British hero. The novel is set in 1856–58, the very years that Ignatiev made his way from St. Petersburg to Orenburg and Central Asia. See George MacDonald Fraser, *Flashman in the Great Game* (London: Harper Collins, 1975).

long trek across the Qazaq ("Kirghiz") steppe. While Ignatiev managed to collect a fair amount of intelligence in Khiva, his efforts to negotiate for an improved Russian commercial relationship failed. He fared considerably better in Bukhara, where he managed to negotiate a treaty of friendship with Amir Nasrallah (r. 1827–60). Among its many features, Ignatiev's account provides insight into Russia's intentions in Central Asia and many of the logistical difficulties and other obstacles that complicated, and occasionally confounded, Russia's Central Asian campaigns.

Preparations

In September, 1857, not wanting to get an official diplomatic post in the Orient, I asked for "a non public office," as an unofficial observer who was well acquainted with the East. I told Gorchakov, "In case of an explosion with Great Britain, only in Asia can we expect to win and harm Turkey. In peace time, difficulties started by Great Britain in Asia and the increase of our influence in those countries which separate Russia from the British Empire, will be the best guarantee of keeping the peace with Great Britain."

I felt that Asia was the only area remaining for our trade activities and development of our industry because we were too weak to enter into successful competition with Great Britain, France, Belgium, and the United States of America. The investigation of Central Asia and the promotion of friendly ties in this region would increase Russian influence and lessen Great Britain's.

In conversations with Prince Konstantin Nikolaevich, Gorchakov, the War Minister, and Kovalevskii, I continually showed the necessity to investigate this region in order to subordinate Central Asia to Russian influence, gain control of Amu Darya (if not in fact, then politically and commercially) for the use of our military ships and finally to threaten Great Britain in order to force it to value our friendship. Kovalevskii agreed with me about the investigation of Central Asia and the importance of the Amu Darya. I wrote several notes proposing to send expeditions to Persia and Afghanistan by spring, and insisted that an Embassy be sent to the Syr Darya and from there to the Amu Darya not later than April 15.

It was decided to send two expeditions: one scientific-political to Herat and possibly later to Afghanistan via Persia; another for the investigation of the Amu Darya, Khiva, and Bukhara under the pretext of returning a Russian Embassy to Central Asia to reciprocate the Embassy of the khanates which had been sent to the coronation of Alexander II.

Knowing that Asiatics react only to material force and that diplomatic discussions rarely bring positive results, I suggested certain measures be taken that would exert influence by the Embassy on the Khiva and Bukhara khans and stipulate as a condition of the Embassy, that in these two Asiatic capitals, our naval ships receive permission to use the Amu Darya. Kovalevskii of the Asiatic Department agreed with my point of view. I also proposed the need for a Flotilla to accompany the Embassy, but details could not be worked out without a preliminary agreement with the naval administration and the Orenberg Governor General. . . .

The long range goal of our Embassy was to find the best independent route to India via the Syr Darya and Amu Darya or via Kashghar, due to the fact that Russia was not permitted to go through Persia. In spite of the fact that the expedition had supplies for one and a half years, I wanted to return from Bukhara in November. If the Khans agree to the visit of our commercial agents in their capitals, then we would seek permission to leave some kind of caravan-base without any official sanctions. Kovalevskii begged me to avoid leaving my place of domicile in Khiva and Bukhara and to "never appear to the Bukharan Emir on horseback in the street."

He decided in case of a lack of money I was to borrow it in the name of the Foreign Ministry in Khiva and Bukhara. To my question, "What should be done if the Khan, in case of some imagined fear, received the Embassy in an insolent or negative fashion or if the approach of our ships to the Khivan shore evoked a response of gunfire?," Kovalevskii answered that "in the event of local hostile activity I was not to pay any attention nor attach any political significance to it; but if I have already reached Khiva and there is a disturbance or a slaughter, that I should learn from spies the nature of the situation and decide in good time to leave the Khivan territory."

Concerning the entrance of ships into the Amu Darya, despite the Khivan Khan, it was decided with great caution that the Khivans would not be allowed to hold up the Embassy by means of a ransom. We were not to risk having the Flotilla spend the winter in the river, and instead were instructed to drop back to the river delta at the entrance into the Aral Sea if this situation should arise.

The Ministry authorized me to promise to lessen the tariffs at the Customs on the frontier for the Khivan and Bukharan goods in return for our opening of navigation on the Amu Darya. To the question of "what point of view we should take in Khiva concerning an extension of the Syr Darya military line by our forces and what should be the Embassy's position if Russian captives of the Khivans run directly to us for protection," Kovalevskii gave the following answers: "No attempt should be made to give our view on extension of the Syr Darya line; it would be better not to aid and abet Russian prisoners in Khiva or give them protection. This might endanger the whole Mission."

In connection with natives from India that we might meet in Central Asia, Kovalevskii advised attempting to sow mistrust of the English, and if any Indians wanted to defect from Khiva or Bukhara, we were to promise them asylum. The Mission was given permission to communicate with Khanykov but was forbidden to send a Russian agent to Balkh, Qunduz, Gissar, and others, and instead, was given orders to wait for a trusted official sent from the above towns, or if we had to send someone it should be a Kirghiz.

Keeping in mind the many rumors that arise in the East, I asked Kovalevskii "whether we should give support to a defensive union among Afghanistan, Persia, Bukhara, and other independent states bordering on India with the goal of being hostile to England, and whether we shouldn't push for a similar grouping of states in Central Asia thus trying to include Khiva and Qoqand in the alliance?" The

Director of the Asiatic Department stated that, "we should attempt the above as far as possible, if it was feasible." ...

Part of my fear stemmed from the fact that our relations with Khiva and Bukhara were far from satisfactory. The activities of our agents in Khiva and Bukhara was a witness to the infertility of our diplomatic conversations.

Khiva, considering itself unassailable, continued to harm us in the Kirghiz steppe as much as possible. They consistently referred to our notes as impertinent and impudent lies and did not pay any attention to the suggestions of the Governor General of Orenberg. The Khivans continuously harassed and robbed our traders, agitated and confused our Kirghiz, and sent our emissaries and tax collectors into the Üst-Yurt and to the Syr Darya. Khiva also bought Russian citizens sold to them by the Turkmen after they were taken prisoner.

Bukhara was more restrained and not as ugly or bold as Khiva. The Bukharan Emir Nasrallah, although he understood the importance of trade relations with Russia, dreamed about his own personal role in Central Asia. He, too, permitted the purchase of Russian prisoners and harassed our traders by charging them twice the tariff for Russian merchants of that for Muslims.

Faith in God and an unabashed desire to serve Russia buoyed my spirits. I would distinguish myself in the upcoming enterprise and felt that intrigue and gossip were beneath my dignity and not worth my attention. The farewell with the Tsar and Grand Duke Konstantin Nikolaevich was very touching and showed their great trust in my expedition. It made a deep impression on me.

Many of my friends said farewell to me as if for the last time, and my parents made the direst predictions. What touched me the most was the quiet Empress Alexandra Fyodorovna. She blessed me with the ikon of the Holy Mother's beautiful miniature portrait, and I knelt before her while she took my head in her hands and blessed and kissed me. Tears of emotion sprang from me when she began to reproach the Tsar, who was just entering the room. She scolded him for sending me away on purpose "into that terrible country where he will uselessly be risking his life while here he would be very needed." The Tsar replied that there was no one else qualified for such a dangerous mission....

Before the departure of the Embassy into Central Asia, political and military goals of the trip had been emphasized, but trade possibilities could not be forgotten. It was hoped we could conclude trade treaties in Khiva and Bukhara which would improve the condition of Russian traders and make easier their relationship with the local inhabitants. Therefore, at my suggestion, two Russian merchants were assigned to my Embassy as agents. I was successful in persuading a local merchant named Deev to accompany us as our agent. This took care of one of the main problems I had in assembling the Embassy, and I felt an experienced salesman like Deev could render valuable services. However, the absence of well informed commercial agents was extremely regrettable and deprived us of any possibility of forging closer trade relations between Russia and the khanates. ...

In order to ensure protection of the Embassy while in Khiva, I requested Katenin to supply me with a letter which would guarantee the Khivan Khan's protection. The letter is as follows:

To the High Ranking Khan of Khiva and the Respected Vizier. In fulfillment of the highest approval expressed in the charter of His Imperial Majesty—Most Esteemed Tsar which was sent by the messenger, Shaykh Ul Islam Fazil' Khodzheir to the highest official of Khiva, the Imperial Embassy whose destination is Khiva in accordance with the desires of the Khan arrived recently in Orenberg and on May 10 departed Orenberg to the Kirghiz steppe. The leader of the Mission who is authorized to conduct negotiations with the High Ranking Khan is Colonel Ignatiev who was personally selected by his Imperial Highness and serves as a Fligel'-Adiutant, i.e., one of his closest and most loyal officials. The retinue of the Embassy consists of a Secretary, two interpreters, two medics, and other officials. The total number is 16 people. The Embassy will be in Kunia-Urgench by June 29. Until that point it will be accompanied by my own personal convoy which at Kunia-Urgench must be substituted for by the convoy guard of the High Ranking Khan. This information was already conveyed to the respected Divan-Beg in a letter of February 22 by me. I consider it my obligation to inform the respected Vizier on the above subject so that the Khivan Government will be aware of the exact number of personnel of His Majesty's Embassy and the exact time of the Embassy's arrival on the frontier of Khiva so that he will have the Convoy-Guard there. Also I find it necessary to warn you that Fligel'-Adiutant Ignatiev is authorized to travel from Khiva to Bukhara and from Bukhara he is to hasten back to Russia. Because of his high rank he is needed in Russia. For the same reason he will in all likelihood be forced to shorten his stay in Khiva and therefore it would be extremely helpful if negotiations with him and the Khivan Government are conducted in the shortest possible time. (Written in Orenberg, May 6, 1858)

The preparations and preliminary conversation with the Governor General lasted two weeks, and on May 15 the Embassy was ready for departure. Its personnel, along with the convoy, included 117 men with 178 horses, 352 camels, and 22 wagons, a hospital wagon, and field kitchen. We made an awkward and impractical looking sight for a campaign through the steppe. . . .

Bukhara

On the eve of our departure from Khiva, I sent a report to Kovalevskii summarizing the events and circumstances of our sojourn in Khiva. I detailed the problems of the Embassy's relationship to the Flotilla and with Butakov in General; informed him of problems with the damaged gifts; discussed our sick personnel and their transport; and described the situation created by the runaway Persian slave. My report also touched upon navigation potentials.

I also wanted to explain the actual meaning of the diplomatic treaties which the Ministry of Foreign Affairs had approved in vain (1841) and wrote:

The Treaty concluded by Danileveskii in 1841 was a political bluff because the treaty in Khiva did not have a European significance. It was never observed and was practically unknown in Khiva. If you want, the concessions forced on the Khivans in the present time could be considered incomparably more important and realistic than those which were made in 1841. It wouldn't do any good to conclude a diplomatic treaty without the right of free navigation on the Amu Darya in order to present to the Ministry of Foreign Affairs a scrap of paper attached to the Khan's seal without any significance for us because of the absence of a guarantee of fulfillment. I hope Your Excellency will not censure me. Maybe in Petersburg they will find that I erred in these activities, but I remain convinced that we entered in good conscience, consistent with a feeling of trust, at least to my mind we did not chase after tawdry results.

Despite the fact that all our information from Bukhara was indirect, word reached me that the situation in Bukhara would not be favorable, and that the Emir of Bukhara opposed free navigation on the Amu Darya. Under these conditions it was necessary to make inquiries about the actual state of affairs in Bukhara and how we would be received. It was rather difficult to achieve this because the Khivans watched over us vigilantly and took measures to block direct relations between us and Bukhara. Through the merchant, Panfilov, and two other Kirghiz I found several efficient Kirghiz who were loyal to Russia and who were not viewed suspiciously by the Khivans. I sent them to Bukhara with my official, confidential, and personal letters to the Vizier in Bukhara, Tokhsab Mirza 'Aziz.

The Kirghiz were instructed, as I told Tokhsab in a personal letter, to present our views and describe our activity in Khiva. We disclosed the intrigues of the Khivans trying to make the point that suspicion and fear were not good reasons for refusing the right of free navigation.

Soon after the arrival of my emissaries, Tokhsab answered me in a very cautious fashion and announced that the Emir instructed him to invite me formally to Bukhara. This answer was sent by an indirect route and arrived when I already was on Bukharan lands. But our messengers had time to return first by the direct route to Khiva, and they told me about the polite reception Nasrulla gave them in Bukhara and that they had related to him all the necessary information. This strengthened me in spite of the obstacles and treacherous tricks of the Khivans. We would go from Khiva to Bukhara on a route never before travelled upon by Europeans.

55   Bayani: The Russian Conquest of Khiva and the Massacre of the Yomut Turkmens

INTRODUCTION

Muhammad Yusuf Bek, known for his poetic pseudonym
"Bayani," was a poet, a writer, and one of the highest administrative officials in

*the court of Khiva, at a time when the khanate was a protectorate of the Russian
Empire. Educated and skilled in several languages, including Russian, Bayani
wrote a history of Khiva from 1911 to 1914 at the request of Isfandiyar Khan,
who wished to render the history of the region and his dynasty in a language that
ordinary people would find intelligible. Bayani based his account on the previous
works by Munis and Agahi, the most noted historians of Khiva in the nineteenth
century. However, since he was unable to find all of Agahi's chronicles, he had to
write the history from 1846 to 1856 and from 1864 onward himself. These parts
are his original contribution, based on information, usually from oral testimonies,
that he had collected himself. Interestingly, one of his sources was none other than
the account of the American journalist J. A. MacGahan, who had accompanied
the Russian troops in their conquest of Khiva in the 1870s and left a detailed
record of the conquest. Bayani apparently consulted an Ottoman Turkish translation of MacGahan's testimony, but was still able to provide a keen and intriguing
local perspective of the conquest, the negotiations between the Russians and the
Khivans, and the massacre of the Yomut Turkmens that followed. This excerpt
is an abridged translation from Bayani's manuscript, which has never been fully
edited or translated.*

His majesty the Khan (Muhammad Rahim Bahadur Khan)
heard that Governor Kaufman together with the Russian army were marching
upon Khorezm. He assembled all the amirs and grandees and took counsel with
them. They all said, "It is better for us not to fight with them." These words seemed
fitting to His Majesty the Khan. He ordered to gather all the Russian prisoners.
There were twenty-one men. He entrusted them to Murtaza Biy Khoja and charged
him to deliver them to the hands of Governor Kaufman. Murtaza Biy honored his
command, took the prisoners, and set off in the direction of Qazaqli.

In the vicinity of Nur-Ata, he met Kaufman and delivered the prisoners to
him after apologizing for the delay in recovering the prisoners. The Khan expected Kaufman to call off the attack, but Kaufman accepted his apology and none-
theless continued with the attack, saying, "We have our instructions from the
Great Emperor." He detained the messenger and continued the march to Khiva.

Hearing nothing of the fate of Murtaza Biy, the Khan realized that the Russians were continuing their advance from two directions: the column led by
Verevkin from the north and the one led by Kaufman from the east. Again he
assembled all the amirs and grandees and after consulting with them decided
to plan a counter attack. He appointed Muhammad Murad Divanbegi the commander of an army consisting of divisions of Chowdur, Göklen (namely, Turkmen tribes), and Uzbeks, and together with Mahmud Yasavul Bashi and Ya'qub
Bay Qalmaq sent them to repel Kaufman's column. As for the column headed by
Verevkin, he appointed Eltüzer Inaq at the head of a force composed of Yomut,
Yemreli (again, Turkmen tribes), and Uzbeks (all in all six thousand men) and together with Baba Mehter sent them to the city of Qongrat. He also gave two thousand men to Amir Turä and Muhammad Riza Turä and sent them to Hazarasp.
Inaq Bek was in command of the troops going to Khoja-eli.

The Defense of the River

In order for Kaufman to reach Khiva he had to cross the Amu Darya river. Therefore, the Khivan army decided to try and prevent it. Since Kaufman was still far, the Khivan army under Muhammad Murad Divanbegi crossed the Amu Darya and stopped at Üch-Uchaq. Muhammad Murad, in agreement with the commanders of the troops and the Turkmen elders, chose from the troops two hundred brave men under the command of Sadiq Qul, who hurried to Adam Kirulen to ambush the Russians. As the Russians' avant-garde under the command of Ivanov approached the place unaware of the ambush, the men attacked at once and managed to generate confusion among the Russians. Since the Khivan commander understood that the Russians were interested in reaching the wells to get a fresh supply of water, he gathered his men and set another ambush near the wells. Soon, the Khivans received a reinforcement of three hundred men. The Russians approached the wells unaware and were attacked. The Khivans managed to kill several Russians while sustaining themselves at first only minor losses; only one brave man from Kunia-Urgench by the name of Pir Niyaz was hit by a bullet.

However, the battle was not over, and more Russian troops arrived. When the Khorezmian troops realized that they were about to run out of ammunition they tried to escape, but were surrounded from every side. A battle began. Many of the Russians' horses, camels, and men perished. Finally, with the help of their better weapons, the Russians inflicted defeat on the Khorezmian troops.

When Kaufman approached the river, Muhammad Divanbegi ordered the artillery men stationed on the other bank to fire. However, the Khorezmians did not manage to achieve even one victory, and the Russians crossed the river in peace. After that Kaufman knew that now he would go to Khiva. When the Khan received the word about what had occurred, he became worried. He consulted with the elders of Khiva and Hazarasp and decided they would dedicate their efforts to the defense of the city of Khiva.

The Verevkin Column

Meanwhile, Verevkin and Lomakin were advancing toward the city of Qongrat. The battle outside the city ended in great defeat for the Khivans. The elders of Qongrat, Chap Niyaz Biy, Sayyid Biy, Taji Murad Biy, Qanchirga Biy, Mansur Biy, and others sent a messenger to Verevkin saying, "Do not enter our city and do not fire upon our citadel . . . we have sent word to His Majesty the Khan in Khiva. We do not have enough ammunition to fight with you right now. Once the Khan sends us supplies we will come out and fight with you." Verevkin ignored their request and decided to enter the city anyway. He did not encounter much resistance, and the elders of the city honored him with gifts.

Meanwhile, Eltüzer Inaq went to Khoja-eli, and together with 'Abdallah Mahram Yemreli and selected troops moved to attack Verevkin. The Khivans charged at an avant-garde composed of two divisions of mounted Cossacks. They managed to kill thirteen of them and injure a few. The Khivans also captured ammunition supplies and thirteen horses. When Verevkin heard about it he became angry. He ordered a search and capture of those responsible and he himself headed the operations against the city of Khoja-eli. After the defense for Khoja-eli failed, the elders came out with presents and gifts and asked Verevkin to spare the city, which he did.

After the battle in defense of Khoja-eli ended in defeat, "the Uzbek troops dispersed. Inaq Bek and the Qoshbegi, together with the Turkmen troops of the Yomuts and Chowdur were on their way back to Khiva and were determined to defeat the Russians." Thus, the Turkmens were the only ones remaining to defend Khiva. A few days later, after Verevkin succeeded in subduing a force of Turkmens defending the city of Manghït, the Orenburg column reached Khiva from the north.

Meanwhile, in Khiva, the Qoshbegi (a high minister) explained to the khan all the events that had happened. The khan decided to multiply the guards at each and every one of Khiva's gates and gave instructions to the watch commanders. The khan sent two more letters of surrender to Kaufman and asked him to halt the attack, but the letters were unanswered. When the khan realized that the conquest of Khiva was imminent, he consulted with his close advisers, and one night left the citadel and escaped with the help of the Yomuts to their sanctuary. When the khan left the city, Amir Turä became khan. After a short enthronement ceremony attended by a few relatives, he gave orders for the peaceful submission of the city and sent a messenger to Kaufman to tell him that Khiva surrendered. After two days Kaufman entered the city of Khiva and Bayani had only this to say, "Such was the will of God most high, there is no escape from the divine decree."

Kaufman came and entered the citadel. He sat himself on the throne of the Khorezmian kings and the others sat around him in their places, while different relatives of the khan came in and paid their respects, carrying food and drink. Kaufman also decided to inspect the treasury of the palace and together with Golovachev, found an assortment of weapons, bejeweled daggers, swords, and hand guns. Kaufman refused to conduct negotiations with the khan's relatives. Eventually, he learned of the Khan's hiding and decided to send a messenger to him, inviting the khan to return and conduct negotiations himself, promising not to hurt him.

The khan inspected the letter and became aware of its contents. He consulted with Sarï Sardar (the commander of the Yomuts hosting him). Sarï Sardar said, "O King, your departure may be a good thing. If they indeed made peace, it cannot be bad for you. Now that it has become so by the will of God, it cannot be good for you to abandon your country and go to Akhal." His Majesty the Khan accepted Sarï Sardar's words, mounted his horse, and set out in the direction of Khiva.

The Meeting between Kaufman and the Khan

The meeting took place in the Khan's summer palace in Khiva. Under the shadow of the trees there was a small pavilion. The Khan approached the pavilion and dismounted.

Kaufman saw him and went out of the tent to meet him. He shook his hand and greeted him.

"Welcome," said Kaufman, and with utmost respect and highest regard and the greatest esteem and appreciation he showed him into the pavilion. He made him sit on a cushion a little higher than himself, and he himself sat on the carpet.

After the refreshments, Kaufman said, "I have planned to come here with my army for three years and now I have come."

The Khan said, "It is the will of God."

Kaufman said, "If you had understood the meaning of my letter three years ago, you would never have seen me, and God would not have made me come here."

The Khan said, "Nothing remains hidden from the will of God. In any case, I am pleased to see you."

Kaufman smiled and said, "The pleasure is not yours alone, it is mine as well. If we continue in this friendly manner, we may be able to turn harm into good."

They ate for a while and then the Khan expressed his country's submission by saying, "We are at the Emperor's command." After exchanging a few more pleasantries, Kaufman decided to create a council of seven Khivan dignitaries. Their first decision was to abolish slavery in the khanate and set free all the Persian slaves. Then they began negotiations on the final conditions for the surrender of Khiva.

The Campaign against the Yomut Turkmens

Kaufman informed the Yomuts that they had to pay 300,000 rubles as war indemnities. The Yomuts sent a delegation of their elders to Kaufman saying that they did not have that kind of cash and that they needed a delay. Kaufman agreed to give them fifteen days to procure the money.

Meanwhile he prepared the army for the battle and instructed Golovachev, Lomakin, and Ivanov to be prepared to fight if they do not pay. According to Bayani, they all agreed that fighting with the Yomuts was not a desirable course of action to take. Two weeks later, Golovachev received an order to destroy all the Turkmens.

Golovachev left with Ya'qub Bay and reached Ghaziabad. There he stopped and said: "It is not good to fight with the Yomuts. We shall stop here and perhaps they will get news of our advance and pay the indemnities. However, if they want a fight we shall give them one." The next day, the Yomuts showed no sign that they were about to pay the indemnities. Therefore, Golovachev set out and together with his army entered the territory of the Yomuts. . . .

The Cossacks who were mounted on their horses dispersed to all sides and set fire to the Yomuts' crops, to their huts and tents; the flames reached the sky from every direction and the smoke could be seen everywhere, so that the meaning of the Qur'anic verse *Wait for the day when the heavens bring forth visible smoke, enveloping mankind* (Qur'an 44:10) became clear. The Cossacks fired at everyone they saw. They stabbed the old and the women and children with their sabers and impaled infants who were still suckling their mother's milk on their lances and tossed them into the burning fire. And they continued to plunder the Yomuts' possessions.

At that time, a group of Yomuts, a few old men, women, and children, escaped. Several Cossacks learned of this and gave chase. When they caught up with them the Yomuts said, crying, "What wrong have we done to you?"

The Cossacks answered, "You rebelled by not paying the indemnities."

The Yomuts said, "The sum was impossible to pay; this does not mean a rebellion. Give us more time. No man can endure such tyranny as we have experienced in this world."

The Cossacks returned to General Golovachev and conveyed these words to him.

Golovachev said, "Their words are true. I did not tell you to burn their crops and their houses nor to massacre their women and children. Now, what is done is done, there is nothing we can do."

After this event the Yomuts were all in agreement and said, "Now that we have encountered the Russians it is better for us to live by the sword. After our women and children were butchered it is our obligation to rise against Russia. It is better to die than to lead such a life in this world." They gathered and were going to Hilali. In order to follow the Yomuts, Golovachev chose from among the Cossacks seven mounted divisions and sent them on their way.

The Cossacks gave chase and every now and then caught up with a group of Yomuts who had broken off from the rest and were lagging behind. Most of them were women and children. They suffered the same fate as previously mentioned. The scene of the massacre harbored many other images: women jumping under the hooves of the horses; women and children trying to hide in the reeds in the lake and are being shot at by the Russian troops from the bank; four Cossack riders thrashing their sabers at one unarmed Yomut man kneeling in their midst; the continued burning of crops, the looting of possessions. Whenever the Yomuts could, they returned a fight, mainly through night attacks on the Russian camps, killing a few Russians and taking their weapons. Eventually, it became clear that the Yomuts had no chance. Those who did not perish fled and regrouped in the hope of returning one day to their land.

GLOSSARY

'amil (Ar.): official, tax collector, prefect

dihqan (Per.): land owners and village heads of lesser nobility; after the 11th century the term came to denote peasants

dirham (Ar.): type of currency, often a silver coin

elchi (Turk.): envoy or ambassador

farsakh (Per.): unit of distance, roughly 5–6 km; see also *farsang/parsang*

farsang (Per.): see *farsakh*

fatwa (Ar.): opinion on a point of law in Islam, issued by a *mufti*

fida'i (Ar.): one who is willing to give up his life in order to take another's; particularly associated with a certain sect of the Isma'ilis.

hadith (Ar.): testimony to what the Prophet said or sanctioned, often as sayings attributed to the Prophet and his companions

hijra (Ar.): Muhammad's migration from Mecca to Medina in September 622, established as the beginning of the Muslim calendar

imam (Ar.): a leader of the Muslim community, often the head of a mosque

jizya (Ar.): poll-tax imposed on non-Muslims in Muslim states

katib (Ar.): secretary, typically in charge of drafting letters and documents

khanqah (Per.): a building reserved for Sufis

kharaj (Ar.): tax, often land tax

khatib (Ar.): a public spokesmen, often the pronouncer of the *khutba*

khutba (Ar.): part of the Muslim Friday sermon, mentioning the ruler's name

kibitka (Rus.): a nomadic tent

kunya (Ar.): patronymic

li (Chin.): Chinese unit of length, roughly 500 meters

madrasa (Ar.): a college

mawla (Ar.): a client (non-Arabs who wished to become part of Arab society needed to have an Arab patron)

mihrab (Ar.): the prayer niche in the mosque

minbar (Ar.): pulpit

mu'azzin (Ar.): the person who performs the call to prayer (*azan*)

namaz (Per.): ritual prayer in Islam

noyan (Mong.): a chieftain or a military rank

qazi (Ar.): judge

qibla (Ar.): the direction of Mecca (in Central Asia, usually south, southwest) the precise direction to the holy *ka'ba* in Mecca

parsang (Per.): see *farsakh*

rak'a (Ar.): bowing and bending while uttering prayer in Muslim worship

sahib-qiran (Ar. & Per.): lord of the auspicious conjunction; in this volume refers mostly to Timur

shar'ia (Ar.): the rules and regulations that govern Muslim life, relying in principal on the Qur'an and *hadith*

silsila (Ar.): the chain of transmission, mostly as a spiritual lineage, in Sufi Islam

sunna (Ar.): the customs of previous generations, introduced by the Prophet

tanga (Per.): a coin (typically silver)

tariqa (Ar.): "way" or "method," referring to a Sufi order

'ulamu' (Ar.): scholars who often also fulfilled religious and judicial duties

verst (Rus.): unit of length, roughly 1 km

waqf (Ar.): religious endowment

yarlïq (Turk.): decree

yasa (Mong.): Chinggisid customary law

Index

Scott C. Levi is Assistant Professor of Central Asian History in the Department of History at the Ohio State University. His publications include *The Indian Diaspora in Central Asia and Its Trade, 1550–1900* and the edited volume *India and Central Asia: Commerce and Culture, 1500–1800.*

Ron Sela is Assistant Professor of Central Asian History in the Department of Central Eurasian Studies at Indiana University Bloomington.

Printed and bound by CPI Group (UK) Ltd, Croydon, CR0 4YY

13/04/2025

14656550-0003

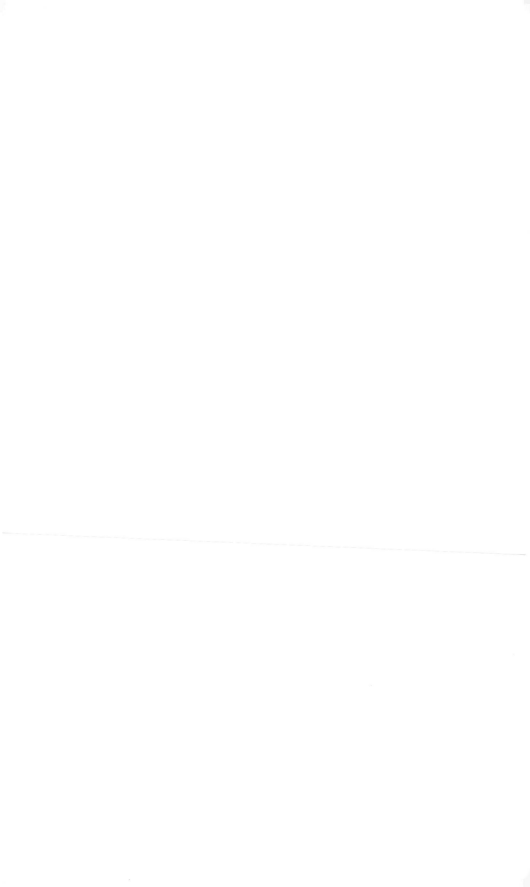